POLITICS, HISTORY, AN

A series from the Internat

at the University of M

Sponsored by the International Institute at the University of Michigan and published by Duke University Press, this series is centered around cultural and historical studies of power, politics, and the state—a field that cuts across the disciplines of history, sociology, anthropology, political science, and cultural studies. The focus on the relationship between state and culture refers both to a methodological approach—the study of politics and the state using culturalist methods—and a substantive one that treats signifying practices as an essential dimension of politics. The dialectic of politics, culture, and history figures prominently in all the books selected for the series.

STATES OF IMAGINATION

Ethnographic Explorations of the Postcolonial State

Edited by Thomas Blom Hansen and Finn Stepputat

Duke University Press *Durham and London 2001*

Printed in the United States of America on acid-free paper ∞
Typeset in Quadraat by G&S Typesetters, Inc.
Library of Congress Cataloging-in-Publication Data appear
on the last printed page of this book.

CONTENTS

PREFACE

The ideas that led to the conception of this volume grew out of the intellectual environment of the research program Livelihood, Identity and Organization in Situations of Instability, which materialized thanks to the Danish Council for Development Research, the Centre for Development Research in Copenhagen, Institute of Anthropology at Copenhagen University, and International Development Studies at Roskilde University. The LIVELY program brought together researchers from a variety of academic fields in an effort to synthesize ongoing theoretical and empirical work on violent conflict, migration, and popular culture. Because these subjects converged on the culture of states yet challenged the idea of the state as something given and immobile, we conceived the idea of an international seminar on the States of Imagination in the postcolonial world and invited a number of prominent and talented scholars for the event.

The idea of States of Imagination was enthusiastically received, and the seminar, which took place in Copenhagen in the midst of winter 1998, elicited a collection of fascinating papers, most of which appear in this volume. We are grateful to the participants of this seminar for contributing to an intellectually stimulating seminar and for challenging and refining the common approach that now emerges from the volume. We would also like to express our appreciation of the support and inspiration we have received from our colleagues in the LIVELY program: Karen Fog Olwig, Bodil Folke Frederiksen, Preben Kaarsholm, Henrik Rønsbo, Ninna Nyberg Sørensen, and Fiona Wilson, as well as Peter Gibbon, Poul Engberg-Pedersen, Jan Ifversen, Karuti

Kanyinga, Thandika Mkandawire, Afonso Moreira, Kirsten Westergaard, and other good colleagues.

Finally, we would like to thank our secretary, Annette Smedegaard Christiansen, for working hard with us throughout these years, as well as the two anonymous reviewers for Duke University Press for their encouraging and constructive suggestions, which have improved the final product.

INTRODUCTION States of Imagination

Thomas Blom Hansen and Finn Stepputat

. . . as if every man should say to every man, I Authorise and give up my Right of Governing my selfe, to this Man, or to this Assembly of men, on this condition, that thou give up thy Right to him, and Authorise all his Actions in like manner.—Thomas Hobbes, *Leviathan*

The state has once again emerged as a central concern in the social sciences. It has also been rediscovered by practitioners of development and powerful international agencies such as the World Bank (1997), which now advocates "good governance" by lean and effective structures of government. However, in the vocabulary of World Bank economists the state and its institutions remain strangely ahistorical entities, a set of functional imperatives of regulation arising from society but devoid of distinct characters and different historical trajectories. In this influential train of thought the state is always the same, a universal function of governance. In the 1970s, theories of the capitalist state also privileged the state's functions in reproducing labor and conditions for accumulation of capital over its forms and historicity. Also, when Evans, Ruschemeyer, and Skocpol (1985) "brought the state back in" as an actor in its own right, their conceptualization of state revolved around certain assumed core functions and historical tasks that every state presumably had to perform.

The current rethinking of the state occurs at a juncture where the very notion of the state as a regulator of social life and a locus of territorial sovereignty and cultural legitimacy is facing unprecedented challenges. Ethnic mobilization, separatist movements, globalization of capital and trade, and intensified movement of people as migrants and refugees all tend to undermine the sovereignty of state power, especially in the postcolonial world. The equations among state, economy, society, and nation that constituted the dominant idea of stateness in the twentieth century have been undermined from below by growing demands for decentralization and autonomy, and from above by the imperatives of supranational coordination of monetary, environmental, and military policies in new configurations after the cold war.

At the same time, the discourse of rights and the proliferating demands for a variety of entitlements have expanded and transformed the meanings of citizenship. The paradox seems to be that while the authority of the state is constantly questioned and functionally undermined, there are growing pressures on states to confer full-fledged rights and entitlements on ever more citizens, to confer recognition and visibility on ever more institutions, movements, or organizations, and a growing demand on states from the so-called international community to address development problems effectively and to promote a "human rights culture," as the latest buzzword goes. This paradox has to do with the persistence of the imagination of the state as an embodiment of sovereignty condensed in the covenant, as Hobbes saw it; as the representation of the *volonté generale* producing citizens as well as subjects; as a source of social order and stability; and as an agency capable of creating a definite and authorized nation-space materialized in boundaries, infrastructure, monuments, and authoritative institutions. This myth of the state seems to persist in the face of everyday experiences of the often profoundly violent and ineffective practices of government or outright collapse of states. It persists because the state, or institutionalized sovereign government, remains pivotal in our very imagination of what a society is. Whether we agree on what the state means or not, "it" is, nonetheless, central to all that is *not* state: civil society, NGOs, the notion of a national economy, the market, and the sense of an international community.

This paradox of inadequacy and indispensability has robbed the state of its naturalness and has enabled scholars from many disciplines to study stateness as a historical and contingent construction. Following Philip Abrams's (1988) important unpacking of the state in theoretical terms and Corrigan and Sayer's (1985) work on the state in Britain, a growing body of work has begun to chart historical trajectories of state formation in various parts of the world. Much of this work has been inspired by Gramscian notions of class power articulated through always fragile and contested hegemonies, as well as Foucauldian notions of governance through knowledge-practices and different governmentalities, that is, the forms of *mentalité* suffusing techniques of *gouvernement* have informed other careful empirical studies of government and stateness. Among these, the works of Timothy Mitchell on Egypt (1988) and Partha Chatterjee on India (e.g., 1993) have gained wide currency within anthropology.

The contributions in this volume all share this denaturalizing approach to state and governance in the postcolonial world; they all study the state, politics, and notions of authority empirically from a variety of ethnographic sites; and they all position themselves in the space between a Gramscian and a Foucauldian position on power, government, and authority where much of the reconceptualization of the state has been taking place. This is, however, a field fraught with tension and contradictions. In Gramsci's understanding, state power emerged from the capacities, the will, and the resources of classes, or segments thereof. This "will to class power" gave birth to projects of political-cultural hegemony and strategies of social transformation aiming at the consolidation of class domination. Gramsci did not merely see the state as an executive of the bourgeoisie, as older Marxist theories had held, but maintained the foundational role of class power becoming realized in the form of a state: "The historical unity of the ruling classes is realized in the State and their history is essentially the history of States . . . the subaltern classes, by definition, are not unified and cannot unite until they are able to become a 'State'" (Gramsci 1971: 52). Gramsci tried in other words to denaturalize the state by pointing to its essentially political, and therefore unstable, partial and always violent character.

This line was also taken by subsequent Marxist and post-Marxist scholarship inspired by Althusser and Poulantzas, wherein the state remained thoroughly "socialized" and epiphenomenal, that is, an expression of social relations and ideological configurations and, hence, less interesting as a phenomenon in its own right. Also, a range of attempts in the 1980s to create a "state-centered" approach to the relationship between state and society failed to escape a simplistic dichotomy between "state" and "society." In most of these writings the state remained, somewhat paradoxically, a rather unexplored but unified "social actor" along with other ubiquitous and abstract social forces whose internal relationship, as in Marxist scholarship, determined the shape and functions of institutions and directions of policies (e.g., Evans et al. 1985; Migdal 1988).

Even in Laclau and Mouffe's (1985) influential poststructuralist rethinking of hegemony and politics beyond social determinism, the question of the state remained submerged in a wider category of "the political," now liberated from the straitjacket of essentialist thinking but also far removed from empirical categories. In this perspective, the state, or just institutions, remain entirely political, that is, alterable and floating, and only appear as relatively stable "nodal points" in discursive formations (Laclau and Mouffe 1985: 112–13) or as relatively routinized forms of power that have become "sedimented" and stable as their political origins have been effaced (Laclau 1990: 34–35).

Foucault found issues of legitimacy and sovereignty less relevant. Instead he explored how modernity was marked by the emergence of a broader field of government of conduct—of the self, of the family, of institutions, of the body, and so on. Foucault famously remarked, "We need to cut off the King's head: in political theory it still needs to be done" (1980: 121). In Foucault's view, the intensified regulation of modern societies was not a result of the penetration of the state as a center of power, but the other way around: the modern state was an ensemble of institutional forms made possible because of the general "governmentalization" of societies, that is, the specific ways human practices became objects of knowledge, regulation, and discipline. In this view, the modern state is not the source of power but the effect of a wider range of dispersed forms of disciplinary power that allow "the state" to appear as a structure that stands apart from, and above, society (Mitchell 1999: 89).

As has been remarked by many of Foucault's interpreters, one finds little interest in the state or in politics in Foucault's writings (see, e.g., Hindess 1996: 96–158; Ransom 1997: 101–53). Although frequently invoked in studies of resistance, Foucault had very little to say about resistance as such beyond mere reactions to new strategies of power, a kind of ubiquitous inertia he at one point likened to chemical processes (1982: 209). Instead, his interest was rather consistently in the conditions of possibilities of politics: how certain disciplinary forms, certain styles of knowledge and governmentalities made specific policies plausible, specific forms of rationality thinkable, and forms of political discourse possible and intelligible.[1]

Can these stances, harboring such different epistemological strategies, be reconciled? The answer is that they obviously cannot be reconciled completely, but also that they may not need to be. Our argument is that keeping these two perspectives in a productive tension with one another affords a somewhat broader perspective on the ambiguities of the state: as both illusory as well as a set of concrete institutions; as both distant and impersonal ideas as well as localized and personified institutions; as both violent and destructive as well as benevolent and productive. Modern forms of state are in a continuous process of construction, and this construction takes place through invocation of a bundle of widespread and globalized registers of governance and authority, or, as we prefer to call it, "languages of stateness." The central proposition of this volume is that the study of the state and its practices must discern and explore these different languages, their localized meanings, genealogies, and trajectories as they appear couched in mythologies of power, as practical, often nonpolitical routines or as violent impositions. This requires that one study how the state tries to make itself real and tangible through symbols, texts, and iconography, but also that one move beyond the state's own prose, categories, and perspective and study how the state appears in everyday and localized forms: in brief, to study the state, or discourses of the state, from "the field" in the sense of localized ethnographic sites, whether "inside" or "outside" of the evanescent boundary between society and the state that usually crumbles when subjected to empirical scrutiny.

Languages of Stateness

In a recent article on the character of the modern state, Pierre Bourdieu outlines in his inimitable style the problem of studying the state as one of escaping the "thought of the state": "To have a chance to really think a state which still thinks itself through those who attempt to think it, then, it is imperative to submit to radical questioning all the presuppositions inscribed in the reality to be thought and in the very thought of the analyst" (1999: 55). Bourdieu remarks wryly that given the ease with which "social problematics"—as they are diagnosed from the point of view of states claiming to represent society and the common good—are taken over by the social sciences and thus given the stamp of quasi-independent thinking, social scientists may in fact be singularly ill-equipped to meet this task.

Bourdieu expands Weber's classic formulation and characterizes the formation of the modern state as a process of concentration whereby "it," the x that is the state, acquires a monopoly of physical and symbolic violence over a territory and its population. The state condenses four types of "capital":

violence, economic capital (tax and regulation), informational capital (curricula, validation of knowledge, etc.), and symbolic capital (juridical discourse, nomination, validation, etc.). Together they constitute, argues Bourdieu, *capital étatique*, state capital, the (meta)authority to validate or invalidate other forms of authority, that is, to have the last word in a territory, to have the last judgment (1999: 67). To maintain this supreme position as the summit of society, each institutional field that sees itself as a part of the state must devise elaborate institutional rites, schemes of classifications, hierarchies of competence, achievement and honor to retain order and a distance between itself and "society" as well as other parts of the state. Bourdieu's concern is not so much whether or how the state governs but rather how the specific authority of the state, its stateness and its hegemonic location at the center of society, is (re)produced through symbols and rituals.

Although Bourdieu's outline of the symbolic registers of the state does not acknowledge its own mirroring of French *étatisme*, it does rather usefully remind us that the disciplinary forms of power of the state constantly are engaged in a perpetuated reproduction of the state, its institutions, its hierarchies, its own languages and forms of identities produced and sanctioned by its procedures. The state not only strives to be a state for its citizen-subjects, it also strives to be a state for itself and is expected by populations, politicians, and bureaucrats to employ "proper" languages of stateness in its practices and symbolic gestures.

As we try to understand how states in contemporary Africa and Asia are imagined and designed we are inadvertently thrown back on the historical development of modern forms of governance and sovereignty in Western Europe. In the eyes of politicians, rebels, planners, and social scientists, the history of European state formation continues to provide powerful images of what a proper state should be. As Crawford Young suggests, "Both colonialism and resistance to it yielded diffusion of a notion of stateness whose lineage lay in the European core" (1994: 16) It is important, therefore, to come to grips with the historical specificities and contingencies that shaped that historical experience, as Mitchell Dean points out in his discussion of Foucault's work on sovereignty and biopolitics in this volume.

Instead of seeing state formation in the postcolonial world as a flawed imitation of a mature Western form, we need to disaggregate and historicize how the idea of the modern state became universalized and how modern forms of governance have proliferated throughout the world. Instead of talking about the state as an entity that always/already consists of certain features, functions, and forms of governance, let us approach each actual state as a historically specific configuration of a range of languages of stateness, some practical, others symbolic and performative, that have been disseminated, translated, interpreted, and combined in widely differing ways and sequences across the globe.

Without pretending to be exhaustive, we single out three practical languages of governance and three symbolic languages of authority as particularly relevant for an ethnography of the state. The former are (1) the assertion of territorial sovereignty by the monopolization of violence by permanent and visible military and police forces; (2) the gathering and control of knowledge of the population—its size, occupations, production, and well-being—of this territory; and (3) the generation of resources and ensuring the reproduction and well-being of the population: in brief, development and management of the "national economy."

These languages of governance, always underpinned by knowledge-generating techniques, have historically been disseminated, exchanged, and transplanted globally, including in the non-Western world. As we know, this has been a highly unequal exchange of technology, flowing mainly from the colonial powers to the colonies, later from the so-called developed world—capitalist and socialist—to so-called underdeveloped countries. Today, NGOs and international aid agencies have emerged as major transmitters of new administrative technologies in the field of development. This technology transfer and exchange has involved export of a range of techniques: how to set up secret services and military logistics, budgetary models and taxation systems, entire packages of "high-intensity" biopolitical governance such as state-of-the-art systems monitoring deforestation, participatory local development projects empowering women, and the structure and procedures adopted by commissions trying to produce the truth about past regimes or atrocities.

The larger and more imprecise imagination of the state as an expression of effective territorial sovereignty and authority capable of protecting and nurturing population and economy became from the 1940s on the dominant global form of political community. Expressed in the programs and rhetoric of nationalist movements in the colonial and postcolonial world, authorized by the UN Charter, the principles of the Non-Aligned Movement and countless other documents, the nation-state is (or should be) a legitimate representation of the will and interests of its citizens. The production of states as not only loci of governance but centers of authoritative power has usually taken place through deployment of three symbolic languages of authority: (1) the institutionalization of law and legal discourse as the authoritative language of the state and the medium through which the state acquires discursive presence and authority to authorize; (2) the materialization of the state in series of permanent signs and rituals: buildings, monuments, letterheads, uniforms, road signs, fences; and (3) the nationalization of the territory and the institutions of the state through inscription of a history and a shared community on landscapes and cultural practices.

The first three are technical languages, the Foucauldian aspect, one may say, of practical governance, discipline, and productive biopolitical governance; the latter three are symbolic languages aiming at reproducing the imagination of the state as that specific authoritative center of a society in principle capable of issuing what Bourdieu calls the "last judgment." None of these languages necessarily goes together or presupposes each other; each has distinct historical trajectories, meanings, and degrees of sophistication in every case and locality. The essential thing is, however, that a state exists only when these "languages" of governance and authority combine and coexist one way or the other. The decisive step in the invention of the modern nation-state was exactly when the sovereign state became entrusted with expanding tasks of managing the social and economic well-being of its people, to protect, reproduce, and educate its citizens, to represent the nation, its history, and its culture(s), and to reproduce boundaries and institutions enabling the political community to be recognized by other states as a proper state.

Exploring the state through ethnographies thus raises the question of the limits of government: Where does the state begin and end? What is the specificity of the state as opposed to other forms of authority and governance that exist alongside it—in communities, within enterprises, in localities, and in families? Standard governmental practices in general are not considered to be part of the political sphere. They may be everyday routine government actions such as census taking, primary health care programs, road construction, alphabetization programs—all routine practices undertaken by inconspicuous government employees. The fact that these routines are considered outside the domain of political contention and its variable languages, however, is of importance. In what ways do people talk about and act on these forms of government practices? Through what genres are narratives and knowledge of the state or the government circulated? How do these genres relate to more elaborate languages of political contention and the style in which state and governmental authority is imagined? These are some of the questions we suggest could be asked and explored anew. As shown by several of the contributions in this volume, stateness does not merely grow out of official, or "stately," strategies of government and representation. The attribution of stateness to various forms of authority also emerges from intense and often localized political struggles over resources, recognition, inclusion, and influence. Whereas certain forms of state intervention may be loathed and resisted, other and more egalitarian forms of governance, or more benign forms of authority, may at the same time be intensely desired and asked for. Everyday forms of state power, in other words, are always suffused with and mediated by politics: contestation of authority, open defiance, as well as attempts to divert or privatize resources.

The centrality of the state to virtually every modern notion of a society thus means that the exploration of forms of state, stateness, and government inadvertently traverses a deeply normative ground. The state and modern governance is not something one can be for or against as such, for the simple reason that we cannot escape it. One can and should criticize specific forms of governance, undesirable institutions, and oppressive state practices, and many contributors in this volume do so. Implied in such critiques are not visions of the absence of government or the state as such, but rather the possibility of other, more humane and democratic forms of governance. While not ignoring that state power harbors the potential of unprecedented brutality in the name of a chilling dehumanized and scientistic utopia, as shown by Scott (1998), we advocate a more disaggregated and less essentializing study of the state by foregrounding the local, the emic, and the vernacular notions of governance, state authority, and resistance to state power. Instead of deploring the crisis or even collapse of postcolonial states in terms of the repercussions for regional stability (see, e.g., Zartman 1994), we find it more pertinent to explore the local and historically embedded ideas of normality, order, intelligible authority, and other languages of stateness. The constant recurrence of notions of stateness as a guarantee of order and ordinary life, shown by several contributors in this volume in various parts of the world, is thus not a barrier to critical engagement with the phenomenon of the state, but its most fundamental condition.

The contributions in this book are organized according to the three dimensions of the state outlined above: first, as technologies of governance encountered in the guise of classifications, forms to be filled in, rules to be obeyed, epistemologies learned, and so on; second, symbolic representations of the state as a locus and arbiter of justice and a symbol of a larger society; third, the invocations of the state as a set of institutions that can recognize, adjudicate, and authorize, that is, invest its authority in and give legitimacy to certain representatives, forms of community, public symbols, and also become loci of resistance and contestation. In the remainder of this introduction we unpack these aspects of state and politics and elaborate a bit on how each of the contributions in this volume feeds into them.

Colonialism, Modernity, and Governance

This volume grows out of an engagement with a range of postcolonial experiences of government, authority, and notions of rights in Africa, Asia, and Latin America. The central question is, of course, to what extent these experiences can be understood and interpreted through theoretical lenses that rely heavily on the historical trajectory of state formation in Western Europe. As we suggested above, the more productive answer to this question is, in our view, to abandon totalizing and culturalist notions of certain enduring "Eastern," "African," or "Western" forms of state and instead disaggregate and trace how various languages of stateness, not necessarily all purely Western in origin, have been spread, combined, and vernacularized in various parts of the world.

At the same time, it is also pertinent to remember that the Western imagination of the state, however traversed by myths and historical fiction, remains the globally most powerful idea of political order in the twentieth century, institutionalized in the international state system after 1945. The most central presupposition underlying this system is that all states in principle are, or will become, similar, or at least mutually intelligible, in their structures and in the rationalities governing their actions. Such an ahistorical understanding of the state was eagerly embraced by the nationalist political elites in the postcolonial world, anxious to transform their states into "normal" nation-states. That task entailed, among other things, that the state was represented effectively to its citizens and communities and that it manifested itself effectively on its territory. As pointed out by Sarah Radcliffe in her piece on Ecuador, many states approached this task through a systematic production of a geographical imagination. Through elaborate cartographies and education, the space of the state was domesticated as the proper place of the nation. This was the spatial matrix within which local communities hence could be inscribed, fixed, and ranked.

Other important interventions aiming at producing "normal" states were performed by development agencies, international donors, and the thrust of development theory that all supported the view of the state as an "agent of modernization," an island of modernity and rationality, a part of the so-called modern sector, and so on. This conception obviously disregarded the fact that most colonial administrations were designed to exercise forms of governance and control of populations and territory that often were crudely extractive and much less fine-grained and less intensive than in the European homelands. As Mahmood Mamdani (1996a) has pointed out forcefully in the context of Africa, colonial administration often relied heavily on indirect rule, on a somewhat random brutality, and on local notables to whom many details of governance and tax collection were entrusted. As colonial administrations were turned into the backbone of the new postcolonial nation-states, their excessive centralization and bifurcation in rural and urban segments, their habits of summary governance at a distance, their lack of independent judiciaries, and the heavy-handed techniques deployed to control the majority of their populations were suddenly diagnosed as developmental flaws, as lack of modernity, as "weak states."

Reflecting on the "flawed" states in the non-Western world, Samuel Huntington opened his controversial book with the sentence "The most important distinction among countries concerns not their form of government but their degree of government" (1968: 1). In his text Huntington acknowledged the capacity of communist movements to transform states into effective vehicles of governance, and he recommended, infamously, that the Western world should realize that states governed by so-called praetorian regimes were more likely to create order, stable institutions, and economic growth than democratic regimes likely to be overwhelmed and destabilized by the overload of expectations from a wide array of interest groups. Huntington was fascinated by the ability of strong governments to "normalize" the state apparatuses of developing societies, that is, to discipline them, extend them, make them capable of effective penetration of evermore social and economic relations.

Turning the state into an autonomous actor capable of swift social reform was, however, an agenda and a desire shared broadly across the political spectrum both within and outside the postcolonial world. Radical regimes in Africa, Asia, and the Middle East swept to power promising rapid modernization and strict social discipline, often blending elements of Soviet planning, militarization, and notions of secular modernity taken from Atatürk and Nasser. In Latin America dreams of using the state, and sometimes the military, in a rapid and pervasive drive for development, modernity, and recognition were nurtured by young radicals, bureaucrats, and officers. In the burgeoning development industry similar ideas of transformation through stronger and more effective governance were prominent, not so much aiming at national grandeur and recognition, but driven by desires to impart economic development, political stability, and techniques of poverty eradication to the postcolonial world. Much of this developmental desire meant that profoundly political issues of social transformation and institutional designs were depoliticized and put in the hands of developmental agencies and experts who transformed them into technocratic designs and further removed governance from the realm of the everyday, the vernacular, and the intelligible (Ferguson 1990).

As we know by now, many of these attempts to strengthen the state turned into outright authoritarian regimes that promoted the interests of narrow elites and, in effect, eroded the institutions and authority of the state. The existence of oligarchic structures of power, the organization of entrenched class interests, and the production of new, self-interested bureaucratic elites were obviously central to this development. Another problem was that the very form of the apparatuses employed to effect this grand transformation of the postcolonial societies bore the indelible mark of colonial designs just as the inventory of techniques employed in these tasks were steeped in colonial notions of control, policing, and summary governance of communities rather than citizens.

Colonial states, however, were never full-fledged states, Crawford Young (1994) reminds us. They had no sovereignty, no autonomy, no embedding in society and remained appendages to powerful European military and administrative complexes. The incompleteness and abnormality of the colonial state was in fact one of the central criticisms waged against imperial rule by nationalists, from the early "Creole nationalists" around Bolivar, to the founders of the Indian National Congress and nationalists throughout Africa. Young argues that "the emergence of the colonial polity as a distinctive species of the state genus occurs as a process paralleling the development of the modern state" (44). This means, argues Young, that our ideas of what a colonial state was, did, and wanted to achieve have to be historicized and seen in the context of the wider development of governmental technologies and political imaginaries at their time. There were, for instance, enormous differences among the maritime Portuguese empire bent on the "revenue imperative" (52), the Spanish empire organized around extension of regal power and the authority of the Church to new territories, and the austere mercantile rationalities governing the early British and Dutch empires. It was, Young reminds us, only in the nineteenth century that the European powers began the systematic construction of specific institutions aimed at governing the colonial populations and territories.

One corollary of this observation is that colonialism in Latin America had a complexion completely different from the high-noon imperialism that hit the African continent in the 1880s. The states of Latin America can hardly be regarded as postcolonial states in the same sense as their counterparts in Africa. The rationalities governing state practices in Latin America developed alongside those of Europe and North America, although in a mimetic relationship, as Michael Taussig (1997) has pointed out. For Taussig, the efforts at creating illusions of proper states in "the European Elsewhere" remain travestic, shot through with utopias and an (often absurd) zeal in the face of a colonial history that refuses to support any narrative of autochthonous authority (57–61). The desire to modernize, the eager embrace of *cientismo* and rational governance among national and local elites in large parts of Latin America were fueled by the circulation of the languages of stateness mentioned above, that is, new techniques of control and knowledge through which societies, communities, and selves could be improved, governed, and appreciated.[2] David Nugent's contribution to this volume gives an arresting illustration of how the desire to become modern also was a powerful impulse in political mobilizations in Peru in the first half of the twentieth century. In a different and yet related context, Tim Mitchell (1988) has shown how nineteenth-century Egypt was (self-)colonized without overt colonialism through the internalization of scientific genres of knowledge, modern methods of administration and surveillance, and styles of cultural self-objectification through European registers by Egyptian intellectuals and administrators.

But the feasibility of governmental technologies was always constrained by the location of a state in the wider international economy and by the resources and revenues at its disposal in the domestic economy. As Fernando Coronil reminds us in his study of the formation of the Venezuelan oil economy, "In capitalist societies, command over persons rests in the hands of the state, while command over resources lies in the hands of capital" (1997: 64). His study forcefully demonstrates how the modern Venezuelan state was restructured and reimagined as the country emerged as a leading oil producer in the world but also a captive in the larger global economy, completely dependent on foreign technology and global oil prices. Not only were state policies reconfigured around this abundant resource, oil was also introduced into the dominant political imagination as Venezuela was reconstructed as a modern "oil nation": the sublated unity of a natural body (s-oil) and a timeless collective body of the people, the nation (67–117).

It is these actually existing forms of governance and the trajectories of institutions and representations of the state in various parts of the postcolonial world that this volume explores. Throughout we try to avoid the usual negative prefixes (weak, disorganized, incoherent, illegitimate, deinstitutionalized, etc.) that still enframe the problematics and the puzzles to be solved in most political science and development studies literature on the postcolonial state. One of the most promising avenues away from this deadlock is to disaggregate the state into the multitude of discrete operations, procedures, and representations in which it appears in the everyday life of ordinary people. By treating the state as a dispersed ensemble of institutional practices and techniques of governance we can also produce multiple ethnographic sites from where the state can be studied and comprehended in terms of its effects, as well as in terms of the processes that shape bureaucratic routines and the designs of policies.

State, Violence, and Justice: Between Imaginary and Apparatus

However analytically useful it is to denaturalize the state and to get beyond the state's own prose and problematics of social order and development, we should not forget that the notion of the state probably remains the most powerful lens through which society, nation, and even the ubiquitous but elusive notion of "the economy" is imagined. The modern state is not just a set of rationalities or institutional forms. It has also acquired vital mythological dimensions that give its authority both historical aura and weight. The "myth of the state" that Ernst Cassirer (1946) saw as a malign product of fascist and organicist ideology is, we would argue, absolutely crucial to the organization and the experience of coherence and order of modern societies in most parts of the world. The entire idea of political legitimacy, of the difference between naked power and authority, the idea that "the Law" is something that stands above the contingencies of everyday life and incarnates a certain collective justice, the crucial discourse of rights as something that once defined and authorized become unassailable and inalienable: all hinge on the perpetuated myth of the state's coherence and ability to stand "above society," as it were.

Since Hobbes theorized the absolutist state, European notions of political power and the state have undoubtedly been starkly reductionist. To paraphrase Hobbes: "Covenants without the sword are but words," and at the basis of the state, of power, of legitimacy, we find, purely and simply, violence. In this view, royal pomp, state rituals, and modern ideological formation essentially serve to efface and occlude this foundational violence, which is the origin of a state. Clifford Geertz has called this "the great simple that remains through all sophistications . . . politics, finally, is about mastery: Women and Horses, Power and War" (1980: 134). This, argues Geertz, has led to an unfortunate blindness toward the importance of symbols and ideas in their own right to statecraft and state power. Geertz retrieves the importance of this in his study of the classical Balinese theater state, the *negara*, a polity whose basis of sovereignty was its status as "an exemplary center—a microcosm of the supernatural order." Pomp, ritual, and spectacle were not devices to represent the state or occlude its violent nature; they constituted the core of the state that was based on the "controlling idea that by providing a model . . . a faultless image of civilized existence, the court shapes the world around it" (13). The dramas of that polity were neither lies nor illusions, concludes Geertz: "They were what there was" (136).

The negara should remind us that there are languages of stateness other than those invented in Europe in the past two centuries but also that the rationality of intent, purpose, and action often imputed to modern states—by the analyst as well as the citizen-subject—tends to occlude the important mythical dimensions of the modern state. Maybe it is the very idea of state actions as guided by an abstract, omniscient, and rational intelligence—ceaselessly celebrated and vilified in novels and films on spies and intelligence agencies—that constitutes the very core of the myth of the modern state.

The widespread idea of the state as *a thing* is indeed at odds with basic tendencies in how states develop. As modern forms of governmentality penetrate and shape human life in unprecedented ways, the practices and sites of governance have also become ever more dispersed, diversified, and fraught with internal inconsistencies and contradictions. This has not necessarily weakened the state in terms of the capacity of policies and designs to create social effects. The strength of the modern state seems, on the contrary, to be its dispersion and ubiquity. The modern states of, say, Western Europe are today more diverse, more imprecise in their boundaries vis-à-vis other forms of organization, more privatized or semiprivatized than ever before, more integrated in supranational structures and yet apparently stronger than ever before. The new role of the state is, Helmut Wilke (1992) has argued, to supervise governance by semiprivate organizations, local authorities, self-governing bodies of all kinds, NGOs, and so on, rather than to actually govern directly.

The neoliberal attempts to restructure and trim the apparatuses of postcolonial states, originally designed for "low-intensity governance," along similar lines, however, have rarely produced a similar flexibility and enhanced capacity. The predominant organization of postcolonial governance as "command policies" have meant that IMF-prescribed delegation of powers to the local level of the state more often than not has produced deep fragmentation, lack of coordination, and an undermining of the notion of the state as a guarantee of social order. For subject populations or citizens, the experience of the state has, in many cases (e.g., in the postcommunist world), changed from a frightening Kafkaesque labyrinth of impersonal power into the random brutality of a state parceled into smaller fiefdoms run by local bureaucrats and police officers. In the more extreme cases of state collapse, as witnessed in western and central Africa in the 1990s, state administration ceases to be a factor in everyday life, which is thrown back in an almost Hobbesian state where raw military might emerge as the ultimate basis of legitimacy. Even then, amid chaos and bloodshed, some warlords attempt to create zones of stability and to erect something resembling a state: taxation instead of random plunder, dispensation of "justice" through courtlike ritual instead of instant killings, territorial control, and, in some cases, appeal to subjects in the name of a shared community or destiny.

There is little doubt that a mythology of the coherence, knowledge, and rationalities of the (ideal) state exists, thrives, and empowers many otherwise widely discrepant practices. This myth is carefully cultivated inside the bureaucracy and among political figures as the state's own myth of itself and is constantly enacted through grand state spectacles, stamps, architecture, hierarchies of rank, systems of etiquette, and procedures within the vast expanse of the bureaucracy. But do these elaborate state rituals actually manage to create or reproduce a state mythology coherent enough for the state to impose itself on populations with effective authority? Or are these spectacles and rituals of the state more for internal consumption among bureaucrats, clerks, accountants, officers—a daily, routinized reassurance of the importance and power of the state that actually serves to strengthen the sense of a unified stateness of dispersed forms of government?

Drawing on Foucault's insights regarding the specifically modern reorganization of space and time into routinized, repetitive, and internalized disciplines and forms of surveillance, Mitchell (1999) argues that the "appearance of structures" on the basis of these micro-operations seems to be one of the most fundamental features of modernity in general and the preeminent feature of the "state effect" that modern governmentality produces. The state is the "abstraction of political practices" analogous to the way capital is the abstraction appearing from labor: "We must analyze the state . . . not as an actual structure, but as the powerful, apparently metaphysical effect of practices" (89). The multiple practices involved in policing and controlling territorial boundaries is that which creates the nation-state as effect,[3] just as the technicality of the legal process is what (re)produces the notion of the Law.

The question is how these insights can be given historical substance and differentiality and how we can create ethnographic sites from where such "state abstractions" can be studied. One obvious, if very underdeveloped type of study is that of the bureaucracy itself: its routines, its personnel and their internal cultures, gestures, and codes, its mode of actual production of authority and effects by the drafting of documents, uses of linguistic genres, and so on: in brief, an anthropology of the policy process that looks at it as ritual and as production of meaning rather than production of effective policies per se. Michael Herzfeld's (1992) work on the symbolic registers developed by Western bureaucracy has laid out valuable conceptual groundwork for such studies but has not been followed by thorough ethnographic work that could demonstrate its wider relevance. Herzfeld's own text manages to produce only brief but highly interesting ethnographic illustrations of the imbrications of bureaucratic categories and idioms and everyday life, mainly from contemporary Greece. Lars Buur's analysis in this volume of the minutiae of the everyday workings of the South African Truth and Reconciliation Commission represents another example of how anthropological sensibilities applied to the routines, rituals, and underlying assumptions of legal-administrative practices can yield valuable insights.

The discourse of rights that has assumed such critical importance in international politics and has given rise to a whole new human rights sector within the development industry is also centrally linked to the myth of the state. As much as the Law as a concept depends on the state's mythical qualities, the practices of solemnly encoding certain rights in constitutions, of entrenching and interpreting these rights in judicial practices and invoking them in political rhetoric also hinges on the efficiency of the imagination of the state as a guarantor of these rights. If that imagination is ineffective, the discourse of rights is inconsequential.

Even more important, if the legal apparatus of the state is unable to translate these abstract rights into actual and effective judgments that prescribe precise entitlements that can affect people's lives or empower them, the appeal to a larger notion of rights makes no sense. Instead, local communities engage in small and inconspicuous acquisitions of entitlements—to land, customs, employment, and so on. Rachel Sieder's contribution analyzes the protracted efforts in Guatemala to develop new and more inclusive forms of citizenship in a society characterized by deep and enduring differences between an elite "owning" the state and the large Indian communities. In Sieder's analysis it is apparent that encoding rights in legislation is not a question of handing down entitlements to grateful subjects, but a complex negotiation of how existing entitlements stipulated in customary law and localized settlements can be codified and inscribed in more durable and abstract rights. Thus, the case illustrates how one of the most powerful languages of stateness—the codification of social relations in law—works in processes of state formation at the turn of the century.

Another way of studying the myth of the state is to regard it as a form of "social fantasy" circulating among citizens and communities. This fantasy is produced and reproduced by numerous encounters, everyday forms of defiance and obedience, ranging from fantasies of the mighty and evil state hatching hyperrational designs (a genre popular among radical groups on the left as well as on the far right) to popular genres of conspiracy theories that often impute almost superhuman omniscience and omnipresence to political leaders and agencies of the state. These genres represent widespread, popular, and highly interesting points of access to how the state is mythologized, externalized, and abstracted from ordinary existence yet is believed to be omnipresent.

Achille Mbembe's (1992) well-known and controversial depiction of the obscenity and absurdity connected with public exercise of state power in the "postcolony," in casu Cameroon, points to the importance of the state as an entity manifesting itself in spectacles. To Mbembe, the impulse of state power in the postcolonial world, due to its origin in a system of excessively violent, colonial power, is organized around an equally excessive fantasy of making the imperatives of the state, *commandement*, the hegemonic center of society. But this is impossible because "the postcolony is chaotically pluralistic and . . . it is in practice impossible to create a single, permanently stable system out of all the signs, images and markers current in the postcolony . . . this is why, too, the postcolony is, *par excellence*, a hollow pretence, a regime of unreality (*régime du simulacre*)" (8).

Mbembe takes popular forms of ridiculing of power, jokes of a sexual nature about the men in power, their bodily functions, appetite, and so on, as examples of how this hollowness of state power is dealt with. In itself, there is nothing African or even postcolonial about such joking about the elevated and yet profane representations of power.[4] But the specifically postcolonial feature, Mbembe suggests, is the way the state is excessively fetishized in pomp, ritual, and entertainment, and the way these spectacles are disarmed but also domesticated through jokes and humor to an extent that there is a coexistence or conviviality between the official and the everyday world: "In fact officialdom and the people have many references, not the least of which is a certain conception of the aesthetics and the stylistics of power . . . it must furnish public proof of its prestige by a sumptuous presentation of status" (9).

Mbembe's argument is that to be legitimate, power must be represented within already established registers of pomp. The holders of power must present themselves as firm but also generous and endowed with an excessive appetite. This resonates with J. F. Bayart's (1991) argument that African politics remain organized around specific discursive registers that often predate colonialism, such as the "politics of the belly," understood both as a practical politics of feeding populations and a symbolics of power around metaphors of eating and digesting. Mbembe uses the execution of two prisoners in Cameroon and the cheering crowds gathered to witness it as an example of this specific mode of postcolonial power that thrives on a certain measure of complicity and involvement of broader sections of the population through enjoyment. Unlike the excruciating torture and execution of Damiens for regicide that Foucault made famous in the opening pages of *Discipline and Punish*, the execution in Cameroon was organized more like a theater celebrating the splendor of the state. To Mbembe, the grotesque (and ineffective) character of power in the postcolony is revealed in its lack of seriousness, its indulgence, its theatrical and obscene nature, and its successful involvement of the population in "cheap imitations of power so as to reproduce its epistemology" (1992: 29).

Taussig has also recently explored how the idea of the state is fetishized through a range of magical transactions and spectacles, from spirit possessions to official textbooks and monuments, in a Latin American country. Not unlike Mbembe's work, a sense of the absurd and surreal suffuses the representations of power that ceaselessly revolve around stories and images of the "Liberator" (Bolivar), his court, his black general Paez, later elevated to the status of El Negro Primero, a figure that connotes a primitivity and virile power of the plains, both loathed and desired by the urban elites (Taussig 1997: 94–95); the death of Bolivar, his second funeral on South American soil as the founding moment of the state, and the rumors that his heart had been removed "to live on in every South American" (104). The story about how a commander of the M-19 guerrillas in 1974, Alvaro Fayad, stole the Liberator's sword, the ultimate fetish of the state, from a museum is particularly arresting. The communist guerrillas were at first indifferent to such symbols, but once in their possession they, too, fetishized the "thing," wrapped it in multiple layers of cloth and plastic so that it literally grew and grew to such a size that it stuck out of the trunk of a car and had to have a small red flag tied to it in traffic! This state "thing" disappeared, and rumor has it that it was given to Castro (190–95). Taussig's point is close to Mbembe's: state power is fetishized through displays and spectacles but becomes effective as authority only because it invades, and is appropriated by, everyday epistemologies of power, of the magical, the spiritual, and the extraordinary.

In his work on the role of spirit mediums during the guerrilla war in Zimbabwe, David Lan (1985) also points to the crucial role of spirit mediums, *mhondoros*, in legitimizing the struggle of the Zimbabwe African National Union (ZANU-PF) in what became known as "the second Chimurenga," the second war of liberation. Lan shows how the spirit mediums, being in contact with the ancestral spirits, gradually shifted their loyalty to the liberation movement, which had a decisive effect on the course of the war. As independence was announced on the newly renamed Zimbabwe Broadcasting Corporation, it was followed by a ZANU song celebrating the spirit of Grandmother Nehanda, who had been in the first Chimurenga (in 1896) and in the second as well (217–18). In the following months and years, this "nationalization of the mhondoros" continued, and the picture of Nehanda was always placed above that of Mugabe at official functions. It appears that some of the spirit mediums later shifted their loyalties away from the ruling party, but nationalization was in a sense complete when the new state authorized the association of traditional healers to practice as doctors, and when spirit mediums were given a special license under this association and the right to use the letters "SM" (!) in advertising and official communication (219–20).

These and other works have opened a field that approaches the construction of the state in everyday life, although they remain within conventional areas of anthropological research: magic, spirits, the body. Several of the contributions in this volume attempt to approach more routinized and less dramatic forms of folk theories of the state and of political authority. Fiona Wilson's analysis in this volume of the narrative of a rural schoolteacher in Peru demonstrates rather strikingly how notions of the proper nation-to-be, of modernity, of the ideal Peruvian peasant exist in forms that in many ways are separated from the actually existing state in the area. Oskar Verkaaik also illustrates the pertinence of rumors of intelligence, informers, and the supposed "capture" of the state by ethnic conspiracies in contemporary Pakistan.

However, in many cases the myth of the state is actually sustained by the rather mundane practices of authorization and recognition carried out by the state: the acts of authorizing marriages and registration of deaths and births, the recognition of deputations or representatives of communities or interests as legitimate and reasonable and thus entitled to be consulted in policy matters, the certification by the state of institutions, professions, exams, standards, and so on. Such practices reproduce the myth of the state by literally implanting it in people's lives, as revered documents carefully stored or proudly displayed on the walls, as stamps, permits, titles from where certain entitlements, social status, and respect flow. The upholding of a certain image of the state as a revered object of respect and authority is often vital to the status, livelihood, and identity of millions of people. Nowhere is the importance and dependence on the mythological dimensions of the state more pathetically represented than in the profound disillusion one can read in the rugged faces of elderly Russians, desperately displaying their medals and distinctions from the Soviet era in the vain hope of extracting a minimum of respect when receiving their pensions that now are reduced to mere crumbs. A great many of the institutions that governed the everyday life of Soviet citizens are still in place and many of the routines are unchanged, but the power of the myth of the state has vanished.

In her thoughtful piece, Aletta Norval deals with another instance of the vanishing of one type of state, the South African apartheid state, and the imaginative attempt to provide the new order, the New South Africa, with a new authorized national history through the narrative built by the proceedings of the Truth and Reconciliation Commission. This is a history of evil and its exorcising, of forgiving and overcoming, but it is also, crucially, an attempt to reduce a more fundamental sense of undecidability and to conceal the impossibility of complete reconciliation.

State, Community, Hegemony, and the Art of Politics

A number of contributions to this volume deal with the relationship between the state and "its other," the social identities, practices, and allegiances that states "are formed *against*," to use Corrigan and Sayer's expression (1985: 7). The notion of community is often used to depict the other of the state, whether local, political, religious, or other communities, that are imagined to be located outside, but in relation to, the state. Much of the recent discussion of the nature and dynamics of this relationship draws on the notion of hegemony, thus posing the question of how noncoercive forms of domination are constituted and how communities are brought within the purview of the state.

In particular, remembering Gramsci's preoccupation with practical politics and the construction of intellectual and moral leadership, we may ask about the importance and dynamics of politics, understood as a distinct social field, in relation to the constitution, negotiation, and change of state-centered hegemonies. In other words, how do political operators control or transform the state on behalf of specific economic and social groups?

In this volume, the relation between politics and the state is explored in two different ways. Several of the contributions deal with popular perceptions of politics as something that tends to "pollute" the state, and the state as something that can be "conquered" or "captured" through politics. In Karachi and Hyderabad, rumors depict the Pakistani state as captured by Punjabis and feed into the sense of displacement and loss so pivotal to Muhajir identity, as shown by Verkaaik. In his essay on legal inquest and policing in contemporary Mumbai, Thomas Blom Hansen shows how police officers and social workers share the conviction that the "politicization of the state" constitutes an obstacle to effective and rational governance. This diagnosis of competitive politics as the very source of the decay, corruption, and weakening of the state is shared widely by bureaucrats, development workers, social scientists, journalists, and certainly millions of ordinary people in contemporary India.

A different way of exploring the relations between politics and the state is in the context of radical political changes when new governments elaborate strategies and policies for profound reforms of the state, in this volume represented by the essays on the current South African transition. Within political science this theme is often discussed under the rubric of regime or form of regime, one of three dimensions of governance: state (the notion of the state as legal and military structures of considerable permanence), government (the wider institutional structures and administrative procedures), and regime (the political organization and will in power). Although this is a necessary unpacking of the term state, it is clearly not radical enough to allow for any ethnographic exploration of the state and state-community relations.

As noted by David Nugent (1994), the bulk of the literature on state-society relations argue on the basis of an implicit model that posits two abstractions, state and community, as two essential and bounded entities in opposition to each other. One is seen as essentially expanding, transforming, and coercive, the other as essentially conservative and actively resisting imposed transformations. This, however, is only one of several possible "junctures" of state-community relations. In the present volume, Nugent himself shows how the imagery of this kind of state-community opposition in the case of Chachapoyas, Peru, is an outcome of a historically specific process of transformation from the 1930s to the 1980s. In the 1930s, in the context of an emerging populist regime, the petit bourgeois Chachapoyanos were actively involved in producing themselves as a community of citizens, as well as the state as an effectively ruling apparatus in the province. But from the late 1960s, relations have deteriorated and the community has developed into an antimodern, antistatist "traditionalism" depicting the state as external and imposing.

Finn Stepputat shows how village populations in postconflict Guatemala engage in a similar, not necessarily coerced, extension of state institutions. Intertwined with struggles for communal leadership and collective recognition, many villagers strive to develop their places into urbanlike, formal sites of governance with public services, offices, parks, and other elements that symbolize the recognition of communities of citizens. In the process, "local community" is stabilized as a territorial, administrative entity, an interface between state and population. In this sense, the labeling and institutionalization of a village-community works as a kind of enframing of segments of the population (Mitchell 1988). The struggle for state-centered yet autonomous urbanization feeds the local appropriations of the system of political representation and contributes to the creation of a space of local politics: the"politics from here" as opposed to the (less legitimate) "politics from there."

Martijn van Beek offers us a different example of state-community relations in which the introduction of bureaucratic categories of inclusion evokes practices of representation and belonging that go beyond the "either resistance or compliance" dichotomy. Analyzing the process leading to political autonomy for Ladakh in India, van Beek shows convincingly that ethnicization and communalization is the price for being included in the liberal democracies of the contemporary world of nations. At the same time, however, the British colonial fear of "communalism" and the posterior denial of communalism in India have premised the specific form of political representation of the Ladakhi. They have been recognized and granted autonomy as eight different tribes. Such exclusive categories are at odds with the disorder of social practices of identification in Ladakh, but because tribalism and communalism are extremely powerful images in this context, the population engages in everyday dissimulations in order to practice the exclusivist categories of political inclusion.

Contrary to the school of subaltern studies, our usage of the notion of community is not a priori; it is not referring to a more or less autonomous repository or space of resistance to domination, homogenization, and disciplinary techniques. In spite of his relational analysis of the formation of community, Partha Chatterjee, for example, sticks to a binary opposition, not between "state and civil society" but between "capital and community" (1993: 13). Like the abstractions of people or "the popular"—usually defined through negativity, as opposed to elite and elite ways of doing things—

community is imagined either as something good, pure, and authentic or as something dangerous, unpredictable, and ungovernable, as in the above case of India. Genealogically, these opposed imageries of community and state can be traced to the tension between romanticism and rationalism in the European tradition (Hansen 1997a).

Insofar as the notion of community is locked in an opposition to modern, rational society it calls for images of localization, boundedness, reciprocity, and so on, but also of tradition, backwardness, parochiality, and immobility. Such images are often invoked in paternalist governmental or nongovernmental interventions on behalf of the communities, such as those promoted by the *indigenista* movement in several Latin American countries. Here anthropologists and other urban intellectuals developed policies and techniques for the integration of "backward" and "humiliated" indigenous people into the nation-state. Several progressive governments have taken this ensemble of images, policies, and techniques on board, for example, in Mexico after the revolution.

An increasing number of studies have shown how state-centered representations have worked to incorporate communities in a hierarchically organized yet homogeneous nation-state through strategies that relate certain identities to certain spaces, time sequences, substances, and so on (e.g., Urban and Scherzer 1991; Coronil and Shursky 1991; Rowe and Schelling 1991; see also Alonso 1994). Who are at the center, who are at the margins? Who belong to the past of the nation, who belong to the future? In this way, representations tend to naturalize some groups occupying positions in government or in the political system and other groups occupying inferior positions. However, we need more studies to scrutinize the institutional aspects of such hegemonic strategies. We have to ask how the opposition and the boundaries between state and communities have come into being, which differences and identities that have been subsumed are the main opposition to the state, how relations are organized and negotiated across the boundaries, how communities are represented, and by whom. Community may well be represented differently by different politicians, by schoolteachers, and by other contenders for leadership positions.

In her study of one of the many marginal regions in contemporary Indonesia, Anna Tsing notes that the formation of local leadership is of vital importance in the incorporation of the region into Indonesia's dominant languages of stateness: "At the border between state rule and the wild stand those who dare to define, defy and demand administration. These are the men whom I call 'leaders' because they are ambitious enough to tell the government that they represent the community and their neighbors that they represent the state" (1993: 72). Tsing shows the multiple roles performed by these men as brokers between governmental agencies and the community they bring into existence in a clear form, but also how these roles produce an authority that is employed in settling local disputes within the communities' own discursive registers and practices, such as marriage cases (127–53). The paradox is that as these marginal areas are subjected to more intensive governance, the importance of these men tends to recede: "Local leaders invoke the authority of the state, but often lose out if the state arrives" (151).[5]

The contributions in this volume share an understanding of hegemony as a *process* of constructing "not a shared ideology but a common material and meaningful framework for living through, talking about, and acting upon social orders characterized by domination" (Roseberry 1994: 361). In this sense state-community relations may be interpreted as hegemonic processes that over time develop "a common discursive framework": a shared, state-authorized language of cognition, control, and contestation. An important feature of such a framework is the formation and delimitation of a distinct field of politics, including the definition of specific spaces for politics and a common "language of contention" for struggle and negotiation among different political actors (363).

This perspective allows us to scrutinize the complex processes through which certain phenomena become objects of political debate and eventually political intervention, and others not; how ideological formations produce distinctions between the politically permissible and nonpermissible, between proper public conduct and improper. Transitions, for example, from conflict to postconflict or from one political regime to another, are privileged contexts for the investigation of ways that regimes pursue and negotiate inclusions and exclusions from the limelight of the political field.

In other words, the delimitation of the field of politics defines the boundary between undisputed, naturalized, and commonsensical *doxa* and the *heterodoxa* of politically disputed alternatives—at least in the discursive genres that symbolically constitute stateness, such as the distinctive bureaucratic "legalese." At the heart of the doxa of the political field are the professional languages and the concepts and categories by which social and political sciences analyze state, economy, and politics. These forms of knowledge do not exist outside or independently of the state but are vital components in dominant ideological formations that try to define the character and limits of the state, how politics is supposed to be conducted, how institutions should function, and so on. They are, in other words, intrinsic to the symbolic production of stateness. As Mitchell (1999) has shown persuasively, the emergence of political science as a discipline in postwar America was indeed informed by the larger fear of communist expansion and by a quest for American global hegemony. It also became a highly influential analytical and disciplinary technique that sought to devise a certain universal and "normalizing" conceptual vocabulary within which "state," "political system," "society," and "economy" could be understood as discrete and concrete entities available for analysis and amenable to governmental intervention (77–80).

In the same vein, but at a different level, Akhil Gupta's analysis in this volume of an extension program for *anganwadis* (day care centers) in North India points usefully to the way in which ostensibly technocratic schemes have profoundly political effects. Gupta shows how the program problematizes gender inequality as a developmental problem, and how the official depiction of increased independence of women as a possible source of development and economic gain slowly encroaches on older discourses on gender. This practical reconceptualization of gender may over time contribute to the transformation of gender relations in North Indian villages, although not necessarily in the emancipatory direction envisaged by the policymakers.

Hegemony thus also works through the development of technocratic programs and institutions that govern by virtue of routines, internal bureaucratic logics, and allotted resources without being directed by political forces in any strict sense. In this sense, hegemony is diffuse and difficult to pin down. If we further consider the complexity of governance in modern, politically pluralist, and decentralized states where politicians and bureaucratic bodies at different administrative levels may dispute decisions, divert programs, and struggle over jurisdictional boundaries, it becomes very difficult to perceive of hegemony as being closed, monolithic, and coordinated. Compared to the older and more centralized apparatus inherited from the colonial powers, it is undoubtedly much more difficult to dominate and control a multilayered and intensely competitive system of democratic government that has emerged in many postcolonial societies.

Partha Chatterjee (1998) has argued recently that conventional distinctions between state and civil society are unable to capture the richness and specificity of the actually existing forms of political struggle one finds in postcolonial societies. The state and civil society belong, he argues, to the same conceptual world of orderly negotiation of interests properly organized and conducted according to certain rules and conventions: "The institutions of modern associational life [were] set up by nationalist elites in the era of colonial modernity . . . [and] embody the desire of this elite to replicate in its own society the forms as well as substance of Western modernity" (62). Against such a yardstick of formal and educated debate and organization most forms of politics and negotiations of power in the postcolonial world inevitably appear chaotic and lacking in purpose and formality, Chatterjee suggests. Instead, he coins the term "political society" for the zone of negotiations and mediations between state and population, wherein the main mediators are movements, political parties, informal networks, and many other channels through which the developmental state and the vast majority of the population interact. This distinction between civil and political society is pertinent and highly relevant. If we are to understand how issues of welfare and questions of rights and democracy are negotiated in the postcolonial world, we need to understand the dynamics, the tacit rules, and the historicity of its many political societies.

However, the rough and tumble of competitive politics at many levels does not necessarily mean that hegemony is ineffective. On the contrary, a low level of political and ideological coordination, a diffuse nature of power, a nonreflexive routinization of governance and political processes, and a commonsensical acceptance of the domination of political life by certain groups and families may well be what make hegemony endure. But if this is the case we must consider the question of how, or if, political operators are able to establish control and alter hegemonic relations through the state apparatus.

The Art of Politics

To understand how political forces deal with the state, how they seek to address and reproduce the constituencies and social interests they consolidated (or created) on their road to political office, we need to analyze more carefully, and with more ethnographic precision, what ruling parties do when they rule.

Assuming political power does not mean that a new government can change institutional routines overnight or that social practices within the bureaucracy can be easily modified. The state is an enormous and amorphous mechanism that functions along a whole range of discrete and often self-perpetuating logics, bereft of any unifying and encompassing rationale. For a new political regime to be effective in implementing parts of its professed objectives, it needs to produce a fairly coherent "state project," as Bob Jessop (1990) has argued. Jessop suggests that political forces that desire to transform a society must let themselves be absorbed in thoroughgoing institutional reforms and in a certain reinvention of the state. Governance and attempts to transform social structures through administrative reform in the main do take place *inside* the technocratic confines of government departments. Only insofar as a thorough reform of institutions take place, as it happens at the behest of ANC in South Africa right now or as the Congress Party gradually brought about in India in the 1950s and 1960s, may we legitimately talk of a political force actually dominating the state in any meaningful sense.

But often, such structural reforms are not carried through. Yesterday's revolutionary regimes end up focusing on political changes of symbolic value or on crude nationalism rather than on implementing structural reform. The case of Zimbabwe, where revolutionary rhetoric has been combined with the persistence of a colonial structure of landholding and agricultural economy, immediately comes to mind. Without exaggeration, we might say that most contemporary societies remain governed by yesterday's administrative systems and procedures.

Bearing this relative "ungovernability" and inertia of the state in mind, the issue of how ruling parties rule and how we can study the ways political operators operate may be restated in a slightly more precise form. We mention only three of the modes of direct political intervention in the processes of governance that authors in this volume touch on:

1. Prior to any major change in policies or institutions, most governments will appoint committees to review an area, conceptualize the problems, and recommend solutions in white papers or reports. Such committees are often staffed by senior bureaucrats whose own entrenchment in the social world and the languages of the bureaucracy ensures that their diagnosis remains within the dominant discourse and the proposed amendments of governmental techniques remain moderate and gradual. Within well-established sectors with complex and closely woven networks of entitlements, systems of rank and promotion, and so on, reforms are often extremely difficult to push through. Certain sectors of the governmental apparatus, due to their origins in the colonial order or a military or authoritarian legacy, have been allotted

considerable autonomy and over time have developed extremely resilient forms of organization, recruitment, and functioning that few political parties dare to confront. The military, the police, the system of prisons and correctional institutions are often such almost self-governing institutions within the larger network of the state. Although the state as a whole may be fragmented and "weak," we need to take note of varying degrees of "softness" and "hardness" in different sectors of the state apparatus. It is in the face of this problem of resilience and reluctance toward reform and scrutiny within the security apparatuses that a range of "truth-producing" technologies and strategies of reconciliation have been employed by new and democratic regimes in Latin America and South Africa. Instead of an all-out confrontation with the often unrepenting executioners of yesteryear, these processes have sought to bypass the security apparatuses and instead create a common platform for a broader and collective catharsis of the excesses of past regimes.

2. It is tempting for political parties eager to show results to create new governmental institutions or programs instead of reforming or terminating those in existence because of the web of entitlements, resources, and institutional routines surrounding a given sector. New programs and discourses are believed to be able to bypass and displace older and existing structures by virtue of the energy and hegemonic strategies pursued by a new regime. This intricate play between older forms of governance and new forms of rationalities seeking to hegemonize a field of intervention lies at the heart of Steffen Jensen's paper in this volume on the attempts to reproblematize the field of crime, policing, and correctional institutions in South Africa.

The result seems to be that each new regime builds a number of new institutions or nurses particular areas with greater care and zeal, often reflecting the larger ideological formations and communities out of which they have emerged. In intensely competitive democratic setups, the result seems to be that each political movement or party seeks to establish and maintain zones of loyalty, reproduced through flows of patronage, in various parts of the bureaucracy. It is a process that, needless to say, often brings forth the intrinsic fragmentation of the state to an extent that sometimes jeopardizes its central mythological dimensions. The long-term result of such competing and successive projects of domination and social reform through constant formation, addition, and restructuring of state institutions is a morphology of governance, that is, historical layers of institutions that left traces and documents as they were reformed or rebuilt. Such morphologies can be invaluable texts in our understanding of the dynamics of broader conflicts between social classes and communities. David Nugent's exploration of state formation and the struggle over political power and designs of institutions in Peru in this century is a fine example of the insights such an approach can yield.

3. The most widely used and most immediately effective method used by political force to exercise power and to consolidate its popularity and support is intervention into the implementation and administration of specific policies and regulations at the local level. When lists of those entitled to new agricultural credits are drawn up, when children are admitted into government schools and colleges, when new clerks are employed in a government department, when liquor licenses are issued, when builders are allowed to build on certain plots—the list is endless—local politicians are often involved in putting pressure on local officials. National-level politicians are involved in similar efforts, only on a larger scale concerning the sanctioning of large industrial projects or large construction projects.

This part of the political vocation involves the ability to construct a large network of contacts, mutual favors, and economic resources that enable political operators to put pressure on a local bureaucrat (threats concerning possible transfers are common) or to win influence in local boards and commissions, to make friends with influential bureaucrats, and to rise in their own political party. From the point of view of the consumer of government services, this local art of politics also requires a certain command of the "rules of game" as well as the discursive register through which bribes and kickbacks are talked about and constructed as reasonable within a local cultural economy, as Gupta's (1995) path-breaking paper on corruption demonstrated. In a similar, if more generalizing, vein, de Sardan (1999) has recently pointed to a range of cultural logics and everyday forms of reciprocity and obligation in sub-Saharan Africa that contribute to the reproduction of what he terms the "corruption complex." A very substantial part of the everyday forms of governance and political power is exercised this way. Police constables are told to look the other way or to arrest someone particular. The name of one farmer is deleted from the loan scheme and the relative of a leading family is entered instead. Municipal authorities are told to ignore the construction of unauthorized buildings. Examples are legion.

This form of power, however, cannot easily be equated with the power of certain classes or communities, nor can it necessarily be taken as proof of the power of one particular party. Most political figures are involved in this "political retailing" that has very little to do with dominating or restructuring the state, but merely with influencing the course of a few of the micro-operations of the state. But the net result of these millions of everyday interventions in the functioning of local institutions is, of course, that governance becomes increasingly "porous" and fragmented at the local level and that the implementation of most policies are deflected, if not stunted.

Resisting Regimes

The category of resistance remains a very unclear and opaque term in spite of the enormous literature on the subject in all the disciplines of the social sciences. Much like the state-community dichotomy discussed above, the very definition and conceptualization of resistance, of defiance or insurgency is vitally dependent on the character and clarity of the regime, or state, that is opposed. Resistance, most anthropologists, historians, and sociologists agree, is a category and a type of social practice that cannot be understood or presupposed outside its historical context. Yet, there is something universal and transhistorical in the way resistance is conceptualized and assumed. This was true of Marxist scholarship but also applies to contemporary work of a poststucturalist persuasion, inspired among other things by Foucault's remark "Where there is power there is resistance, and yet, or rather consequently, this resistance is never in a position of exteriority in relation to power" (1978: 95–96). This remark seems to affirm resistance as an anthropological universal, something that is always/already out there. If we cannot see "it," our conceptual tools must be inadequate and insensitive to the localized and emic categories that are the medium of resistance. But Foucault's notion of the imbrication of resistance in every operation of power has, along with work by James Scott, Michel de Certeau, and others, made resistance into a much wider and more ambiguous category than it used to be. Lila Abu-Lughod observes: "What one finds now is a concern with unlikely forms of resistance, subversions rather than large-scale collective insurrection, small and local resistance not tied to the overthrow of systems or even to ideologies of emancipation" (1990: 41). Abu-Lughod demonstrates that the use of lingerie and dreams of romantic love among young Bedouin women indeed is a form of resistance to patriarchal forms of domination, but that these practices also entail submission to other dominant ideologies, such as the privatization of the individual and the family and market-driven consumption (43–55).

In the face of such obvious ambiguities of both resistance and power it seems that imposing a universal dialectic of power and resistance on diverse and complex situations may narrow rather than open the scope for interpretation. In his foreword to a new edition of Ranajit Guha's path-breaking *Elementary Aspects of Peasant Insurgency in Colonial India*, James Scott argues that Guha has avoided such a narrowing of perspective and has avoided reading the past in terms of the present: "At every turn *Elementary Aspects* emphasizes the dangers of reading the process of insurgency with a political grammar based on mid–twentieth century nation-state political forms. In the place of formal organization . . . Guha finds informal networks . . . in the place of formal messages and public conflict, Guha finds the world of rumor" (1999: xiii).

Both Guha's (1999) rich interpretation of a century of peasant insurgencies in colonial India read "against the grain" in official reports, and Scott's (1985, 1990) work on everyday forms of defiance, joking, and other kinds of "low-intensity resistance" have recorded a valuable range of acts of defiance, or passive insubordination, in local and emic terms far removed from the world of formal politics and organized opposition. The question is, Does the universal category of resistance or insurgency actually obtain in all these contexts? Do we not tend to inscribe a somewhat heroic dimension into actions that local actors may see as mundane, unexceptional, and maybe deeply ambivalent? Guha is aware of such ambiguities in acts of defiance, the blurring of lines between regular crime and collective resistance against authorities (1999: 77–108). Insurgence and resistance remain, nonetheless, the overall lens through which he interprets the British colonial reports on dacoitry, looting, killing of aristocrats—events that often were mediated through idioms of religion and community.

Our argument is that we need to be more sensitive to the historicity and polyvalent nature of the expressions, symbols, and acts we intuitively may register as resistance. The lives and acts of ordinary people may as well be intertwined with the lives of the powerful in the "illicit cohabitation" that Mbembe writes about, and revolts or resistance may well serve ends, reproduce structures of domination, or create new forms of power that are more repressive and violent than those preceding them. The works of Guha, Scott, and others have been crucial in wrestling the question of resistance and revolt out of the clutches of a powerful teleology that saw "primitive" revolts of peasants or marginal people as prepolitical stages of emancipation that could emerge fully as political/proletarian consciousness only in the modern (and Western) age.[6] Our argument, however, is that we should go one step further.

As we try to make the state a less natural entity we should also endeavor to reverse the tendency toward reading resistance to the state into every mundane social act and instead listen to and record the discourses, the organization, and the context of that which from a distance appears as resistance. The result will inevitably be more perplexing and unclear but also more interesting, as Sherry Ortner (1995) argues in her critique of what she terms the "ethnographic refusal" to engage resistance empirically.

Let us briefly mention two of the ambiguities involved in resistance and revolts against states: first, the logic of emulation of dominant orders by rebels and revolutionaries; second, the collapse of states and emergence of warlordism that has (re)appeared in the late twentieth century. As pointed out by Eric Wolf (1969) in his classic work on peasant wars in the twentieth century, these rebellions grew out of a complex and layered interaction between localized disgruntlement and the desire for upward mobility among "middle peasants" that was given a certain interpretation, direction, and shape by an educated, ideologically sophisticated leadership. The ordinary peasant had little idea of socialism or the catharsis of revolution but often desired a return to an idealized state of social equilibrium governed by proper moral conduct of patrons and officials, albeit in unequal relations (1969: 276–303).

Guha points to how revolts inevitably take place within social imaginaries structured by prevailing arrangements of power and only rarely transgress established notions of authority but rather tend to reproduce these: "Peasant kings were a characteristic product of rural revolt . . . and an anticipation of power was indexed on some occasions by the rebels designating themselves as a formally constituted army (*fauj*), their commanders as law-enforcing personnel (e.g., *daroga, subhadar, nazir,* etc.)—all by way of simulating the functions of a state apparatus" (1999: 10).

This logic of negative emulation and reproduction of structures of governance and, in effect, languages of stateness seem to be a recurrent feature of rebels and revolutionaries in many parts of the world: from the emperor crowned by rebellious slaves in Haiti in the late eighteenth century, to the peasant leader of the nineteenth-century Taiping revolution in China whose millenarian dreams of a new utopian state led him to regard himself as a new emperor, a new "Son of Heaven," to countless local revolts that produced similar effects of negative emulation. Such effects were, of course, also highly productive in terms of giving idea, coherence, and structure to the parallel systems of governance, control, and sovereignty set up by rebels and revolutionaries. As the general ideas about what a state was, what it could do and should do expanded and diversified in nineteenth-century Europe, rebels and revolutionaries also developed ever more refined ideas about the utopian "counterrepublics" they desired to set up, with the Paris Commune in 1871 as a paradigmatic example.

Twentieth-century guerrilla warfare, famously theorized by Mao Ze-dong, set new standards for the sophistication of the "parallel state" organized by revolutionaries in liberated zones or as "night governments" in contested areas. These were state structures that used some existing structures of governance (taxation, territorial control, village councils, etc.) but also often aimed at introducing radically modern discourses, for example, of gender equality into marginal peasant communities by the use of "state-of-the-art" techniques of organization and surveillance, new procedures of justice, and more. In many cases, guerrilla movements inspired by Maoist doctrines became exceptionally effective builders of such parallel states by pursuing draconian reform of social structures, removal of competing centers of authority, such as religious institutions, and extension of control and political surveillance. During thirty years of guerrilla warfare the Eritrean People's Liberation Front created such a "shadow state," partly organized around the *kerbeles* of the lineage society of the highlands and around the imperatives of war and production, but always controlled by the disciplined cadre structure of the movement. These structures became the backbone of the new independent state in 1993 (Iyob 1995).

Here, as among the Tamil Tigers in the Jaffna peninsula of Sri Lanka and the Sendero Luminoso in the Andean provinces in Peru, an all-pervasive logic of militarization, a strong ideology of personal sacrifice and the ennobling death in struggle, and devotion to what was believed to be an elevated leadership at the heart of the shadow state created organizations that were both effective and terrifying in their determination to control people, resources, and territory (Degregori 1991). Peasant populations in these areas came to realize that the governance practiced by these organizations often was harsher, more effective, and less negotiable than that of the old regime. In Peru, for instance, this harshness worked against the Senderistas, as did the imprisonment of Sendero Luminoso's mythical leader Guzman, the father and "teacher" of the new shadow state, in 1992.

If some of these militant movements almost suffocated their new subject populations in too much and too tight governance, the opposite seems to be true of some of the "collapsed" states in Africa. Here, warlords and strongmen have broken the territorial sovereignty of the state, throwing large territories into an almost Hobbesian predicament of apparently randomized but also ethnicized violence. Rather than shadow states, we are dealing here with shadow economies. The control of territories, people, and natural resources is not bureaucratized but relies on alliances, engagement in transnational economic networks, and coercion (Richards 1996; Bayart et al. 1998). Chilling practices of literally inscribing the sovereignty of the warlord into populations by maiming and disfiguration—as in Sierra Leone, Liberia, and the Lord's Resistance Army in northern Uganda—seem to be integral to these more mobile and floating sovereignties.

These "commercial-military complexes," free from the weight of bureaucracies and creditor demands, are much more flexible than their developmentalist opponents, and throughout the 1990s several of the latter have mimicked the practices of the warlords (Duffield 2001). William Reno (1998) and Mark Duffield (1998, 2001) have argued that this kind of warlord society may be seen as an innovative system of political authority corresponding to the neoliberal world order, rather than as abnormal, and temporal, deviations from the governmentalized state.

This does not mean, however, that the languages and images of stateness evaporate. The weight of the international system of states and their all-encompassing rituals of authorization reinforce the need for articulations and complicity between the warlord systems and state institutions. Furthermore, representatives of the nonbureaucratic warlord systems may justify their actions with reference to previous violation of their rights and their exclusion from state systems. As Monique Nuijten (1998) has illustrated in her study of land, domination, and politics in rural Mexico, state subjects do not necessarily give up claiming rights and entitlements just because the state representatives never fulfill their promises. In this sense, she argues, the state may best be understood as a "hope-generating machine."

The Great Enframer

The study of localized political struggles, of the functioning of local institutions of governance, of often disorderly and ambiguous forms of defiance or insubordination, of celebration of the myth of the state and its physical representations should caution us when it comes to drawing conclusions regarding the uniformity of how the current global languages of stateness are spoken, understood, and converted into policy and authority. If subjected to an ethnographic gaze, a strict Foucauldian view of modern governance as the inexorable global spread and proliferation of certain discursive rationalities and certain technologies tends to crumble. These forms of governmentality do exist and their techniques and rationales do circulate, but they only effect practical policies or administrative practices in a rather slow and often indirect way: sometimes as justifications for new measures or norms, sometimes simply as a form of "scientific" diagnosis, but always in competition with older practices and other rationalities.

We have pointed out in this introduction that the state, governance, and the effects and subjectivities shaped by the languages of stateness of our time need to be denaturalized and studied in rich ethnographic detail as an integrated part of the cultural economy of postcolonial societies. We have also pointed out that we cannot assume that an institution, a policy paper, a discursive construction, a protest, or the practices of a government official are "the same" all over the world. We have emphasized that the state is not a universal construction and that states have widely different histories, internal logics, and practices that need to be understood and studied. Yet there are many similarities, a real and effective circulation of a range of languages of stateness around the world, and very real and enduring mythologies of state. If the state as an actual social form is not universal, we may suggest that the desire of stateness has become a truly global and universal phenomenon.

In that light, we should perhaps regard the rhetoric of state officials, the nicely crafted white papers and policy documents, the ostensibly scientific forms of governance, the grand schemes and organizational efforts of governments, with all their paraphernalia of vehicles, titles, and little rituals, as parts of a continuous state spectacle asserting and affirming the authority of the state. These spectacles only occasionally succeed in producing the specific social effects they aim at, but always reproduce the imagination of the state as the great enframer of our lives.

Notes

1. This is how Foucault put it in an interview with Paul Rabinow shortly before his death (Rabinow 1984: 381–90).
2. For an incisive argument concerning the transformation of logics of state formation and governance from the late Spanish empire to the early national state in Central America, see Rønsbo (1997).
3. The genealogy of one of the great fetishes of the modern mobile world, the passport, has recently been explored by John Torpey (2000). In fascinating detail Torpey explores how states

in Europe, along different but also converging lines, in the nineteenth century gradually establish a monopoly over what he terms "the legitimate means of mobility."

4. As demonstrated by Kantorowich (1957) in his classic study of medieval English law, royal authority embodied by the king was divided into a sublime eternal body and a profane, human body that also was the object of innumerable tales, jokes, and the popular wit. See Hansen's essay in this volume for further discussion of the relevance of Kantorowich's work for the study of state practices.
5. Political anthropology has provided valuable contributions that are useful for the analysis of the interaction between local authorities and institutions of the modern state. See, for example, Vincent 1990, and Gledhill 1994.
6. This is the case, for instance, in Hobsbawm's (1965) otherwise celebrated book *Primitive Rebels*.

I STATE AND GOVERNANCE

"DEMONIC SOCIETIES" Liberalism, Biopolitics, and Sovereignty

Mitchell Dean

In a lecture at Stanford in 1978 Michel Foucault said: "Our societies have proved to be really demonic since they happen to combine those two games—the city-citizen game and the shepherd-flock game—in what we call modern states" (1988c: 71).

What could such a statement possibly mean? Was this a case of hyperbole, an attempt to catch the ear of an American audience, designed to convince them of his critical intent and credentials? Was it something we were meant to pass over quickly and move on to the more detailed analysis of different forms of what he called "political rationality"? Or did this statement summarize and encapsulate a certain dimension of what Foucault would identify as the arts of government, as I suggest in this essay? As is well-known, the modern literature on these "arts of governing" arises, for Foucault, with the crisis of spiritual government and the pastorate in the fifteenth and sixteenth centuries. It inquires into a multiplicity of problems "concerning the 'right way' to govern children, a family, a domain, a principality" (Foucault: 1997a: 68).[1] Foucault's theme, therefore, is of "a more general questioning of government and self-government, of guidance and self-guidance," of all the attempts at the calculated direction of conduct undertaken by various authorities. This extends "beyond the state" to the programmatic activity of communities and community organizations, unions, corporations, and associations of all kinds. It even extends to those attempts we ourselves make to transform our own conduct with different objectives in mind so that we might become a different kind of person. In brief, government for Foucault refers us to the theme of the "conduct of conduct."

This essay is in large part a critical exposition of Foucault's general schema for understanding these arts of governing. It argues that this schema cannot be properly understood without reference to concepts such as biopolitics and sovereignty. The point of this exposition is not philological, however. Rather, it is to deepen our understanding of the resources that an analytics of government has to draw on and of some of its critical bases. It is also to suggest some of the limits of Foucault's interpretation of political rationality. Foucault's 1978 statement is a useful epigraph for this task.

This statement is not without its problems. Foucault assumes that we know what he means by "our societies." In common with the vast majority of European and North American theorists, he was resolutely "metropolitan" and Eurocentric. His analyses tend to assume that one can talk relatively coherently about forms of government, rule, and power that are internal to, as he puts it, "what we call modern states," in isolation from the relations between states and other political formations. As many have suggested, most notably Ann Laura Stoler (1995), the study of colonial power relations and colonial bodies is largely absent from Foucault's studies of discipline and sexuality. More recently, a number of writers have noted that Foucault's account of the art of government finds its limit in a relative neglect of issues of international government, and the international forms of government that are among the constitutive conditions of sovereign states.[2] It is thus fair to say that Foucault's analyses of the arts of government, with some significant exceptions and indications in his lectures, are largely "internalist." That is, they ignore the international arts of government that are the condition of these relatively autonomous, sovereign, territorially bounded states, and the practices that assign populations to specific states in the modern system of states. When Foucault discusses "our societies," we know he means the populations that are assigned to the territorial unities of liberal-democratic states of Europe and North America and perhaps certain of their antipodean derivatives. More deeply, he also appears often to assume that these states unproblematically coincide with relatively autonomous and bounded unities called societies.

Turning to the term "demonic," it would perhaps be permissible to read this term as analogous to Socrates' "daemon," which, as Pierre Hadot puts it, was both a kind of inspiration that came over him in an irrational manner and his real "character" (1995: 164–65). The demonic would thus be the irrational and inspirational character of modern states, even accounting for something of their dynamism and capacity for political invention. There is something in this interpretation. Here, however, I argue that we should also understand this term in a much stronger sense, as a reference to what bedevils modern forms of government and rule, and to that which, at least in part, can help us pose the problem of political danger and evil. I suggest that Foucault sought to pose the problem of the political danger as that which lurks in our rationalities and techniques of government in the various attempts to combine elements of the "shepherd-flock" and "city-citizen games." This understanding is borne out by certain other texts that are in a not distant proximity to this one. The Stanford lectures, with their focus on pastoral power, reason of state, and *Polizeiwissenschaft*, are based on material from Foucault's course on "Security, Territory, Population" in 1978 (1997a: 67–73). There is more than a trace of the same problem of political evil in evidence in the extraordinary final lecture Foucault gave in his previous course in 1976 (1997b: 213–35) and the final chapter in the first volume of his *History of Sexuality* (1979b).[3] There, the shepherd-flock game takes the form of the modern life politics, biopolitics, and the city-citizen game is cast in the language and practice of sovereignty. In both of these earlier texts, Foucault uses National Socialism as a key example of certain of the dangers perhaps more discretely manifest in other doctrines of rule.

This further elaboration raises other types of problems. These arise from a potentially "totalizing" reading of the above statement. On the one hand, such a statement might appear to suggest that we do not have to engage in a genealogy of the specific ways in which the arts of government are shaped and imagined within particular contexts. It is of course necessary to consider not only the pervasiveness of different rationalities of rule, such as sovereignty and biopolitics, but also how they are articulated in specific contexts. This is the case, particularly in the colonial and postcolonial era, when such rationalities are articulated with alternative, older, or "indigenous" forms of authority and government.[4] On the other hand, such a statement might be read in a manner that underplays the contingent, unruly nature of these rationalities and the manner in which they become available to be used by different political actors in contestation. Indeed, to follow Hindess (1997), one might suggest that the use of the term "political rationality" in this context is rather limited in that the identification by Foucault of political rationality with rationalities of government does not leave room for the political per se. An example of this is when a liberal rationality of government is concerned to limit or regulate the effects of the partisan action of factions on the work of government. We need to consider the way rationalities of how we govern and are governed are articulated with rationalities and forces that seek in some manner to affect the employment of such rationalities. Thus, we need to consider what Weber called "politically oriented action," that which "aims to exert influence on the government of a political organization; especially at the appropriation, redistribution or allocation of the powers of government" (1968a: 55). Thus, we need to examine action that is oriented to affecting the government of an organization, as much as action oriented to shaping conduct. Or, to put it in Foucault's terms (1988a: 19), we need to discuss the ways in which these rationalities and technologies of government are articulated with "strategic games between liberties," that is, how they enter into a field of political forces.

My exposition above suggests that the demonic character of modern societies, according to Foucault, stems from the unholy combination of two distinct trajectories: that of sovereignty and that of biopolitics. It may be that such a view cannot be maintained. The effect of Giorgio Agamben's (1998) argument would appear to be that there is a much closer and longer bond between politics and life than Foucault allows. Drawing on Aristotle, Agamben argues that the Greek understanding of politics contained two conceptions of life: *zoe*, or bare life, is distinguished from *bios*, or politically or morally qualified life. The constitution of the political is made possible by a kind of exclusion of bare life from political life that simultaneously makes bare life a condition of politics. Life is included in politics, not by the eighteenth-century emergence of biopolitics, but at the very genesis of Western conceptions of politics, by its very exclusion.

This is not the place to rehearse the details of Agamben's appreciative critique of Foucault, but he does indicate the possibility that Foucault has underestimated the extent to which sovereign forms of power were constituted in relation to notions of life. In so doing, Agamben might be read as contributing to an analysis of how modern democratic conceptions of sovereignty already contain assumptions about life in relation to politics that open them to readily and somewhat surreptitious colonization by biopolitical imperatives. However, Agamben himself may risk a lack of attentiveness to the specific character of modern biopolitics.

Despite all the possibilities of reductive readings of ethnocentrism, of an unexamined focus on nation, and of a form of totalization that threatens to neglect historical singularity and the field of contestation, this statement of two forms of rule advances our understanding of our imagination of the political in two ways. First, it establishes the importance of the *longue durée* of two very broad—and intertwined—trajectories of rule. Second, it argues that many current problems and dangers are located not in one or the other of these trajectories but in the attempt to put together elements of the rationalities found along these trajectories in the government of the state. That is, whether political actors take the form of an incumbent regime, a party, or a social movement, those who attempt to affect the government of the state are forced, in very different contexts, to try to force together aspects found along these two trajectories. And, to allow for Agamben, the point of articulation is found in the different conceptions of life.

Foucault's statement, then, locates the problem of political danger in the combination, the "tricky adjustment" between two modes of exercising rule. The shepherd-flock game, or what he elsewhere calls pastoral power, has its birth in Hebraic and early Christian religious communities. Its genealogy concerns its transformation into a centralized and largely secular exercise of power over populations concerned with the life and welfare of "each and all" with the development of the administrative state in Europe in the seventeenth and eighteenth centuries. The city-citizen game has its sources in Greco-Roman antiquity and notions of the polis and res publica and concerns the treatment of individuals as autonomous and responsible political actors within a self-determining political community. This mode of exercising power has been transformed by modern liberal and republican doctrines, notions of direct and representative democracy, and, most crucially, by the key status of citizenship being granted to certain members of the population within the territorial state.

One way in which the attempted articulation of these elements may be viewed as demonic concerns the vacillation over the status of the welfare state. On the one hand, national governments are loath, for a variety of reasons, to do anything that might undermine the responsible freedom of those who can exercise active citizenship and even seek to reform social provisions so that it might transform certain groups into active citizens. On the other hand, governments must find a way of providing for those with needs whether due to human frailty and mortality or the nature of the capitalist labor market itself. The genealogy of the welfare state seems to be bedeviled by this problem of trying to find a norm of provision that can adjust the competing demands of a subject of needs with the free political citizen. We can note that that genealogy would also show that this problem of welfare states is also a problem of the relations and competition among sovereign states, most recently reconfigured as an issue of economic globalization.

Important as this welfare state problem and its ramifications are, I want to focus here on another aspect of this demonic character of modern states. This is the character of what I call, for want of a better term, authoritarian forms of rule.[5] This term encompasses those practices and rationalities immanent to liberal government itself that are applied to certain populations held to be without the attributes of responsible freedom. More directly, it refers to nonliberal and explicitly authoritarian types of rule that seek to operate through obedient rather than free subjects or, at a minimum, endeavor to neutralize opposition to authority.

Very broadly, then, this retranslation of Foucault's sentence on the demonic nature of modern states amounts to something like the following: All versions of what might loosely be called modern arts of government must articulate a biopolitics of the population with questions of sovereignty. And it is the combination of these elements of biopolitics and sovereignty that is fraught with dangers and risks. I turn first to the triad liberalism, biopolitics, and sovereignty before examining nonliberal types of rule.

Liberalism, Biopolitics, Sovereignty

From the end of the eighteenth century until perhaps quite recently, there existed a common conception of government. This was true for those who criticized and sought to limit existing forms of government and those who argued for their extension, their coordination and centralization. Government would be regarded as a unitary, centralized, and localized set of institutions that acted in a field that was exterior to itself. It would no longer be purely concerned with "the right disposition of things arranged to a convenient end," as La Perrière had argued (cited in Foucault 1991: 93). The government of things would meet the government of processes. To govern would mean to cultivate, facilitate, and work through the diverse processes that were to be found in this domain exterior to the institutions of government. These processes would variously be conceived as vital, natural, organic, historical, economic, psychological, biological, cultural, or social. They would be processes that both established the paradoxical position of life as at once an autonomous domain and a target and objective of systems of rule, as at once excluded and included within the exercise of sovereign power.

One key domain in which these processes exterior to but necessary to government are constituted is biopolitics. This term designates the very broad terrain on and against which we can locate the liberal critique of too much government and its advocacy of Benjamin Franklin's "frugal government" (Foucault 1997a: 77). Biopolitics is a politics concerning the administration of life, particularly as it appears at the level of populations. It is "the endeavor, begun in the eighteenth century, to rationalize problems presented to governmental practice by the phenomena characteristic of a group of living human beings constituted as a population: health, sanitation, birthrate, longevity, race" (73). It is concerned with matters of life and death, with birth and propagation, with health and illness, both physical and mental, and with the processes that sustain or retard the optimization of the life of a population. Biopolitics must then concern the biological, social, cultural, economic, and geographic conditions under which humans live, procreate, become ill, maintain health or become healthy, and die. From this perspective, biopolitics is concerned with heredity and environment, with the family, reproduction and genetics, with housing, living and working conditions, with what we call "lifestyle," with public health issues, patterns of migration, levels of economic growth, and the standard of living. It is concerned with the biosphere in which humans dwell.

Drawing on the work of Robyn Lui-Bright (1997), we might say that there is an internal and an external side of biopolitics. There is a social form of government concerned to govern the life and welfare of the populations that are assigned to certain states; there is also a kind of international biopolitics that governs the movement, transitions, settlement, and repatriation of various populations, including refugees, legal and illegal immigrants, guest workers, tourists, and students. This international biopolitics is a condition of the assignation of populations to states and thus of social government of any form.

Biopolitics is a fundamental dimension or even trajectory of government from the eighteenth century concerned with a government of and through the processes of life and the evolution of life. It constitutes as its objects and targets such entities as the population, the species, and the race. In Foucault's narrative, however, the detailed administration of life by biopolitical (and, it should be added, disciplinary) practices is not coextensive with the entire field of politics and government. There are at least two other dimensions of rule that are important here: *economic government*, which is internal to the field of government conceived as the art of conducting individuals and populations, and the theory and practices of *sovereignty*. Both are invoked by liberalism as a means of criticizing and halting the effects of the generalization of the biopolitical norm of the optimization of life. However, both economic rationality and sovereign power, however democratized, might also be viewed as ultimately referring to another conception of life—that of the zoe or bare life. Economic rationality presupposes a world of limited resources and relative scarcity in the face of human needs and justifies itself in terms of the "standard of living" or even "quality of life." The discourses of sovereignty, particularly in notions of human rights, presuppose juridical and political status of individuals and populations by virtue of their mere existence as human beings.

Biopolitics, then, first meets quite distinct forms of political rationality and knowledge concerned with the role of commerce in civil society. These take as their theoretical object the notion of the economy as a self-regulating system largely coincident with the boundaries of the nation. In doing so, political economy presents limits to the biopolitical aim of the optimization of the life of the population. These limits are most clearly articulated by Malthus and his absolutely crucial discovery, in the relation between the processes that impel the growth of population and those natural ones that provide the subsistence for the increasing quantity of human life, of a realm of scarcity and necessity. The bioeconomic reality discovered and enshrined in the work of the English political economists of the early nineteenth century will be used to generate new norms of government. Such norms must be factored against the optimization of the life of the population by biopolitical means, even if they are consistent with this goal of the optimization of life.

The notion of sovereignty has its own history and its own effects: it is characterized by a power of life and death that, according to Foucault, was "in reality the right to *take* life and *let* live" (1979a: 136). Sovereignty undergoes its own transformation: in the juridical theories of the seventeenth and eighteenth centuries, such as those of Thomas Hobbes and Samuel von Pufendorf, he finds a more limited account of the sovereign right of death as conditioned by the defense of the sovereign. The end of sovereignty is, however, the continuation of sovereignty itself: it is caught in a kind of "self-referring circularity" (Foucault 1991: 95). Thus, Foucault argues that, if we take Pufendorf's definition of the end of sovereign authority as "public utility" and seek to define the content of public utility, we find little more than that subjects obey laws, fulfill their expected tasks, and respect the political order.

The notion of sovereignty is far from a universal and, like other concepts, should be understood in its historical variation according to specific regimes of practices and forms of political rationality. Furthermore, as the state's concern for its own preservation, sovereignty might be a particular end of government. Indeed, securing the sovereignty of states is an end of the art of international government. The existence of a system of sovereign states has as its condition a form of governmental regulation of the international order. Foucault suggests that internally, however, in western European societies from the Middle Ages sovereignty is principally conceived as a transcendent form of authority exercised over subjects within a definite territory. Its main instruments are laws, decrees, and regulations backed up by coercive sanctions ultimately grounded in the right of death exercised by the sovereign. It operates through spectacle and ritual, it prohibits forms of action, it seizes things, bodies, and ultimately life itself. The symbolic language through which sovereignty operates is one of the sword, of blood, of family and alliance. In certain states, from the end of the eighteenth century, we know that sovereignty has been "democratized" in that we have witnessed the development of mechanisms of representation by which those deemed to possess the required attributes can participate in the choice of who should stand in the place of the sovereign. One aspect of the democratization of sovereignty has been to create a universal language of rights by which efforts are made to regulate the conduct of sovereign states by various international governmental agencies. Another is that sovereignty and the language of rights has proven polyvalent enough to accommodate the claims of movements for self-determination among indigenous and other colonized peoples.

The other aspect of sovereignty mentioned but not emphasized by Foucault is that the notion of a nominally separate state with territorial integrity, subject to noninterference by outside powers, is itself a governmental product and a consequence of the "external" dimension of doctrines of "reason of state" (Foucault 1991: 104). The city-citizen game not only entails relations among putatively self-governing citizens, as Foucault tends to stress, but the formation of and relations among what aspire to be self-governing political communities. One of the features of the modern political world, which may be dated from the agreements of Westphalia concluded in 1648 following the Thirty Years War, is that these fictive self-governing political communities have come to be represented as independent states. That is, they are political unities with definite territorial boundaries, secured by the principle of noninterference of one sovereign state in the internal affairs of another. Claims to sovereignty by such communities have thus become identical with claims to be a state. The city-citizen game therefore concerns the panoply of techniques by which the members of a population are formed or form themselves into a political community, and by which they seek to exercise sovereignty. It also includes the arts of international government by which certain populations are assigned to these nominally independent sovereign states and that regulate the coexistence of states with one another.

The relation of the arts of governing and sovereignty is not the replacement of one by the other but each acting as a condition of the other. On the one hand, the existence of nominally independent sovereign states is a condition of forcing open those geopolitical spaces on which the arts of government can operate. On the other hand, a set of supranational agreements and regulations of populations is a necessary condition of the world inhabited by these sovereign states.

We are now in a position to locate the third term of our triad, liberalism. As Foucault puts it in regard to biopolitical problems: "'Liberalism' enters the picture here, because it was in connection with liberalism that they began to have the look of a challenge. In a system anxious to have the respect of legal subjects and to ensure the free enterprise of individuals, how can the 'population' phenomenon, with its specific effects and problems, be taken into account? On behalf of what, and according to what rules, can it be managed?" (1997a: 73).

According to Foucault, liberalism can be understood as a form of critique of excessive government. It should be approached, however, as a critique not only of earlier forms of government such as police and reason of state but of existing and potential forms of biopolitical government. That is, liberalism criticizes other possible forms that the government of the processes of life might take. It might criticize those forms, for example, in which biopolitical norms will be compromised by a lack of understanding of economic norms. It might also criticize the detailed regulation of the biological processes of the species, and the tendencies toward state racism found in biopolitics, by an appeal to the framework of right—either legal or natural—that it will codify as the theory and practice of democratic sovereignty. If liberalism emerged less as a doctrine or form of the minimal state than as an ethos of review, this ethos needs to be situated in the rationalization of the field of biopolitical problems. For liberalism, it is always necessary to suspect that one is governing too much. This is because the imperatives of biopolitical norms that lead to the creation of a coordinated and centralized administration of life need to be weighed against the norms of economic processes and the freedoms on which they depend and the norms derived from the sovereign subject of rights. This is why, for liberalism, the problem will not be a rejection of biopolitical regulation but a way of managing it.

Liberal government is a particular form of articulation of the shepherd-flock game and the city-citizen game. It assembles a pastoral power that takes the forms of a biopolitics of the administration of life and a form of sovereignty that deploys the law and rights to limit, to offer guarantees, to make safe, and, above all, to justify the operations of biopolitical programs and disciplinary practices. Liberalism, however, can never fully check the "demonic" possibilities contained within this mix, as recent revelations about the way in which liberal-democratic states (like those in Scandinavia) have, in the course of the twentieth century, practiced forced sterilization in the name of a eugenic utopia on certain of its populations. Even more pervasive has been the tendency within certain national states (Australia, Canada), having ceased to attempt actual genocide, to commit forms of cultural genocide on indigenous populations within their borders in the name of their own well-being, such as in the case of the removal of children from their parents and families. Although the biopolitical imperative does not account for all that bedevils liberal-democratic states, it is remarkable how much of what is done of an illiberal character is done with the best of biopolitical intentions.

But why is this so? First, note, following Mariana Valverde (1996), that liberalism has itself never been entirely identical with itself. Valverde shows how the liberal conception of the juridical and political subject has a form of ethical despotism at its core, contained in notions of the possibility of improvement and habit. The history of liberalism as an art of government shows how a range of illiberal techniques can be applied to those individuals and populations who are deemed capable of improvement and of attaining self-government (from women and children to certain classes of criminals and paupers). Moreover, as a form of colonial governmentality, liberalism can justify authoritarian types of government for those regions deemed unimproved, like Africa, or degenerate and static, like China, to use John Stuart Mill's judgment. For such nations, "their only hope of making any steps in advance depends on the chances of a good despot" (cited in Valverde 1996: 361).

Second, and we might think fortunately, things have not quite turned out the way Mill envisaged. The appeal to rights within the democratized framework of sovereignty has proved a resource that has enabled some degree of success on the part of political movements in liberal democracies such as those of women, colonized peoples, racial and ethnic minorities, and people with disabilities. However, although rights claims within sovereignty discourses might enhance and protect the position of certain groups, others have not been so fortunate. This is especially so of those whose political identity is defined as without citizenship, state, or even means of subsistence, that is, merely by the fact that they are living. This would appear to apply to prisoners, illegal immigrants, and even today unemployed people, all groups defined by bare life.

Finally, although liberalism may try to make safe the biopolitical imperative of the optimization of life, it has shown itself permanently incapable of arresting—from eugenics to contemporary genetics—the emergence of rationalities that make the optimization of the life of some dependent on the disallowing of the life of others. I can only suggest some general reasons for this. Liberalism is fundamentally concerned to govern through what it conceives as processes that are external to the sphere of government limited by the respect for the rights and liberties of individual subjects. Liberal rule thus fosters forms of knowledge of vital processes and seeks to govern through their application. Moreover, to the extent that liberalism depends on the formation of responsible and autonomous subjects through biopolitics and discipline, it fosters the type of governmental practices that are the ground of such rationalities. Further, and perhaps most simply, we might consider the possibility that sovereignty and biopolitics are so heterogeneous to one another that the derivation of political norms from the democratization of the former cannot act as a prophylactic for the possible outcomes of the latter. We might also consider the alternative to this thesis, that biopolitics captures and expands the division between political life and mere existence, already found within sovereignty. In either case, the framework of right and law can act as a resource for forces engaged in contestation of the effects of biopower; it cannot provide a guarantee as the efficacy of such struggle and may even be the means for the consolidation of those effects.

Sovereignty and Biopolitics in Nonliberal Rule

There are, of course, plenty of examples of the exercise of sovereignty in the twentieth century that have practiced a decidedly nonliberal form and program of national government both in relation to their own populations and those of other states. Does this mean that the form of government of such states is assembled from elements that are radically different from the ones we have discussed here? Does this mean that state socialism and National Socialism, for example, cannot be subject to an analysis of the arts of government? The answer to both these questions, I believe, is no. The general argument of this essay is that the exercise of government in all modern states entails the articulation of a form of pastoral power with one of sovereign power. Liberalism, as we have just seen, makes that articulation in a specific way. Other types of rule have a no less distinctive response to the combination of elements of a biopolitics concerned with the detailed administration of life and sovereign power that reserves the right of death to itself.

Consider again the contrastive terms in which it is possible to view biopolitics and sovereignty. The final chapter in the first volume of the *History of Sexuality* that contrasts sovereignty and biopolitics is titled "Right of Death and Power over Life." The initial terms of the contrast between the two registers of government is thus between one that could employ power to put subjects to death, even if this right to kill was conditioned by the defense of the sovereign, and one that was concerned with the fostering of life. Nevertheless, each part of the contrast can be further broken down. The right of death can also be understood as "the right to take life or let live"; the power over life as the power "to foster life or disallow it." Sovereign power is a power that distinguishes between political life (bios) and mere existence or bare life (zoe). Bare life is included in the constitution of sovereign power by its very exclusion from political life. In contrast, biopolitics might be thought to include zoe in bios: stripped down mere existence becomes a matter of political reality. Thus, the contrast between biopolitics and sovereignty is not one of a power of life versus a power of death but concerns the way the different forms of power treat matters of life and death and entail different conceptions of life. Thus, biopolitics reinscribes the earlier right of death and power over life and places it within a new and different form that attempts to include what had earlier been sacred and taboo, bare life, in political existence. It is no longer so much the right of the sovereign to put to death his enemies but to disqualify the life—the mere existence—of those who are a threat to the life of the population, to disallow those deemed "unworthy of life," those whose bare life is not worth living.

This allows us, first, to consider what might be thought of as the dark side of biopolitics (Foucault 1979a: 136–37). In Foucault's account, biopolitics does not put an end to the practice of war: it provides it with new and more sophisticated killing machines. These machines allow killing itself to be reposed at the level of entire populations. Wars become genocidal in the twentieth century. The same state that takes on the duty to enhance the life of the population also exercises the power of death over whole populations. Atomic weapons are the key weapons of this process of the power to put whole populations to death. We might also consider here the aptly named biological and chemical weapons that seek an extermination of populations by visiting plagues upon them or polluting the biosphere in which they live to the point at which bare life is no longer sustainable. Nor does the birth of biopolitics put an end to the killing of one's own populations. Rather, it intensifies that killing—whether by an "ethnic cleansing" that visits holocausts upon whole groups or by the mass slaughters of classes and groups conducted in the name of the utopia to be achieved.

There is a certain restraint in sovereign power. The right of death is only occasionally exercised as the right to kill and then often in a ritual fashion that suggests a relation to the sacred. More often, sovereign power is manifest in the *refraining* from the right to kill. The biopolitical imperative knows no such restraint. Power is exercised at the level of populations and hence wars will be waged at that level, on behalf of everyone and their lives. This point brings us to the heart of Foucault's provocative thesis about biopolitics: that there is an intimate connection between the exercise of a life-administering power and the commission of genocide: "If genocide is indeed the dream of modern powers, this is not because of a recent return of the ancient right to kill: it is because power is situated and exercised at the level of life, the species, the race, and the large-scale phenomena of population" (1979a: 137). Foucault completes this same passage with an expression that deserves more notice: "massacres become vital."

There is thus a kind of perverse homogeneity between the power over life and the power to take life characteristic of biopower. The emergence of a biopolitical racism in the nineteenth and twentieth centuries can be approached as a trajectory in which this homogeneity always threatened to tip over into a dreadful necessity. This racism can be approached as a fundamental mechanism of power that is inscribed in the biopolitical domain (Stoler 1995: 84–85). For Foucault, the primary function of this form of racism is to establish a division between those who must live and those who must die, and to distinguish the superior from the inferior, the fit from the unfit. The notion and techniques of population had given rise, at the end of the nineteenth century, to a new linkage among population, the internal organization of states, and the competition between states. Darwinism, as an imperial social and political program, would plot the ranking of individuals, populations, and nations along the common gradient of *fitness* and thus measure *efficiency*.[6] However, the series "population, evolution, and race" is not simply a way of thinking about the superiority of the "white races" or of justifying colonialism, but also of thinking about how to treat the degenerates and the abnormals in one's own population and prevent the further degeneration of the race.

The second and most important function for Foucault of this biopolitical racism in the nineteenth century is that "it establishes a positive relation between the right to kill and the assurance of life" (Stoler 1995: 84). The life of the population, its vigor, its health, its capacities to survive, becomes necessarily linked to the elimination of internal and external threats. This power to disallow life is perhaps best encapsulated in the injunctions of the eugenic project: identify those who are degenerate, abnormal, feeble-minded, or of an inferior race and subject them to forced sterilization; encourage those who are superior, fit, and intelligent to propagate. Identify those whose life is but mere existence and disqualify their propagation; encourage those who can partake of a sovereign existence and of moral and political life. But this last example does not necessarily establish a positive justification for the right to kill, only the right to disallow life.

If we are to begin to understand the type of racism engaged in by Nazism, however, we need to take into account another kind of denouement between the biopolitical management of population and the exercise of sovereignty. This version of sovereignty is no longer the transformed and democratized form founded on the liberty of the juridical subject, as it is for liberalism, but a sovereignty that takes up and transforms a further element of sovereignty, its "symbolics of blood" (Foucault 1979a: 148).

For Foucault, sovereignty is grounded in blood—as a reality and as a symbol—just as one might say that sexuality becomes the key field on which biopolitical management of populations is articulated. When power is exercised through repression and deduction, through a law over which hangs the sword, when it is exercised on the scaffold by the torturer and the executioner, and when relations between households and families were forged through alliance, "blood was *a reality with a symbolic function*." By contrast, for biopolitics with its themes of health, vigor, fitness, vitality, progeny, survival, and race, "power spoke *of* sexuality and *to* sexuality" (Foucault 1979a: 147).

For Foucault (1979a: 149–50), the novelty of National Socialism was the way it articulated "the oneiric exaltation of blood," of fatherland, and of the triumph of the race in an immensely cynical and naïve fashion, with the paroxysms of a disciplinary and biopolitical power concerned with the detailed administration of the life of the population and the regulation of sexuality, family, marriage, and education.[7] Nazism generalized biopower without the limit-critique posed by the juridical subject of right, but it could not do away with sovereignty. Instead, it established a set of permanent interventions into the conduct of the individual within the population and articulated this with the "mythical concern for blood and the triumph of the race." Thus, the shepherd-flock game and the city-citizen game are transmuted into the eugenic ordering of biological existence (of mere living and subsistence) and articulated on the themes of the purity of blood and the myth of the fatherland.

In such an articulation of these elements of sovereign and biopolitical forms of power, the relation between the administration of life and the right to kill entire populations is no longer simply one of a dreadful homogeneity. It has become a necessary relation. The administration of life comes to require a bloodbath. It is not simply that power, and therefore war, will be exercised at the level of an entire population. It is that the act of disqualifying the right to life of other races becomes necessary for the fostering of the life of the race. Moreover, the elimination of other races is only one face of the purification of one's own race (Foucault 1997b: 231). The other part is to expose the latter to a universal and absolute danger, to expose it to the risk of death and total destruction. For Foucault, with the Nazi state we have an "absolutely racist state, an absolutely murderous state and an absolutely suicidal state" (232), all of which are superimposed and converge on the Final Solution. With the Final Solution, the state tries to eliminate, through the Jews, all the other races, for whom the Jews were the symbol and the manifestation. This includes, in one of Hitler's last acts, the order to destroy the bases of bare life for the German people itself. "Final Solution for other races, the absolute suicide of the German race" is inscribed, according to Foucault, in the functioning of the modern state (232).

Foucault's analysis of the political rationality of National Socialism finds confirmation in the work of recent German historians on at least one point, that of the fundamental role of the human sciences in the atrocities of that regime (Peters 1995). The late Detlev Peukert drew on studies of psychiatry under National Socialism, the history of compulsory sterilization programs, genetics, eugenics, medicine, social policy, and education, and his own work on social-welfare education, to argue that "what was new about 'Final Solution' in world-historical terms was the fact that it resulted from the fatal racist dynamism present within the human and social sciences" (1993: 236). Again we witness a fundamental division of the population, on this occasion made on a particular qualitative distinction between "value" and "nonvalue" and a treatment of the *Volkskörper* or body of the nation that consisted in "selection" and "eradication." Peukert argues that twentieth-century medical and human sciences are confronted by what he calls a "logodicy" that tries to resolve the dilemma between the rationalist dream of the perfectibility of humankind and the empirical existence of human finitude, of illness, suffering, and death. One resolution of this dilemma is the projection of the rationalist project away from the finite individual onto a potential immortal body. In the German case, what Foucault called the species body of the population is mapped onto the body of the *Volk* or race. The biopolitical imperative is rearticulated with a kind of mythicized version of sovereignty. Like Foucault, Peukert argues that the logic of National Socialism, with its concern for the nurture and improvement of the immortal Volkskörper, had a double significance: heroic death on one side and eradication on the other (242).

National Socialism is one contingent, historical trajectory of the development of the biopolitical dimension of the social, medical, psychological, and human sciences that occurs under a particular set of historical circumstances. One should not underestimate the factors operative in German society, the historical legacy of war and revolutionary movements, the nature of German polity, or the economic crises of the early twentieth century. Nevertheless, Peukert and Foucault would both agree that the kind of state racism practiced by the Nazis that would lead to the Final Solution was quite different from traditional anti-Semitism insofar as it took the form of a "biological politics," as the German historians call it, that drew on the full resources of the human, social, and behavioral sciences.

In this regard, Peukert's retrieval of the process by which the human sciences move from a concern with "mass well-being" to acting as the instrument of "mass annihilation" remains extremely interesting. In the case of "social-welfare education," he identifies a number of phases (1993: 243–

45). First, there was the formulation of the problem of the control of youth in the late nineteenth century within a progressivist discourse in which every child had a right to physical, mental, and social fitness. This was followed by a phase of routinization and a crisis of confidence exemplified by the failure of legal schemes of detention or protection of those who were "unfit" or "ineducable." The third phase, coinciding with the final years of the Weimar Republic, has disturbing overtones for our own period. Here there were a series of scandals in young people's homes and a debate about the limits of educability coupled with welfare state retrenchment. This debate introduced a new cost-benefits trade-off with services allocated on the basis of immediate return, and the criterion of "value" was brought into the calculative framework. Value at this stage may or may not be determined on the basis of race or genetics, but the ineducable were excluded in 1932 from reform school education. After 1933 those who opposed the racial version of determining value were forced into silence, compulsory sterilization of the genetically unhealthy was practiced, and concentration camps for the racially inferior established. However, even this program faced a crisis of confidence and the utopian goals came up against their limits and the catalogue of deviance became greater and more detailed. The positive racism of youth welfare provision now met the negative radicalization of a policy of eradication of those who, in the language of the order that represents the crucial step in the Final Solution, are deemed "unworthy of life" (*lebensunwertes Leben*). The biopolitical government of life had arrived at the point at which it decided who was worth living. With the technology of murder up and running, the social and human sciences "are engaged in a parallel process of theoretical and institutional generalization that is aimed at an all-embracing racist restructuring of social policy, of educational policy, and health and welfare policy" (Peukert 1993: 245). The term *Gemeinschaftsfremde* (community alien) came to embrace failures, ne'er-do-wells, parasites, good-for-nothings, troublemakers, and those with criminal tendencies and threatened all these with detention, imprisonment, or death.

The phrase "those unworthy of life" is striking because it so clearly resonates with the biopolitical attempt to govern life. It suggests a distinction between those who are merely living and those who are worthy of existence as a part of a social or political community. We should be clear that there was nothing necessary in the path of National Socialism and that there were crucial steps of the conversion of knowledge and services concerned with the care of the needy into a technology of mass annihilation. However, given that many, if not all, the forms of knowledge and technologies of government (including the concentration camp) were the product of polities characterized at least broadly by liberal forms of rule, this does suggest there is no room for complacency and that the liberal critique of biopolitics cannot offer the kind of guarantees it claims to. Foucault is right to provoke us with the idea that the assurance of life is connected with the death command and to claim that "the coexistence in political structures of large destructive mechanisms and institutions oriented toward the care of individual life is something puzzling and needs some investigation" (1988b: 147). Mass slaughters may not necessarily or logically follow from the forms of political rationality and types of knowledge we employ, but they do not arise from a sphere that is opposed to that rationality and knowledge. It is crucial to realize, as Peukert argues in his book *Inside Nazi Germany*, that racism was a social policy, that is, a policy that was concerned with the elimination of all those who deviated from an ever more detailed set of norms and the reshaping of society into a "people of German blood and Nordic race; four-square in body and soul" (1989: 208).

What Peukert cannot address is the rationality of what he conceives as the irrational component of Nazism. Although he understands the role of the human sciences in the formation of Nazi biological politics, he tends to consign the themes of blood, race, and Volk to an irrational sublimation contained within them rather than viewing them, as Foucault does, as rearticulated elements of sovereign power. This brings us to the central distinctiveness of Foucault's comments. National Socialism is not regarded as the pinnacle of the total administration of life undertaken with the help of the human sciences and biopolitical technologies, as it might be by the Frankfurt School and their descendants. The key point for Foucault is that National Socialism is regarded as a particular articulation of specific elements of biopolitics and its knowledge of populations and individuals and sovereignty. It is not simply the logic of the bureaucratic application of the human sciences that is at issue but the reinscription of racial discourse within a biopolitics of the population and its linkage with themes of sovereign identity, autonomy, and political community. This form of sovereignty has been drained of all its potential to claim and protect rights by the removal, following Bauman (1989: 111), of all counterbalancing resourceful and influential social forces.[8] A political discourse that divides populations on the basis of race has certain fairly obvious political dangers. However, one that makes the welfare and life of a racialized population the basis for national sovereignty and political community could be viewed as more clearly "demonic."

Unfortunately, this story of biopolitical racism does not end with Nazism. Foucault also insists that the possibilities of state racism are found in many versions of the articulation of biopolitics and sovereignty, including many varieties of socialism (1997b: 233–34; Stoler 1995: 96–97). For Foucault, the problem with socialism is that it has a kind of state racism inscribed in its premises and that, even if it has sometimes criticized biopower, it has not reexamined the foundations and modes of functioning of racism. When socialism analyzes its own emergence as a result of economic transformation, it does not have need for an immediate recourse to these racist motifs. When it insists on the necessity of struggle to socialist transformation, a struggle that is against the enemies within the capitalist state, Foucault argues, it necessarily revives the theme of racism. Moreover, when socialism takes upon itself the task of managing, multiplying, and fostering life, of limiting chances and risks, and governing biological processes, it ends up practicing a form of racism that is not properly ethnic but evolutionary and biological.[9] The enemies within on which this racism will be practiced are the mentally ill, the criminal, political adversaries, and—with, say, China's one-child policy—imprudent parents and their potential offspring (Sigley 1996). In the last case, we find a form of government that combines market-based norms and biopolitical interventions into the intimate life of the population in a nonliberal manner in order to realize the objective of the quantity and quality of the population necessary for the socialist plan.

This kind of evolutionary and eugenic racism is one that can be practiced against one's own population in the name of optimizing its quantity and quality. Thus, the Chinese government "claims that, not only is it possible to know in detail the object to be governed, but, further, it is possible to predict the precise outcome of any possible intervention" (Sigley 1996: 473). This kind of rule is nonliberal in that, first, it does not use any version of the liberal subject to limit or try to offer guarantees for or make safe population programs, and, second, it seeks to unite market-style economic norms with biopolitical ones. Thus, national authorities assign numerical targets, provincial authorities translate these into birth quotas that are distributed among prefectures and counties, which in turn divide the quota among communes, townships, and so on. The policy is implemented at the microlevel of brigades, or street or lane committees, and their subgroups (474–75). The latter are responsible for "one hundred or so households . . . to keep records of their family plans, contraceptive use and monthly cycles" (475). This detailed chain of command uses such instruments as local meetings of married couples, certificates of permission to become pregnant, allowances for couples of single children, and harsh fines for those conceiving without a certificate and those with more than one child.

The Chinese policy thus inscribes sovereign elements (of decree, interdiction, punishment, and reward) within a detailed biopolitical intervention into the intimate lives of its population. It does this not in the name of the fatherland, blood, and racial purity, but in terms of the targets envisaged by the plan. On one point, it is clear that Chinese policy is nonliberal in that it does not rely on the choices, aspirations, or capacities of the individual subject. This does not stop it having some similarity with early liberal policies, particularly Malthusian-informed poor policies. In both cases, the process of economic liberalization and the recommendation of prudential procreation are linked. One tries to privatize the costs of imprudent propagation onto individuals, families, and their offspring; the other tries to prevent burdens on the developmental dreams of the socialist state.

The study of governmentality has yet to open up the extensive discussion of authoritarian and nonliberal governmentality. Foucault's analysis of National Socialism is a striking contribution to this problem for a number of reasons. First, it shows that this case of what might be thought of as, to put it mildly, a nonliberal or authoritarian form of rule is composed, like liberal rule, of biopolitical and sovereign elements. It also places National Socialism, like liberalism, within the development of a government of biopolitical processes. This does not mean that we should efface the differences between liberal and nonliberal rule. Nor is this analysis an attempt to undermine critical distinctions between such forms. What it does illustrate, however, are the dangers inherent in biopolitical rule and in the articulation of the shepherd-flock and city-citizen games that Foucault held as central to modern politics. The continuities between authoritarian and liberal governmentality, together with the recovery of the illiberal components of liberalism, remind us of the dangers of not calling into question the self-understanding of liberalism as a limited government acting through a knowledge of the processes of life, yet, at the same time, safeguarding the rights of the political and juridical subject.

There is no necessity that means that our most general rationalities of rule such as sovereignty and biopolitics will ineluctably lead to the truly demonic eventualities we have continued to witness right to the beginning of the twenty-first century. Nor, however, is there any guarantee that the appeal to rights within liberal democracies and the international community of states will guard against such eventualities, as the contemporary confinement of illegal immigrants in camps in liberal democracies attests. Elements within sovereignty and biopolitics will continue to provide resources for political rationality and action in Weber's sense of the attempt to influence the government of organizations. But there can be no system of safeguards that offer us a zone of comfort when we engage in political action. When we do so, Foucault's position here seems to suggest, we enter a zone of uncertainty and danger because of the governmental resources we have at our disposal. We might add that the price of not engaging in political action is equally great, if not greater. A condition of informed political action remains an analysis of the actors involved, the contexts of their action, the resources at hand, the tactics used, and the ends sought. Though handling this relation between biopolitics and sovereignty remains tricky, we must establish an analysis of the way an implementation of programs of the administration of life opens fresh arenas of contestation, negotiation, and redefinition around citizenship, democracy, and rights. We must also be prepared to admit, nevertheless, that the appeal to rights might link this form of contestation to the powers it contests, particularly when such an appeal concerns the rights of those without any status but their mere existence.

The more general argument advanced here is that modern politics must combine the resources of a biopolitics based on population, life, procreation, and sexuality with the deductive logic of sovereignty based on right, territory, death, and blood. Moreover, this biopolitics captures life stripped naked (or the zoe that was the exception of sovereign power) and makes it a matter of political life (bios). It follows that, given that we continue to live in a system of modern states, we must face up to forms of biopolitical racism, that is, a racism that follows not simply from discrimination, scapegoating, or institutions, but from the elements by which we are compelled to think about and imagine states and their populations and seek to govern them. This is as true for liberal arts of government as for nonliberal rule. The liberal arts of governing through freedom means that liberalism always contains a division between those capable or deserving of the responsibilities and freedoms of mature citizenship and those who are not. For those who are not, this will often mean despotic provision for their special needs with the aim of rendering them autonomous by fostering capacities of responsibility and self-governance. Under certain conditions, however, frustrations with such programs of improvement may lead to forms of knowledge and political rationality that identify certain groups as without value and beyond improvement, as those who are merely living, whose existence is but zoe. Liberal regimes of government can thus slide from the "good despot" for the improvable to sovereign interventions to confine, to contain, to coerce, and to eliminate, if only by prevention, those deemed without value. It is true, perhaps, that many of our worst nightmares tend to be realized when these elements of sovereignty and biopolitical rule are articulated somewhat differently from the way they are in liberal democracies today. This should offer no reason for complacency even for those who find themselves marked as the mature subjects within the boundaries contained by liberal-democratic constitutionalism, let alone those who currently remain in need of a good despot within and outside these boundaries. It offers even less room for complacency for those who find themselves occupying the position of the good despot.

Notes

1. For the most succinct and instructive summary of his reflections on the arts of government in English, see *Security, Territory, Population* and *The Birth of Bio-Politics*, the summaries of his 1978 and 1979 courses at the Collège de France in Foucault (1997a: 66–79). See also his justly famous lecture on the development of early modern discussion of government and his introduction of the concept of governmentality (1991).
2. I would draw attention to three important papers in this area by Hindess (1998), Lui-Bright (1997), and Dillon (1995) that have opened up this question of the relations between international government and a system of sovereign states.
3. The 1976 lectures on war, race, and the modern state have been brought to our attention by Ann Laura Stoler in *Race and the Education of Desire* (1995).
4. An excellent example of this is the exemplary genealogy of the language of modern constitutionalism provided by James Tully (1995) from the perspective afforded by the politics of cultural diversity and the resources of the alternative traditions of common constitutionalism. Tully draws on the work of the later Wittgenstein to challenge the assumptions of modern constitutionalism. I should also mention Pat O'Malley's (1998) study of the articulation of programs of government of aboriginal people in western Australia and forms of indigenous governance.
5. For an extended discussion of notions of "authoritarian governmentality" as a framework for understanding Indonesian politics, see Philpott (1997, especially chap. 4).

6. On changing conceptions of population at the end of the nineteenth century and their relation to Darwinism, social reform, and eugenics, see Rose, *The Psychological Complex* (1985).
7. For an admirably documented account, see Pine, *Nazi Family Policy* (1997).
8. I have not the space here to discuss the similarities and differences between Zygmunt Bauman's (1989) important account of the Holocaust and the present understanding of the specific character of Nazi racism as a rationality of extermination. Bauman's account concurs with the one presented here insofar as it presents the Holocaust as something that must be understood as endogenous to Western civilization and its processes of rationalization rather than as an aberrant psychological, social, or political pathology. Moreover, to the extent that his account stresses the collapse or nonemergence of democracy, it indicates the failure of the democratization of sovereignty as a fundamental precondition of Nazi rule, a theme that echoes those of Hannah Arendt's famous book, *The Origins of Totalitarianism* (1958). Foucault's brief remarks seem to add to or qualify Bauman's account in two ways. They first offer the possibility of a closer specification of the kind of rationality and technology that make possible a racialized politics and policy by demonstrating its biopolitical character. Such a view enables us to get a clearer understanding of the role of the human sciences in such a politics. They also suggest that Nazi politics articulates this biological politics with alternative traditions and frameworks of sovereignty such as those of fatherland, Volk, and blood. It is not simply the imperative of the totalistic administration of life that accounts for the mentality of Nazi rule, but the way the biopolitical discourses and sovereign themes are reinscribed and modified within one another.
9. Note that Foucault's point here extends one made by Hannah Arendt. "Practically speaking," she states, "it will make little difference whether totalitarian movements adopt the pattern of Nazism or Bolshevism, organize the masses in the name of race or class, pretend to follow the laws of life and nature or of dialectics and economics" (1958: 313). Biopolitical state racism can be justified in terms of the goal of the evolution to an ideal society or optimizing the quality of the population as much as the evolution of the race. The practice of state racism on populations retarding social and political evolution does not necessarily always speak the language of race.

GOVERNING POPULATION The Integrated Child Development Services Program in India

Akhil Gupta

I returned to Alipur village in western Uttar Pradesh for a short spell of fieldwork in the summer of 1989. Villagers excitedly told me about all the changes that had occurred in the four years since I had last been there doing a study on agricultural change. Among the new features of Alipur were an *anganwadi*, a center that provided day care, nutrition, and inoculations to children and supplementary nutrition and health care to pregnant women and mothers of infants. I was so intrigued by this new development that in my second fieldwork project on the ethnography of the state I included the Integrated Child Development Services (ICDS), more popularly known as the anganwadi program, among the development projects that I studied.

The ICDS program is interesting for a number of reasons. It is one of the fastest growing development programs run by the Indian state. Launched with only 33 projects in 1985, the ICDS program had expanded to 1,356 projects in the next ten years, and to 5,614 by 1995 (Government of India 1985: 4). The anganwadi program grew even when the Indian government started cutting the budgets of other social welfare programs in the postliberalization era initiated in 1991. Allocations for ICDS in 1998–1999 went up to more than twice their 1990–1991 levels.[1] Another reason for paying attention to the ICDS program is that it was one of the first interventions that attempted to control population growth rates by paying attention to the *quality* of the population. It thus provides us with one of the first large-scale examples of the kind of approach to population planning that, after the Cairo Conference, has attained the status of official dogma. Theoretically, the ICDS program helps provide us with a nearly perfect example of the regulation, care, and documentation of the population, especially those members of the population (women and children) who are poorly represented in official statistics. Such attention to the welfare of the population is a form of biopower, one of the hallmarks of "governmentality," a term introduced by Michel Foucault (1991) to analyze modes of government that are not necessarily part of the state apparatus.

The enlargement of the scope of governmental regulation and concern represented by the ICDS program produces new kinds of subjects and new kinds of resistances. Among the new subjects produced are bureaucrats whose job is to focus on the weak and disempowered members (women and children) of the weakest and most disempowered groups within rural north Indian society (lower and scheduled castes); anganwadi workers, who are implementers of the ICDS project but also themselves beneficiaries of state benevolence; and, finally, the poor women and children who find themselves objects of state attention and discipline but also beneficiaries of supplementary nutrition, educational services, and health care that may not be available to their economically better-off rural neighbors. These new subjects are placed in structurally dependent but antagonistic positions. Bureaucrats attempt to discipline and control the anganwadi workers, who, in turn, attempt to discipline and control their rural charges. Those in subordinate positions, in turn, resist the mechanisms of surveillance that are employed on them. What do such acts of resistance by the women who are the objects of state surveillance, protection, and investment mean for an understanding of governmentality? And how does one tie the ethnographic analysis of everyday practices of resistance to a structural understanding of inequalities of gender and class? The analysis that I develop in the rest of this essay pursues these questions in greater detail.

The section that follows attempts to lay out some of the more general features of governmentality, so that my use of this still somewhat unusual term is clear in the remaining parts. The section that follows contextualizes the ICDS program in the history of family planning campaigns conducted by the Indian government and provides some details about the bureaucratic structure of ICDS. The third section provides a close look at actual practices of one ICDS office. In particular, I am interested in the practices of surveillance, exemplified in the "surprise inspection," the most common instrument of rule and regulation. I follow one officer on her inspection visits and record some of her reactions, as well as the reactions of the anganwadi workers who are subjected to these visits. The section that follows shifts attention away from surveillance to enumeration, one of the most important instruments of government. I show what kinds of data are collected by anganwadi workers and what happens to these data once they are passed up the hierarchy. Finally, I consider the question of resistance: how it is to be understood within the governmentality literature and what form it takes in the case of the anganwadi program.

Governmentality

The term "governmentality" comes from a lecture by Foucault (1991) in which he drew attention to all the processes by which the conduct of a population is governed: by institutions and agencies, including the state; by discourses, norms, and identities; and by self-regulation, techniques for the disciplining and care of the self. Political economy as knowledge and apparatuses of security as technical means operate on the population as a target to constitute governmentality as the dominant mode of power since the eighteenth century (102). Rather than attempt to exhaustively define governmentality, a job that has been well done by others, especially Mitchell Dean in *Governmentality* (1999), and by others such as Nikolas Rose (1996), Peter Miller and Nikolas Rose (1990), Pat O'Malley, Lorna Weir, and Clifford Shearling (1997), I wish to emphasize a few features of governmentality.

Foucault argues that since the eighteenth century, population became the object of sovereign power and discipline in a new way, so that the growth of the welfare of the population within a given territory, the optimization of its capabilities and productivity, became the goal of government (1991: 100–101). The goal of "good government" became not simply the exercise of authority over the people within a territory or the ability to discipline and regulate them, but fostering their prosperity and happiness.[2] Thanks to the rise of the science of statistics, "population" became an independent realm and force in social life separate from the state and the family. As an aggregate statistic, the population had its own intrinsic rhythms and regularities and exerted its own effects on the economy and on the nation. Population becomes the new aim of government: an object whose control, regulation, welfare, and conduct become the main goal of government.

Governmentality is concerned most of all with "the conduct of conduct," that is, with the myriad ways in which human conduct is directed by calculated means (Dean 1999: 10). Such a definition of government harks back to the original meaning of the term, before it became hitched to a particular relationship with the state: before, that is, the words "government" and "state" started being used almost as synonyms in academic discourse. Miller and Rose (1990: 1) point out that in advanced liberal democracies, "political power is exercised . . . through a multitude of agencies and techniques, some of which are only loosely associated with the executives and bureaucracies of the formal organs of state." In fact, the state has to be seen as "a particular form that government has taken, and one that does not exhaust the field of calculations and interventions that constitute it" (3). Like Weber, Foucault is interested in mechanisms of government that are found within state institutions and outside them, that in fact cut across domains that we would regard as separate: the state, civil society, the family, down to the intimate details of what we regard as personal life.

As an example of governmentality, take family planning. There may be state policies that promote or regulate an optimal family size through tax incentives, advertising campaigns, public health policies, zoning laws, and so on. But there are also corporate policies that may promote a particular family size in the form of leave policies, the provision of insurance, and the like; women's magazines and popular culture may influence how many children a couple desire; the comments of neighbors, coworkers, and teachers might draw attention to those who violate "societal norms" by having too many children or not enough. All these are forces of governmentality, and between the concern with the population—its health, longevity, productivity, resources—that is so central to state policy, think tanks, and private agencies and the desires that inform and regulate the sexual behavior and intimate relations within the "private" and "domestic" realms of (heteronormative) families and marriages are a series of relays that transmit and translate ideas, practices, and policies from one realm to the other. Governmentality allows us to bring under one analytical lens the entire domain, showing the operation and role of state agencies within a wider field of action and intervention made possible by a range of social actors and discourses.

It should be clear that governmentality does not name a negative relationship of power, one characterized entirely by discipline and regulation. The emphasis, rather, is on its productive dimension: governmentality is about a *concern* with the population, with its health, longevity, happiness, productivity, and size. But managing a population involves an immersion in the details and minutiae of people's lives. Here mechanisms of discipline and regulation are important not merely as repressive measures but as facilitators of new modes of accountability and enumeration. Although neither Foucault nor various commentators on governmentality have had much to say about this topic, any discussion of discipline and regulation must entail a corresponding emphasis on questions of resistance (O'Malley 1998). What forms of resistance do the new technologies of governmentality engender? And, if we don't take governmentality to be a system that was set in place once and for all in the Enlightenment, but as an ever renewing and ever deepening process, then we have to consider how governmentality is itself a conjunctural and crisis-ridden enterprise, how it engenders its own modes of resistance and makes, meets, molds, or is contested by new subjects.

"A Silent Revolution"

If one were seeking a model of governmentality today, it would be hard to come up with a better example than the ICDS program. We can see this very clearly when ICDS is located in its historical context and positioned more explicitly within state agendas. The ICDS was launched in 1975, soon after the formulation of the National Policy for Children. It was spurred by awareness that India exhibited some of the world's highest rates of infant mortality, morbidity, and malnutrition and extremely high rates of maternal mortality during birth. According to the United Nations Development Program *Human Development Report for 2000*, the infant mortality and under-five mortality rates are still 69[3] and 105 per 1,000, respectively, and the maternal mortality rate stands at 410 per 100,000.

The goal of the anganwadi program was to provide a set of services that consisted of supplementary nutrition for pregnant women and young children and education, immunizations, and preventive medicine for poor and lower-caste children. The immunization program was operated by the Health Department, which ran the Primary Health Centers (PHCs). It thus took advantage of the presence of a large number of children and "at-risk" women in the anganwadis to inoculate children, pregnant women, and nursing mothers against the most common diseases.[4] After experimenting with supplementary nutrition programs that produced generally poor results (Tandon, Ramachandran, and Bhatnagar 1981: 382), the ICDS program was initiated to provide a package of well-integrated services that would combine nutrition, health, education, and day care for children under six years of age and nutrition and health care for pregnant women (Heaver 1989; Sharma 1986; Tandon, Ramachandran, and Bhatnagar 1981).[5]

The ICDS program in any one block (a block consists of an administrative unit of approximately one hundred villages) was considered a "project," and each project received funding independently. In Mandi subdistrict (*tehsil*), there were two ICDS programs. In Mandi block, the program had been operating since 1985, whereas it had begun in the other block in 1990–1991. The structure of command of the ICDS bureaucracy at the district level was as follows: it was to be headed by a district program officer (DPO); the two child development project officers (CDPOs), who headed the program at the level of the block reported to the DPO; the CDPO was the head of the office and supervised a clerical staff, which included an account clerk, another clerk who did other jobs, a peon, and a driver; the CDPO was responsible for overseeing the work of the four supervisors (*Mukhya Sevikas*), the eighty-six anganwadi workers in the block, and their eighty-six helpers; the anganwadi workers were responsible for the day-to-day functioning of centers in villages, which targeted poor and low-caste women and children as beneficiaries. The anganwadi centers were supposed to operate every day from 9 A.M. to 1 P.M. Because it was not feasible for a single anganwadi worker to run a center, take care of as many as forty-five children, teach the children, cook food for them, supervise their medical care, and maintain the records, the anganwadi worker was provided with a helper. The helper's duties included doing all the odd jobs associated with the anganwadi, including rounding up the children to attend the center, doing the cooking when the centers were supplied with food, and cleaning the "school." In Mandi, all the helpers, anganwadi workers, and supervisors, as well as the CDPO were women; the rest of the office staff were men.

Apart from humanitarian concerns with the high mortality of infants and pregnant women, other factors may have contributed to the support given to the anganwadi program by the Indian government and by international development agencies such as UNICEF. The chief factor, no doubt, was a concern with population control.[6] At the time the ICDS scheme was launched, the Indian government already had substantial experience with an aggressive birth control campaign. It had used a modernization theory model, according to which exposing people to information would change their attitudes, which, in turn, could change people's practices (this was called the knowledge-attitude-practices, or KAP model). When I was growing up in India in the 1960s and 1970s, it was impossible to miss the inverted red triangle that was a symbol of birth control. It was accompanied by the slogan, *Hum do, hamaare do* ("Us two, our two"). Sometimes, there was an additional graphic displaying a man, a woman, a boy, and a girl. However, when it became clear that methods of population control built on modernization theory were ineffective, that better knowledge of contraception and the inculcation of "modern" attitudes failed to alter birth control practices, a sense of frustration set in among policymakers, culminating in the draconian measures adopted during the Emergency in 1975–1977. By all accounts, the forced sterilization of men during the Emergency, especially among the poor and politically weak segments of the population, only impeded subsequent government interventions in this field.[7]

In the post-Emergency period, there was a lull in family planning campaigns. However, in the next decade, a new consensus emerged among governments and international development agencies that focused on the *quality* of the population (Dasgupta 1990). The logic, since inscribed as official dogma by the Cairo Conference, simply states that lower birthrates are highly correlated with higher status for women, accompanied by better nutrition, education, and health care for them and their children (Cliquet and Thienpont 1955; Sen 1994). In other words, investment in the development of "human resources" of "human capital" was expected to pay high dividends, especially when targeted to women and children. This was, in fact, the explicit language in which the "ICDS Experience" was summarized in a government brochure: "The experience of ICDS during its first decade (1975–1985) indicates that it has the potential of becoming a silent revolution, a profound instrument of community development and human resource development" (Government of India 1985: 24).

The adverse impact of rapid growth on the welfare of the population had long been recognized: Indian policymakers and politicians routinely emphasize how development efforts are slowed by rapid population growth. The debate then concerned what the best methods were for reducing the rate of growth of the population. Having failed to persuade people to adopt birth control practices by a vigorous advertising campaign, an increasingly desperate political leadership attempted to use authoritarian measures to sterilize people during the Emergency under the leadership of Indira Gandhi's younger son, Sanjay Gandhi. However, the resulting backlash forced Mrs. Gandhi out of power in the elections of 1977. Since then, the ICDS program took over as a technology of birth control that sought to reduce gross birthrates by focusing on the quality of life for those children already born, that is, by reducing the mortality and morbidity rates for infants and by reducing maternal mortality. If governmentality draws attention to how to govern and how we are governed (Dean 1999: 2), then ICDS is an excellent example of how the governance of the population came to be reformulated after a moment of crisis.

In fact, if one does not frame the population question narrowly, one can appreciate how the ICDS brings forth an explicit conjunction between the development of human resources, communities, and the nation. The relationship between the population, political economy, and sovereignty so central to governmentality is revealed quite clearly. In a country like India, children under fourteen constitute a large proportion of the population (42 percent, according to the 1971 census, and 38.6 percent at the end of the 1970s). More than 80 percent of all children live in rural areas and have poorer access to government services than their urban counterparts (Dasgupta 1990: 1302). The Government of India's National Policy for Children proposed fifteen measures to achieve the goals of fulfilling children's needs. It stated:

> The nation's children are a supremely important *asset*. . . . Children's programmes should find a prominent part in our national plans for the development of human resources, so that our children grow up to become robust citizens, physically fit, mentally alert and normally healthy, endowed with the skills and motivations needed by *society*. . . . It shall be the policy of the State to provide adequate services to children, both before and after birth and through the period of growth, to ensure their full physical, mental and social development. (Baig 1979: 339–41; emphasis added)

Such a statement reinforced directives in the Constitution of India that provided for, among other things, free and compulsory education for all children up to age fourteen. The authors of the Constitution directed the government to attempt the provisioning of educational services to all children within ten years from the commencement of the Constitution (Dasgupta 1990: 1304). The point I wish to make here is that concerns with the needs of "national development" were not incidental to programs aimed at children. In fact, the National Policy for Children explicitly conceived of the ICDS scheme as a response to its first three directives, which proposed a comprehensive health program, supplementary nutrition to remove deficiencies, and provision for the care and nutrition of expectant and nursing mothers (Baig 1979: 340). These themes were spelled out even more explicitly in a memorandum attached to the National Policy by the Indian Council for Child Welfare (ICCW), which argued that "the child is an investment in the future of the nation and must, therefore, be an integral part of *economic* planning" (Baig 1979: 334–35).

The relationship between ICDS and economic planning for the nation was seen in its relationship to other development programs. The supplementary nutrition aspect of ICDS was funded from a range of sources. For instance, in Mandi block, the program had switched in the late 1980s to a "wheat-based" program. This was mentioned several times by the ICDS staff in Mandi, and at first I could not understand why they were placing so much emphasis on this fact. I later learned that what was significant about the program was that the wheat allocated to it came from the Food Corporation of India (FCI). The FCI was the body that purchased wheat from farmers in the area at support prices set by the government. This policy of buying all the wheat that farmers could sell at preannounced prices was one of the cornerstones of the green revolution and had led to the accumulation of large surpluses in government go-downs. The state's use of this "surplus" wheat for the ICDS thus took the results of agricultural development policies and, quite literally, fed them into its welfare policies. Therefore, the development of agriculture and the development of human resources were placed in a synergistic relationship that would lead to the development of the nation. The wealth of the nation was thus tied to the welfare of its population.

Because the goal of governmentality is to manage "the population," mechanisms for intervening into the affairs of communities and individuals are necessary. The ICDS program depended on community intervention for its efficacy. Anganwadi workers were recruited from the villages in which they served to garner local support for the program. One of the most important components of local participation was that the space for the anganwadi was to be supplied by the community; thus, there was no provision for rent in the ICDS budget. Apart from reducing the cost of administering the program, such a requirement was intended to provide the community with a stake in the operation of the anganwadis. This created a great deal of difficulty for anganwadi workers and was one of their chief sources of complaints about the program.[8]

The efforts to involve the community in the program did not always work very well. Instead of allowing nongovernmental agencies, voluntary organizations, and community groups to influence the design of the program and the methods and kinds of services it delivered, the ICDS scheme, like many other government programs, imposed a top-down administrative structure with elaborate bureaucratic procedures that had a "slot" for community participation (Dasgupta 1990: 1315). Ironically, such a slot was deemed necessary to make the program conform to the requirements of "participatory development" that, according to development orthodoxy, was one of the lessons learned from the high failure rate of development projects in the past. Community participation was essential if government was to be seen not as something external and imposed but as an intrinsic mode of discipline that led to regular and predictable patterns of conduct and that grew out of, and came "naturally" to, communities and selves.

Governmentality and State Surveillance

The concern with the size and quality of the population embodied in the ICDS program was exhibited in techniques of *regulation*, *enumeration*, and *accountability*. There were a host of procedures and rules about the day-to-day functioning of the anganwadis that made little sense when viewed from a bottom-line perspective of gains in health and nutrition. Yet such regulations were not incidental to the ICDS. As important as were the goals of the ICDS program—reducing infant mortality and maternal mortality, increasing educational achievements for girls, providing supplementary nutrition to decrease morbidity—the methods to achieve those goals were equally important. The size of the population was being controlled, but, perhaps more important, new subjects were being created. And the only way to ensure regulation, enumeration, and accountability was through a process of surveillance. Although the methods of surveillance would never reach the Benthamite ideal of the panopticon, which ensured that subjects would regulate their own behavior because they never knew when they were being observed (Foucault 1979a), the goal of the program was to achieve similar results. If anganwadi workers, children who were being served by the anganwadi, expectant mothers, and the families of the "clients" would all behave "naturally" in regular, predictable, patterned ways, then surveillance would have been most successful (and hence unnecessary). But surveillance didn't always achieve exactly what it set out to do, and that is what makes this story really interesting.

The ICDS office in Mandi was located in one of the side streets that led off the busy road that served as the major shopping center of the "modern" part of town. When I first went looking for the ICDS office, I walked right past it; this happened on more than one occasion. I had been told to look for the blue UNICEF jeep that served as the unofficial mascot for the ICDS program. I missed the office because the jeep was missing, and, unlike other government offices that displayed large signs, there was no outward indication that an office existed in that building. It was a nondescript space, consisting of a small driveway barely large enough for a vehicle and a narrow flight of stairs to one side. One went up the stairs to a terrace, no wider than eight feet, which had a series of doors opening up to it on the left. There were three rooms. The first room housed the main office, where the two clerks had their desks and where the peon usually stood. The second room was used primarily as a storage space. The third room, furthest from the stairs, was the office of the dynamic and articulate CDPO of Mandi block, Asha Agarwal. She was a thin, small-boned woman in her thirties who spoke with a confident and engaging tone, sitting behind a fairly large desk in a sparsely furnished and decorated room. Like other officers, she had a buzzer on her desk, which she pressed whenever she needed to get the attention of the peon.

Inspection Trips

The chief instrument of bureaucratic surveillance was the surprise inspection, which functioned to ensure that the goals of regulation, enumeration, and accountability were met. Regulation took the form of seeing that the anganwadi centers functioned at regular days and times and that the workers and children were obeying instructions about how the day care center ought to be run, how the schooling was to be accomplished, how the facilities had to be maintained. Enumeration was important in that one of the officer's primary responsibilities was to monitor the degree to which the anganwadi workers collected data, especially information about women and children who were the targets of the ICDS program. In this sense, the object of the officer's surveillance was the degree to which the anganwadi worker monitored her client population. As we will see, in practice, this model worked quite unevenly. Accountability was accomplished by a series of checks that ensured that the data recorded by the anganwadi worker matched what could be observed during the inspection. For example, if the worker claimed that forty children regularly attended the center and ate their meals there, she might be asked to explain why only twenty students were there during a surprise inspection, or the claims of the worker about what she taught the students might be tested by giving the students an impromptu test.

One of the greatest challenges facing the bureaucrats was to ensure that the village women who had been hired to run the anganwadis were in fact operating them. Asha Agarwal would often impress upon me the importance of inspections for ensuring the "proper operation" of anganwadi centers in her block. She reinforced her point by relating the following anecdote to me. When she had taken over the Mandi office, it had been without a CDPO for several months; the government had appointed one of the previous supervisors to be a temporary CDPO. Asha pointed out that appointing a supervisor to monitor the functioning of anganwadis was doomed to failure because "in-charges," as the temporary CDPOs were termed, were at the same level in the official hierarchy as other supervisors and, hence, lacked the authority to "pull up" (*khainchnaa*) other supervisors and anganwadi workers. In addition, the office jeep had not been operating for a year because the money to repair it had not been sanctioned by the state government; the previous in-charge had used the lack of a vehicle to justify not making inspection trips. This, in turn, had enabled the supervisors to slack off, and the clerks too felt that they could get away with not fulfilling their responsibilities. Once supervisors stopped going on inspection trips, anganwadi workers felt they had nothing to fear and they ceased operating the centers. Thus, claimed Asha, because the in-charge had not made inspection trips, the "whole system" ground to a halt.

During Asha's first few months in Mandi, the ICDS jeep was still inoperable, so she, too, had not conducted any inspection trips. But when it appeared that the vehicle would not be repaired in the foreseeable future, she started taking public transportation to pay "surprise visits" to the centers. She went to four centers and was horrified to find that none was functioning. She felt that it was useless going to other centers because she would then end up having to give warnings to all the workers under her charge. So, at the next monthly meeting of anganwadi workers, she announced that if she found centers that were not functioning, she would take disciplinary action against the workers concerned. Following that warning, she resumed going on inspection trips. At first, she found attendance at the centers spotty. However, once the word spread that she had started issuing warnings and docking workers' pay, the centers started operating again. Thus, even without an official vehicle, Asha managed to use inspection trips effectively and, although she could not inspect as many centers as she would have been able to with a vehicle, she still managed to monitor quite a few.

I accompanied Asha Agarwal on a couple of inspection trips. She had carefully planned our itinerary so that we would visit centers that had a record of good performance, but the fact that these were "surprise visits" meant that they could not serve as public relations exercises. The first trip was on a cold and overcast day in February 1992, soon after the office had received a fresh disbursement of funds for purchasing petrol. The blue ICDS jeep, which had been lying idle because of insufficient funds for repairs and petrol, was coaxed into life by the driver. Because anganwadis were supposed to operate from nine in the morning to one in the afternoon, we left the Mandi office just before nine. Asha and I sat alongside the driver in front, while the supervisor responsible for the areas we were visiting was in the back. Our first stop was the petrol station. Asha informed me that the state government had requested all offices to cut their expenditures by 20 percent. Because the office's annual report was due at the end of March, they had to run around even more than usual. She wondered aloud: How did the state government expect her to cut expenditures so drastically and still get all the work done for the annual report?

The first village we stopped was Kalanda. There were two anganwadis in Kalanda that had been operating since 1985, when the ICDS project began in Mandi block. I was told that it was a primarily Muslim village, and we encountered an impressive mosque at the entrance to the village rather than the temple often seen in Hindu-majority villages. The village was most unusual for the well-maintained quality of its inner roads and the complete absence of sewage water and garbage on the streets. I was told that many men in the village were masons and had volunteered their labor to lay the roads and the drains. Some of them had gone to work as laborers in the Middle East and had come back with small fortunes, which accounted both for the relative grandeur of the mosque and the neat-looking houses.

The first anganwadi that we went to inspect was housed in a dark room that served as the storage area for a farm family. A huge pile of lentils (*arhar*) occupied half the room, completely covering one wall and a good proportion of the floor space. The anganwadi worker, a pleasant and energetic woman, quickly sent the helper to round up additional children to add to the fourteen who were already there. Asha asked the children to count numbers and to recite the alphabet, which they did with practiced ease. One child in particular, who was a little older than the rest, had written down numbers all the way to one hundred on his slate, and had also memorized all the poems and songs they had been taught. While we were at this center, a number of children came in, looking washed and scrubbed. Asha told me that the teacher had only a high school degree, but seemed to be doing a good job with the children. She castigated the anganwadi worker for not removing the charts, which functioned as teaching aides, from the wall where the lentils had been piled. "It is your job to look after the charts," she told her. "When you knew that the crop was going to be stored there, why didn't you remove the charts beforehand?" After inspecting the attendance registers and writing a brief report in the inspection register, which noted when the inspection took place, how many children were there, and what the children had demonstrated, we left that center and headed for the second one.

The second center in Kalanda was in the porch of a house. When we reached there, the anganwadi worker was nowhere to be seen. There were a handful of very young children present, along with the helper. When asked where the worker was, the helped claimed that she did not know. Asha and the supervisor attempted to coax some of the children to stand up and recite the number table or identify objects on an alphabet chart; however, none of them opened their mouths. It was hard to tell whether this was out of fear of the visitors or because of the unfamiliarity with the task. We waited for a few minutes, then headed back to the jeep. As we were leaving, the anganwadi worker came hurrying toward us. She apologized profusely and blamed her delay on the fact that the bus she was traveling on had broken down. Asha chastised her in no uncertain terms. Even if her bus had broken down, she said, that was no excuse for reaching the center at 11:15 instead of 9. The worker lamented her fate, saying that it was her bad luck that the one day when she started late was the day we happened to arrive. She tried to persuade us to come back to the anganwadi for a few minutes, but Asha wanted to see centers in other villages that day, and it was fast approaching closing time.

On our way to the jeep, Asha noted wryly how much better seemed the center operated by the woman who was only "high-school pass" compared to the second one, despite the fact that the second anganwadi worker had a master's degree. The children at the first center seemed better taught and the teacher displayed more enthusiasm, observed Asha. She appeared surprised at this because, in the past, she had found that the better-educated "teacher" had done a really good job.

That day, we visited another village with two more centers and had a remarkably similar experience in that the two anganwadis that were well run had workers who had high school degrees, whereas the anganwadi workers in the other two were women whose qualifications exceeded the minimum required for the job. Asha's explanation for this was that highly trained women often felt that this job was below their dignity. They usually preferred other, better-paying jobs, but accepted the position of an anganwadi worker for lack of other opportunities. Asha said that it was probably a mistake to hire people who were overqualified, because such people would never be happy in a job where their skills were underutilized and in which they felt underappreciated.

During her inspection trips, Asha referred to the attendance registers, in which anganwadi workers had to record the number of children who came to the center in order to evaluate the performance of an anganwadi. If she did not find a center open or functioning properly during a surprise visit, she docked the anganwadi worker's pay for that day and left a note requesting an explanation (*spashtikaran*) for why the worker was not there. Repeated absences or delays in responding to the CDPO's demand for an explanation resulted in extended pay cuts; however, a decision to terminate employment required a great deal of documentation and careful groundwork on the part of the CDPO.

One example of repeated abstention from duty was provided by Sona Devi, an older, widowed woman with three children who lived in a large village called Hamirpur that had three anganwadi centers. Asha told me that she had found Sona Devi's center closed during her last three inspection visits. Asha opened her inspection ledger and showed it to me as evidence: it indicated that Asha had reached the center at 12:30 and found it closed. When she asked why there were no children at her center, Sona Devi replied that they had all gone to see a play (*nat*) being performed in the village. But when Asha checked this story with workers at the other centers, they were unaware of any play being performed in the village at that time. Yet, despite Sona Devi's poor record, Asha had so far resisted firing her; all she had done was cut her pay for not performing her job.

Asha then proceeded to give me more examples of how difficult it was for her to fire, and therefore discipline, anganwadi workers even when she knew they were not doing their jobs. One, Balvanti, used to manage a center in her natal village. When she got married and left for her husband's village, her father requested that his younger daughter be made the anganwadi worker in place of the older. Asha told him that she could not do that because she was required to advertise the position, and that, furthermore, all new positions were reserved for scheduled caste applicants.[9] Asha waited for, but did not receive, a letter of resignation from Balvanti. After her marriage, Balvanti returned to her natal village for a few months before she moved permanently to her new home.[10] During the time that Balvanti was back in her parents' home, she resumed operation of the anganwadi. Asha added that Balvanti had been a conscientious worker and had done a very good job of running the anganwadi. But eventually, Balvanti had left permanently for her husband's village. Whenever she returned to her parents' home for brief periods during the year, she would reopen the center and operate it for a few days. But for most of the year the anganwadi remained closed. Once, when Asha had gone on an inspection tour and found the center closed, she went to Balvanti's house to verify her whereabouts. She was told that Balvanti had just left for the fields on some urgent business. But a small child who was standing there piped up, "She hasn't gone to the field, she has gone to her own home!" Thus, her family member's lie was exposed. During previous inspection visits, Asha had tried to persuade Balvanti's family that she would be better off resigning than getting fired. She told them, "This is a government department. By resigning, she leaves with her self-respect intact. By getting fired, she brings disrespect to herself." Yet, eighteen months after that incident, Asha had not yet received a resignation letter. Asha added that it was imperative that she fire Balvanti before a new consignment of food was allocated to the ICDS program because, if she waited to relieve her until after the food had been supplied, the chances were that Balvanti, knowing that she would have to resign soon, would appropriate the food. Asha also knew that Balvanti would come back to her parents' home for Holi (the spring harvest festival) and was afraid that she might restart the anganwadi for a few days; Asha would then have to conduct three more inspections to fire her. Asha underlined the difficulty of her task by noting that the two registered letters she had sent Balvanti were not returned to the office, nor was there evidence that they had been delivered. Asha surmised that Balvanti's family probably knew the village postman and had cajoled him to hand the letter over without their signing a receipt. She had drafted another letter terminating Balvanti's employment and was about to send it to her boss, who would have it signed and delivered officially.

Asha showed me examples of letters in which she had put two anganwadi workers on notice and had demanded a written explanation for why they had been absent from their centers. Both women responded within a day, saying that they could not be at the anganwadi because their children had suddenly taken ill. Asha told me that this was the excuse that she was given most frequently. If, during a surprise visit, she found a center that was not functioning, she would visit it again in a few days, usually within a fortnight. If she found that the center was still not operating, she would leave a warning and would dock the worker's pay for yet another day. Shortly thereafter, she would visit the same anganwadi for a third time; if it was still not operating, she would leave a third warning and would thereby prepare the way for suspending the worker. Anganwadi workers were not government employees and, hence, could be fired after the third warning. However, Asha usually gave them another chance. "When we go to higher officials to get rid of someone," she explained, "they tell us, 'First make the file thicker.'" In other words, get more material, more paperwork, before taking any action. "The thicker the file," she said, "the easier it is to get a decision to fire someone."

Thus, the surveillance exercised by the CDPO through her inspection trips was not always matched by a capacity to discipline and fire workers. The CDPO's authority was limited to withholding the pay of workers who were not doing their job. To relieve a worker of her job, the CDPO had to first assemble an unimpeachable record of the worker's misdemeanor and then convince her boss that such drastic action was justified.

On one of my visits to the ICDS office on a warm day in February 1992, the staff had pulled the desks and chairs onto the narrow porch to take advantage of the sunny weather. While I was talking to Asha, a man came up the stairs and headed into the office. After consulting with the clerk, he handed a slip of paper to Asha. It was an application for leave on behalf of his wife, who was an anganwadi worker. The application requested leave for a few days because she was ill. Accompanying the application was an impressive stack of papers, including an X-ray, which the man plopped down in front of Asha. He said that if Asha didn't believe him, she could look at the medical papers and convince herself that his wife was telling the truth. Asha categorically refused to believe the man. She said that she had made surprise visits to that center on two occasions and found it closed both times. What was more, many villagers had come to her complaining that the center did not function. She told the man that if his wife could not operate the center because she was ill, she should have applied for medical leave, and Asha would have been happy to endorse such an application. Alternatively, his wife could have applied for "casual" leave (which, however, was limited to twenty days every year). But, Asha emphasized, the worker could not keep the anganwadi closed indefinitely because she was ill *and* continue to draw a salary as if the center were open. Asha added that she had not yet received a response (*spashtikaran*) to the letters she had left at the center. She demanded to know why, if the worker was ill, the center was not being run by her helper: "If your wife cannot make it to the anganwadi on certain days, why is the helper absent? I should find the helper [at the center] even if the anganwadi worker is not there." The man defended his wife, saying that she could not force the helper to show up. But Asha did not give up her line of questioning. If his wife went to the anganwadi regularly, why did the attendance registers not demonstrate that fact by listing the names of the children who were present? "When I went there," Asha said, "none of the registers had been filled." That charge finally broke the man's resistance. He then switched tactics and claimed that it was hard to entice children to come to the anganwadi when there was no food (*poshtahaar*) provided to them. Asha claimed that, by that logic, none of the anganwadis in Mandi should have been operating, as there was no food being distributed at any of them. Defeated by that battery of arguments, the man left. When he had gone, I asked Asha if she intended to fire that particular anganwadi worker. To my surprise, she said that she did not think it necessary to resort to such a drastic step. "This was only my second warning to her," she said. "We have to allow for the possibility that there are often genuine reasons why the center is not open." Anganwadi workers sometimes came back on track after repeated warnings and, in that particular case, she would wait a little longer.

Asha proceeded to tell me about other centers that were in trouble, drawing on the cases of Balvanti and Sona Devi referred to earlier, and emphasized the difficulties she had in doing anything to remedy the situation. Asha had already been to Balvanti's village twice, and a supervisor had visited once, and they had both found the anganwadi closed. In addition, when Asha went to inspect the center, villagers complained that it no longer functioned properly. However, oral complaints were of little use, and Asha was frustrated in her efforts to persuade villagers to write down what they told her. "The problem," she said, "is that when you ask someone to give you a complaint in writing, they at once withdraw what is otherwise vociferous criticism. With government work, unless you have something in writing, you cannot build a case and take any action."

The recalcitrance of subordinates was only one instance in which the hands of CDPOs were tied. Sona Devi, whose pay had been docked by Asha, had decided to put political pressure on Asha to restore her stipend. One day, five men arrived and told Asha that she had no right to speak to Sona Devi in an "insulting tone." Asha presented her case to them and asked them what they wanted her to do, given the fact that Sona Devi's anganwadi was found to not be functioning on three different occasions. Ignoring her question, the men said that they were not asking her to do anything, they just wanted to warn her to not "misbehave" with her workers. Asha became enraged as she recounted what happened: "First, she [Sona Devi] does something wrong, and then she tries to put [political] pressure on me! That makes me even more angry."

Surprise inspections and registers were two devices by which regulation and accountability were pursued through devices of enumeration. It was not only that superior officers at "higher" levels traveled in jeeps, it was also that they traveled to conduct inspections, to discipline, reward, encourage, and punish. Registers helped them do just that, for registers enabled them to check their observations against what had been noted. For example, Asha complained that workers who ran anganwadi centers in their homes often brought in additional children when they saw the dust of the jeep in the distance. Thus, by the time the CDPO actually reached the center, there were many children there even if the anganwadi had not been operating. However, she managed to catch the worker's "deception" in such cases by checking the names of the children present against the names (if any) entered in the attendance register. The CDPO's ability to swoop down on the space of the anganwadi worker was thus mediated by the semiotic of dust: a smoke signal delivered by that very device, the jeep, that enabled her to suddenly enter the space of the worker.

The surveillance exercised by superior officers on their subordinates was part of the routine functioning of the Indian state. However, this kind of monitoring did not easily translate into control and discipline. The authority of the CDPO, as of any superior officer in the hierarchy, could be subverted, deferred, or denied through a range of tactics. The workers who were the objects of surveillance by their superiors did not merely conform and police themselves as expected. Rather than simply regulating and normalizing, the power of superior officers to exercise surveillance on their workers sometimes provoked disruptive reactions that threatened the hierarchical assumptions of bureaucratic order. Government by state bureaucracies did not smoothly translate into self-government by anganwadi workers; there were significant points of tension and friction in the art of government.

I found a similarly contested relationship between anganwadi workers and villagers. As part of their job, workers were required to collect vast amounts of data, particularly about women and children, segments of the population that had not been as extensively surveyed, counted, classified, measured, injected, or schooled in the past. The monitoring that superior officers exercised on workers was meant partially to ensure that they were, in turn, conscientiously monitoring the population they were "serving." The next section deals explicitly with the relationship between anganwadi workers and "their" villagers.

State Mechanisms: A Numbers Game?

Although they were not government employees, anganwadi workers were expected to behave as such in one important regard: they had the crucial responsibility of generating official statistics for the state. In an appropriate image, Hacking (1982) has characterized the activities of the modern state as generating an "avalanche of numbers."[11] In the anganwadi program, record keeping often appeared to be an end in itself; it also had far-reaching effects in mapping, surveying, and tabulating the population and, most important, in potentially monitoring the lives of women and children.

Enumeration is a critical modality of governmentality; it is through the collection of statistics that the conduct of conduct can be effected. What kinds of statistics are collected, who collects them, and how they are used all affect the regulation of populations, techniques of accountability, and the formation of group identities. Foucault has pointed out the family resemblance between statistics and the state: the rise of statistics is integral to the science of the state that developed in Europe at the end of the sixteenth century (1991: 96). Kaviraj (1994) links enumeration to a specifically modern form of community identity, which he opposes to "fuzzy" communities. It is through the purposeful counting of peoples as members of certain kinds of groups that arguments can be made about representativeness, about majorities and minorities, about who is falling behind and who is ahead in income data, educational achievements, and so on. Statistics are not just collected by the state, and they certainly are not always collected or employed in the *interests* of the state. Aggrieved groups can quite effectively marshal statistics against the state to justify a range of actions. My argument is that statistics function to gauge things like activity levels and health, monitor the actions of social agents, and regulate the behavior of populations. All these functions extend beyond the state and belong to the realm of government more generally.

The most time-consuming activity of anganwadi workers consisted of documenting and generating statistics. A plethora of registers recorded such things as how many children attended the center each day and who they were: their name, father's name, and caste. A nutrition register recorded how much food and fuel was consumed each day. A third register was used to record the birth dates of each child born in the village and the parents' names, ages, and castes. Similar records were kept of all deaths. The name, age, and caste of each pregnant woman and a record of the outcome of the pregnancy were recorded in another register. A travel log maintained a record of when and why an anganwadi worker was missing from a center. An inspection register was maintained where supervisors, the CDPO, and other visitors recorded their impressions about the functioning of the anganwadi.

Maintaining all these records posed a daunting challenge to most anganwadi workers, particularly those who lacked the requisite cultural capital in the form of mathematical skills. Sharda Devi was a worker in the village of Bhaipur, a few miles from Mandi. Her husband was a self-taught "doctor" who was also the community health worker for the village. When I met her during one of my visits to the center, she complained to me about the mathematics involved in the supplementary nutrition program. Different quantities of food, measured in grams, had to be given to children, pregnant women, and nursing mothers. Then the totals had to be added up for each category and for all groups each day. These totals were next tallied against the amount of food actually left in the center. When the CDPO came on her inspection trips, one of the things she looked for was discrepancies in the registers and the actual amount of food remaining at the center. Sharda Devi's husband asked pointedly, "How do they expect a person with an eighth-grade education to do all this? If I didn't help her, she would never be able to manage the books." However, everyone, including the CDPO, understood that the object of the exercise was not so much to detect "corruption" as to keep the record straight so that no aspersions of corruption could reasonably be made. Thick files and carefully totaled numbers were more important than actual action, because the logic of bureaucratic justification demanded written evidence, a fact often lost on semiliterate or illiterate people in rural areas.

But there was more to the functioning of anganwadis than generating numbers so that tables and columns totaled up correctly. A silent revolution was indeed taking place through this program, and it was not just in the "development of human resources." Perhaps for the first time in the history of the nation records were being kept on births and deaths in rural areas. Anyone who has attempted to do a census of an Indian village knows how difficult it is to record precise ages and dates of birth, as the techniques of the modern, Western imaginary of the nation and "its" population are (mis)-translated into incommensurable modes and methods of recording the passage of time as it intersects with life histories. I looked at several registers in anganwadis that recorded information about births. The mothers' ages, which may have ranged from fifteen and up, were all carefully recorded as over the legal age of marriage: eighteen years and six months, or nineteen, or twenty-two. However, the birth of children in the village since the anganwadi program began in Mandi was recorded to the day, and sometimes to the hour. The registers contained similar, relatively accurate information about deaths. In other registers were to be found data on inoculations, the weight of infants and pregnant women, attendance at the anganwadi, and so on. The anganwadi program had resulted in a quantum leap in data on women and children, particularly with respect to fertility and infant mortality.

It may be objected that because anganwadi workers were not trained census takers, the quality of the data they collected was suspect. And, indeed, because there were no mechanisms to check whether a worker had recorded *all* the births and deaths in a village or had accurately noted down the exact birth date of individuals, it would have been impossible to tell if a birth or death had been recorded correctly. However, what needs to be pointed out is that, unlike census takers, anganwadi workers either lived in the village in which they worked or went daily to the village to operate the anganwadi. They could gather a great deal of information from the children who came to the anganwadi. Further, births and deaths were major public occasions in villages in western Uttar Pradesh and thus could be hidden only with great difficulty. Finally, anganwadi workers had no incentive to not record or to misrecord such events. Thus, although there were few mechanisms to double-check the records kept by workers, there was little reason to be suspicious of the figures that had been entered in the registers.

The broader point that I wish to make here is that, seemingly by-products of the functioning of the anganwadi program were series of numbers, modes of enumeration, classification, and recording that operated on a segment of the population whose low level of literacy and lack of participation in the formal economy had kept it relatively insulated from the chronotope of state surveillance. What differentiated the anganwadi worker from the census taker was precisely the degree of *familiarity* with the village that no outsider could ever obtain. Even when the worker kept her distance from the social life of the village, its politics and divisions, she still knew a great deal more about individuals and families than any other state official could possibly know. More important, the worker learned a great deal about women in the village, a segment of the population relatively insulated from the gaze of other (male) state officials.

However, just as there were limits to the state's surveillance of the running of anganwadi centers through the direct supervision of the CDPO, there were limits to its surveillance through practices of data gathering by anganwadi workers. The anganwadi program did not merely or mainly result in the incorporation of women and children into the relentless march of the machinery of state surveillance. I give two reasons below why such a conclusion would exaggerate claims about increasing state control and underestimate the spaces for resistance and ambivalence created by these very processes. Whether or not the state's role in rural life was increased by the anganwadi program, it is clear that new modes of governmentality were being introduced by the program, techniques of enumeration and data gathering, and novel technologies of regulation and accountability.

Despite anganwadi workers' best efforts, villagers often resisted their efforts to collect statistics. At one of the monthly meetings of workers that I attended, several stood up to document the difficulties they experienced in collecting the information they were required to enter in the registers. One worker said that villagers refused to allow their children's weight to be measured. One day, as part of her duties, she had weighed some children; the next day, a little boy fell ill, and his sibling told the rest of the family that the child had been weighed the previous day. Measuring children's weight and pronouncing them healthy was considered reason enough to attract envy, the "evil eye" so feared by people in western Uttar Pradesh.[12] After that day, none of the households in the village would allow their children to attend the anganwadi. They told the worker, "When you don't feed the children, why do you weigh them?" She could not convince them that no harm would come to children by weighing them.

Similarly, some workers reported that when they went from door to door to do a survey of the population, people often refused to cooperate with them. "Why do you come to our house to do the survey when we have to come to you for inoculations and injections?" the workers were asked with impeccable logic. "You should just sit at the center and do the survey there." Workers also described their difficulties in asking questions about all members of a family. They were challenged by villagers with the words, "When you feed only the children, why do you want to take a survey that includes everyone? Why do you want to find out who has died—are you going to feed the dead too?" The workers said that they had no good response to such questions and were sometimes unable to persuade villagers to cooperate with them.

State surveillance did not increase by virtue of the fact of data collection. When analysts use the concept of the state, the impression conveyed is of a unitary and cohesive institution that has potentially great capacities for controlling, monitoring, and manipulating its population. However, when one disaggregates the state and analyzes the workings of individual bureaucracies and programs like the ICDS, it becomes more difficult to conceptualize a coordinated, systematic institution that can exploit the data collected by its various apparatuses. In fact, the level of coordination between agencies and bureaucracies of the state implied by the term surveillance, with its connotation of linkages between data collection and repression, suggests capabilities that the state may not possess. The ICDS project at the block level diligently accumulated the data collected by the anganwadi workers and passed them on to the district level, from where they were fed into national statistics on the program. However, it was not clear if anyone at the district level was processing the data and using them for any purpose whatsoever. I was told of mountains of data awaiting processing, from which conclusions might be drawn and lessons extracted. Hacking's (1982) image of an "avalanche of numbers" is appropriate: it suggests an undirected and undisciplined flow, triggered by the smallest disturbance in a mountain of numbers threatening to cascade down without being directed to any end by any agency.

Governmentality and Resistance

The examples of resistance offered in the previous section raise the question of the role of resistance in understandings of governmentality. O'Malley argues that resistance has too often been seen as a "negative externality" that causes programs to fail, rather than as a constitutive part of rule, of "government from below" (1998: 157). To see resistance mainly in terms of that which causes state programs to fail privileges the perspective of planners and bureaucrats and fails to acknowledge the central role played by resistance in shaping discourses, institutions, and programs of rule. At its limit, O'Malley suggests, resistance can so fundamentally transform regimes of rule that it can create a "significant source of instability" (170) for those regimes. Resistance, in other words, might provoke a shift in strategy of modes of governance that alter them so fundamentally as to be constitutive rather than acting merely as a source of constraint.

Resistance, of course, provokes reactions from those in charge of programs and policies. One such fascinating tussle about the meaning of work in the anganwadi concerned ICDS's component of schooling. Contrary to the state's efforts to portray them as voluntary workers, most anganwadi workers that I interviewed referred to themselves as teachers, consciously eliding the difference between themselves and schoolteachers. The state, on the other hand, employed the discourse of motherhood in representing the efforts of anganwadi workers as voluntary. By this logic, what workers did in the crèches was deemed an extension of what a "good mother" would have done at home: the only difference was that the worker performed that function for more children than would normally be found in a household. By the state's logic, therefore, the work done by a worker differed in scope from what she did at home but was *qualitatively equivalent* to mothering. In contrast, by referring to themselves as teachers, anganwadi workers emphasized how similar their work was to that performed by teachers in elementary schools. Thus, anganwadi workers chose to emphasize the *qualitatively different* nature of work in the anganwadi as compared to the home.

Anganwadi workers were proud of those students who had either refused to leave their centers to go to a "Montessori" (the name for any school that charged tuition and claimed to teach English as a subject) or returned to the anganwadi because they had learned so much there. Once, toward the end of January 1992, I dropped in to visit the anganwadi in Alipur. Sharmila, the Brahmin woman who was the anganwadi worker, pointed to one of the girls in her class. Before she joined the anganwadi, the girl used to walk a fair distance to a Montessori in an adjacent village. When she started attending the anganwadi regularly, she discovered that her classmates knew more than she did. She was, in fact, asked by one of the other little girls if she had learned anything at all at the Montessori! Sharmila commented that, because the Montessori charged Rs. 15 a month in tuition and the anganwadi school taught children for free, people in the village assumed that the education students received at the Montessori was better. "They don't value this education because it is free," Sharmila concluded. At another center in Kalanda, described above, the "star student" had been removed from the anganwadi and sent to the village school by his parents. However, he ran away from there and came back to the anganwadi because he liked being at the center.

At one of their monthly meetings, anganwadi workers complained that, ironically, the superior education provided at the anganwadis actually created problems. The workers claimed that as soon as the children learned a little bit at the anganwadi, their parents felt that they were "too bright" to stay there and would transfer them to a Montessori or a government-run primary school. This resulted in high turnover, as many children left the anganwadis soon after beginning their education. The workers added that this was bad for the children because, in the government schools, they were packed eighty to a class and the teachers were usually found sipping tea in the courtyard instead of teaching. They point out that teachers in the government schools were paid thousands of rupees for their "efforts," whereas anganwadi workers were compensated little for giving children individual attention.

The tension between "voluntary worker" and "teacher" was symptomatic of a more general contradiction that underlay the design of the anganwadi program. On the one hand, the anganwadi program was clearly built on the notion that women, as the "natural" caregivers for children, would be best suited to bring health and educational interventions to young children and to pregnant women and nursing mothers. On the other hand, anganwadi workers were expected to be "professional" in carrying out their duties and were bound to an even more impressive array of bureaucratic procedures and record keeping than their better-paid counterparts in government service.

The tensions between anganwadi workers' status as voluntary workers or paid professionals were manifest in the selection of sites for anganwadis. One day, as we walked to an anganwadi center, Asha took the opportunity to return to one of her favorite themes: the difficulties created by the fact that there was no provision to rent space for the anganwadis. "When someone gives you a place for free," she said, "you can't tell them that they don't have a right to use that space for their personal use. And then the result is that even if the children don't have a place to sit, there is little you can say to the owner of the house."

On another occasion, she explained why "it was a bad idea" for a woman to run an anganwadi center in her own house. She said that in such a center, it became impossible to determine when a woman was actually working and when she was doing her own housework. In addition, Asha felt that if the center was at the worker's home, there was no way to ensure that she was not diverting the food provided for supplementary nutrition of children for her own family's needs. "It is far better for the woman to go to a center somewhere else because then she goes with the attitude that she has to work for the next three hours." Not only would it make it easier to keep surveillance on the worker, it would also maintain the center as a separate space imbued with the authority of the state.

The problem, she said, was that when she told women not to establish centers at their own homes, they replied, "What can we do? Get us another place, and we'll move." Thus, one of Asha's biggest frustrations with the program was that no money had been allocated for rent. The space for the anganwadi was supposed to be donated by the village to ensure local participation in the program. However, in Mandi block, where the program had been operating for six years, landlords, nervous of government intentions toward their property and aware of laws that favored tenants, were systematically taking back the spaces they had loaned to the centers.

Women who worked in the anganwadi program were thus expected to perform home-like duties in the centers, extending their "natural" roles of caring for children and cooking meals. However, they were also expected to *maintain* the boundary between their home and their workplace, because blurring those boundaries made surveillance and control impossible. In harnessing women's energies by extending their domestic roles to the public sphere for the development of the community and the nation, the anganwadi program was unable to mediate the tensions created by domesticating the state, as conflicts between control and performance became intractable. Control required women to operate the centers in a workspace, a nondomestic setting; however, the tasks they were expected to perform were considered domestic and home-like duties. Predictably, anganwadi workers resisted such a formulation by taking the opposite position on those issues, arguing for an elision of work and domestic spaces on the grounds that it was hard to run a center in borrowed space and insisting on a distinction between domestic work and the teaching they did in the center. Thus, even the best efforts of state officials to govern the conduct of anganwadi workers, who were, after all, their own employees, did not bring about the results they had hoped for.

Instead of the program's objectives becoming the objectives of the workers through a process of internalization and self-discipline, recalcitrant workers redefined their activities and changed the site of the anganwadi to their own home. Here is a case where resistance took not the form of refusal, but largely of *reinterpretation*. It was not that anganwadi workers necessarily changed what they were doing; they were in a semiotic struggle about the *meaning* of their actions.

Conclusion

Governmentality, Dean and Hindess (1998) remind us, is equally about the government of conduct and the conduct of government. Examining the ICDS program allows us to see precisely how the latter shapes the former. In other words, how does the functioning of one government program shape the conduct of workers, clients, and bureaucrats? State efforts to alter, regulate, monitor, measure, record, and reward the conduct of politically disempowered groups of lower-caste women and children emerged from an effort to manage the size and quality of the population. At the same time, the conduct of government itself was changed as a result of this interaction, as these groups imbued the state with their own agendas, interpretations, and actions.

I began this essay by noting the importance of a "benevolent" program like the ICDS in the face of certain incontrovertible and tragic facts relating to the high mortality and morbidity rates for children and pregnant women in India. The program promised to inexpensively increase the human capital of the nation and, thus, promote its rapid development. Investing in children, the logic went, was investing in the nation's future. Another, closely related payoff was its potential to bring down fertility rates. Better health and education and increased rates of survival for children were expected to have long-term effects in slowing down population growth. As Suman Nayyar, a training officer in the ICDS directorate, succinctly put it: "If a couple know that their children won't survive, they'll have more. Education is the best contraceptive" (Inter-Press Service, January 7, 1987).[13]

The ideology of humanitarian intervention, given an economic rationale as an investment in the future of the nation, was accompanied by a discourse of protection. The premise of benevolent protection implicit in the ICDS scheme almost never drew comment from any of its planners or participants. The commitment to protection explained why the ICDS program targeted women (especially pregnant women) and children, and why the program was geared so heavily to poor and lower-caste groups. These were the groups who most needed protection, as they were "at-risk," "vulnerable," and least able to help themselves.

Investment in human capital and benevolent protection colluded with the third feature that was a necessary effect of such a program, and that was the vast increase in the monitoring, surveillance, and regulation of the target population.[14] This happened through a variety of mechanisms. Anganwadi workers were required to collect a staggering array of statistics. It is significant that most of the data collected by workers dealt with the segment of the population that was least represented in official records. Almost any type of record kept by the state—land titles, school records, bank accounts, postal savings accounts, electricity connections, loans—recorded the name, age, residence, and sometimes caste of the father. Typical records read: "Ravinder, age 16, s/o [son of] Gavinder, Village Khurd," or "Poonam, age 10, d/o Gavinder, Village Khurd." Men were present in a variety of capacities: as sons, husbands, fathers, and even grandfathers. Significantly, women were largely absent or were mentioned only occasionally as wives and daughters. Because women were less likely to attend institutions of formal learning or to transact business at a bank or post office, they were far less visible in the official record. It was precisely this segment of the population, heretofore insulated from the apparatuses of state surveillance, that the anganwadi workers' statistics were systematically bringing under the gaze of the state.

There was another aspect to the increased ambit of state surveillance. This had to do with the anganwadi workers, who were themselves ambivalently positioned as simultaneously implementers of the ICDS program and beneficiaries of state benevolence. Workers were not treated as state employees; what they did at the centers was defined as volunteer work for which they were recompensed not with a salary but with a stipend. Participation in the program subjected them to an intensive regime of regulation and surveillance. Inspection trips to monitor the performance of anganwadis were made by several levels of officials, who thus subjected them to a level of monitoring that exceeded even that exerted on regular employees of the state.

However, state surveillance was not without its ambiguities and ambivalences. In coping with the requirements for paperwork placed on them and the insistence on procedure followed by Indian bureaucracies, anganwadi workers gained a great deal of competence in navigating and circumventing the procedures of the bureaucracy. They learned too to create paper trails that prevented them from being cowed by the high-handed methods of the bureaucracy and its demands for literacy. In addition, the requirement that workers travel to training centers for three months at the beginning of their tenure and to the office in Mandi for their monthly meeting had several unintended consequences. In western Uttar Pradesh, women almost never made such trips on their own, that is, without the "protection" of an accompanying male. And yet, because they were required to do so, women in groups of two or more embarked on these trips. In so doing, they began to traverse a public space formerly closed to them by the constraints of "honor" and threats of gendered violence. Finally, one cannot understate the transformative impact on the lives of anganwadi workers of the discovery that they could teach, and often teach better than (relatively) highly paid teachers in government schools. As described above, workers' greatest source of pride rested in the favorable comparisons made by students and parents between their centers and the private schools that charged tuition.

In addition to these features of ambivalence and ambiguity were instances of resistance that defied the monitoring and surveillance functions of the ICDS program. Such resistance ranged from villagers who refused to answer survey questions, to anganwadi workers who challenged the CDPO at the monthly meetings, to workers who used the rules of the bureaucracy to resist being fired from their unrecognized "jobs." Resistance also found expression in the workers' refusal to see their work at the centers as an extension of the work of child care, cooking, nurturing, and attending to the sick that they did at home. Workers insisted on calling themselves teachers and thus underlined the similarity of their work to that performed by primary school teachers.

I trust it is clear that my emphasis on ambiguity and resistance is not intended to efface the state's surveillance and regulation, the productive proliferation of statistics, and the preoccupation with questions of the population. I have emphasized throughout that governmentality is never just about control, it is most of all about a *concern* with the population, with its size, but also with its health, happiness, and productivity. It is precisely this relationship between the state's increased capacity for the surveillance and control of women's lives and its concern with saving the lives of children, particularly girls, and protecting millions of others from more acute forms of malnutrition and disease (Sen 1990) that becomes hard to grasp in conventional academic discussions that pit the state against civil society. An understanding of governmentality demonstrates to the contrary that these are two features of a singular process, a process, moreover, that does not reside in the state. In the government of conduct, the state is only one among a number of heterogeneous institutions and cannot simply be assumed to be the dominant player. Nor can it be assumed that the conduct desired by planners, policymakers, and bureaucrats is actually achieved, for the subjects of these policies may well alter the nature of the programs themselves, and thus change the conduct of government as much as government changes them.

Notes

1. The exact amounts were as follows: expenditures in 1990–1991 were Rs. 268 crore vs. Rs. 603 crore in 1998–1999 (approximately $151 million).
2. What is interesting in this discussion of governmentality is the extent to which the welfare of populations within territorial states is discussed in isolation from the wider context in which those states existed. In particular, if one is thinking of European states in the eighteenth century, the welfare of the population within those states was intimately linked to the welfare of those other populations who were the object of their state's actions: their colonial subjects.
3. For the purposes of comparison, the UNDP report puts the infant mortality rate in 1960 at 165 per 1,000 live births, indicating that it has been more than halved in the past forty years.
4. The health component for children included the administration of large doses of Vitamin A, iron and folic acid tablets, DPT and BCG immunization shots, and the monitoring of malnutrition by weighing or measuring midarm circumference; for pregnant women, measures included iron and folic acid tablets and tetanus shots.
5. In a survey conducted in twenty-seven of the thirty-three blocks in which the ICDS program began, Tandon, Ramachandran, and Bhatnagar (1981: 380) reported that 76 percent of children under three years of age in rural areas and 78 percent of those under six were malnourished. Severe malnutrition was found in 21 percent of rural children under three and in 26 percent of tribal children in the same age group.
6. Concern with the size of the population arose both from fears of the inadequacy of the food supply as well as from its potential to impose demands on state services. India's population was 442 million in 1960, 884 million in 1992, and has grown to over a billion by the year 2000.
7. The overwhelming defeat of the Congress in the elections that followed has been attributed by most political observers to the coercive tactics used for birth control during the Emergency. Sanjay Gandhi's followers often invoked China as an example of "successful" population control, and democracy was held to be the chief reason for India's failure. For a fascinating analysis of China's efforts in this field, see Greenhalgh (1999).
8. This issue is analyzed in greater detail later in this essay.
9. Scheduled castes are the lowest castes in the caste hierarchy.

10. This custom is known as *gaunaa* in western Uttar Pradesh.
11. See also the work of Cohn (1987) and Appadurai (1993) on the Indian state. Appadurai states the problem particularly well when he says "Statistics were generated in amounts that far defeated any unified bureaucratic purpose" (316).
12. The belief in the "evil eye" is not limited to people in western Uttar Pradesh, but is common in large parts of the South Asian subcontinent.
13. There are various versions of this basic formula. I have heard the same sentiment being expressed as "Development is the best contraceptive."
14. Although I cannot develop this line of argument here, I note that the use of military and missionizing metaphors in development projects is remarkably similar to those employed in colonial conquest: God, guns, and glory.

THE BATTLEFIELD AND THE PRIZE

ANC's Bid to Reform the South African State

Steffen Jensen

The new South African state is one in which formal expressions of democracy and human rights should be backed up by mass involvement in policy formulation and implementation. It is a state which should mobilize the nation's resources to expand the wealth base in the form of a growing economy. It is a state which should continually strive to improve people's quality of life. Such a state should ensure that all citizens are accorded equal opportunities within the context of correcting the historical injustice.—African National Congress, *Strategies and Tactics*

When the African National Congress (ANC) assumed power after South Africa's first democratic election in April 1994, one of the party's main tasks was transformation of the state apparatus (ANC 1997). The ANC[1] leadership viewed the old state apparatus as its antithesis: exclusive, without legitimacy, and the instrument of an inherently racist white minority. The party set itself the historical task of transforming the state into a state for all South Africans, without vested interests and fair. This begets the question, and the main focus of this essay, of how a political party can bring about reform of the state. I argue that reform is happening on many different levels, often as unintended consequences and not as deliberate as the ANC seems to think. Most of the time, transformation is effected through very localized, not always heroic, power struggles.

I focus on the transformation of the field of safety and security, or issues of crime and violence in a broad sense, as a privileged point of entry. Nowhere was the former state more compromised than when it dealt with crime and violence (see Cawthra 1993; Shearing and Brogden 1993). In a way, the security apparatus came to incarnate the apartheid state in its most condensed and brutalizing form. Yet, another reason for analyzing the field of safety and security, although on a contrary note, is that crime is perceived as endangering South Africa's fragile transition to democracy (National Crime Prevention Strategy 1996). It is contrary because prevention of crime is not a heroic issue relating to the party's struggle against apartheid. Like all issues of everyday governance, it is piecemeal and contingent. When the ANC ascended to power, the party was quite unprepared to deal with these piecemeal issues that were unheroic, often tainting, problems of governance.

Before beginning my investigation of the more detailed processes of transformation, I consider some questions pertinent to this problem. A first set of questions evolves around how the ANC conceives its own role in transformation and what perception it has of its antagonist, the apartheid state. A second set of questions evolves around the character of this apartheid state, not least the security forces, the police, and how they maintained order. Finally, I go to the murky and contradictory world of Richmond in the KwaZulu Natal Midlands, which was and is one of the most contested areas of South Africa. A virtual civil war has been fought during the past two decades among the apartheid police, the ANC in its different forms, the conservative and ethnic-based Inkatha Freedom party (IFP), and, of late, the United Democratic Movement (UDM). I look at Richmond because it is exemplary of the contradictory nature of South African politics, both before and after 1994. Only after dealing with these issues do I venture into analyzing transformation in more detail. But let me begin with the ANC.

A Historical Charge

In the *Strategy and Tactics* paper from the fiftieth congress, the ANC states the following about its role in South African society: "The ANC is . . . called upon to win over to its side those who previously benefited from the system of apartheid: to persuade them to appreciate that their long-term security and comfort are closely tied up with the security and comfort of society as a whole. In this sense therefore, the ANC is not a leader of itself, nor just of its supporters. History has bequeathed on it the mission to lead South African society as a whole in the quest for a truly non-racial, non-sexist and democratic nation" (ANC 1997: 12). Thus, the ANC is not simply a political organization but is charged with something altogether more important: the well-being of all South Africans, and being the keepers of what is termed the "national democratic revolution" (7).[2] This also influences ANC's understanding of the state:

> The new democratic government is faced with the challenge of changing [the injustices of the past], as part of its strategic task of creating a united, non-racial, non-sexist and democratic society. In the first instance, this government derives its legitimacy and legality from the democratic processes which saw to its birth. However, the state machinery we inherited contains many features of the past. Formally, it is a state based on a democratic constitution, a state which is obliged to serve the aspirations of the majority. However, the emergence of a truly democratic state depends on the transformation of the old machinery, a critical part of the NDR [national democratic revolution]. Such transformation should see the location of *the motive forces of the revolution at the helm of the state*, as the classes and strata which wield real power. The challenge that faces these forces in this phase is to ensure that the elements of power they have captured are utilized rapidly to transform the state, while at the same time *placing it at the centre of the transformation* of South Africa's political, economic and societal relations. (ANC 1997; emphasis added)

What is clear from the quote is that the ANC believes in the state as a tool to be employed by a political party in the interest of the people. Here, we hear clear reminiscences of a state controlled by a vanguard organization—much like a Jacobin idea of a "few good men" at the helm of the state.

This Jacobin understanding of the state also informs the ANC's perception of the apartheid state, on the one hand, as designed solely to preserve a white minority's privileges, and, on the other hand, as omnipotent, reaching from top to bottom of society. Apart from explaining that the security forces were particularly successful in hunting down activists and infiltrating ANC structures, the image of an omnipotent state as the adversary of the ANC also gives the party the legitimacy to rule and reform.

A Draconian State

Especially within the ANC, the apartheid state is legendary for its ability to act relentlessly, without hesitation or remorse. The political will, wielding the state, decided to move three million people under the Group Areas Act—and it did. It decided to lift a vast number of white Afrikaners out of deep poverty—and it did so in just thirty years (Norval 1996; Sparks 1990), and did so to such an extent that, as Malan sarcastically writes, "Only the dumbest white men failed to prosper" (1990: 129). This happened on the backs of nonwhite people in a system of racial exploitation, but it was also effected through a radical expansion of the state apparatus that made room for the employment of Afrikaners in a gigantic affirmative action move. Thus, at the end of the 1980s, about half the Afrikaner workforce was employed in the state sector (Saff 1998: 21). A significant number ended up in the security apparatus, either in the police or in the military, with a considerable stake in upholding the system of apartheid.

As Cawthra writes, the police and the military "came to regard themselves as defenders of the 'free world' and 'Christian civilization' against the communist threat" (1993: 2). This made the security apparatus's prime task political and, as Cawthra writes, "overlaid with military imperatives" (2), with military-style wars waged against liberation forces, first in the frontier states of what are now Zimbabwe, Namibia, Angola, and Mozambique and later inside the townships of urban South Africa. The entire political task was articulated through a Christian-nationalistic discourse of apartheid. As Minister Kruger said in 1977 about the South African police, shortly after the internationally condemned Soweto massacre where many, mainly children, had died: "It is so that the all-knowing God thought fit to exercise His authority on earth using the service of people, parents, officials of the Government. Therefore the wearers of the fine uniforms of the police are also the mandate holders of God" (in Argus 1977; qtd. in Shearing and Brogden 1993: 41).

Although more than 50 percent of the force was nonwhite (Shearing and Brogden 1993), Afrikaner nationalism was prevalent within the police force. The style of policing, developing "from bush-war to counter-insurgency" (Cawthra 1993), resembled colonial policing where much of the actual violence was carried out by nonwhite help troops (in South Africa called *kitskonstabels* or special constables), who by their acts were alienated even further from their own communities. Poverty brought them to the force and alienation kept them there. That blacks policed blacks also went well with the ideology of separate development, where each population group should govern its own affairs. But it was not only the black police personnel that lived the lives of colonial police officers. Drawn from the most vulnerable circles of Afrikaner society (Cawthra 1993: 3), given a special mission, often isolated in military-style compounds, and on duty in the special forces in the townships for months on end, white police officers also lived out a colonial police officer existence. According to more personal statements from police officers working in the riot units, this isolation distorted the world and turned all blacks into enemies.[3] Also a signature of colonial policing, vigilante groups were armed and trained to target mostly ANC-aligned organizations like the UDM (Cawthra 1993: 109–26).

The apartheid state also employed other counterinsurgency strategies besides mere repression and violence. Up through the 1980s, the so-called total strategy[4] or "Winning the Hearts and Minds" (WHAM) strategy became increasingly important. When an area had been "calmed down," a concerted effort was to be made to win the population of the area over to the government's point of view through substantial social and economic development (Sparks 1990: 354).[5] As hindsight tells us, this strategy backfired. The colonized people rejected the offer of inclusion in this form of selective economic development, and instead of "stabilizing" the areas, they often became more violent as the security forces clamped down even harder (Norval 1996). This made activists call the strategy WHAM BAM. The way the strategy was implemented, with a highly arbitrary allocation of resources, only increased the levels of violence and internal strife. The security forces were not too unhappy about this, as the strategy also aimed at destabilizing antiapartheid structures, but as we shall see below in relation to Richmond, the security forces also lost control to a large extent.

The picture that emerges is one of a police force enmeshed in political counterinsurgency toward a colonized majority of nonwhite people. This included a minimum of crime prevention and detection (Cawthra 1993: 5). Most efforts were aimed at inciting violence and quenching the first of an increasingly hostile population.

There were, however, important differences. Policing in white areas was similar to policing in most other Western countries,[6] with one big difference: white people were told to police their own areas as well. For that purpose, the government set up the National Security Management System, encouraged neighborhood watches, and let private security companies play a still bigger part in policing, all of which resulted in a profound militarization of white South Africa (Norval 1996: 24–47).

Nonwhite people were also policed for different purposes. One example of this was that the policing in the "coloured"[7] areas was directed toward criminal offenders. This was carried out to such an extent as to turn the coloured population into what must be one of the most imprisoned populations in the entire world (Pinnock 1984; Midgley 1975).[8] What is important for our purpose is that although few coloureds were charged with political offenses, the methods employed by the police were not very different from those employed in the policing of political insurgence. Thus, Fernandez (1991) has documented how the police in the Western Cape employed the most gruesome torture (electricity, rape, beatings, animals, etc.) against suspected coloured criminals.

To summarize, the police had wide-ranging powers that could be used with discretion on the part of the individual officer. These powers were employed in the policing of nonwhite people in the harshest and most violent way, regardless of whether the offense was political or criminal. Consequently, vast numbers of nonwhite people were imprisoned, beaten, tortured, or killed, and many political organizations were infiltrated and often destroyed (Truth and Reconciliation Commission [TRC], vols. 2 and 3, 1998). It is partly because of this that the image emerged of an omnipotent apartheid state, controlled by purpose and will of an Afrikaner elite. This (ANC) perception of the apartheid state, however, is rather oversimplified. To exemplify this, let me investigate how South African politics were played out in Richmond, one of the country's most contested localities. This also provides a sinister illustration of the problems facing any attempt to transform South African society.

Sifiso Nkabinde: The End of Politics?

On January 23, 1999, Sifiso Nkabinde, one of the most famous South African political figures, was murdered in Richmond, KwaZulu-Natal. This marked the end of a remarkable saga in South African history. In August 1999, the *Mail and Guardian* could report that the local police had known about the suspects for four months prior to an arrest ("Police 'Sat on' Nkabinde Docket" 1999: 2). The newspaper could also reveal that the local police even had dockets on the suspects but had failed to arrest them, and that it was only when there was a change of guard that they were arrested. As it turned out, they were all closely linked to the ANC, one of them a bodyguard for the mayor of Richmond, Andrew Ragavaloo (2).

Sifiso Nkabinde began his political career in 1987, when he took part in the virtual civil war of Richmond on the side of the conservative and ethnically

Zulu-based Inkatha (which, with the advent of democracy, became IFP). Over the past two decades, this virtual civil war has cost thousands of people their lives and repeatedly made even more into temporary refugees as they tried to escape the violence (e.g., Goodenough 1999a, 1999b; Strudsholm 1997). In 1987, Nkabinde organized rallies and led groups of young Inkatha supporters against the supporters of the UDM (the internal wing of the then exiled ANC). This continued until 1989, when he was talked into joining the ANC by the ANC strongman in the KwaZulu Midlands, Harry Gwala. Gwala enjoyed much influence internally in the ANC, with friends right up to the top of the party. Nkabinde's decision to change his allegiance was probably the turning point for the ANC in the KwaZulu Midlands. In the famous Battle of the Forest in March 1991, Inkatha, which until then had controlled most of Richmond, lost twenty-three men (Goodenough 1999a). As the years passed, rumors of Nkabinde's criminal links and violent exploits, also against his own, became more and more frequent. The murder in 1994 of the Midland's ANC youth leader, Mzwandile Mbongwa, was indicative of how Nkabinde turned his violence against his own instead of the now largely defeated IFP. This murder was committed by Nkabinde's SDU (Self-Defense Unit), which by then had become a small army accountable to no one but themselves.[9]

During the 1990s, ever more people were displaced from their homes by the violence, and ever more people were killed. In 1997, Nkabinde was expelled from the ANC after having obtained a seat in the provincial legislature. The ANC finally moved to expel him after rumors that he had informed on the ANC during the latter part of the 1980s and in the 1990s. The problem for the ANC was that they had known for six years that he informed on them. In an interview, Jacob Zuma, the deputy chairman of the ANC, explained that the ANC only very seldom expels people but tries to deal with them inside the organization (Strudsholm 1997). It is also fairly well substantiated that the ANC knew about the violence being inflicted on their own, as in the case of Mbongwa. Strudsholm suggests that the real reason the ANC failed to expel Nkabinde was fear of losing support in the KwaZulu Midlands if they did. Another explanation is that his mentor, Harry Gwala, had been able to protect him until then. After Gwala's death in 1996, nobody in the ANC would exonerate Nkabinde anymore.

After Nkabinde was expelled in 1997, he joined the ANC's new rival party, the UDM, where he obtained a position as national secretary general.[10] Soon after, his Richmond past caught up with him again, and he was charged with sixteen cases of murder. To the dismay of the ANC, he was released from prison a year later due to lack of evidence. The ANC began talking about "Third Force" elements in the old state (see below) that had an interest in fueling the violence in the Midlands. The role of the police was certainly far from admirable. The Human Rights Committee (HRC) and the Network of Independent Monitors (NIM) investigated the issue of police involvement in the Nkabinde saga. The report proves again and again that specific police officers indeed had helped Nkabinde. The allegations of his informing for the police were also proved beyond doubt (HRC/NIM 1998). Minister of Safety and Security Sydney Mufamadi and National Commissioner of the Police George Fivaz closed down the Richmond police station in 1998, after yet another killing spree in Richmond following Nkabinde's release. This was not the first time police officers had been removed from the station. The same happened in 1997, and since 1995 all investigations into political violence have been handled by different national units (HRC/NIM 1998). All this occurred because there were serious indications that the police "worked hand in hand with Nkabinde," as the ANC put it in their motivation for the removal of the head of the Richmond investigating officers, Johan Meeding (quoted in HRC/NIM 1998: 31).

But the ambivalent role of the police is not restricted to the fanning of violence. Before 1994, the areas controlled by Nkabinde were for all purposes no-go areas for the police, who had to obtain permission from Nkabinde to enter Richmond. This changed when the police and Nkabinde made an agreement at a Community Policing meeting in 1994. Suddenly, the police had "freer" access to the area. In the words of Meeding, the police "went from a caseload of 400 unsolved cases to 100. The solving rate went up from 20 percent to 80 percent" (HRC/NIM 1998: 31). The police officer who finally arrested Nkabinde on the sixteen counts of murder "noted that he had the impression, Nkabinde and his SDU led the Richmond police by the nose" (31). This indicates that not only did the police use Nkabinde; he used them as well. No doubt the police, and before 1994 the apartheid police, helped create Sifiso Nkabinde for the purpose of destabilizing the different antiapartheid organizations. Involuntarily, they also facilitated the development of a niche in which Nkabinde was allowed to roam freely, and, as time went by, they lost access to Richmond and control over him. In the end, they, like everybody else in Richmond, were at the mercy of Sifiso Nkabinde.

By disregarding his brutality and connections with the police, the ANC were instrumental in the creation of the self-proclaimed warlord (Strudsholm 1999). In other words, a picture emerges in which the statements from the fiftieth national congress, quoted above, have no resonance. This schism between ANC discourse and practice has not passed unnoticed, as testified to in the following statement by the leader of the UDM, Bantu Holomisa, commenting on the role of the ANC in the violence in Richmond: "It should be noted that while the ANC leaders are parading the Capitals of the world as human rights activists, they on the other hand had taken the decision to eliminate their political opponents by instructing their juniors to do their dirty work" (1998: 8). Holomisa's comments must, of course, be seen as an attempt to exonerate Nkabinde and UDM of guilt in the violence in Richmond, but Holomisa makes a further charge. Contrary to its own discourse, the ANC is not acting fairly and in the interests of all South Africans; they are involved in local politics and, as such, are part of the violence in Richmond.

The ideological construction of an omnipotent state resisted by a heroic movement dissipates when confronted with the murky world of local Richmond politics. Although the police have now arrested the suspected ANC-aligned killers of Nkabinde, many other people had reasons for wanting Nkabinde dead: he was involved in a taxi rank dispute;[11] he had grievances with the provincial leadership inside his new party, the UDM, whom he had managed to sideline; and he had a dispute with his own bodyguards, whom he had apparently just fired (Strudsholm 1999). Everything points to the realization that politics in Richmond cannot be interpreted as a simple bipolar conflict between the ANC and different antagonists, as political and academic commentators usually do (e.g., Goodenough 1999a, 1999b; HRC/NIM 1998). This is not the "end of politics," but another kind of politics, far from the politics envisaged by the ANC leadership. It is contingent, fragmented, and essentially determined by the local setting.

Postapartheid Politics Revisited

Richmond may be an extreme example of the intricacies of South African postapartheid politics, but it is by no means unique. In other places as well, ANC people were involved in local power struggles. Given the social and historical complexities, there is even a certain inevitability to this. Therefore, rather than questioning the ANC's political legitimacy (only the South African electorate can do that), the reading I propose is one that sees the ANC as having to engage in a number of often localized and fragmented power struggles, emerging as *the* antagonist of the omnipotent apartheid state and therefore the transforming force of society per se. Let me look at two related ways of asserting the ANC's position as "Leaders of the Transformation."

One way of doing this has been to celebrate the antiapartheid struggle in such a way as to underline the achievements, unity, and courage of the members in their struggle against the omnipotent state. The public holiday calendar since 1994 offers an insight into this form of celebration. As the ANC assumed power, most Christian and all apartheid holidays were abandoned. Instead, South Africa now celebrates Human Rights Day, Freedom Day, Workers Day, Youth Day, National Women's Day, Heritage Day, Reconciliation Day, and the date of the 1999 election. All these national holidays celebrate the new South Africa with its respect for its citizenry—all in opposition to the former regime.

These holidays, as well as the national policies launched at the fiftieth congress, for that matter, are what we might term state spectacles. They are not only for the consumption of the electorate and signs of change, but are also meant for internal consumption in the state apparatus and the ANC. Their purpose is to instill in the ANC and the bureaucracy the feeling that they are part of a "new thing" in delivering equal services to the people and generally working for the common good of the people (ANC 1997). Furthermore, the state spectacles have the purpose of appeasing all the localized power struggles that constantly tear at the party's image as a unified body.

The fiftieth congress in Mafikeng is an illustration of this. Before the congress, the newspapers abounded with stories of internal strife in the party, and it was with a fair amount of trepidation that the party commenced its congress. Thus, the *Electronic Mail and Guardian* could ask "Can New Leadership Heal the ANC?" (1997e). After the congress, Minister of Environmental Affairs Pallo Jordan exclaimed that "the conference demonstrated maturity of the ANC's membership who were not side-tracked and distracted from their course by demagogy and posturing by anybody" ("The ANC Triumphs at Mafikeng" 1997). On the one hand, these state spectacles give the image of the new state as normalized in contrast to the apartheid state, which the ANC viewed as pathological. On the other hand, the spectacles are aimed at portraying the ANC as "a political will" that had taken over the reins of government and now determined the course of the state.

The ANC has dealt with the contingent local politics in yet another way. The leadership always confirms the support of their own people, as they did with Nkabinde six years before he was expelled, when he became counterrevolutionary. Holomisa reflects this when he says that whenever somebody reminds the ANC "of their unfulfilled promises to the masses, they are termed counter revolutionary" (1998: 9). Holomisa's charge that it is "a form of defense mechanism by the ANC" is less important here. What is important is that the ANC does not seem to have a public language to deal with the intense local power struggles but must revert to the bipolar language of the struggle against apartheid. Thus, those who are with the ANC are, by definition, in favor of transformation, and those who are against the ANC are opposed. The ANC knows that this categorization is problematic, but publicly, they must appear undivided behind transformation.

This means that the past very much informs the present (postapartheid politics), both discursively and in actions: discursively because the past is constantly recycled as struggle narratives, and in actions because old alliances and the modus operandi of the struggle against apartheid are not easily forgotten. Thus, there is a great deal of inertia in the ANC stemming from the time when the ends (the defeat of apartheid or mere survival) justified the means. This is necessary to keep in mind when evaluating the ANC's attempts to fulfill its historical mission.

The State Conceptualized: The State as Battlefield and Prize

I have attempted to problematize the ANC's implicit understanding of statehood, by which the state is perceived as potentially omnipotent, be that for better or for worse. I have also questioned the general assumption that the struggle was an affair between the ANC and the apartheid regime. Instead, a much more complex picture emerged.

In line with the introduction to this volume, I propose a double perspective on the state inspired by Foucault and Laclau respectively. I agree with a Foucauldian interpretation (e.g., Foucault 1979a) of the state as a set of fragmented, noncoordinated institutional practices, contested through local-level power struggles. But the bureaucratic knowledge and experience inscribed in institutional practices produces an inertia within the institutions that is very difficult to change. It is these institutional practices that the ANC must engage with throughout the state apparatus.

Institutional inertia has yet another twist to it in South Africa: the negotiated settlement. This settlement brought the ANC to power in a fairly peaceful manner. It emerged during the period up to the election in 1994, when there were very real fears that South Africa would descend into civil war. The settlement was a compromise in which different positions had to be balanced, and the ANC leadership could not dictate the settlement. Under the threat, on the one hand, of Afrikaner right-wing violence, and on the other, of an imminent bureaucratic collapse, the party had to accept that it could not terminate loyal employees of the former regime. As a matter of realpolitik, the negotiated settlement basically stated that their experience from the apartheid era was useful as apolitical bureaucratic expertise. South Africa had to "let bygones be bygones," as Mandela (1994) put it in his inauguration speech. Although there have been serious attempts to deal with the past, most notably through the Truth and Reconciliation Commission[12] (see Lars Buur's and Aletta Norval's pieces in this volume), the past is still a source of tension that informs the power struggles over transformation in both implicit and explicit ways.

But the state is not only institutionalized knowledge and practices. It also has, following Laclau (1985: 110–12), a symbolic function of forming a kind of moral high ground. Thus, by taking control of the state, the ANC can perform the task of spearheading the NDR of society. Thomas Blom Hansen talks of something similar when he asserts, in his contribution to this volume, that there is a constitutive split between a profane dimension of the state—incoherent, brutal, and partial—and a sublime state principle. In this sense, I discuss the state not only as a battleground but also as a prize.[13]

Thus, one must have in sight both dimensions of statehood, both as fragmented power struggles over institutionalized practices and as sublime state principle, when analyzing the ANC's reform endeavors. But one more issue is important to consider: transformation depends on how the field to be reformed is perceived, problematized, and categorized. In other words, it matters whether it is reform of welfare policies or the security apparatus. Let me therefore briefly consider the field of safety and security as the ANC began to conceive it when the party ascended to power in 1994.

Violence as a Problem of Governance

Before 1994, the ANC never really conceived of safety and security as a problem. Violence and crime were primarily read as a necessary consequence of the unrest in the country, and as such fit well with the ANC strategy of making the country ungovernable. Furthermore, as we saw in the case of Richmond, violence was a legitimate means of securing areas under their control. Only after 1994 did the party begin seeing crime and violence as issues of order. There were several reasons for this change in approach. First, violence and crime undermined the party's legitimate claim to rule. Second, large segments of the South African population became preoccupied with crime and violence as the most serious problem facing society.[14] That the ANC now had to deal with violence and crime as an issue of order (as opposed to ungovernability and revolution) and the ascension of crime and violence unto the political agenda meant that the party had to rely on the despised security apparatus, which had been predominantly involved in counterinsurgency and, because of the negotiated settlement, remained largely unreformed, even exonerated and professionalized. As an illustration of how difficult that made the transformation process, Minister of Justice Dullah Omar expressed deep mistrust to his own staff at the beginning of his term in 1994: "I cannot trust anybody here" (interview with former staff member, October 1997). It was, in other words, a highly complex terrain in which the party had to effect change—not only of the system but also of the levels of violence and crime.

Let me now turn to an ethnographically detailed examination of the processes of transformation and how the ANC attempts to effect change. I take my point of departure (as one among other possible examples) in the ANC's attempt to imagine and create new, unambiguous, and normalized institutions, in casu the Secretariat for Safety and Security. This institution, the new government's attempt to exercise some civilian, political control over the police, was soon enmeshed in local political power struggles. It is these power struggles that I propose to follow. To the end of the essay, I will show how the ANC leadership seeks to exonerate the blame for present failures, combating crime and transforming the police, by recycling the problems through "struggle [Third Force] narratives."

The Secretariat for Safety and Security: Eradicating the Past through Institution Building

If new institutions are to be created in accordance with the negotiated settlement's principle of reconciliation, they must not be seen as creating or reinforcing divisions. The creation of the Secretariat for Safety and Security is a case in point. The official purpose of the Secretariat was to create "civilian oversight" of and a policymaking mechanism for the police, thereby dealing with the most serious problems of the past. The Secretariat's policy director asserts: "It was a response to . . . [the historical problems of the police] that a very strong oversight was created, controlled by several people, democratically elected through our democratic process, with a minister directing in his capacity to analyze and to formulate policy" (interview with Desiree Daniels, September 1997).

In other words, the hitherto unaccountable police force was now to be submitted to political priorities. The priorities were not only about controlling the police but also aimed at changing the focus of the police force. In line with the National Crime Prevention Strategy (NCPS 1996), which outlined the new government's all-inclusive plan to combat crime in ways departing from past atrocities,[15] nonwhite South Africa should be policed in the same way as white South Africa: accountable and service- and victim-oriented in direct contrast to the hitherto colonial-style policing, where the focus was on counterinsurgency and control. This also meant a reallocation of resources and personnel. To bring this about, the national and provincial Secretariats were given three roles: policy planning, monitoring of implementation, and coordination. Also, the police accepted the construction with civilian political oversight formulating policies and with the police as operational entity. In a status report, the police describe their relationship with the Secretariat: "The Department 'South African Police Service' has been renamed the 'Department of Safety and Security,' consisting of the South African Police Service and a 'Secretariat for Safety and Security'[16] . . . distinct and separate of the operational component. This Secretariat comprises civilian employees, thus establishing civilian oversight and enhancing the democratization of the Service" (South African Police Service [SAPS] 1997a: 31).

This is echoed in the *Police Plan 1996/97*, where the question is asked whether this relationship with the Secretariat will not lead to a politicization of the police (something that has a bad ring to it in South Africa since apartheid). This, the plan asserts, has two aspects: "On the one hand it is the role of politicians to distil the wants, demands and needs of the communities." The politicians must, however, "take seriously the professional judgment of skilled and experienced police officers in the determination of policies" (SAPS 1997b: 28).

It is evident that the police accept the civilian oversight and prioritization as necessary in the democratization of the police; at the same time, they demand that their professional expertise be acknowledged. In other words, the Secretariat works for reconciliation and does not reinforce the divisions of the past. Furthermore, the police, as a professional state agency, are partly exonerated of past guilt in the sense that the experiences obtained in the past are useful. The police can work democratically and impartially for the benefit of all South Africans. What is asserted here is that the police have mended their ways, and/or that the transgressions of the past were the deeds of a few wayward individuals. Thus, the now cleansed police should be able to work in the interest of the entire South African population.

This is the official, nonconflictual version: politicians in the ANC-led government working together with the police in the pursuit of the common goal of ridding South African society of the curse of crime in a democratic and accountable way and with a clear understanding of who is doing what. However, just under the nonconflictual surface, confusion and disagreement seem to reign—not least in understanding and coming to terms with the role of the Secretariat: "From the beginning there was an adversarial relationship between the police and the Secretariat. With the passing of time, its role will become clearer or less needed. From the beginning the Secretariat did as much policy as it could and the police continued oblivious and unconscious, without caring what the Secretariat was doing" (interview with Wilfried Schärf, Institute of Criminology, University of Cape Town, October 1997).

In other words, the Secretariat had great difficulties asserting itself vis-à-vis the police. At the institutional level and in terms of competencies, the Secretariat had no direct influence over the police. Thus, the national commissioner reports directly to the president rather than to the minister of safety and security. This means that the role of the Secretariat is merely consultative, or, as the police plan puts it, "to 'direct'" the commissioner (SAPS 1997b: 28; quotation marks in original).[17] Due to the ambiguities, the minister and the national commissioner have both fought over the right to leadership and over the blame for the failure to combat crime. These power struggles have been fought out in the press but also through secret investigations. The ANC minister's chief accusation against the police has been their "inability to transform," whereas the police's main problem has been what they see as "political interference" in their work[18] ("Fivaz Takes on Mbeki Police Squad" 1997).

The image emerging from these power struggles stands in stark contrast to the official version of the new institutions, where politicization is no problem and the police are basically innocent. The power struggles are embedded in past antagonisms between the ANC and the police, where the Secretariat is part of the ANC's attempt to democratize and control the police. This means that forgetting the past to work for a new South Africa has some inherent contradictions that make such an operation very difficult.

However, we cannot assume that the creation of the Secretariat did not have any transforming effects. Wilfried Schärf asserts that it is an ongoing process that does not end in insurmountable antagonisms. Thus, "as the Secretariat grew aware of how the police operates and how changes within the police are brought about, the Secretariat began establishing key partnerships with opinion changers within the police" (interview with W. Schärf). The Secretariat also moved in another direction. Throughout 1997, a number of provincial crime prevention summits were held at which the Secretariat asserted its position as the lead department. By having a closer look at what came out of these summits, we can learn something about both transformation and the work of the Secretariat in terms of priorities and functions. The Western Cape provides a good illustration, as the province is run by the National Party. Thus, the inherent problems of state transformation in terms of institutional inertia exist in a condensed form there.

The summit in the Western Cape was held in October 1997. Out of it came a number of projects and programs aimed at crime prevention. As an employee of the Western Cape provincial administration put it: "Originally the Secretariat was to function as civilian oversight and to do support functions. This is not so much the function anymore. Now the focus is on crime prevention much more than monitoring. That means that there is no longer the same level of contradictions between the police and the Secretariat" (interviews with Ronel Schoeman, March 1998).

Of course, it is difficult, Schoeman goes on, to separate the two completely, but the emphasis has changed from civilian oversight to a more socioeconomic approach, referred to as "programs" or crime prevention. Schoeman stresses that the approach adopted by the Western Cape Secretariat has been implemented as the model for the rest of the country's secretariats. Thus, the secretariats have forged a space in which they can have a role beside the police, without being in opposition to them. This choice is, however, neither uncontested nor politically neutral, and especially not in an institution conceived by the ANC in a province run by the National Party.[19]

One of the most important programs in the Secretariat's crime prevention unit's plan to defeat crime was the so-called MADAM structure (multiagency delivery action mechanism). It was launched in 1998 and focused on ten areas of concern: marine poaching, the festive season (December to February), street children, safer schools, Cardboard City (a squatter area in the middle of Cape Town), surveillance cameras in the inner city, the Safer Cities projects (report back), rent-a-cop (where citizens pay for a bobby on the beat), and different initiatives under the Ministry of Justice (interview with Ronel Schoeman, January 1999).

When looking at the list of priorities, one realizes that little attention is given to what could be termed nonwhite problems of crime.[20] My fieldwork in 1997, 1998, and 1999 and various crime statistics (e.g., Institute for Security Studies [ISS] 1998) indicate that these have to do with taxi violence, train violence, gangs, vigilante groups, *shebeens* (informal liquor outlets), and corrupt, brutal, and inconsistent policing. None of these problems is addressed by the province's unit for crime prevention. Furthermore, civilian oversight of the police has been toned down considerably from its original center-stage position. This change from the Secretariat's inception as being charged with both safety *and* security, that is, making the police more safety-oriented, is also evident in the recent renaming of the Secretariat from Safety and Security to Community Safety. How can we explain this apparent shift in approach to its functions?

There are two factors we need to look at: first, the political environment in which the Secretariat works; second, how resources are allocated.[21] The National Party governs the Western Cape, and the MEC (member of the Executive Committee) of the Department of Community Safety is Mark Wiley, a former member of the armed forces and white. According to some people close to the department, he has been promoting issues dear to the hearts of the white constituency in spite of promises to do the opposite, and has de facto neglected or stopped most projects that were aimed at what could be termed nonwhite priorities. As an NGO person said during an interview, for example, the gang commission aimed at the rampant gangsterism, particularly in coloured areas in Cape Town, was neglected to such an extent that it fell flat without ever achieving anything (interview with Gaynor Wasser, Western Cape Anti-crime Forum, April 1999).

But the racialization of the Secretariat goes right to the core of the department. As one informant said, "It is a very racially divided department. They just hired two more whites in 'programs.' When the department was established they secured it with white people on all the director posts." This is a typical feature of Western Cape provincial administration. Most employees are either Afrikaners or coloureds, and the main language is Afrikaans. As the National Party is still firmly in control, little has changed since the transition to democracy.[22] Of course, it is not evident that people with a stake in the former regime are incapable of focusing on nonwhite issues, but there certainly seems to be a correlation between the two, and maybe especially so in the case of the Secretariat and Mark Wiley. As another informant put it, "Mark Wiley refuses completely to level criticism against any man in a uniform, be it military or police. But also, he is afraid of working with any structure that just smells of ANC. Although most people in the coloured areas voted for the National Party, most of the neighborhood watches and civics are in some way associated with the ANC. They don't want to strengthen these structures because they are afraid of losing the election [on June 2, 1999]."

The way the supposedly disinterested bureaucracy is traversed by politics is specific to the Western Cape, with the result being a lack of prioritization of nonwhite areas. Furthermore, most of those coming from the former regime, whether whites or coloureds, have very little knowledge of the townships, where what I have called nonwhite issues are prevalent. It is thus difficult to do anything about crime and violence in these areas. However, we should not confine these problems of prioritization to the Western Cape. Many of the problems exist elsewhere in South Africa, although maybe not in the condensed form of those in the Western Cape.

However, the Secretariat for Community Safety is not only white. Although underresourced and spatially marginalized at the bottom of the provincial administration, the Directorate of Civilian Oversight (employing only former activists) has managed to maintain a focus on nonwhite issues. Among these are police actions in relation to rape in Khayalitsha (a huge squatter camp twenty-five kilometers outside Cape Town), attempts to build partnership with the neighborhood watches in nonwhite areas in a bid to avoid their turning into vigilante groups (which some of them already are), mediation between police stations and nonwhite communities, and complaints over mishandling of junior officers (from a list of Directorate activities, April 1999). In other words, despite political, practical, and personal reluctance to police the townships without armed vehicles and riot squads, there is scope for another approach.

Although the political leadership of provincial administration generally attempts (whether by design or not) not to allocate many resources to nonwhite priorities, and although the administration has worked toward establishing a nonconflictual relationship with the police, a space was created with the inception of the secretariats in 1994 by the national ANC government. New priorities cannot eliminate this space completely, meaning that the former activists in civilian oversight have a platform from which to engage in power struggles over policing priorities in the Western Cape. Here, it is important to note that these power struggles among different parts of the provincial administration, traversed as they are by (Western Cape) politics, cannot be explicitly political but must take other forms. Most often, these are departmental investigations[23] into lack of professionalism, bad administration, and malpractice. These strategies of deprofessionalizing the political adversary's work are necessary because the new state is not supposed to be entangled in the politics of the past, but rather is to be a professional bureaucracy. However, although the Western Cape is heavily dominated, both on the political and bureaucratic levels, by people from the former regime coupled with the discourse of a depoliticized bureaucracy, the secretariats conceived by the ANC national leadership have opened a space that cannot easily be disregarded, and can be used in the reform of the police and the state.

Third Force: Recycling the Past as Political Strategy

Both in the section on Richmond and in the analysis of the local power struggles over transformation, I refer to the perception that the police are not only against transformation but are actively working against it through violence. In South Africa this is called Third Force. The concept emerged to designate how agencies within the apartheid security apparatus fanned violence among different nonwhite organizations. The fight between the IFP and the ANC in Richmond is one such example. This kind of Third Force activity began in the 1980s to split the liberation forces, and continued on through the 1990s in an attempt to destabilize the ANC and show the party's inability to govern. There is substantial evidence that these Third Force allegations were true. In Richmond, there is no doubt that the police worked with Nkabinde (HRC/NIM 1998) and that the police trained and armed IFP supporters in KwaZulu Natal (e.g., Ellis 1998; TRC 1998). However, the story from Richmond shows that the police often lost control of their own protégés. Furthermore, the corrupt police officers in Richmond and their cooperation with Nkabinde do not amount to Third Force in the sense described above. In the present situation, one might say that the concept of Third Force has been "deterritorialized." It no longer signifies anything concrete but has become an "empty signifier"[24] (Laclau 1996) used to explain the inexplicable, such as why crime does not decrease. See, for instance, this short article in the *Electronic Mail and Guardian:*

> Safety and Security Minister Sydney Mufamadi is to investigate claims that prisoners are being used as hitmen as part of "Third Force" operations on the violence-torn Cape Flats. The announcement was made after a meeting on Thursday between Justice Minister Dullah Omar and deputy Minister for Intelligence, Joe Nhlamhla. Omar said he had briefed Mufamadi on recent allegations of Third Force activity, and in particular a claim that prisoners are being released from prison at night to perpetrate violence against specific targets before returning to jail. Omar said he had told his colleagues that though these allegations are untested, they are serious enough to warrant urgent action. ("Third Force on the Cape Flats" 1997)

Several remarks are required here. First, allegations of Third Force seem to emerge when unusual levels of spectacular violence happen (in this case, vigilante and gang violence in Cape Town). Second, and more interesting, the violence is explained by pointing to covert operations orchestrated by someone with apparent interest in creating mayhem: someone released prisoners so they could perpetrate violence on unspecified "specific targets" ("Third Force" 1997). In other words, an unspecified finger is pointed at an unspecified perpetrator with, it is assumed, an interest in discrediting the government and causing chaos on the Cape Flats (or in South Africa in general). By pointing to Third Force activities, the government and the ANC place the blame outside themselves; they exonerate themselves of any guilt for the crime and violence, in the case of Omar, on the Cape Flats. Furthermore, what could just as well be highly contingent events of violence are localized in one locus of evil. In a resolution from an ANC crime summit, it is thus stated that these Third Force activities emanate from "networks of the past" (ANC 1996). This means that although the allegations are unspecified, they clearly point to circles around the police. This is far from lost on the police themselves. As an anonymous constable tells the *Mail and Guardian:* "The government treats the police as if all of us were involved in third force activities. . . . They are useless" ("Death and Drudgery on the Beat" 1997). The point is that by not pointing to specific individuals or specific networks the government and the ANC blame the entire police force for preventing them from reaching the goal of a crime-free South Africa. In this way, the government dispels the notion that the police have reformed and that only a few "rotten apples" are left. A group of the enemies of transformation has been created to which all the "bad" things can be referred, thereby leaving the ANC and the government blameless.

The question, then, is whether there is any reality to these allegations. One researcher, normally close to the government, in response to Minister of Safety and Security Mufamadi's blaming the increases in crime on the nexus between Third Force and organized crime, asserts that it "smacks of a political ploy, an expedient cop out" (Jakkie Cilliers, quoted in "Blasting a Hole in Crime Stats" 1997). Also, Minister of Justice Dullah Omar asserts that although the allegations are "untested," they do not need urgent investigation but "urgent action" ("Third Force on the Cape Flats" 1997). It does not matter, in other words, whether the allegations are true or not. This points to an interesting double feature of crime in the transformation of the South African state. Although crime is a huge problem for the government and a test that the government has to pass to expand its legitimacy, it can also be a resource in the struggles over the transformation of the state. Any claim made by people unspecifically accused of Third Force activities loses all legitimacy. By referring the blame for crime to a category outside the influence of the government—to its oldest foe, the apartheid regime's security apparatus—the government and the ANC leadership exonerate themselves of guilt and place it with a group of people, who, because of the negotiated settlement, they normally cannot blame for anything.

This kind of construction produces a strong resonance in the general population as well. Third Force has become a category in which everything working against the "people" is placed. I have often encountered statements such as "Third Force is clearly involved in this." When I probed, people responded, "Just some Third Force." But Third Force is always related to the former regime. One example is the Muslims in Cape Town, who are generally accused of "urban terrorism."[25] They always caution me that "one has to think further here. Things are not always as they seem. We have information that there is Third Force involved, wanting to discredit the Muslims" (interview with Muslim woman on the Cape Flats, October 1997). In times of high levels of violence, it seems as though the unspeakable divisions of the present are recycled through struggle narratives. Thus, Third Force seems not only to be a political strategy but also a way of asking questions that are normally difficult to pose, such as why there is violence in the reconciled South Africa, or why the police do not (want to) work for the benefit of all South Africans—and even more, why the ANC has not succeeded in creating a normalized state that is universal and fair, a state that can guarantee the safety of its citizens.

By Way of Conclusion: Transforming the South African State

I began this essay by asking how the ANC, as a political party, can transform the South African state into a "normalized" state. I argued that the rather Jacobin representation of itself as a party, of the state as such, of its opponent, the apartheid regime, and of the conflicts of the past can only be sustained on a purely discursive level. These representations crumble when they come into contact with the contingencies of local South African politics. The subsequent gap has to be mended through constant celebration of unity, legitimacy, and ability to govern in what I have termed state spectacles where the party's historical mission is (re)affirmed.

The ANC's actions also seem to be informed by an inability to talk about the truly fragmented nature of the South African society and state. It is as though the party does not have a vocabulary that can express all the locally specific contingencies in the public sphere. Instead, the party reverts to the bipolar language of the struggle against apartheid: everybody who does not support the ANC is against transformation or counterrevolutionary, as it were, and everybody in favor of the ANC, as a matter of definition, is in favor of transformation. Furthermore, due to the inherently fragmented nature of the state, the transforming efforts of the leadership do not filter through the system unchanged but are appropriated by (ANC) people in different departments of the state involved in power struggles informed by local logics.

Through the ethnographic account of the power struggles between the police and the ANC and inside the Secretariat of Safety and Security, I have attempted to illustrate how difficult transformation is and how the reform endeavors of the ANC encountered serious obstacles. However, the secretariat(s) forged strategic alliances locally with people in the police, and, as the case from the Western Cape illustrates, although people with a stake in the former regime appropriated the Secretariat, its mere existence created a platform from which power struggles could be fought. Transformation does happen, but contrary to the ideas of the ANC leadership, it happens very gradually and in a very dispersed manner.

As we saw in relation to the Secretariat, most battles about transformation of the state take on a highly bureaucratic and depoliticized character. However, just under the surface, the entire process is traversed by politics, and because of institutional inertia and the negotiated settlement, it is difficult for all parties to verbalize political disagreements. Thus, many of the power struggles take the form of departmental investigations into alleged bureaucratic malpractice. However, the ANC leadership can express its discontent openly through the Third Force signifier. The allegations of Third Force need neither to be specified nor tested. It is simply enough, in the paranoid political climate of South Africa, to allege the presence of Third Force to taint virtually anybody with any stake in the former regime. They will then be relegated to the subversive out-group of "people against transformation."

This strategy of creating a group of people inside the state who are opposed to transformation helps the ANC leadership to verbalize politically charged complaints. Furthermore, this exonerates the ANC of guilt for not making South Africa into the place it should be: normalized, safe, and for all. In other words, the past is being recycled as metaphors of the struggle, enabling people in South Africa, notably the ANC, to talk about a difficult present.

This exercise is necessary for a number of reasons. Although the ANC has made giant leaps in terms of transformation and securing the peaceful transition to democracy to an extent that one can still talk of a "South African miracle," many hard issues remain unsolved. The distance between what is and what should be seems to have diminished only marginally. The gap between rich and poor has not decreased; only the composition of who is poor and who is rich has changed through the creation of a nonwhite middle and upper class. Entire areas are being consumed by fear of crime and violence; South Africa's marginal place in the global economy has become more exposed; AIDS is threatening the entire makeup of society; public education is still in shambles. The ANC leadership has no or very little influence over most of these problems. They are beyond its reach in either the IMF and the international finance sector or the localized power struggles that take place inside specific departments or on the ground of South African politics. Here, the leadership can work only for the discrete, and often unintended, transformation outlined above. But the leadership is still made accountable, by its own admission and by the general population. Therefore, the "people against transformation," or "counterrevolutionary forces" as an out-group will still be a necessary element in the highly fragmented transition to "a truly non-racial, non-sexist and democratic nation."

Notes

1. In the following, "the ANC" refers to the policy formulators at the top of the party. This is, as it turns out, an important and necessary qualification. The party is so divided and consists of so many different factions that talking about one party is absurd.
2. The South African historian Alister Sparks attempts to explain this sense of being a vanguard by referring to the ANC's history of exile and the important communist influences on its organizational structures. This top-down approach, Sparks says, "is a concept that makes for authoritarianism" (1990: 403).
3. Personal communication with police officers working in Cape Town and east of Johannesburg in the Internal Stability Units.
4. Total strategy was devised by President Botha in the early 1980s on the basis of an analysis that there was a total onslaught against South Africa by communism. This onslaught had to be countered on all fronts by a total strategy.
5. The WHAM strategy was heavily influenced by an American counterinsurgency theory, the oil spot theory, developed by Lieutenant Colonel McCuen. Oil spotting, of course, has the connotation of oiling troubled water.
6. This is what made the director of investigation of Western Cape Province tell me that in terms of detection and prevention, nothing had changed from the 1980s: the police still worked in the same manner (interview with André du Toit, October 1997).
7. The term "coloured" is one of the most contested concepts in South Africa. Throughout this piece, I use the British spelling of the word to indicate that the coloureds form part of a specific racial grouping in South Africa. In this, I do not mean to indicate that I consider the racial categories original. They have been produced historically throughout the past century. This means, again, that specific life conditions for coloureds have emerged. It is in that sense that I speak of coloureds as a specific group. For elaboration, see Jensen and Turner (1996).
8. I cannot go into any detail now, as this is largely uncharted academic territory, where indeed very few studies have been made. One promising work-in-progress in this regard is Azeem Badroodien's study of reformatories in the coloured community. This is also by and large the subject of my Ph.D. thesis, tentatively entitled "What Place in the World: Of Young Men, State Transformation and Violence."
9. These Self-Defense Units were created in the 1990s by the ANC to protect itself against attacks particularly by IFP-aligned Self-Protection Units. Their history has been fraught with ambivalence and violence, enmeshed as they were in local politics. For more elaboration, see TRC (1998a). For a more critical analysis, see, e.g., Jensen (1999b) and Schärf (1997).
10. The UDM presented itself as a radical departure from what existed before. The party's leader, Bantu Holomisa, proposed that it was the only one not caught up in the past, the only party that represented a new beginning. That Nkabinde not only joined up but attained the position of national secretary-general destroyed a lot of people's hope in the UDM and created the impression of a party that enrolled all the disgruntled bad guys from other parties.

11. The taxi industry has its roots in the fact that no transport service was provided for the booming nonwhite townships. Transportation was for many years a part of the informal economy and one area where some people could earn a lot of money. The competition among different companies and taxies was so hard that large-scale violence often erupted, leaving hundreds dead.
12. Buur argues that the TRC was to a large extent an attempt to institutionalize the horrors of the past and thereby create a space in which other issues could be discussed without constant reference to apartheid. This is similar to when Žižek, through Lacan, talks about transferring the deepest emotions to others. He uses the example of the "weeper": "In so-called primitive societies we find the . . . phenomenon in the form of weepers, women hired to cry instead of us: so through the medium of the other, we accomplish our duty of mourning, while we can spend time on more profitable exploits—disputing the division of the inheritance of the deceased for example" (1989: 35). By institutionalizing the horrors of the past, former antagonists, most notably labor unions and mainly English corporate business, can get down to business and divide the inheritance after the now deceased apartheid regime.
13. Of course, there are dissenting voices within the ANC grassroots, especially among those we could term the communitarians, who think the state is always against the "people" (see, e.g., Nina 1995).
14. One opinion poll institute investigated the issue and found that in 1994 only 6 percent thought violence and crime to be a serious issue. In 1998, the figure had risen to 64 percent (Institute of Democratic Alternative in South Africa 1998). Another report, furthermore, concluded that this preoccupation was relatively equally distributed along racial lines. Thus, crime and violence were no longer only "white issues" (Nedcor Project 1996).
15. The National Crime Prevention strategy was passed in 1996 at the very moment when crime and violence became the most important preoccupation of South Africans. The aims of the plan were to "establish a comprehensive policy framework" that could generate "a shared understanding among South Africans" on how to combat crime. By "integrating the policy objectives" in all sections of the state—vertically (national, provincial, local) as well as horizontally (in different departments)—a "common vision around crime prevention which . . . [could] be embraced by the whole of society" should be created (NCPS 1996: 5). This constituted a radical departure from the past, when "no organized or systematic approach to the prevention of crime . . . existed." The new plan would focus on "stemming the tide . . . through the application of more policing capacity to selected problems" (7). Although the NCPS, which for a while monopolized the discourse on crime and violence, failed to achieve its (high-reaching) goals, it nonetheless managed to change the ways in which crime prevention was talked about locally in the ministries. Thus, a subtle process of transformation was set in motion or helped along by the largely forgotten plan.
16. This is not quite so. The ministry was called the Ministry of Law and Order and consisted solely of the South African police. The executive branch, the police, was renamed the South African Police Service to indicate that it provided service to communities. Safety and Security as a term was forged to indicate that issues of security were made much broader than simply law enforcement. Apart from the symbolic intervention as strategy in the reformation of the state through renaming, the mixup is perhaps indicative of the confusion about reform, here expressed in renaming procedures.

17. There is a point to be made about the kind of imprecise language used. The term "civilian oversight" is another example. Its imprecision could either mean that people drafting the policies did not think about it, or more likely that it was impossible to agree on a specific term that would either allow the politicians direct control or bluntly state that they should not get involved in control.
18. Here, we note the technocratic pledge to be outside politics. This is far from unique for South Africa. In many ways, it is the constitutive element in the self-perception of civil servants all over the world.
19. In the first general election in 1994 the former apartheid party, the National Party, became the majority party in the Western Cape with just over 53 percent of the votes. This was largely due to the fact that the coloured voted en bloc for the party. The Western Cape is thus the only province where the party has any significant support. In the next election, in June 1999, the National Party lost a lot of support, but due to an alliance with the Democratic Party, it managed to keep the premiership and control over the province.
20. It is a bit problematic to make this distinction, of course. One of the main reasons for the priorities of the MADAM strategy is the tourism industry, which is not only Cape Town's problem but the whole country's, because the city is the world's access point to the whole country. The tourist as concept plays a very big role in the imaginations of all sectors of society. However, the argument here is that although tourists are important, securing them is not making anybody in nonwhite Cape Town safer.
21. This section is based on interviews with people in or close to the Secretariat, documents, and newspaper articles.
22. There are deep historical reasons for this. The former regime used the public service extensively to promote the economic uplift of, first, the poor white Afrikaners, and later the coloureds, through what was known as the Department of Coloured Affairs. The latter is a typical product of apartheid, where each group was supposed to manage its own affairs. With the amalgamation of bureaucratic institutions after the breakdown of the former regime, the former white Provincial Administration and the Coloured Affairs Department were amalgamated and now largely make up the Western Cape Provincial Administration. Thus, most employees have a stake in the former regime. Also, the administration has always been used to further certain groups' economic position.
23. These investigations go on from the top to the bottom of the bureaucracy. At the time of my fieldwork, one staff member of civilian oversight was the subject of such an investigation, allegedly because he in turn had investigated a high-ranking police officer. The power struggles between former Minister Sydney Mufamadi and the National Commissioner also took the form of their investigating each other ("Fivaz Takes on Mbeki Police Squad" 1997).
24. An empty signifier denotes a "signifier without signified," i.e., a signifier that has been detached from its original meaning and can now be redeployed in new ways with no structural limits (Laclau 1996: chap. 3).
25. For an analysis of the "urban terrorism" and the Muslim population, see Jensen (1999a).

IMAGINING THE STATE AS A SPACE

Territoriality and the Formation of the State in Ecuador

Sarah A. Radcliffe

States encompass a space in which they carry out their actions and throughout which they claim sovereignty and power (Agnew 1999). In their regimes of power, states draw on space to construct their control by means of techniques of power that disperse citizens and resources and order the regimes of everyday life (Foucault 1984, 1991). According to a state-centric picture, the state views itself as establishing a spatial matrix into which subjects are slotted and in which the national economy, polity, and society are made (Massey et al. 1999; Agnew 1999). Yet the establishment of that spatial outreach, and the techniques of control that work through—and over—the territory, are questions about how over time a state responds to the challenges of territorial integration and internal contests for power. Just as state formation has recently been analyzed as an ongoing series of cultural acts and material practices (Corrigan 1994; Joseph and Nugent 1994b), so too it is possible to examine the process of *spatial* formation of the state, that is, how the state is made as a space. As Stepputat (1999a, drawing on Certeau 1984) argues, we are dealing not only with the creation of abstract space but also the practices through which space is consumed and its organization disrupted.

Drawing on recent work on Latin American state formation, this essay examines the spatial "forms of rule and ruling" that have been accomplished in Ecuador since the mid–nineteenth century. One productive effect of state power is the establishment of territory as self-evidently sovereign and made up of varied component elements of regions, cities, and natural resources into an integrated whole. In parallel with Joseph and Nugent's recent discussion of the cultural process of state formation, this essay addresses the ways in which "practical and processual dimensions of state formation" (1994a: 19) are inherently spatial, based on specific geographical tools and knowledges, *and* on imaginative geographies and images. Corrigan (1994: xviii) outlines the various means by which rule is accomplished, namely, through a regime's use of a repertoire of terms, the learning of skills and discourses from "outside" the state, and the hierarchical nature of political subjectivities. The history of the independent Ecuadorian state is a story of the deployment of geographical terms and the selective adoption of ideas of spatial science from abroad, notably Europe. In the postcolonial period,[1] the project of Latin American nation building has been a profoundly *spatial* project, in which a lack of physical integration has been compounded by regional conflicts over the nature of the state project (see Mallon 1994; on Ecuador, see Quintero and Silva 1991; Maiguashca 1983). In this context, the question of spatial control and geographic technologies of rule have been of continued, and significant, interest to the region's states.

In theoretical terms, the nation-building project of the state is seen to derive from the confirmation of its territorial and political sovereignty over space (produced as the modular area of the nation, within recognized and secure international boundaries) and the monopoly of means of violence and physical control. With regard to the construction of abstract space—Anderson's (1991) homogeneous space of the nation—the nation-state relies on certain technologies and rules. The methods of cartography, inventory, and census data, as well as the physical integration of territories (by means of currency, transport, or education) can all be identified in the case of Ecuador as tools of the state to confirm its power over—and knowledge of—its extent. The consolidation of these methods, and their institutionalization within the nation-state over the past 150 years, provides a picture of the Latin American nation-state. As the editors point out in their introduction, the "universalization" of modern forms of rule has rested contradictorily on unequal North-South relations as well as a discursive endowment of sovereign power to citizens (Hansen and Stepputat, this volume; also Anderson 1991; Breuilly 1982). In the late twentieth century, Ecuador is experiencing another contradictory twist in this doubleness of the nation-state, as mappings of state and citizenship are moving out of the state's hands and increasingly into a transnational space informed by indigenous social movements and multilateral development agencies. As the negotiation of terms of rule are increasingly subject to indigenous and social movement input, so too the spatial vocabularies of rule of the state are transformed. Ecuador thus provides an example of how, as "modern governmentality . . . has penetrated and shaped human life in unprecedented ways, the practices and sites of governance have also become ever more dispersed, diversified, and fraught with internal inconsistencies and contradictions" (Hansen and Stepputat, this volume).

This essay is organized around a historical overview of Ecuador's technologies of spatial power, documenting the key periods in which geographic techniques and discourses provided crucial tools for the consolidation of territorial sovereignty and means of social integration.[2] The process of "making the map" is then contextualized by a brief discussion of the ways citizens are inducted into the "spatial vocabulary" of the state. In this section on "Seeing the Map," the extent to which citizenship is constructed around a geographic imagination and a spatial vocabulary is examined. It is clear that "forms of local consciousness" (Joseph and Nugent 1994a: 22) contribute to the forms of state rule. A consideration of statehood in Ecuador at the current time is incomplete without an acknowledgment of the diverse ways in which state maps have been redrawn and the geographic technologies of power seized by nonstate actors, often in engagement with transnational flows of information and resources. The final section, "Remaking the Map," outlines the ways in which indigenous confederations, in some cases with transnational networks, have reworked the spatial configuration of the state and, indeed, the nature of its power. Tracing the history of spatial strategies of states is not, of course, a neutral process, and raises questions about the spatial tactics that can be taken for empowerment. By critically analyzing the ways in which space underwrites power relations, this essay hopes to contribute to a more liberatory and decentered set of sociospatial relations.

Making the Map: State Technologies of Spatial Order

That official discourses and practices of nationhood have their own spatiality is not as widely recognized as the historicity of national imaginings (on the latter, see Smith 1991; Hobsbawm 1990). Although analysts recognize the territorial foundations of official nations, the diverse levels of this category and its functioning in the circulation of signs and power practices have more recently been analyzed, particularly through the concept of territoriality.[3] Territoriality operates in three ways: through classifications of space, through a sense of place, and through the enforcement of control over space (by means of surveillance and legitimization). In a Foucauldian account, territoriality brings in its train certain productive effects. In this context, state territoriality produces the effect of a sovereign nation-state: "It [is] by means of a process of subjective representation, recognition and cartographic design, however, that the invention of the contents of a 'natural' state territory [takes] place and that a legitimate discourse about national sovereignty [is] developed" (Escolar, Quintero, and Reboratti 1994: 347).

The state's "will to order" operates across a number of sociospatial relations engaging with the productive social differences of gender, sexuality, class, race-ethnicity, and location.[4] Surveillance by the state—its all-seeing and all-knowing overview of, and discursive claims over, its territory—is thus analyzed as a power effect, the outcome of particular dispositions of maps, personnel, networks, and discourses. State territoriality is thus not a given but rather something to be worked for, and the tools and behaviors through which it is made are constantly being rethought and remade. In this light, Ecuador is a highly contested space, with various groups generating polyphonic mappings and images of the national space. At the same time, the nation-state over the past 150 years has extended and elaborated the means of knowing and mapping its land. Foucauldian approaches have of course been criticized for failing to acknowledge different actors' contestations of power and whose tactics offer alternative avenues for sociospatial organization. It is only in the more recent period that these spatial tactics can be more readily uncovered.

By means of classifications, sense of place, and control, territoriality operates to establish and extend state power by means of physical and discursive control over (mapped) areas and the production of "grounded" subjectivities. National subjectivities gain a distinct "sense of place" vis-à-vis their international borders and the internal landscapes (see Smith 1991). Territorial disposition and orders rest on quotidian work and social reproduction by various institutions of the nation-state, but these practices and technologies have not existed since the foundation of independent nation-states in Latin America (nor indeed elsewhere). Rather, in Ecuador there have been four key periods in which the state has either introduced new methods of spatial order or has reconfigured the utilization of these spatial technologies to bring them into line with the state project. I argue that the spatial imagination of the state is, first, always in a process of readjustment, and second, that our analysis of the imagination of the state requires an understanding of these geographies. The four periods under consideration here are 1860–1875; 1930s–mid 1940s; 1960s and 1970s; and 1980s and 1990s.

Whereas the late twentieth century is arguably characterized by the "unbundling of sovereignty," postcolonial states such as Ecuador have spent the past 150 years attempting to consolidate sovereignty, by "bundling up" territory and power through geographic techniques (see Anderson 1991: 164; Radcliffe and Westwood 1996). While professional geographers engaged in mapping and spatial practices, the state utilization of geography also encompassed a range of groups, including cultural workers, the military, and administrative functionaries (Dijkink 1996).

Making the Geographic Tools of Statehood Scientific, 1860–1875

Although geography as a discipline was only slowly being professionalized in Europe in the nineteenth century, the opportunities for the application of the newly emerging practice of "scientific" geography did not go unnoticed in the slowly consolidating nation-state of Ecuador. Independent since 1821, Ecuadorian statehood began to be centralized in midcentury under the dictatorship of Gabriel García Moreno, himself a lawyer and consummate politician. In line with other states in Latin America, the territorial question was an urgent one, and states turned in large measure to the positivist ideologies of observation and experiment for an answer (Hale 1996: 148).

In effect, during the mid–nineteenth century, the Ecuadorian state faced the task of retaining the country as a geopolitical entity in the face of expansionist claims by Peru and Colombia and as a coherent set of institutions that brought together often fractious regional elites. When Peru and Colombia threatened to divide the newly independent state of Ecuador between them, the atomized regional elites unified around García Moreno, whose power rested on a combination of Church backing,[5] the army, and landowner families. The state's need for spatial integration and secure boundaries was paramount; as Quintero and Silva note, "The national question in 1860–1865 *was* the territorial question" (1994: 114). As geographic work before this date had largely comprised gentleman-naturalist assistance for French geodesic missions (see Radcliffe 1996), García Moreno turned to the emerging scientific community in Europe. Establishing the Escuela Nacional Politécnica (National Polytechnic School, the first non-church-established university) entailed the recruitment of Europeans, largely Germans and Jesuits, to the new state institution. Geographers, botanists, and naturalists as well as mathematicians were employed, and physics and chemistry were taught systematically for the first time.[6]

Theodore Wolf, a German geologist, was central to the establishment of geographic techniques in the state in Ecuador. Arriving in 1870, he generated a discourse (including Darwinism) and practice of scientific skills in the geographic and geologic sciences that was to be used by the state in its territorial consolidation. Together with colleagues, such as Wilhelm Reiss, his work in mapping the country was invaluable, establishing centralized knowledge about the layout and makeup of the country. Reports were regularly sent to García Moreno. The appointment of Padre Menton to the directorship of the new Astronomical Observatory in Quito consolidated this move (Terán 1983). By 1870, the government established the post of state geologist, held by Wolf, who was sent to study the mines of Loja. The inventories of state resources were complemented by an emerging role for geographers in public works administration (a role that was to become highly significant in the mid–twentieth century). Wolf, for example, was made director of a drinking water project in Guayaquil after 1879.

The introduction of specialists in the new science of geography was soon put to good use in the making of new spatial connections across the highly fragmented territory. During his regime, García Moreno oversaw the unprecedented building of bridges, roads, and a railway line. Eleven bridges were constructed between 1869 and 1875, and roads were built in four provinces, including forty-four kilometers of the Cuenca–Quito road, although their coverage remained extremely patchy (Quintero and Silva 1994: 161); the rail link between Quito and Guayaquil, for example, was not completed until 1908.

Cartography was a prime new tool of the state, which had previously been reliant on eighteenth-century maps by Pedro Vicente Maldonado, who prepared them while taking part in the French geodesic mission of 1763, and an (arguably inaccurate) midcentury update by Villavicencio (Terán 1983). Using the new maps and political power, García Moreno changed the electoral geography of the country in 1860, soon after becoming president. Rather than continue the system of three equal representative blocs (Quito, Guayaquil, and Cuenca), he established the province (*provincia*) as the basis of administration and political power, a move strongly opposed by Guayaquil (Quintero and Silva 1994: 123). Spatial politics were further reshaped in the Constitution that permitted in theory some degree of regional decentralization, although this was not acted on (124).

Social aspects of national integration were also being developed at this stage, although they reflected the fragile sense of unity in the state, which comprised a shifting set of coalitions among landowning and new commercial elites on the coast and in the Highlands (Quintero and Silva 1994). The currency, *sucre*, was established only in 1884, although the Banco del Ecuador had been founded in 1868 for the issuance of notes (53, 161). A national anthem was performed for the first time on 10 August 1866, whose words were written by the poet and politician Juan Leon Mera (García González 1992).[7] Primary education was encouraged, although this remained firmly in the hands of the Catholic Church. Although these means of establishing a "community" of Ecuadorians were adopted, they remained extremely remote from the bulk of the population, who were excluded from nationhood by racism, poverty, and lack of civil rights.

Overall, the Ecuadorian state by the mid–nineteenth century was just beginning to organize the abstract space of statehood. The means at its disposal were relatively rudimentary, but have continued to be used up to the eve of the twenty-first century, namely, the consolidation of geographic knowledge and skills in the arms of a few professionals, and the mapping of territory. These spatial techniques were conceived by García Moreno and later presidents as offering a regulatory power, wielded by the elites in their defensive protection of Ecuador as a geopolitical entity. Notably in this geopolitical power game, the state cartography did not provide a visual vocabulary for the citizenship of the country, although it appears that García Moreno, the main initiator of this process, personally possessed a strong geographic imagination of the state. Although the national currency and the national anthem circulated as signs of a national community, they were meaningless to the bulk of the population. By the end of this period, Ecuador as a sovereign nation-state was considerably more established, due in part to the deployment of spatial techniques of knowledge production and to the consolidation of political ties in new geographies.

The 1930s to mid-1940s: Modernization of State Geographies

The next major period of state usage of spatial techniques came in the 1930s, with certain elements joining the state repertoire of "methods of statehood" in the decades before and after. The use of mapping was much more extensive by this time, in both the global North and South, and the application of cartography to statehood increasingly was bound up in a move to create a sense of national identity among citizens. Around the world, newly independent states in the twentieth century found geography a "necessary tool for clarifying and fostering their national identity" (Hoosen 1994: 4). Ecuador's twentieth-century state similarly professionalized geography in line with its state-building practices, producing geographic knowledges and inventories. Moreover, these skills and inventories were associated with the military, whose central role in nation building was taken as self-evident. What we see by this time, too, is a growing awareness of the social dimensions to nation: as homogeneous space was established, more emphasis was placed on the social groupings within that space.

In the 1920s, the Ecuadorian army was appointed by the state to create a national topographic map (Cortés 1960: 27). In pressing their case for the job, the army's representatives argued that the knowledge of "patriotic frontiers" and an inventory of the country's natural wealth (geology, hydrology, forestry, agriculture, minerals) would be in the state's interest. Moreover, German technical skills sharing and exchanges were important in the wake of the German mission for this purpose in 1925 (N. Gómez, interview 1994). Consequently in 1927, a technical commission for the national map was formed, followed in 1928 by the inauguration of training programs in topography and cartography and the placing of the Geographical Military Service (Servicio Geográfico Militar) under the army high command. The Servicio later became the Instituto Geográfico Militar (IGM, Geographical Military Institute) as the association among state mapping, geographic knowledges, and the military drew closer during the cold war (see below). From the start, the Servicio was tied to similar organizations across the Americas, as it had links with the Instituto Pan-Americano de Geografía e Historia (Pan-American Institute of Geography and History) and the Inter-American Geodesic Service, both of which gained increasing significance in training and resource distribution during the cold war.

At the end of the 1930s and into the 1940s, geography gained a further, civilian boost through the extension of teaching of the discipline to secondary school teachers. Francisco Terán, first as a teacher and then as a lecturer in the training college, became a key figure in the establishment of a civilian group of geographers. His book, *Geografía del Ecuador*, was first published in 1948 and subsequently went through twenty more editions. Terán was later appointed to sit on the National Cultural Council in the mid-1970s, as social integration superseded spatial integration in state agendas.

Although by 1940 Ecuador expected that its territorial sovereignty was relatively secure and was consequently establishing resource inventories for development, the war with Peru in 1941 abruptly changed that situation. With the extensive territorial loss in the Amazon basin, both Ecuador's discourses of national territory and the practices of surveillance required to secure the remainder of the country changed. In the wake of the conflict, the Servicio Geográfico Militar had the knowledge and personnel to place the concrete boundary markers along the new (disputed) frontier. However, the process of representing this new border and explaining the abrupt change of shape of national maps became an overriding concern that continued until the conflict's resolution in 1998 (see Radcliffe 1998, for a brief history). After this date, the IGM produced maps showing the "dismembering of the territory of Ecuador," developing a vocabulary through which the relations of spatial rule could be encoded in forceful, emotional terms. Maps indicated two types of territorial loss; first, the territories "ceded" to Brazil (in 1777 and 1904) and to Colombia (in 1916, clarified in 1922); second, the "territories in Peru's power" (under the 1830 protocol, and the 1942 event; see map in Quintero and Silva 1994: 451–52). After the Rio Protocol of 1942, Ecuador continued to dispute Peru's claim to territory by marking one segment of the (disputed) border with the words "zone in which the Rio Protocol is inapplicable" (*zona en qué el protocolo de Rio de Janeiro es inejucutable*). The geopolitical interests of the state were clear in this cartography (see Hepple 1992); moreover, the map continually kept the issue alive for Ecuadorians, whose education texts constantly repeated the "history of the borders" in which the conflict with Peru featured heavily. In talking of the relationships among myth, history, and identity, Friedman argues that the *temporal* continuity of identity is established (or reestablished) by means of *spatial dis*continuity (1992: 194). In Ecuador's national repertoire, the post-1942 visual and spatial discourses highlighted a strongly spatial discontinuity (real and highly symbolic) with neighboring countries, especially Peru.

In summary, the period of the 1930s and 1940s was one in which the production of abstract space for and by the state continued, although increasingly under military command, in particular after the conflict with Peru. International exchanges of knowledge were built up under the U.S. policy of overseeing its "backyard," a process that increased in the 1960s and 1970s.

Yet the state did not deal with the production of territoriality as exclusively a concern for its military: geographic knowledges and nationalist interpretation of maps slowly came into the public arena through schools and the distribution of the "logo map" showing Ecuador's new configuration.

1960s and 1970s: Attempting a Social Integration of State Territory

This period saw increased military control of the techniques of geographic knowledge under the cold war logic of anticommunism. These decades were also characterized by the application of spatial principles to the "problem" of development, and particularly to the perceived need to integrate poor Ecuadorians into the modernizing nation. In the urgent agenda for social and spatial integration, spatial knowledges and imageries were increasingly displayed for public consumption, although their production was increasingly centralized.

In the context of cold war geopolitics and the nexus of military power with "development," it is not surprising to see that the map and cartographic techniques come further under the surveillance of the (military arm of the) state. Since the 1950s the United States had been organizing fifteen Latin American states in its Geodesic Survey, also providing grants to students to attend courses in the latest techniques in Panama. Even in 1960, the IGM was arguing in state national security debates for a more significant role for mapping, and suggested that "the fortificatory project has to be better when the map on which it is designed is exact" (Cortés 1960: 23). The Law of National Cartography of 1978 was a response to these issues. The law explicitly stated that cartography served the demands of the national development plan and national security. Map making was to be centralized in one state institution, a task given to the IGM, which was funded by the Ministry of National Defense. The armed forces were given overall responsibility for the security of maps and aerial photographs, and, together with the Foreign Ministry, the IGM took over the designation of international borders. With a large staff and modern offices, the IGM gained from its association with a centrist state ethos of modernist development, objective science, and the tutoring of citizens. Legislation endorsed its role as the holder of a monopoly on geographic techniques in the state, and other institutions were established to extend its work in new directions (Radcliffe 1996). Under the Law of Cartography too, the IGM took on a role in the publication and preparation of information and educational texts.

Explaining the role of the military mapmakers, the law described a need "to control cartography and geographical publications, which circulate or are exhibited, so that they correspond to geographical reality, and that the international borders are correct and recognized by the Ecuadorian state." Moreover, the authority of the maps with the Rio Protocol rested on the judicial system, under which the sale of maps *without* the Rio Protocol line was considered traitorous and carried a sentence of up to sixteen years in prison. Under law, maps had to include the Ecuadorian territory from before 1941, a law that was enforced through regular inspections by the authorities of bookshops and other outlets.

Cartographies produced by the modernist IGM were oriented toward both the national security of the geopolitical region of Ecuador and the consumption by citizens of "nationalist" imagined geographies. With regard to national security, the Institute for Advanced National Studies (Instituto de Altos Estudios Nacionales, IAEN) coordinated with IGM geographers for territorial and aerial photographic information. Formed in May 1972 under a military government, the IAEN was explicitly designed to elaborate a national security doctrine (NSD), as well as "to prepare the ruling classes (cadres) of the nation" (Quintero and Silva 1991: 223). As elsewhere in cold war Latin America, the NSD became a state-centered mission to block external threats to national sovereignty and expand the state into the full frontiers (Hepple 1992), justifying and legitimizing surveillance and military expenditure. The elaboration of the NSD created a discourse in which the military emerged as homologous with the *patria*, in which interests of the military epitomized the national interest, and where the armed forces could speak on behalf of the country. Following from the idea of an essential, natural "national soul" of *ecuatorianidad*, the IAEN viewed itself as coterminous with the very territory it was responsible for mapping. Despite contradictory shifts in emphasis toward social development, the armed forces continued to expound their cartographics of state power in a state-centered notion of sovereignty, with the military regarding itself as the sole competent agent for overseeing the nation's security and development. In the course of the 1970s and 1980s, when rising ethnic group demands and weak unification were perceived as blocks to complete national expression, the military had bound itself so closely to state territoriality that it remained central (Quintero and Silva 1991: 231).[8]

Visual referents to the security of national borders were widely disseminated, along with accompanying nationalist stories, during this period. The first six Republican constitutions had not mentioned the Amazon region, but the eastern region, the Oriente, was increasingly represented in state discourse as a core area in the nation's geographies. "Ecuador was, is and will be an Amazonian country" became a slogan on government-headed notepaper in the 1970s (Whitten 1981). Oil-based development permitted extension of state sovereignty over the territory for the first time in the modern era (Quintero and Silva 1991: 165). The new focus was echoed in the geography-history curriculum, where special emphasis was placed on the "Ecuadorian discovery" of the Amazon River by one of Pizarro's officers. The myth of prior Ecuadorian claim to the Amazon lowlands east of the Andes of course reiterated an anti-Peruvian sentiment. In addition to a geopolitical concern with the basin, policy discourses highlighting the promise of future national development emerged, not least due to the new petrol economy of these years (Restrepo 1993: 154). The ubiquity and banality (Billig 1995) of the country's map and landscapes (in weather maps, on school walls and barracks) was established in this decade. The Oriente represented an area of security weakness as well as future development prospects.

Although the 1960s and 1970s were undoubtedly shaped by the geopolitical concerns of the post–World War II period, there was nevertheless in Ecuador an extensive effort by military and civilian regimes alike to overcome the profound development problems facing the country. Florencia Mallon (1999) sees this period of Latin America's history as one of "national liberation" in which states address national questions in a more expansive (and at times progressive) agenda. With oil revenues to hand, Ecuador engaged in a number of measures intended in part to create an inclusionary nation-state. Although it had security overtones, a range of policies contributed directly to strengthening civil rights and inducting a sense of national place among citizens. Suffrage was extended to illiterates in the 1978 general election, thereby including many rural and female voters for the first time, a third of whom had previously been excluded from the vote. The physical integration of the country was quickened through the trebling of road mileage between 1959 and 1978 (Quintero and Silva 1991: 238). North American geographers were commissioned by the state agency for development, the Junta de Planificación, to carry out research into the persistent problems of regionalism (interview, April 1994).

Geography in planning was perceived as a tool to overcome uneven development. As one geographer active at that time said, geography "can help enormously to overcome many problems, principally the localist problems.

Also regionalism of countries. For example, here we have regionalism around Guayaquil and Quito" (interview, April 1994). The extension of education around the country also spread the nationalist ideas about geography to a wider population. A geographic training college for teachers was established in 1973 by the government, with a representative of the IGM on the board (interview, April 1994). The training college Centro Panamericana para Estudios e Investigación Geographica (CEPEIGE) had an explicitly nationalist idea of its role. As one director explained, "Geography is a very interesting science that helps to strengthen the spirit of Ecuadorian nationhood" (interview, April 1994). State co-optation of intellectuals was generally high at this time (Quintero and Silva 1994: 299), although in the case of geographers, the endorsement of state policies appears to have been particularly enthusiastic.

Social integration was encouraged through the above-mentioned dissemination of imagined (Amazon) geographies, as well as through extensive social programs. From 1963, the Civil Action programs deployed military contingents in development projects, a pattern that was expanded in the later *Alas para la salud* (health) and *Alas para la cultura* (culture) programs. Kibbutz-type settlements were also established in sensitive border zones to incorporate young peasants into military and development agendas. This Conscripción Agraria Militar Ecuatoriana (CAME, Ecuadorian Military Agrarian Conscription) began in 1966, and within ten years had three centers in the Sierra, one on the coast, and one in the Oriente. Where possible, civilian populations were also involved, such as through festivals, old peoples homes, and links with peasant leaders (Quintero and Silva 1994: 221–23). A more enduring institution was the establishment of a "national" football team by the military in 1972, a team that still exists today although it became associated with Quito, thereby undermining its original intention.

In summary, a brief overview of Ecuador's use and deployment of geographic skills and spatial knowledges has demonstrated the varying yet persistent agenda of mapping by the state. Different institutions have been charged with this task, and their relationships with the state have been at times contradictory and diffuse. Nevertheless, the spatial imagination of the state has arguably been central in a wide—and significant—range of aspects of the state project. In the establishment of state territoriality, the state has used geography and geographers to map resources, to guarantee geopolitical security, to overcome localisms, to control international borders, to inculcate a love of country, and to provide a basis for development planning. Although the geographic imagination of the state was initially a controlling impetus locked into territorial defense, that agenda has increasingly taken second place to the socioeconomic development concerns of the state.

Seeing the Map

As noted above, while in the process of nation building, the Ecuadorian state has attempted to instigate affiliations and structures of feeling of nationalism in its citizens. As has become clear in recent research, these structures of feeling are profoundly geographic, based on a popular sense of geopolitics, knowledge of a "national" landscape (Smith 1991), and recognition of the national map (Anderson 1991), as well as rituals of commemoration (Gillis 1994). Geographic imaginations and tools can thereby provide the basis for the "collective internalization of a territorial identity" (Escolar et al. 1994: 352; see Breuilly 1993). As argued by Gupta and Ferguson, "States play a crucial role in the popular politics of place-making and in the creation of naturalized links between places and peoples" (1992: 12). Through its discourses around Amazonian development promise and the visual referent of the national (truncated) map, the state attempted to generate a community of cosubjects united by a primary affiliation to the nation-state (see Crain 1990).

One visual technique for the establishment of state power in Ecuador is the truncated map, showing the territory lost to Peru in the 1941 conflict. Whether in school textbooks, on murals of public buildings, or adorning the side of barracks, the map of Ecuador is widespread across the territory. This visual referent to nationhood echoes Benedict Anderson's (1991) suggestion that national maps become "logos" for national identity in an era of print capitalism and easy reproducibility of images. Marked with the Rio Protocol line and minimal features internally, the logo map resonates with a memory of truncation; more than a guide to place, the map functions as a commemorative frame for spatial identity (Radcliffe 1996).[9] Schools, geographic institutes, and the media created maps of the national space while implicit spatial metaphors and place-bound images circulated (Radcliffe and Westwood 1996).

Another means through which subjects construct their sense of national place is the school curriculum, which includes a section on the "history of the borders" (*historia de límites*). Referring to the long history of territorial disputes with neighboring countries, the history of the borders reiterates a geopolitical imagination picked up by citizens. In this way, local or regional horizons were brought into line with the national territory. Thus, in rural Andean communities, around 80 percent of mestizo and indigenous groups recognized the national flag and the shield. Additionally, over 75 percent recognized the map of the country (although 20 percent did not) in the mid-1990s, reflecting high rates of primary education and frequent migration (Radcliffe and Westwood 1996).

In summary, the geographic techniques deployed by the state operated not only to establish territorial sovereignty vis-à-vis other states, but to construct internal integration among the populations inside its borders.

Remaking the Map

Despite attempts to inculcate visual cartographies and geographical stories about the national territory in citizens' minds, these attempts are not hegemonic, or ruling people's geographical imaginations. Alternative geographies have erupted in Ecuador during the past twenty years in ways that contest the spatial order established by the state. Relations of citizenship and space have been reworked in processes that illustrate the ways in which "emergent popular cultures and processes of state formation" interact (Joseph and Nugent 1994a: 3). Challenging state-centered notions of a unified discrete space, distinct voices and practices of "popular geographical identities" (Radcliffe and Westwood 1996) create new spaces through which to express notions of community, citizenship, and identity (Painter and Philo 1995). Popular geographies may attempt to "redraw the map" of state power—figuratively or literally—by generating new spatial order (and mapping that) as well as by voicing distinctive affiliations to territory.

The use of cartographic maps by Ecuador's indigenous federations to lay claim to land illustrates this process and the hybrid nature of popular geographies of identities (Lavie and Swedenburg 1996). To recuperate land from colonizers or to gain land title, indigenous organizations such as the Confederación de Nacionalidades Indígenas de la Amazonía Ecuatoriana (CONFENIAE, Confederation of the Indigenous Nationalities of the Ecuadorian Amazon) and the Organización de Pueblos Indígenas de Pastaza (OPIP, Pastaza Indigenous Peoples Organization) prepare their own maps showing the extent of their land claims, thereby denying validity to the IGM maps. Originally trained by a German development consultant based in the Amazon lowlands, indigenous cartographic teams gained the necessary skills and political motivations to engage in map making. The confederation cartographers also designated territory on the ground with marks on village trees in consultation with local populations. Map making thereby entered into the dynamics of memory, space, and identity by reminding younger villagers of their village limits (interview with OPIP, 1994).

The confederations' map making and land titling projects generate metaphorical and material means to contest state projects that deny indigenous identity and colonize lands. These alternative nonstate cartographies have at their core a spatial project different from the state's. By providing visual proof of alternatives to land colonization by settler farmers and to state development projects that see in the Amazon basin an "empty space" promising unlimited opportunities for national development, these maps provide a distinct palimpsest to that organized by the state. Mapmakers in the indigenous confederations are key actors in the realization of indigenous projects. They produce maps of spaces that are to be read both as representations of material territories and as metaphoric and symbolic referents to a sociality constituted by, and constitutive of, a particular geography (see Pratt 1992).

In the interplay between the indigenous and the state, the rituals of rule have changed, in that the state has acknowledged the confederations' maps and conceded to part of their demands, although without transforming its primary concern in geopolitics. Whereas original concessions were of individual land parcels to families, later grants of land from the state were made to legally registered communities. Additionally, the state cartographers began to work with the OPIP topographic group, although this did not make the indigenous and official projects of creating an indigenous space the same. As expressed by one CONFENIAE leader, "The granting of [land] titles isn't the solution to the problem of indigenous territories" (Uquillas 1993: 185).

In summary, although the preparation and deployment of maps of national territory were once the exclusive preserve of the military arm of the Ecuadorian state, that situation has now changed. The engagement of indigenous popular mappings with state forms of rule resulted in the titling of indigenous land and a greater social inclusion of indigenous populations as full citizens.[10] In a broad social movement, indigenous organizations since the 1980s have contested the centralized and racist hierarchies of rule embedded in the Ecuadorian state. Through marches, demonstrations, and coalition building both within and outside the country with a variety of social actors, the indigenous movement has transformed the political culture of the country. Formally, the institutions of state rule now include indigenous leaders, such as the Indian representatives elected into national Congress and the leaders appointed to key posts in state administration (see below; for a summary of these changes, see Santana 1995; Almeida 1991; Albán Gómez et al. 1993; Zamosc 1994). In the next section, I examine the resultant dynamics for the territoriality of the Ecuadorian state at the turn of the twenty-first century.

Globalizing the Map: New Configurations of (National) Society and Space

As outlined above, the spatial organization of the Ecuadorian state has been characterized by the "bundling up" of sovereignty through the use of geographic forms of knowledge and the institution of spatial vocabularies of citizenship. In an era of growing global interconnections of production, images, and populations, spatial closure can no longer be constituted around neat state boundaries (Agnew and Corbridge 1995). As a consequence of political-economic changes and social movements, Ecuador's territoriality has been profoundly reworked, giving rise to what are, as yet, preliminary indications of what could be consolidated into new forms of spatial rule and social relations.

Restructuring of the world economy along neoliberal lines has dragged Ecuador in its wake, albeit later than other countries in the region. The opening up of the economy to global markets (connected particularly with oil, timber, shrimp, and banana production) has entailed the removal of state powers from certain sectors and the reinforcement of state intervention in others (government attitudes to privatization remain ambivalent). Foreign direct investment doubled to U.S.$9.1 million by 1993, when the state Consejo Nacional de Modernización (CONAM) "modernization" agency began its remit of further liberalizing of the economy.[11] Key shapers of the spatialities of state power are the World Bank and IMF, promoting neoliberalism with a human face.

As Ecuador was encouraged to enter global markets, a measure of local grassroots democratization was promoted by multilateral agencies. The World Bank initiated programs for the disbursement of funds primarily via nonstate groups comprising nongovernmental organizations, state agencies, and grassroots organizations, with goals of capacity building and institutional strengthening. Learning from the social funds experience to alleviate the impacts of neoliberal restructuring, the programs were initially concerned with administrative "good governance" but became more engaged in shaping civil society-state relations. Through its Indigenous Program work, for example, the World Bank promoted intercultural and bilingual education projects, participatory democratization and multicultural legislation and practice throughout Latin America, including Ecuador from the 1990s.

Moreover, internationally networked advocacy and nongovernmental groups have supplied information, support, and resources as diverse as training, airfares, policy interpretations, and computers to civil society in the Andean countries, including indigenous organizations. As international resources and information have flowed in, indigenous organizations have negotiated a changed position vis-à-vis a (reduced) state (Serrano 1993). As a cold war scenario of suppression of internal dissent gives way to an inclusionary[12] discourse of participatory democracy and rights, indigenous organizations have come into positions that grant them a capacity to rework the formation of the state, at least partially. This is particularly true in Ecuador, where, in comparison with, for example, Bolivia, the state has been less centralized and homogeneous (Andolina 1999). Moreover, indigenous actors negotiate with the state in a space defined by its networks among activists in both North and South and different Latin American countries. Involved in transnational networks with other countries' indigenous groups, NGOs, and solidarity activists, Ecuadorian indigenous populations are exchanging information, strategies, and proposals with nonstate (and, in some cases, antistate) actors (compare Slater 1997).

One brief example can illustrate the process. Following from the developmentalist and increasingly inclusive agenda, the Ecuadorian state in the mid-1990s founded an institution dedicated to the problems of indigenous and black Ecuadorian affairs. This state agency was empowered to deal with indigenous and black Ecuadorian issues in ways that belied their past as backwaters of state administration, deprived of funds and political clout. Consejo de Planificacion Nacional para Indigenas y Negros (CONPLADEIN), later Consejo de Desarrollo de las Naciones y Pueblos del Ecuador (CODENPE, Council for the Development of the Nations and Peoples of Ecuador), stated its objective as "To put in place a process leading to the constitutional recognition of Ecuador as a plurinational, plurilingual and pluricultural society, incorporating this redefinition in global society, in national objectives and in the political, juridical and administrative structure of the state, [and] in the Plan for National Development and in regional and local plans" (CONPLADEIN 1997: 6).

The development project that grew out of this process became the Proyecto de Desarrollo de los Pueblos Indígenas y Negros del Ecuador (PRODEPINE, Development Project for the Indian and Black Groups of Ecuador), working with $50 million from the International Fund for Agricultural Development, the World Bank, the Ecuadorian government, and indigenous organizations (van Nieuwkoop and Uquillas 2000). Drawing on the experiences of grassroots organizations, "base groups," and regional NGOs and federations, the PRODEPINE agenda was designed precisely to reconfigure the spaces of decision making, power, and territory in Ecuador. The PRODEPINE spatial formation was based on a decentralized alternative to existing parish and provincial administration, with regional offices and local development projects formulated by indigenous communities themselves. The aim was to target poverty-alleviation measures and social training projects across the three major regions, focusing on 288 parishes. The parishes were chosen on four criteria: concentrations of black and indigenous groups; high levels of poverty; high levels of social deprivation; and degree of grassroots organization (CONPLADEIN 1997). The policy was thus formulated on a combination of needs-based criteria but also, crucially, on the notion that the populations to be involved in development were to be active agents in the process (having "a degree of grassroots organization") and not passive recipients.

The new spatiality offered by these arrangements forms an explicit part of the discourse of PRODEPINE. According to PRODEPINE documents, "Networks allow the gaining of space, presence, information, greater reflection and capacity of consultation." A network extending beyond the national borders linking diverse social actors is an integral part of the geographic imagination of the movement, in which international assessment and experiences are seen as particularly beneficial (CONPLADEIN 1997: 38). The geographic imagination informed by indigenous and other popular social movements in the 1980s and 1990s is demonstrated in other statements. The project analyzed the relationship between "local" scales and institutions at higher scales in terms of local, national, and global relationships and the balance to be sought among them. Premising their discussion on a linkage between global and local development, the project argues that "no local project is valid unless it has possibilities for regional or micro-regional growth," while there is a need to systematize any knowledges "*a escala*" (in relation to scale; 39).

Despite extensive criticisms of PRODEPINE, in part from interest groups in the state who resent such decentralization and multicultural policies, such remapping of the geographies of resource distribution and decision making hold out the prospect of territorial reorganization in Ecuador. On the one hand, power has been explicitly decentralized to racial groups marginalized by previous administrative and political geographies; on the other hand, these same groups are becoming increasingly engaged in a transnational flow of information, resources, and contacts through which to define their spatial and development objectives. Negotiations over the appropriateness of different types of development intervention are ongoing as a result. Indigenous opposition to neoliberal reforms of water and land resources, combined with environmentalist support for their opposition to oil extraction in the Amazon area, illustrate these processes. Spatial organization, according to PRODEPINE and indigenous practice, is organized in terms of networks, in which flows between global and local actors work around, as well as strategically alongside, the state. In such reformation of state geographies, there is less of a centralized homogeneous state space, but the possibility of a more heterogeneous and empowering space. In summary, while the indigenous development agendas are currently being discussed heatedly, it has been suggested that the extent of change to state forms of rule under neoliberal reform and multilateral agency agendas are significant. As state territorial sovereignty over political economy is unbundled, so the processes of state formation are increasingly informed by "the emergence of forms of [indigenous] local consciousness" (Joseph and Nugent 1994a: 22), themselves constructed in a transnational field of knowledge creation.

Conclusion

The relations among state, space, and power in Ecuador have shown a shifting pattern of spatial techniques, geographic imaginations, and types of power invested in different geographic texts and images. Throughout the Republican period, the imagination of the Ecuadorian state has been a geographic imagination, in which the territoriality of the country has been mapped and managed in various ways. From the centralizing and integrative, almost recuperative, project of President García Moreno in the mid–nineteenth century to the localizations of development policy in the indigenous social movement, it is clear that space is not a passive backdrop to the processes of state formation. Rather, the practices of gaining geographic knowledge and then representing it in maps, documents, and policies have been integral to the historical transformation of Ecuador, and will continue to be so into the next century. Geographers have been employed by the state to carry out this task, but they are not the only actors involved; engineers, politicians, planners, the armed forces, and others have all had varying roles. Most recently, indigenous movements prepared their own maps of local communities. The formulations of state spatial power are not created and fixed once and for all, but rest on quotidian work—including ideological, representational, and material work—carried out by diverse social subjects, themselves reproduced within the inventories and power effects of state territoriality.

In this analysis, the processual and dynamic nature of state geographies and territorialities has been emphasized. During much of the Republican period, territoriality was about the military-state classification of space, about a (fragile) national sense of space, and about military surveillance over the ground and its population. Nevertheless, even within this repertoire of discourse and action, the institutions and actors engaged in a centralized, hierarchical sense of state power changed and developed over time. Nonmilitary contributions to geographic knowledge increased over the mid–twentieth century as the educational curriculum, rituals of national celebration, and increased population migration all transformed patterns of spatial integration. Classifications of space began to include indigenous confederation mappings and land titles. A sense of place was indelibly marked with the 1942 Rio Protocol line, yet other senses of local identities enriched the geographic imaginations of citizens (Radcliffe and Westwood 1996).

The lack of closure around such state geographies reflects the very spatial nature of its task, that is, the unevenness of state power, as well as the existence of alternative geographies that make "other" spaces and identities. The quotidian practice of geographic knowledge-making procedures attempts to centralize the arrangement and regularization of state space. Simultaneously, discourses and repertoires of visual imagery set about creating meaning around these spaces as places. In other words, space and place get called up in the practical, discursive, and representational aspects of power, the dimensions that underpin state power. Within the processes of state constructions, it is thus not only the externally oriented question of geopolitical sovereignty that conditions state practice, but also, crucially, the internally oriented justifications and explanations of territory that matter. Such internal and external elements are intimately interconnected in terms of the personnel involved in defining the state repertoire and in terms of the audiences for their reception and the practices that underpin them. Moreover, with the fast-changing transnationalization of economies, states, and indigenous politics, the boundaries of the map are rapidly transformed into new, unprecedented fields of action as yet not fully explored by social actors nor mapped by social analysts. In conclusion, nation-states are *states of geographic imaginations*, subject to constant redrawings and new cartographies created in the power-invested spaces of territoriality.

Notes

I am grateful to the organizers of the conference on States of Imagination at which this paper was first presented and commented on so wisely. Thanks are also due to Finn Stepputat and an anonymous reader for further comments on later drafts. The research from which this chapter is drawn was generously funded by the Economic and Social Research Council in projects on "Remaking the Nation" (1993–1995, No. R000/23/4321) and currently, under the Transnational Communities Programme, in the project "Transnational Indigenous Communities in Ecuador and Bolivia" (1999–2001, No. L214/25/2023). All translations are mine unless otherwise noted.

1. The postcolonial period in Latin America is generally defined as the 1780s to 1990s. Formal independence for the Spanish colonies was gained in the 1820s and 1830s.
2. For an alternative chronology of regionalism and territory in Ecuador, see J. Maiguashca (1983), who identifies 1830–1925, 1925–1945, and 1945–1972 as significant periods.
3. I use the term territoriality in a critical sense that attempts to question the ways in which geopolitics and space are utilized in power games.
4. In this regard, recent work in the discipline of geography has highlighted the role of surveillance, representation, narrative, racialization, (hetero)sexualization, and gendering as key practices through which power constitutes its social and spatial effects (see Massey et al. 1999).
5. García Moreno signed a concordat with the Pope, granting the Catholic Church status of sole religion in the nation and control over all religious life, education, and the readership of books (Quintero and Silva 1994).
6. In this, Ecuador was not alone, although it was possibly an early advocate of the trend. By the 1870s and 1880s, various republics had created new higher education institutions to provide leadership informed by modern science. The emphasis in these institutions was on encyclopedic knowledge of subjects, on scientific and practical concerns, and on secularism and state control (Hale 1996: 149).
7. Juan Leon Mera was also author of a book entitled *Catechism of Geography of the Republic of Ecuador* (Terán 1983: 183).

8. International talks around securing the Ecuador-Peru border dispute—with the mediation of the United States, Chile, Argentina, and Brazil—resulted in a resolution that undercut traditional notions of territorial sovereignty. The Ecuadorians agreed to drop their claims to sovereign access to the Maranon River in favor of a "free navigation accord" with Peru (*The Guardian*, 29 January 1998).
9. Recent resolution of the Ecuador-Peru conflict over the border raises interesting questions about the form the logo could now take.
10. However, internal security concerns did not completely disappear even then. In the aftermath of the 1990 Indigenous Uprising (Levantamiento Indígena), rural highland areas were militarized, especially in those areas, such as the Central Andes, where indigenous support for the uprising was strongest. State presence and surveillance of Indian communities increased through roadblocks, new "development" projects (viewed by many rural dwellers as a means to enter villages and defuse political organization), replacement of rural civilian teachers with military personnel, and military searches of private houses.
11. Over the period 1982–1988, Ecuador underwent eight adjustment and restructuring programs, although it retained a trade surplus by 1993. In 1986–1991, exports to the Andean countries quadrupled.
12. The extent of "inclusion" is, of course, subject to negotiation, not least with regard to gender issues, which are often remote from debates on "indigenous" politics.

II STATE AND JUSTICE

THE SOUTH AFRICAN TRUTH AND RECONCILIATION COMMISSION A Technique of Nation-State Formation

Lars Buur

The South African Truth and Reconciliation Commission (SATRC) is one of the most prominent features of the South African transition. The processes initiated by the SATRC have had significant influence in transforming the idea and expectations of the new South Africa nation and state. The work of the commission is therefore an interesting site for understanding how an idea about a transformed nation-state is produced.

The SATRC's general task, according to the Promotion of National Unity and Reconciliation Act No. 34, 1995, was to "[establish] as complete a picture as possible of the causes, nature and extent of the gross violations of human rights . . . including the antecedents, circumstances, factors and context of such violations [and decide] whether such violations were the result of deliberate planning on the part of the State or a former state or any of their organs" (Act 1995: 805–6, 809). One could say that the aim of establishing "as complete a picture as possible" of atrocities committed in the past was to create a shared sense of the past in the midst of an extreme diversity of experiences. The SATRC took it upon itself to construct a common national history based on the "truth" about the past human rights violations committed by the past regime and its former opponents. This truth was, ideally, to lead to a shared understanding of the extreme diversity of experiences in South Africa.

The biggest dilemma of this imperative was the question of how the new democracy would manage to deal both with individuals belonging to liberation movements and with those from state institutions, given that both groups were responsible for disappearances, death squads, psychological and physical torture, and other violations of human rights. This problem was inherently related to questions of how a sense of justice could be established that neither granted blanket amnesty nor prosecuted every person who had incited or committed human rights violations.

The Negotiated Settlement

One might say that this process was necessary, but also that it was complicated by the fact that *nobody* could claim he or she had come out of the past conflict a clear and unconditional winner. Unlike the Second World War, there was no official winner of the war against apartheid, and hence it was not possible to establish a war tribunal like the paradigmatic Nuremberg courts-martial. In South Africa, the era of apartheid was brought to an end through a negotiated political compromise including nearly all recognized political players in the country.[1] In spite of, or perhaps because of this settlement,[2] tensions related to the work of the SATRC have continued to emerge. These tensions can be diagnosed as a conflict between implicit and explicit understandings by different people, groups, and political parties of the nature of the negotiated settlement.

In brief, the *explicit* official expression is that there were no winners of the past conflict. Therefore, as SATRC Deputy Chair Alex Boraine formulated it, the work of the SATRC is "an honest assessment and diagnosis of the sickness within our society in an attempt to give people, both perpetrators and victims, an opportunity to face the past and to start afresh" (1996a: 2). I suggest that the *implicit* understanding is that there was indeed a winner, and everybody knows it was the ANC, which is still celebrating the change from institutionalized separate ethnic development to nonracial democracy through sports events, public holidays, and the SATRC. However, due to the nature of the negotiated settlement, this celebration cannot be made overtly in the work of the SATRC, lest it be criticized for not looking toward the future, and lest it alienate supporters of the former regime.[3]

This essay examines the relation between the "onstage," visible, public spectacle of the SATRC process, and the "backstage," invisible, inside of the bureaucratic machinery of truth production.[4] First, I examine the public representations emerging from the SATRC process. I suggest that it was the establishment of the SATRC and the public representations emerging from its strong, onstage presence in the public eye that served to mark the transformation of the state and the nation. The new state sought to present itself as a truth-seeking, impartial judge, dispensing political and social justice, in contrast to the exclusive apartheid state.

Second, I explore how a space was created in which the ambiguous conflicts of the past and present could be dealt with. I suggest that the SATRC was conceptualized as a body disconnected from the state and society through a range of technical and legislative devices. Third, I examine in detail the invisible backstage, everyday practices of the SATRC: how the material for the new national history was produced and cleaned of ambiguities. Here I suggest that the everyday practices were characterized by being highly complicated translations and negotiations, which were informed by both rational ideas about how modern bureaucracy should function and more localized concerns of a political nature.

Finally, I discuss the effectiveness of the separation between the visible and the invisible nature of the SATRC. As a consequence of the perspective chosen, this essay to a large extent leaves out a range of highly relevant questions related to accountability, the need for justice in a transitional society, morality, and discussions related to what has been described as the South African "miracle." Instead, I concentrate on the nitty-gritty of the backstage performance of bureaucratic micropolitics.

The National Spectacle and the Other of the Rainbow Nation

Truth commissions, as pointed out by several authors, have proven far more effective than court proceedings and tribunals in furnishing a dramatic medium for communicating the new official history and law that a transitional society might want to implement (R. Wilson 1996; Hayner 1994).[5] The SATRC has proven particularly effective in this regard. One reason for this was its quasi-legal status, which helped prevent the interruption of storytelling sessions by lawyers drawing attention to legal technicalities (R. Wilson 1996: 16).[6] This gave the process unprecedented media appeal, nationally as well as internationally (Theissen 1999). On the other hand, it also gave the SATRC an enormous ideological responsibility, something to which the usual courtroom in South Africa was not quite as accustomed (R. Wilson 1996).[7] Through these public spectacles, the SATRC provided a controlled environment, which enabled talking about the past in new ways. That is, quite apart from its overt objective of creating an understanding of the "nature, causes and extent of gross violations of human rights" (Act 1995) in South Africa, and documenting violations and abuses in an official state setting, this process allowed a particular picture of the new South Africa to emerge.

In the human rights violation hearings, the victims of abuses were allowed to come forward and publicly reenact a carefully selected catalogue of abuses. In the amnesty hearings, the perpetrators of human rights violations could be granted amnesty according to certain criteria, one of which was telling the "whole" truth. These were not just "media stunts" displaying "the tissue war," as they were popularly known (a reference to the constant dishing out of paper hankies to victims in public hearings). Besides referring to the starkly contrasting displays of weeping victims telling painful stories and amnesty applicants showing little emotion while confessing to gruesome killings and torture, the picture that emerged was one that demonstrated how the balance of power had changed from the perpetrators to the victims—from one class and racial group to another.[8] This display is closely related to the way in which the new South African nation-state, the "rainbow nation," is imagined.

"Othering"

To create a new national history, a "radical other" was needed as the constitutive outside of the new South Africa. In South Africa, the identification of the other of the new nation-state has been the task of the SATRC. More precisely, a certain construction of the other has started to emerge from the work of the commission. This construction has been a positive identification of what the "new" nation-state is, compared to the "old" apartheid state. However, because of the negotiated settlement, this process could not be carried out through clear reference to the present, because current conflicts were extremely difficult to deal with. Instead, present conflicts were constantly rearticulated in the form of the past. The other, in this sense, became the past as opposed to the present focus on transformation.

The psychoanalytic vocabulary of *trauma* combined with the legal language of *human rights* provided legitimate languages for articulating this paradox. In particular, a whole range of illness metaphors has been used to diagnose affairs of the past, which have a bearing on the society of today. The prevalence of these metaphors is illustrated amply in Boraine, Levy, and Scheffer

(1994), Boraine and Levy (1995), and Boraine (1996b). These writings assert that something must be removed from society, the sick must be expiated to let the rainbow nation become healthy. An examination of two such media personifications of sickness, security police officers Gideon Nieuwoudt and Eugene de Kock, is illustrative. I suggest that each looks exactly like the Afrikaner incarnate—the "good" and the "bad" sides.

Personification of Violence and Evil

Today, Nieuwoudt is serving a life sentence for a range of brutal killings in the Eastern Cape during the apartheid era. He has been denied amnesty by the Amnesty Committee of the SATRC for not "disclosing the whole truth" about how he and others tortured and killed human rights activists and cadres of Umkhonto We Sizwe[9] and who gave him the orders to commit human rights violations. Internationally, the most prominent case has been the killing of black consciousness leader Steven Bantu Biko. During these hearings, one had only to listen to and look at Nieuwoudt to understand why he is one of the most hated persons in South Africa. Speaking in Afrikaans at hearings, often with an aggressive and arrogant attitude toward the victims of his brutal actions, every word had to be dragged out of him, and he was never willing to reveal anything or to implicate anybody.[10] Although in some quarters this attitude would create respect, in the context of the SATRC process, Nieuwoudt becomes the incarnation of the "culture of mendacity": the "bad" and evil side of Afrikaner culture.

De Kock came across in much the same manner at the beginning of the SATRC process, but he has since shifted attitude. Also serving a life sentence in prison (212 years), he is currently speaking freely at amnesty hearings, making one disclosure after another, implicating former apartheid cabinet ministers and superiors. His bodily attitude is relaxed and his "naked determination to tell the truth" has been seen as an accommodating gesture toward the victims of his deeds ("A Word, a Nudge" 1999: 24).[11]

De Kock's shift makes it difficult for people to come to grips with him today, and to deal with their own conflicting impulses to condemn him for his evil deeds at the same time as praise him because he has "further opened the doors" to the dark side of South Africa's past ("A Word, a Nudge" 1999: 24). However, should de Kock be granted amnesty for over one hundred cases of killings, torture, and inciting killings for which he has applied, many South Africans would, today, accept it. This is so mainly because he has come to personify the "culture of truth telling" that characterizes the new South Africa. As two brothers of the same culture, the one stands out as an evil of the past, whereas the other is pointing toward the future "with a lightning fast twinkle in his eyes [who has yet] to be caught out in a lie [promising to tell] more at a later stage" (24).[12] Let me give an example of how ambiguities like the ones described above play themselves out inside the SATRC.[13]

An Honest Man

During the "Guguletu Seven"[14] amnesty hearing in Cape Town on 17–19 November 1997, de Kock was subpoenaed to give evidence. He had supplied the SATRC with information about Vlakplaas[15] involvement in the killing of the seven activists in 1986. His testimonies challenged some of the white security officers' versions of the incident, because they denied the killings were preplanned.

My first meeting with de Kock happened on the first day of the hearing. He walked around in his green military uniform, apparently alone. Passing him, I did not at first recognize him, but I remember noticing that I had seen the face before without being able to fix it as de Kock's. A few minutes later I passed a group of staff members of the SATRC regional office in Cape Town. They were talking about the person I had passed a few minutes earlier:

> "Lars, don't you recognize him?"
>
> I said: "Who?"
>
> "The person down there," nodding with their heads toward the other end of the corridor.
>
> I said: "Oh yes, I have seen him before, but who is he actually?"
>
> One of them, a secretary for one of the commissioners, said: "That's de Kock. He is here because he is going to testify in the Guguletu Seven amnesty hearing. He is challenging the local policemen's stories. He is going to make a fool out of them, challenging their lies."
>
> I said: "Oh, is it really him? Are you sure? He looks very different from the person I have seen in the newspapers and in [the documentary television program] *Prime Evil*."
>
> The secretary responded: "Yes, it is him. He looks different because he is in prison now, he has lost so much weight. Before, he was bigger and taller. His time in prison has really taken its toll on him. What a shame, he is much smaller now."

> Half an hour later I met the same secretary together with a logistics officer in the door to the hearings room on the tenth floor. The hearing had just started and they were whispering, discussing de Kock.
>
> The secretary said, "What a shame he is so small now. Before, he was tall and looked really strong. That was before they put him in jail."
>
> The logistics officer, who had been active during the struggle in the ANC and had lost several of her friends while others had been tortured, was furious. "*Kak, man!* [Shit!] How can you defend him? He is a killer with blood on his hands. He is evil. I could go up and kill him for what he has done. He is a *fucking Boer.*" She turned away from us in disgust and sat down in the last row of chairs, right at the back of the room, facing de Kock. Her last words were, "Don't listen to her [the secretary]. He [de Kock] is a *fucking Boer.*"
>
> The secretary tried to explain: "He did awful things, but it is not fair to lock him up alone. He has changed now. He is the only one speaking, telling the truth. He is not like de Klerk and P. W. [Botha]. He is telling the truth, so they should treat him with more dignity and not lock him up like a criminal. I am not saying it is right what he did, but he is telling the truth and that is good." (Based on fieldwork notes 1997)

This story can be interpreted in many different ways. One could, for example, blame the secretary for being naïve, but that would be to miss the point. Apart from telling something important about the highly complicated process of the SATRC and how particular classifications change over time, I would like to highlight the particular configuration of individual Afrikaner security personnel and its intimate relation to the overall classification of the Afrikaners, the "Boer." One way of identifying the malaise of the South African society is to "villainize" somebody. This somebody, I suggest, is the Afrikaner, a name that became shorthand for the old apartheid state and its wrongdoings—the past of the present.

Chains of Equivalence[16]

One of the most striking features of the public amnesty hearings has been the focus on individual Afrikaners as representations of the old apartheid state. In particular, the peculiar configuration of individual Afrikaner security personnel, who were mainly hostile to the SATRC process and seldom free-speaking, was linked to distinct state institutions as human rights violators.[17]

In the work emerging from the SATRC, the specific entity of "Afrikaner human rights violator" was presented adjacent to another closely related entity: the strikingly silent and supposedly ignorant group of ordinary Afrikaners. The Afrikaner as human rights violator and the ignorant Afrikaner form a single entity: the Afrikaner of the old apartheid state. The behavior of this entity is made "real" by linking patterns of action to a specific "culture": the old apartheid state's "culture of mendacity." Deeds and actions of the Afrikaner security personnel became the *operational definition* of Afrikaner and the old apartheid regime. In this way, a paradigmatic image of the Afrikaner as an evil belonging to the past, of what the new nation-state is not, and of what the SATRC process was implemented to identify and leave behind is created.

This process of classification has its dialectical counterpart in a similar chain of equivalence, consisting of a particular combination of individual victims of apartheid, the black majority, and the new South African state. This combination primarily includes women, most often mothers, who voluntarily go to the SATRC. They are presented as representatives of the forgiving and reconciliation-seeking black population, an image through which the SATRC has been able to represent the new South Africa. Instead of the culture of mendacity, embodied in the old apartheid state, the new South African state is characterized by a "culture of truth telling." Rather than being the ultimate victims of apartheid, this group of women stands out as a paradigmatic example of the new national subject, the subject to be served by the new state.

The Afrikaner is constituted as the past against which the new state is seen. Specifically, the democratic state formulates itself in opposition to human rights violations, behavior that infected the "past." In this sense, the formulation of a culture of mendacity also identifies that which is now presumably left behind. Therefore, when human rights violations happen in the present, those actions are deemed "left over" from the past, most often assigned to "Third Force" elements of the past, or as yet uneducated and transformed groups formerly serving the apartheid state.

The power of this particular configuration of the past and the present imbued with two distinct cultures is more intriguing when one realizes that most amnesty applicants coming forward to the SATRC are not white security personnel; many of those were indemnified before the SATRC started. The majority of applicants for amnesty are black, alleged members of the different liberation movements (TRC 2000). The oppositional play outlined above, which structures the past and present, raises one question: To the extent that individual Afrikaners are broadly identified as the source of evil, as evil itself, how can reconciliation be achieved?

If a personification of evil is necessary, this would suggest that the possibility of reconciliation with other Afrikaners and Africans requires a simultaneous celebration of the good elements of the Afrikaner, good elements that can be incorporated in the new rainbow nation's culture of truth telling. This, however, would require that the evil be personified in *certain people*, whose wickedness is then explained by reference to the Afrikaner past, like Nieuwoudt. Hence, the behavior of individuals would be justified, to some extent, as being beyond their personal control, as *deformations* of essentially good Afrikaners. Then, individuals could be "cured," to draw on the medical metaphor, and the healthy Afrikaner could bloom together with the rest of the present rainbow nation, just as de Kock does.

During the SATRC process, "Do not villainize the Afrikaners" was constantly stressed. This statement, however, has the precise effect of vilifying Afrikaners, because the "group," however disorganized and heterogeneous it may be, is by implication pointed out as different from the rest, something to take notice of. On the one hand, by representing the Afrikaner in such categorical terms, the problem is no longer in individual human beings, but in an entire culture of old Afrikaners opposed to the transformation of the new South Africa. On the other hand, this classification process also creates a new category, the new nation-state, an object of identification and service for the Afrikaners.

"Afrikaners Are Africans"

In what is now known as the "Afrikaners are Africans" speech, South African President Thabo Mbeki spoke to "the Afrikanerbond" in Pretoria on 27 July 1999.[18] In the speech Mbeki opened the door to the biggest "group" of Afrikaners who had not yet volunteered their services to the new South Africa.[19] He asked whether South Africans "are to remain tied to the divisions and conflicts of the past, or whether they now can be fused into one South African journey leading into a common future" (Mbeki 1999). Apart from the language used, which reminds us of the language of the SATRC, his speech is interesting because we find here a transformation from "truth telling" and a focus on the past to "the emergence of new ways of doing things, and finding new, creative ways of expressing ourselves and our plans for the future" (Mbeki 1999). It is no longer the past and truth telling, but a question of the future, of becoming involved in development and the uplift of the black majority. His answer is a clear yes: the Afrikaners can become part of the new South Africa because "Afrikaners are Africans." It is only a question of drawing on the good side of the Afrikaner heritage:

> I have been told for a long time there has been an interesting way of describing a loyal Afrikaner. It is always said: "Hy is 'n goeie Afrikaner" [He is a good Afrikaner]. This was often used to describe someone who should be elected to a school committee, parliament or any other leadership position. To some extent it is the same in the ANC when someone is referred to as a "good comrade."
>
> But should a "good comrade" and a "goeie Afrikaner" work merely for their respective interests, or should they not be good comrades and goeie Afrikaners for the entire South Africa? (Mbeki 1999)

A month later, the reply came from the Afrikanerbond, who pledged to work closely with the ANC government in bringing economic and social development to the country ("Afrikanerbond forges ties with ANC" 1999). Thabo Mbeki's speech displaces the question from truth telling to actual everyday dedication in the form of hard work, a language that, given their Calvinistic Christian background, is familiar to Afrikaners. The point is that this displacement could not have happened without the work of the SATRC, with its "public grilling" of the "bad" sides of Afrikanerdom. The subtle shift from truth telling to work ethic needed a resonating background, and this was provided by the SATRC.

Ritualized public representations emerging from the public SATRC process(es) are effective performances of the new nation-state. But the visible character of the spectacles of the SATRC as I have described and analyzed it above is one thing. Another side of this story is the invisible daily work going on behind closed doors. When I visited South Africa and the SATRC for the first time in September 1996 I was surprised when highly esteemed scientists writing papers and participating in the public debate about the commission did not even know where the headquarters of the SATRC were situated (based on fieldwork notes 1996).

Even though the SATRC was the single most public and debated institution in South Africa during 1996 and 1997, with a radio channel sending directly from public hearings and a weekly internationally awarded television program broadcast on national television every Sunday, very few people knew where the national head office of SATRC was situated. It is this phenomenon I turn to now, exploring first the technical construction of the SATRC as separated from the state and later the actual work going on inside the public access points of the SATRC. Based on the above assessment of the South African transition, I suggest that the function of the SATRC has been to institutionalize[20] the conflict over the past and the highly ambivalent present. More precisely, the displacement and separation of these issues from state and society have been produced through a range of both technical and legislative devices.

A Constitutive Separation

The daily work of the SATRC, including the processing of data about human rights violations with the aim of accumulating a comprehensive official historical database, was governed by a scientific, positivistic ideal.[21] The parameters of this ideal are outlined in the mandate of the SATRC.[22] According to the Act of National Unity and Reconciliation, the SATRC was required to "function without political or other bias" and in an objective and even-handed manner (Act 1995: 843). It was therefore obliged to be an *independent* body, separated from the political environment that constituted it and that granted it time extensions (which happened several times) and funding. The Act states that to fulfill its obligations—documenting and laying the foundation for a morally just society—the commission shall be "independent from any party, government, administration, or any other functionary or body directly or indirectly representing the interests of any such entity" (843).[23] This constitutive separation was produced by a suspension of *temporality* and a suspension of *place* to create new *time-spaces* at the margins of the political and social domains of society.

The temporal suspension can be seen in a range of factors characterizing the commission. First, the legally preordained end date locates the commission outside the "normal" temporality of the nation-state. Second, this was further enforced by vesting the commission with special investigative powers because the SATRC could subpoena people without obtaining clearance from other authorities.[24] The special investigative powers enhanced the exceptional position of the SATRC, indicating that we are dealing with an institution where time is compressed and where many tasks have to be done in a hurry, with no time for following the "normal" schedules and procedures of the state.

The suspension of place refers to the fact that most official truth commissions do not work in state buildings, but rent their own premises and lease their own equipment. In South Africa, the SATRC set up four privately owned offices furnished with equipment leased or purchased with foreign donor money. This way of ideally *disconnecting* the SATRC from the state's localized social activities created an idea about a new time-space at the margin of the nation-state, placed outside the nitty-gritty of everyday political struggles. The symbolic importance of this form of technical disconnectedness cannot be underestimated. When the SATRC closed down some of the regional offices before the release of the final report in October 1998, it was decided to transfer the amnesty section of the SATRC to the new premises of Magistrate Court in Durban, KwaZulu Natal. Among staff members in the Durban office this raised discussions about whether they could maintain their independence in the work and whether people outside the commission would perceive the SATRC as a prolongation of the justice system. In other words, they were afraid that by the transference they would not only compromise the work of the SATRC, but also create, in the public mind, a sense of the SATRC's being a "normal" court, judging people (interviews, Durban, 1998).

The Legal Discourse

The sense of the SATRC as disconnected and legitimate cannot be explained with reference to its technical separation from society and state alone. The quasi-scientific working procedures are only one side of the story. Minimally, the legitimacy of the SATRC is based on a convention that rests on the common interest in there being an institution to deal with questions about the past and the dilemma of guilt and responsibility in a nonretributive manner.[25]

Mary Douglas has suggested that for an institution to turn into a legitimate social institution, it needs "a parallel cognitive convention to sustain it," so that conventions and practices are naturalized in social classification (1966: 46). For an institution to be legitimate, "every kind of institution needs a formula that found its rightness in reason and in nature" (45). In other words, there needs to be an "analogy by which the formal structure of a crucial set of social relations is found in the physical world, or in the supernatural world, or in eternity, anywhere, so long as it is not seen as a socially contrived arrangement" (48). I contend that this analogy is the encapsulation of historical truth in a legal discourse and set of practices, that is, in the law. In the case of the SATRC, legitimacy is based on the founding principles of the

Constitution of South Africa, with the invocation of nation building, peaceful coexistence, and a new nation-state built on the rule of law, including the invocation of human rights as the measurement of "universal justice."

There are many references to the judicial discourse and set of practices in the work of the SATRC. Besides the obvious references to amnesty legislation, the judicial power vested in the power of subpoena and in the revocation and framing of the work of the SATRC within international law and in particular the Geneva Convention of Human Rights, the judicial discourse and set of practices was apparent in the public hearings process. Every hearing, for example, starts by claiming "This is not a Court of Law," but the way the hearings room is set up—with commissioners and committee members, applicants, victims, and lawyers placed as if it were a courtroom—makes it difficult to distinguish from a court. This image is supported by the language used, oath taking, and expected behavior, such as participants asking questions through a lawyer.

Through this double invocation of technical separation and legal discourse, the SATRC became a means of accommodating conflict. It was a way of regulating and neutralizing current conflicts related to past responsibility and guilt, so that these conflicts could be contained and dealt with within one segregated domain. In this way, the past and its conflicts were encoded, ordered, and organized, so that past experiences could be encapsulated in the rules and legislation of the Constitution on which the SATRC was based. Though the ideal was not always maintained, despite the best intentions of the SATRC staff, nonetheless it allowed these conflicts to be controlled and their consequences made relatively predictable. A consequence of this process is that the past is determined by legislative provisions and by the particular manner in which legislation is interpreted.

This point is often forgotten in the comparative study of truth commissions. Nearly all descriptions and analyses of official truth commissions rest on the implicit proposition that norms, action, and representations are basically the same (see, e.g., Hayner 1994, 1996, 1997). This means that what a commission should do, what it actually did, and the manner in which people in charge of commissions represent and reflect on the work done all belong to the same level of reality. The result of this is that descriptions and analyses of the work of these commissions end up being far too coherent, and further, that important information is excluded about how mandates (and their internal tensions) are handled by staff members while commissions are working.

The Invisible Inside

The intensity of this public process has also created a certain kind of blindness around the work of the SATRC. The ritualized public representations only describe one aspect of its work. The private process of selecting victims who would tell stories publicly was basically a strategic process where judgments were made by SATRC staff members to identify the good and the bad protagonists of the past. Of the 22,000 statements the SATRC received from victims of human rights violations, approximately 10 percent appeared in public hearings; the remaining 90 percent were processed behind the scenes. This processing behind closed doors was about finding the truth about the past, but more specifically, it was about dividing things up into relevant and irrelevant truth and about removing the debris of national history that was not deemed to fall within the human rights violation schema of the SATRC. This selective, creative, and publicly unobserved production of specific kinds of truth claims is explored in the following sections.

Individualized Truth

The new South Africa describes itself as a *rainbow nation* consisting of many different and highly diverse fragments (people, histories, and ethnicities). To create a shared sense of the past in the midst of this diversity, the commission needs unambiguous information that must then be classified according to a human rights–based "trichotomy": victim, witness, and perpetrator—a human rights violation–based classification schema.

It is important to keep in mind that in the landscape of a negotiated settlement, the road the SATRC has chosen is, in essence, a liberal way of dealing with the past (Mamdani 1996b: 4–5; 1997: 22) because the SATRC has chosen to interpret its mandate from an individualized perspective.[26] This has been done in two ways. First, the commission primarily documented the abuses committed by the apartheid state institutions and its foremost opponents in individual terms. Second, it tried to capture as many stories as possible from individual victims of gross human rights violations (GHRVs), a process of "transparent" data collection that produced material for writing up a new common national history. Not everything enters the national script. The stories forwarded to the SATRC needed to contain certain information that suited clear-cut definitions of victims, perpetrators, and abuses to fit the national script. In this way, a certain grammar was used for the production of the "correct" script.

In the process of truth production, historical events had to be reconstructed. Some events became classified as GHRV, and others did not. This required a series of interpretations and judgments by everyday workers in the SATRC. Even though the SATRC carried out many of its tasks in the public eye, the everyday work of the commission has, until recently, largely escaped scrutiny.[27] This has been so partly because the daily work of the SATRC was to a large extent inaccessible. The everyday practice of objectifying and processing past experiences from the apartheid period in the SATRC was done without any public attention. In other words, the commission's everyday work functions were *retracted* (invisible) from society, in contrast to the theatrical nature of everyday bureaucratic public routines (see, e.g., Herzfeld 1992). This raises questions, such as what characterizes the truth that constitutes the foundation of the new nation-state? What makes the truth produced by the SATRC a legitimate and authoritative truth in national and international arenas? This is what I answer in the following section by examining the ways in which the categories of GHRV were negotiated in the everyday bureaucratic practice of the SATRC.

The Everyday Practices of Truth Production

The following example illustrates the everyday practices that were applied in the Data Processor Unit (DPU) of the SATRC to objectify reliable information about past human rights atrocities. The task of the DPU was to analyze the statements received by the SATRC from alleged victims of GHRVs and to classify and enter the information in a database. The DPU was only one of several units working together on this project. Its work was the second step in an ongoing process of verification of the received statements. At the end of this process statements were either dismissed as being "out of mandate" or classified according to victims, witnesses, or perpetrators of the GHRV(s) who appeared in the statement.

Therefore, the incoming statements, on which all the units depend, were central to the work of the DPU. The cooperation among the different units consisted of different layers of "corroboration" of the information captured.[28] This was done through a database, applying the well-known software program Oracle, which classified and analyzed incoming empirical material in such a way that different units/persons could communicate and change the captured information.

The methodology is, in essence, "positivistic." Each step in the ongoing data processing permitted a systematic cross-correlation and confirmation of the raw data captured by the statement takers and refined by the data processors.[29] The aim of the cross-correlation was to produce a neutral and objective process of fact finding, as required in the mandate of the SATRC. The complex negotiations that this positivistic methodology implied can be illustrated by the following sequence.

The Data Processors

Sheila has received a statement, which at first seems problem-free.[30] She types a reference number into the correct rubric on the computer screen and the deponent, who is also the victim, is thus automatically given a reference number. She then goes through the statement to find other victims. Every time a name is mentioned she writes the new person's name down on a piece of paper and makes the first classification: *who* is victim, *who* is perpetrator, *who* is witness, and so forth. She then begins the creation of their "identities" on the screen by giving them a victim, witness, or perpetrator number, so that they will have their own page in the database. Extracts from my field notes illustrate this process:

> A problem emerges when the screen (the data program) on page 2 asks for more details about the incident. Sheila rereads the statement and begins doubting whether she is dealing with a GHRV incident or a job conflict between different workers in a bar.
>
> Sheila thinks out loud: "It seems more like an event than an GHRV. How can a bar fight over jobs be classified as a GHRV?" She answers herself: "In some cases it seems so, Lars, because boycotts[31] were used as a weapon by the UDF [United Democratic Front], so everything depends on the political context. What do you think, Lars?"
>
> "I don't know."
>
> Sheila looks around the room and goes to Julia, the leader of the unit, who is sitting at the back of the room. They quickly go through the statement together and consult the ten pages of GHRV classifications. After a long discussion and several consultations with the GHRV classifications, they decide *not* to create "personal details"—the witness, victim, and perpetrator identities—because it is *not* a GHRV statement.
>
> But before Sheila has left Julia's desk, Julia changes her mind. She is not satisfied; still doubting, she decides to call Shaida, the person who

registers all statements from the Western Cape, on the telephone and ask her what to do.

During the discussion it is decided that Sheila should write a "throng summary," which would explain *why* the statement is not a GHRV statement, or, in other words, why the statement is out of mandate. The final decision would then be taken by commissioner Mary Burton later on. Mary (or another human rights violation committee member) is the only person who can take the final decision on whether a statement is out of mandate or not.

Sheila then goes to the computer and begins writing the summary. One sentence stands out: "*The bar was predominantly for whites.*" When finished, she decides to create the necessary *identities* on pages 2 and 3 in the database, because the bar was for whites and it could have been a conflict with a political motive. She then consults the room again—this time discussing with several data processors—and it is decided that she should go and talk to some of the more experienced data processors, who work on another floor with the Investigative Unit on corroboration of statements.

We talk to the investigative data processor and show her a printout of Sheila's work. She tells Sheila that she has done good work and promises to talk to Mary Burton after the corroboration has been done by the Investigative Unit. Sheila tells me she feels relieved, because it is "no longer my problem, and because I have done nothing wrong."

I then ask her about the sentence she wrote that guided the rest of her classificatory work: "The bar was *predominantly* for whites." The narrative of the statement did not contain this information; the statement had not said anything about which kind of bar we were dealing with. In Sheila's explanation, she refers to her own knowledge about bars during the time of apartheid. She explains to me that "some bars were for whites only and others were for coloreds and blacks."

Employees in bureaucratic institutions like the SATRC try to fulfill the ideal of the constitutive separation between politics and science, well knowing that it is impossible. They strive hard to follow the rules, even while simultaneously acknowledging that it is impossible to classify and thereby postulate that the nature of apartheid's heritage consists of discrete and distinct entities that can easily be ordered. In part, this commitment owes to an awareness of the implications of not fulfilling the ideal if it comes to public knowledge—the fear of "messing up," as it is popularly expressed among employees of the SATRC. And partly, the commitment owes to a belief in the correctness of this way of working: the bureaucratic ordering of the world. But just as important is commission members' awareness that they have a mission that is bigger than themselves. In this sense, the ideal is a guiding framework—a necessary fiction—for their meticulous work, which informs actions and decisions even when it cannot be preserved in reality.

Classification

The above sequence describes the negotiations involved in the classification of information contained in a statement. Each statement usually involves several classifications, with their own contextual story. Contextual stories contain important information if one does not want to simply dismiss the work of the employees as "bad" or "unprofessional," and if one wants to understand the metamorphic process this statement undergoes before its information becomes an (arti)fact.[32]

The first classification originates with Sheila, but is later transformed by communication with other persons from the unit (Julia, other people in the data processing room and on other floors). At first, the information contained in the statement does *not* describe a human rights violation; this is verified by Julia after a rather long negotiation. It does not fit the definition of a GHRV, which is "the killing, abduction, torture or severe ill-treatment of any person, or any attempt, conspiracy, incitement, instigation, command or procurement to commit an act referred to" among the four basic classifications (Act 1995: 1).

When Sheila classifies the event as a GHRV after all, Julia recognizes the classification as a GHRV. She then immediately sends the decision to another person for further verification. When I later asked Sheila how she knew that it was a GHRV, she responded by saying that she could not know with certainty, but that her own knowledge about bars in South Africa during the years of apartheid made her sure, as a colored person, that this was the case. In this categorization, the arti(fact) that we are dealing with—"*a bar predominantly for whites*"—is an active participant in the negotiations between her and Julia. In this sense, personal history and local knowledge—all the unconsidered factors that organize daily life in South Africa—mingle with the classification schema.

From the moment the categorization is completed, the discourse changes from the question of dealing with a statement out of mandate, to the question of how to secure its acceptance in the classification system, so that identities of victims, perpetrators, and witnesses can be captured in the database.

Another determinant in the process is the specific history of the "normative classification scheme" applied by the SATRC.[33] This contextual history, which refers to unspoken practices, is also a crucial factor in the classification process. Since the data processors began their work in 1996, the normative classification scheme developed from two to ten pages. Nearly every week, new domains of violence were included or removed or the interpretations of the categories changed. But information about the changes was not always passed on to staff, who had to implement the changes in their daily work. When a change did filter down in the internal hierarchy, it generally took one to two weeks to reach staff members.[34] The consequences were, first, that the data processors were always insecure about whether they were doing their work correctly, and second, that they were forced to constantly rewrite the work they had already completed to make it match the latest revisions to the classification scheme. Thus, bureaucracy is a process rather than a rigid set of rules and regulations.

The dilemma for the people working in the DPU was that they had to make decisions that had to be aligned with the rules and classification schema. This required judgments and interpretations, which reshaped the past in particular directions and which are part of the reinvention of the past.[35] This raises a question: Is bending the past, as we have seen in the above example, done deliberately in bad faith? I would say no. I suggest that instead a certain "will to order" seems to be at stake in this process of bureaucratic classification. This leads us to the creation of identities in the form of categories of victims, perpetrators, and witnesses and the specific context of this classification system.

The Will to Order

Week after week, those working for the SATRC are confronted with painful stories of people whose lives have been broken down during the years of apartheid—and there is not much they can do for them.[36] Among ordinary staff members, frustrations started to surface in the beginning of 1997, when the victim-driven hearings were finalized and the amnesty process took off. In contrast with the victim-driven hearings, considerable resources were used on amnesty applicants in the form of legal representation to make the process fair according to international human rights standards. A sense of betrayal was common among staff members, who felt they had often exploited the victims by putting pressure on them to recount experiences publicly, without giving them anything back.[37]

However, *if* people are classified as victims they will at least come into consideration later, when reparations are decided on. After the victim, witness, and perpetrator identities have been defined, the data processors produce the list of dependents (their identities). This list guides the distribution of reparation to victims (TRC 1998b).[38] Therefore, when a person is turned away, this may have enormous consequences not only for the victims themselves, but for their families as well. Without the victim classification they will miss out on the chance of a whole range of future entitlements, including school bursaries, medical treatment, clean penal certificates, and jobs, all of which inform the prospect of a different future.

There is, therefore, what I call the "will to a certain order"[39] at stake among the employees of the SATRC and commissioners: a will to classify people as victims. This happens in a conflictual balance among a range of strategies, such as the imperative of being objective, the feeling of betraying victims, and the will to give victims a chance to access the new state welfare systems. In this sense, classifications are settled and find their stability without any*body* necessarily formulating this preference openly.

On the other hand, for every victim identified there has to be a perpetrator, a person whose life can be ruined if wrongly (or rightly) classified as such. The classification of perpetrators is not just coincidental; it springs from the logic of how GHRVs are identified and counted. When dealing with a GHRV there has to be an agent. As the key words guiding the database indicate: "Who did What to Whom?" Often, no*body* is mentioned in the statements, but still the database requires a perpetrator, a request that comes up on the screen automatically. In these cases, an "unknown" South African policeman, South African National Defense Force member, SDU person, or other is written into the database, helping to establish the overall patterns of GHRVs.

The importance of the identity of witnesses and the implications for people classified as such are less clear. The role of the witness category was downplayed in the work of the SATRC from the beginning of the process. Exceptions were the cases where there was no "objective" material for verification, such as medical records, death certificates, or mortuary, court, or prison files. In such cases, the SATRC had to rely on the affidavits captured from witnesses. The identity of witnesses was in this sense initially less important because the proof provided by a witness within this positivistic methodology ranked lower in the hierarchy than other kinds of evidence. However, this changed in the last months of the work of the SATRC, when it was realized that they had to dismiss thousands of statements as out of mandate due to the lack of objective material verifying the victim statements. Then the witness category became important. The SATRC even went so far, in cases where there was neither objective proof nor witnesses, to say that if people signed a solemn declaration the SATRC would accept the statements as true and entitle them to reparation (based on fieldwork notes and interviews with staff members, 1997–1998).

Before I continue the analysis, I will give another example of how localized knowledge and the will to a certain order, when applied together with specific bureaucratic competencies, not only influenced the classification process, but also made it a powerful tool. The example is taken from the regional Investigative Unit (IU) of Cape Town and is partly based on my own observations and partly on the retrospective reflections of the investigator whose work I observed.

The Legal Mind

The IU was tasked with analyzing and corroborating statements to find out whether a statement fell within the mandate of the SATRC. This was the last step in the chain of data processing before the GHRV cases were submitted to final decision making by committee members and commissioners. On several occasions I shared an office with members of the IU in Cape Town. The following event took place in 1997, just before the investigative process was to be finalized.

The leader of the unit came into the office with a bundle of cases. The cases were handed over to the investigator with the words "Take a look at these cases with your legal mind. I am not satisfied with the decisions taken. See what you can do." This particular investigator was one of three persons in the unit who were trained in law. The cases all belonged to statements received from the rural areas of the Southern and Northern Cape, areas where the SATRC had used very few resources and therefore had few cases documenting GHRVs.

Over the following days the investigator looked through the cases and was struggling with them. He told me: "All the cases clearly speak about GHRVs but none of them have any objective material to support their claims." The investigator in charge of the original investigations, a foreigner, had classified them as out of mandate, which, according to my office fellow, was "reasonable enough," but it was only because the foreign investigator "did not understand the history of violations in South Africa." He then wrote up the cases and handed them back to the unit leader.

When I later interviewed the investigator about the event, he told the following story:

> The worst part of actually doing a case is that you are sitting and *reducing* everything that you've experienced on paper. I think that was ultimately the most difficult part of my work. One person is showing us exactly where he was shot in the eye, the family members have to go and stand in welfare queues, the husband and father is now an invalid, and nobody can support the family. As an investigator you have been there, you have seen it. Every time you deal with these people you're moved.
>
> The fact that they are helpless is very difficult. There is nothing you can do and that sense of helplessness both makes you powerful and leaves you feeling shitty. You know exactly what can be done, you know that this fucking matter falls outside the mandate, there's nothing that the Truth Commission can do for this person. That's why you're walking around with your list of the Human Rights Commission, Land Commission, lawyers that can take this matter further, the type of structures that these people did not have access to [before]. But access is not everything, access does not help them either. You are their last chance.
>
> You can't get angry at the person [for wasting your time], but once you leave, you just get so pissed off and you think there's nobody to blame but the system. And then you obviously relive [the stories from the field] when you sit with a case and have to take a decision. This is why it is always important to have a background, *a South African background*, so that you can actually identify with what was happening. The fact that we could identify with people's plights obviously influenced the report writing as well.
>
> You have to judge whether a case is political or not, and you obviously don't want to mislead the commission because I am here to do a service to the Truth Commission and to the people [of South Africa]. But I'm not going to lie. There are some times when you can actually bend the rules.
>
> Let me give an example. There was this woman who had been

whipped, but there was no documentary proof, she was not arrested. She had been tear-gassed and complained of bad health and that type of thing. Well, there was one witness who saw that she was whipped. You obviously had to corroborate this witness, but not much came out of it. Then she showed me the marks on her back and, it wasn't like electrodes placed on your stomach or on your fingernails, but it was assault. One could say that there was a political motive, because she was a political candidate, but no direct link. If you leave it like that it's a bit too vague, not so vague, but it is not bolstered enough as to actually justify a reason, classify the case as a violation [within the context of the SATRC]. But if you contextualize it, if you go into her psyche, if you go into the times when it happened, if you use the graphic insight detail you have of these people—the trauma that these people went through—highlight their position, how it affected them and you bolstered the case with this information, then maybe.

If you go out of your way basically to have a person classified and there are no gray areas, then either you are a victim or you are not. If you detail a case like that, then a report becomes a tool with which you classify people. You make the recommendation; it is a GHRV, and ten to one your recommendation will be sent to the human rights violation committee [who take the final decision]. (Based on fieldwork notes from 1997 and interview material from 1997–1998)

To let "a report become a tool" and "bend the rules," as it is described above, takes particular skill and knowledge about how bureaucratic systems function and what is required to let a case pass. It requires the ability to balance subtly between too much and too little: to find the middle ground between conflicting demands. In retrospect, it can easily be misinterpreted as deliberate fraud, but in my view this would be a misinterpretation. What I want to highlight is the capacity for settlement that I have called a certain will to order, which gave the past a direction and a clear, unambiguous content.

Metamorphosis and the Creation of Bureaucratic (Arti)Facts

We are now in a position to answer the question: What characterizes the facts produced by the SATRC? The facts on which the new nation-state are founded are (arti)facts. These (arti)facts—the database, the identities in the form of victims, witnesses, and perpetrators, and the memory of the process—are constructed through complex processes of interaction and negotiation. We have witnessed a metamorphic process, where answers are wrested from the narratives of victims captured in statements. It is a metamorphosis in the sense that the initial narratives were characterized by a high degree of ambiguity (and instability), which, through the classification process (of which the DPU and the IU are only a small part), were finally transformed into a set of clear and unambiguous identities.

As we have seen, this stability did not come easily. Complicated translations and negotiations took place to "find the truth about the past." Bureaucratically constructed truth necessitates, in the discourse of rights, unequivocal categories so that entitlements in the form of reparation can be distributed. However, when viewed from the perspective of everyday bureaucratic practices, the bureaucracy, which was ideally perceived to be filtered for the "disturbing noise" of political contention and personal histories, turned out to be something far more complicated.

It is in this landscape of will to order, uncertainty, decisions, controversies, personal stories, political preferences, an Act, a database that demands information, normative classifications, and high stress levels that the foundation of the new nation-state is created. The point is relatively simple. When the complex translations and negotiations among different role-players are complete, all that is left on the computer screen, in the investigative reports, or in the final report of the SATRC are the categories: victim, witness, and perpetrator. The negotiations described here vanish and we have the hard social facts, which in the future will circulate in new networks of statistics, history books, policymaking, crime prevention, political election arguments, and the national history.

The Visible and the Invisible

The public debate on the SATRC discusses whether the commission fulfills the imperative of writing up a new history in a neutral and even-handed manner, disconnected from the political and social forces at play in South Africa. In general, it is astonishing how much attention each step of the seventeen (in the end, there were only fifteen) commissioners or each press release attracts in the media. The SATRC has been hailed as the most transparent official commission so far. Through a whole range of "access points,"[40] such as public hearings, public processes of consultation, and media coverage on an unprecedented scale, including both radio and television broadcasts, the SATRC has created a sense of transparency around its activities. Here, I analyze the relation between the visible—the ritualized access points—and the invisible bureaucratic routines.

The constitutive separation between politics and scientific procedures cannot be maintained if one looks behind the on-stage dimensions emerging from various kinds of official public representations (whether media, academic, final report, or ritual representations) and public transparency. Nevertheless, the separation is a necessary fiction. An echo of Max Weber can almost be heard here. He pointed out: "The march of bureaucracy has destroyed structures of domination which had no rational character. . . . Every bureaucracy seeks to increase the superiority of the professionally informed by keeping their knowledge and intentions secret. Bureaucratic administration always tends to be an administration of 'secret sessions'; in so far as it can, it hides its knowledge and actions from criticism" (1968a: 244).

What Weber so rightly brings to our attention is the double nature of bureaucratic institutions. On the one hand, bureaucratic institutions accentuate their rational side—here, in the form of transparent criteria for defining who are victims and perpetrators. The flip side of the transparency of bureaucratic institutions like the SATRC is the public erasure of irrational actions and decisions, mainly by controlling the circulation of knowledge.[41] This is done by hiding what is going on inside the SATRC, by making the irrational actions invisible, through a whole range of naturalized and logical strategies such as "disconnecting" the work of the SATRC from other state institutions, security checks, media departments, and other kinds of ritualized "access points," and partly by emphasizing openness and transparency. One could call it paradoxical that it is the maintaining of the second separation, this partly invisible and partly transparent Janus face of the SATRC, that makes the truth produced by the SATRC legitimate and authoritative. But as Michael Taussig (1997) has illustrated, the production and reproduction of the idea about the modern state is based on more magic than we normally think. The importance of this observation points to the significance of looking at and analyzing modern bureaucratic state institutions as something other than highly rational bodies.

Final Words

I have attempted to open up the ready-made facts about the past that constitute the foundation of the new nation-state of South Africa. I have analyzed how facts are manufactured and have reconstructed the double separation between science and politics on the one hand, and between what is visible and invisible on the other. I did this by moving behind the ritualized access points provided by the SATRC, toward a place where the truths on which the new nation-state is based are constructed. Although the first constitutive division—between science and politics—is unable to account for the negotiations, links, and influences between the SATRC and politics, it is nevertheless important to bear in mind the words of Bruno Latour: "It would be a mistake to deny the effectiveness of this separation" (1993: 13). By separating science and politics and keeping the interface between the two domains invisible, an extremely efficient, successful, and often "trusted" kind of institution is created. The SATRC has indeed been effective in gathering an important, officially sanctioned body of knowledge about the apartheid past. It is equally important to bear in mind when we are talking about state-governed bureaucratic institutions that the separations between science and politics, or what is visible and invisible, do not have a rigid or totalitarian character. We do not encounter a state that has an all-embracing character, nor do we fail to follow the bureaucratic procedures stated in the law. What we do encounter is the *ideal* of the state as all-embracing, and this is something quite different.

The robustness of the work of the SATRC—the representation that is under construction in South Africa to legitimize the new nation-state—relies on the work of "experts" working for the commission and the visions and images they present in their work. The veracity of this representation has been on trial since the release of the *Final Report* in October 1998: legally, historically, sociologically, and so on. I am sure that to a large extent it will pass this scrutiny—and with good reason, because it is a meticulous and gigantic work, the real effects of which we cannot yet begin to assess. However, because most assessments of official commission work will be of a normative kind, many of the processes dealt with in this essay will escape scrutiny. For exactly this reason I think there is a lesson to be learned from the SATRC, the general features of which could have wider analytical resonance.

One reason for pursuing this analytical perspective is that a reading of the growing literature on official truth commissions shows that it seldom, if ever, deals with the interface between the scientific-bureaucratic rationale and concrete bureaucratic practices—between what commissions claim to do and what they actually do. In other words, there is a gap in the literature when it comes to the ways facts are constructed. Common to the growing literature on official commissions is the fact that the relationship between the practical techniques applied to objectifying past abuses and the resulting claim to truth has seldom been questioned. Taking these invisible and at times hidden processes into account is not the same as being a cultural *spielverderber* (spoilsport), as certain sociological and anthropological perspectives could suggest,[42] but to take seriously the power of modern bureaucratic institutions with their insistence on all-embracing coherence, knowledge, and truth. It is also to acknowledge that, even though they are impossible to maintain in practice, as indicated by Aletta Norval in her essay in this volume, they can still be meaningful practices to strive for. One major analytical consequence has to be taken note of in this analysis. The information revealed through the access points of the SATRC is not interesting as such, as Truth with a capital T. Instead, the information made public in the hearing process, the media, and the *Final Report* is important because it is here that the representation of the new nation-state is displayed, both the "heroic" inclusions and the excluded "other" of the nation-state.

Revisiting the National Script

At first glance, hard social facts nearly always present themselves as innocent. It would therefore be reasonable to ask how hard social facts, in the form of the GHRV classifications presented above, interact with the national script and with the construction of the past (i.e., Afrikaner culture) as the Other of the new nation-state.

For the new national script to be accepted so that South Africa becomes internationally recognized as a modern national state, it has to pass through the legitimate media of official truth and reconciliation commissions. In other words, truth and reconciliation commissions have become one of the means, together with international tribunals, whereby new nation-states can be accepted as bona fide nation-states. Apartheid was classified by the United Nations as a crime against humanity and the apartheid regime placed outside the international community of democratic nation-states, with all the attached implications of economic and cultural sanctions and so on. Thus, through the work of the SATRC and its internationally recognized celebration of a "culture of truth-telling," South Africa becomes liberated from its problematic past and finds its proper humanitarian self. Formerly shamefully misused and appropriated by the omnipotent apartheid regime, it takes its due place among other nation-states.

The work of the SATRC is intended to mark a definitive break with the past to define the new nation-state in contrast to the former apartheid regime. By looking carefully at the everyday work of the SATRC and relating its invisible character to its public performance, it is my hope that it has been possible to understand some of the quasi-magical steps that make the clear separation between new and old possible. What is hidden behind the access points is the material not deemed valuable for the national script. The work of the SATRC is in this sense in a double maneuver of both displaying and removing: magnification and effacement in the same movement. In other words, the SATRC is simultaneously about both remembering and forgetting.

Notes

1. The groupings that excluded themselves were the radical left and the militant right, both of which opposed the negotiated settlement: the former because the reforms negotiated in the settlement did not go far enough, and the latter because the changes went too far.
2. There are several definitions of the South African "negotiated settlement." The concept of "settlement" as I use it here refers to "the striking of a compromise, steering towards a subtle balance between opportunities and dangers, between conflicting demands—not radical solutions" (Bauman 1995: 127). The fact that apartheid was ended as a result of a negotiated settlement meant that the negotiating parties agreed to maintain the state apparatus intact and to gradually redistribute jobs through affirmative action to formerly disadvantaged social groups, mainly black people.
3. During interviews, staff members and commissioners of the SATRC stressed the importance of the work of the commission in relation to writing a new history legitimizing the transition to democracy while at the same time stressing the importance of doing so in an even-handed manner (based on fieldwork interviews, 1996, 1997, 1998, 1999).
4. I suggest that once one declines to accept the limited depth of reified public representations, not only is one forced to take into account "backstage" acts, but "onstage" dimensions, too, change character. Often seemingly incomprehensible, invisible and insignificant onstage dimensions become visible and take on new meaning. The usage of the terms onstage and backstage is an analytical distinction between official, public representations and acts and the invisible everyday practices and acts, which often are conducted by the same actors. The distinction does not imply that backstage practices are more authentic or right than onstage representations and acts; often the tensions and contradictions between them that observers encounter do not arise for the persons moving between the different domains.
5. Osiel is of the opposite opinion, stressing that trial is a more effective public spectacle, because it can "stimulate public discussion in ways that foster the liberal virtues of tolerance, moderation, and civic respect" (1997: 2).
6. The amnesty process, on the contrary, turned out to be far more legalistic than expected. To avoid the type of criticism incurred by the Nuremberg trials for not allowing accused Nazi leaders proper legal representation, the new state, through the Legal Aid Board, has spent a stupendous amount of money on legal representation for amnesty applicants.
7. One has to be careful making such a statement, because the apartheid regime made frequent

use of the courtroom for graphic demonstrations of its policy and for scapegoating opponents of its law. However, the new democratic government has amply demonstrated its inability to reinstate the rule of law, taking into account fraud trials such as the 1997–1998 case against former activist Allan Boesak, as well as the trial of former apartheid minister General Magnus Malan and ten other high-ranking former officials for the massive misappropriation of state funds to train and equip an illegal army during the late 1980s (see, e.g., R. Wilson 1995a: 42).

8. Due to the continued control of the economic field by an affluent white elite and multinational corporations and the poverty most black victims of apartheid are still subject to, the change is ultimately symbolic. This change is concerned with codifying the popular memory of apartheid suffering—which has been characterized by being fluid, unfixed, and fragmentary—to create an official history, or what is often referred to as "global truth." See R. Wilson (1996: 17) and Buur (1999) for an elaborate analysis of how codification took place in the SATRC.
9. Umkhonto We Sizwe is the name of ANC's underground army, popularly called MK, which means "the spear of the nation."
10. This section is based on field notes from two of the Biko amnesty hearings and transcripts from the amnesty hearings; see SATRC website: www.truth.org.za.
11. De Kock was found guilty before the SATRC amnesty process began and was jailed for 212 years, whereas Nieuwoudt could face a criminal trial should the SATRC deny him amnesty.
12. When, for example, the deeds of English-speaking perpetrators such as Craig Williamson, which were no less horrendous than Nieuwoudt's or de Kock's, were publicized by a SATRC hearing, he was seldom presented as anything other than a James Bond-type superspy (see, e.g., "Ex-Spy Williamson Clashes with Pik," 27 December 1995).
13. The data discussed in this essay were collected in the SATRC in 1996, 1997, 1998 and 1999 during field research conducted under the auspices of the Ph.D. project *To Establish a Truth: Victims, Perpetrators, Experts and the Work of the South African Truth and Reconciliation Commission*, Department of Ethnography and Social Anthropology, Aarhus University, Denmark, which was submitted in 2000. I am indebted to Dr. Torben Vestergaard, Department of Ethnography and Social Anthropology, Aarhus University; Dr. Martijn van Beek, Department of Ethnography and Social Anthropology, Aarhus University; Dr. Kristoffer Brix Bertelsen, The Danish Cultural Institute, Copenhagen; Professor Andre du Toit, University of Cape Town; and Ph.D. student Steffen Jensen at the Centre for Development Research, Copenhagen, for their critical comments on earlier versions of this text.
14. Seven young ANC activists were killed in a police ambush in the black township of Guguletu, twenty kilometers outside Cape Town on 3 March 1986. The police claimed then that the young men set up an ambush for the police, during which they killed them in self-defense (see TRC 1998a, 3: 451–53).
15. Vlakplaas is a farm in the Orange Free State from where the C-section of the Security Police operated and planned covert operations against enemies of the apartheid regime. De Kock was the last leader of the unit.
16. This concept is developed by Ernesto Laclau and Chantal Mouffe (1985: 127–34).
17. I do not claim that this has been a deliberate effort of the SATRC. My point is that it is a

picture emerging from a combination of several processes for which the SATRC, due to its public profile, provided the space.

18. The Afrikanerbond was formerly called the Broederbond. It was an exclusive organization for white, male Afrikaners with pro-apartheid leanings. The organization has a long history, but in today's South Africa it is known as a secretive alliance of conservative, Christian professionals and intellectuals opposed to transformation. The Afrikanerbond was established for the promotion of Afrikaner political, cultural, and economic interests, with close links to the National Party that led the apartheid government between 1948 and 1994. Since 1993 the fraternity has opened up for colored members and women ("Afrikanerbond Forges Ties with ANC" 1999).

19. Many Afrikaners have dedicated themselves to the new South Africa, and Thabo Mbeki mentions in his speech several professions from where "good" Afrikaners have emerged, including politicians, journalists, writers, and business people.

20. Institutionalization refers here to a "legitimized social grouping," assuming that if challenged, it is able to rest its claims to legitimacy on something more than just a purely instrumental or practical arrangement, for example, by being "able to rest their claims to legitimacy on their fit with the nature of the universe" (Douglas 1986: 46). Here it is enough to say that I hereby exclude the idea of an institution as merely an instrumental or provisional practical arrangement.

21. I do not claim that everyone working for the SATRC espouses the ideal of separating politics and science. Instead, I follow Schmidt, who describes idealization as being negatively defined (1993: 6). The point is that no one disputes the value of separating politics and science. The separation is therefore not a unifying ideal in the traditional sense, but something that is held in common by being indisputable. In Schmidt's analysis of architecture and its values and ideals, he defines indisputability: "What we find is the not yet experienced disagreement—the disagreement is unarticulated and need under certain circumstances not be articulated. But *if* the values have to be articulated, we immediately discover that all disagree as to what they were not disagreeing on—and they won't ever agree that they do, in fact, disagree" (7).

22. Although it is true that the everyday work of processing information in the SATRC was spelled out in an appendix to the *Final Report*, as being positivistic, it is not automatically given that this scientific positivistic ideal is actually mandated by the Act, even though this is the claim that the commission makes in the *Final Report*. In fact, the Act itself does not refer to the positivistic scientific ideal. Instead, individuals within the commission made choices when interpreting general concepts such as "objectivity," "even-handed," and "independence" in this way. The problem is that by stressing the positivistic ideal guiding the work of the SATRC, one could expect that it guided all facets of the SATRC. I stress that there are major tensions among the *process* (especially the victim hearings), the *everyday work*, and the *product* (the *Report*), and that the process itself went through different and distinct stages depending on what part of the SATRC process one analyzes. In this essay I therefore locate my concern with the bureaucratic logic as a core part of this complex and uneven process, but I do not claim that the positivistic methodology was hegemonic all along (for further elaboration, see Buur 1999).

23. Because a state institution cannot be used by the new government to investigate itself due to

the negotiated settlement, one could say that the SATRC represents the state on a higher level (it is still a state institution but a state institution working outside the state).

24. One of the fifteen official commissions analyzed by Hayner in her comparative study of official truth commissions did not share this characteristic: the Ugandan Commission of Inquiry into Violations of Human Rights, implemented in 1986 (Hayner 1994: 601, 618–20).
25. One might debate whether the SATRC is a nonretributive institution in light of the amount of public blaming and "grilling" inherent in the hearings process.
26. As Mamdani (1996b) rightly stresses, the liberal, individualized human rights perspective of the SATRC—with reference to Hannah Arendt's honored concept of the "banality of evil"—does not capture the gross institutionalized injustice of apartheid as a system. Mamdani mentions in particular "forced removals," "the pass laws," and the economic legacy of apartheid. Instead of making it possible to actively deal with the deprived living conditions of 30 million people and to deal powerfully with the causes, the individualized human rights perspective of the SATRC reaches only 22,000 victims. It therefore works as an ideological smokescreen justifying the social and economic order of today—therefore the reference to "banalities of evil."
27. The first real exposure of the fragility of the everyday work surfaced during the Heidelberg Tavern massacre amnesty hearing in Cape Town in 1997. Here, one of the commissioners, Head of the Investigative Unit Dumisa Ntzebeza, was implicated by a gardener, who alleged that he had seen Ntzebeza driving the car transporting the weapons used in the attack. He later retracted his testimony, but the implication of the leading black member of the SATRC brought one of the most serious race rows to the surface among the everyday staff members of the SATRC, who divided into two groups: black and white, for or against Ntzebeza.
28. The intentions were from the beginning to properly "investigate" each case of GHRV. But by the end of 1997 this methodology was dropped in favor of a corroboration strategy, when it became apparent that there were not enough resources available for such a resource-intensive strategy. It has to be mentioned that one reason for this shift was the resource-intensive "hearings-driven" public work of the SATRC, which began in April 1996, making it nearly impossible for the Investigative Unit to deal with cases that were not going to be presented in public. A backlog of thousands of cases (around 90 percent of the cases did not enter this public process) accumulated in the offices of the SATRC, which had to be dealt with to fulfill the mandate of the SATRC (based on fieldwork material from 1996, 1997, 1998 and interviews with investigators and leaders of the different investigative units of the SATRC).
29. This was done to identify the data, which can be categorized as "false" data. This classification is continually negotiated among the statement, the normative classifications, and the data analyst or processor. In this process, the statement is experimented with and used in different ways, just as the normative classifications are negotiated among the different role-players: commissioners, statements takers, data processors, investigators, human rights organizations, victims and perpetrators, and so on. To understand the complex process of establishing the facts about GHRVs it is important to remember that in the construction and negotiation of what "false" data are, the statement as well as the processors and analysts and the computer software are active participants in the game.
30. The names of the everyday workers have been changed.

31. One could have expected the use of "labor strikes" to be more appropriate here than the use of "boycott." Boycott as a strategy during the campaign of the United Democratic Front was "a campaign not to buy or use certain products or services" and was an inherent part of the language in the DPU room, where most of the data processors were sitting.
32. The intention behind using this spelling of (arti)facts for artifact without brackets is that I want to direct attention to the double nature of the concept. It is both a human construction as well as a "fact" that connotes something more solid.
33. The "normative classification scheme" was the emic name among data processors in the Cape Town office for what was known as the "controlled vocabulary of violations" by more computer-literate and human rights database–trained staff.
34. At management and commissioner levels of the SATRC the "classification scheme" or "controlled vocabulary" was actually reduced, not augmented, from over two hundred violations to fewer than fifty, of which only twenty-five were used in any meaningful way to classify people on the database (based on Internet discussions with one of the creators of the database, Patrick Ball, 1999). One explanation could be that a range of subcategories was developed for each of the main categories in the "controlled vocabulary." According to Ball, the head data processor in the Johannesburg office organized the effort and directed its application among data processors all over the country, but, as mentioned above, the diffusion of the changes was rather slow. This apparent contradiction tells its own story about how differently hierarchically placed people within the same institution can interpret and work with the "same" heuristic tool, call it something different, and interpret its development differently.
35. Because it is not possible to define every instance as a GHRV, there are, as mentioned, many checks and balances in place within the structure: persons, normative classifications, meetings, and so on designed to pick up "mistakes."
36. Right from the beginning of the SATRC it was planned to grant what were called "urgent relief reparations" to victims of GHRVs. Several countries, including Denmark and Switzerland, granted up to $1 million each to the Presidents Fund for this purpose, but the process never really materialized. The first payment of 2000 Rands (approximately U.S.$350) was rather symbolically paid just a few days before the official closure of the work of the SATRC in July 1998.
37. Among staff members a phrase often repeated when they aired these sentiments was: "The circus comes to town." This phrase refers to the intervention process, when the SATRC would set up a hearing in a specific locality in a period of a few weeks. Statement takers, logistics officers, investigators, researchers, the media, and finally the commissioners in "their big BMWs or Mercedeses" would arrive for the hearing. The day after the hearing "the circus" would leave town and the local community would be "forgotten" (based on fieldwork notes, 1997).

    A workshop was held in Cape Town for staff members in 1997 in which several commissioners and committee members participated. The aim of the workshop was to create an internal forum where the frustrations arising after the shift from victim-driven hearings to amnesty hearings could be dealt with openly.
38. It is proposed by the Reparation and Rehabilitation Committee that the maximum amount a

victim can receive is 120,000 Rands (approximately U.S.$20,000) over a period of six years, and the lowest amount is 80,000 Rands (approximately U.S.$13,500). Whether the government will implement the SATRC recommendation regarding final reparations remains an issue in South Africa, much to the anger of people classified by the SATRC as victims of GHRVs, who feel betrayed by the SATRC promising relief without following through.

39. The concept is taken from Lars-Henrik Schmidt (1993), who relies on the work of Michel Foucault.

40. The concept of "access points" is developed by Giddens and refers to "points of connection between lay individuals or collectives and the representatives of abstract systems. They are places of vulnerability for abstract systems, but also junctions at which trust can be maintained or built up" (1992: 88).

41. By emphasizing the question of control, I can be said to differ from Weber, who, as the quote indicates, saw bureaucratic institutions as "keeping their knowledge and intentions secret" (1968a: 244).

42. Most prominently Pierre Bourdieu who, inspired by Durkheim, states that a practical belief, in this case, that the constitutive separation between science and politics is maintained, is "an inherent part of belonging" (1990: 67). Processes of belonging are, in Bourdieu's understanding, double-edged. On the one hand, they confirm the taken-for-granted understanding people have of their own life conditions, and on the other hand, they create "misrecognition," a kind of amnesia toward that which may confront the taken-for-granted relation to the world. "Genesis implies amnesia of genesis," he polemically writes (1977: 19). The relation Bourdieu points at is the relation between what one can speak about and the unspeakable, and the role of the anthropologist, who is committed to do more than just reproduce the self-understanding of groups of people, their taken-for-granted relation to the world. By speaking about what people take for granted and objectifying it, the anthropologist can easily end up being seen as a cultural *spielverderber*—telling people that they misunderstand their own life conditions. The question is whether Bourdieu in his theory of practice does not put too much emphasis on belonging and the reproduction of a sense of belonging, thereby ending up with an understanding of individuals and groups as well-integrated entities. The question is whether people, and groups of people, can both accept the loss of innocence that objectification implies—for example, by acknowledging that the constitutive separation between politics and science cannot be maintained—and at the same time still be committed to it without this adjustment necessarily having fatal consequences for their belief in, for example, the work of the SATRC. Thomas Blom Hansen's contribution to this volume seems to imply so.

RECONSTRUCTING NATIONAL IDENTITY AND RENEGOTIATING MEMORY The Work of the TRC

Aletta J. Norval

In this essay I attempt to disaggregate several important dimensions of the manner in which the memory of the past is being negotiated and reconstructed in and through the work of the South African Truth and Reconciliation Commission (TRC), established by an Act of Parliament to investigate and expose gross violations of human rights[1] that took place under the apartheid regime, covering the period from March 1960 to May 10, 1994.[2] I argue that to do justice to the complexities of this process one has to explore the relation between memory and identity and, more specifically, memory and *national* identity. In short, I wish to bring to the fore the fact that the institution of a new national imaginary that has to articulate a relation to apartheid history is no simple matter. The issue is complicated even further if we want that process to facilitate an opening up onto a postapartheid, postnational society. I intend to offer a certain reading of the logic of apartheid and the negotiation of its memory in the work of the TRC that may point to such an opening, to a future that is no longer dominated by apartheid.[3] However, I argue that this is realizable only on condition that certain of the inherent limitations of the work of the TRC and, by implication, that of the discourse of nonracialism, are overcome.

Reinventing the Myth of Nationhood

As Hansen and Stepputat point out in their introduction to this volume, the myth of the state may be considered a form of "social fantasy" circulating among citizens and communities. Conceptions of nationhood form part and parcel of this social fantasy, and the TRC is a participant in the struggle for instituting a hegemonic conception of that fantasy or, as I prefer to call it, social imaginary. Drawing on the distinction between myth and imaginary developed in the work of Laclau, I argue that South Africa faces a struggle between a multiplicity of myths of nationhood.[4] That is, the posttransition period has been marked by a series of struggles around conceptions of community, nationhood, ethnicity, and so forth, each of which contributes to and contests the institution of an overarching conception of identity. New myths typically emerge during and as a result of periods of deep dislocation and may be regarded as attempts to suture the fissures that have opened up as a result of those dislocations. There is no doubt that during the 1980s and 1990s South Africa faced an organic crisis, part of which entailed a putting into question of the apartheid imaginary.[5] During the final years of the crisis the discourse of nationhood articulated by the African National Congress (ANC), that of nonracialism, dominated the political landscape as *the* alternative to apartheid. However, even this apparent dominance was contested by alternative discourses such as that of "self-determination" increasingly shared between the Inkatha Freedom Party and the far-right Afrikaner Freedom Front.[6] In the years following the first democratic elections the unquestioned acceptance of the discourse of nonracialism has come increasingly under pressure. Without the immediate presence of "an enemy," the apartheid state, it has become more difficult to hold together "the people," for the unity of the people depend, at least in part, on its opposition to the forces of oppression. Having to assume the mantle of government in a period of transition characterized by its search for reconciliation among different sectors of the society made the task of reconstructing a widely acceptable conception of nationhood even more difficult. It is in this terrain that the work of the TRC has to be placed if it is to be understood properly.

Critics of the TRC have suggested that it is nothing but an instrument of the state, and of the ANC in particular.[7] This criticism is based upon a particularly primitive conception of the state and often ignores its legal and moral autonomy, as well as efforts to establish and maintain its political impartiality, yet there may well be a grain of truth in the accusation. However, this is not to be found where critics of the TRC usually locate it: in an inability to take a critical distance from the ANC, leading to an unquestioned acceptance of their "version" of the past.[8] Rather, it is to be found in the conception of nationhood emerging from the pronouncements and publications of the TRC. To substantiate this claim, it is necessary briefly to highlight some of the main contours of the conception of nonracialism that has informed ANC political discourse historically.[9] In contrast to the identitarian conception of nationhood structuring the apartheid imaginary, nonracialism aims at opening a space for difference of a linguistic, cultural, and religious nature without, however, conceding ground on the basis of race. In so doing, it acknowledges the historical legacy of apartheid but seeks to overcome it through an emphasis on political equality regardless of race, creed, and religion, stressing the need for the four "historic groups"—Africans, whites, coloureds, and Indians—to build a common society.[10]

To the extent that the TRC participates in the building and reconstruction of a "common society," it is necessary to place its activities in the context of a posttransitional democratic government facing social demands for an official recognition of the truth about human rights violations committed by the previous regime, and for dealing with those guilty of ordering and committing those violations.[11] The last two decades of this century have been marked by a growing interest in these issues and how they affect transitions. It is not possible to give a detailed account of the different contexts in which these issues arose over the past ten years. Suffice it to say that historically such processes have taken many different forms, ranging from special national tribunals (Argentina), to international tribunals (Nuremberg and Hague tribunals), to individuals (Chile, Paraguay, and Uruguay) and nongovernmental groups (Honduras, Uruguay, Paraguay) taking their cases to national or international courts.[12]

There are, equally, many ways in which these processes may be approached analytically. One could, for instance, focus on the political conditions that permitted or inhibited the realization of practices of truth telling under successor regimes. Such a focus would demand a detailed examination of the repressive, constitutional, and political legacies of specific transitional contexts, as well as of how democratizing political conditions shape the ability of governments to deal with issues of truth and justice.[13] Alternatively, or in addition to this, one may focus on the manner in which collective identities, national self-images, and political cultures are negotiated, reworked, and reconstructed in the course of investigations into past abuses of human rights. To paraphrase Perelli, the resignification of the past does not serve only to explain the present; it is, indeed, a struggle for control over the future.[14] Thus, reconstructing collective memory and instituting new foundational myths do more than "deal with the past"; they act as legitimizing moments for and shape the character of new regimes. It is on these issues that I wish to focus in this essay.

Why a Truth Commission?

It is now two years since the TRC brought out its final report.[15] Its task, in the words of Vice-Chairperson of the Commission Alex Boraine, was to contribute to the healing process in South Africa through "an honest assessment and diagnosis of the sickness within our society in an attempt to give people, both perpetrators and victims, an opportunity to face the past and its consequences and to start afresh. The Truth and Reconciliation Commission is an opportunity to make a contribution to deal finally with the past without dwelling in it and to help to create the conditions for a truly new South Africa."[16]

In attempting to address questions central to the process of transition, namely, how emerging democracies come to terms with past violations of human rights, how new democratic governments deal with leaders and individuals who were responsible for disappearances, death squads, and psychological and physical torture, and how it deals with the fact that some of its perpetrators continue to play important roles in public life, South Africa has decided that the way forward is to be through the work of this commission, rather than through Nuremberg-style trials.[17] After extensive discussion, the idea of such trials was rejected on several grounds. The first was a concern with the difficulty of proving guilt in the context of a criminal legal justice system. As the Nuremberg trials showed, in cases of political trials where large numbers of people acted as members of political organizations, it is very difficult to determine individual legal responsibility. A second reason was the difficulty in gaining evidence of such acts. It was generally agreed that there was very little likelihood of new evidence coming to light or of witnesses being prepared to testify in the context of criminal trials. Most important, however, is the consideration that the granting of amnesty was a central part of the very process that made the negotiated transition possible. As Desmond Tutu pointed out, "Many of those now calling for justice through criminal trials supported the negotiated settlement at Kempton Park, and seem to forget that amnesty was a crucial ingredient of the compromise which reversed the country's inevitable descent into a bloodbath."[18]

Instead, it was agreed that the TRC should proceed through attempting to answer, on the one hand, the demands of those who lost family and friends to know the truth surrounding those circumstances and, on the other, to provide an opportunity for perpetrators of abuses to make full disclosures of their crimes in return for amnesty.[19] It is only in and through full disclosure (truth telling) that justice as acknowledgment can be attained; this, in turn, opens up the possibility of reconciliation.[20] I argue that public recognition and acknowledgment of injustices thus constitute the basis for the attainment of justice.[21] That is why the role of public acknowledgment of memories of the past in the reconstruction of the present and the future is absolutely crucial to the whole process. With the creation of this commission, South Africa, in the words of a commentator, "has decided to say no to amnesia and yes to remembrance; to say no to full-scale prosecutions and yes to forgiveness."[22] This sentiment was already clearly expressed in the new Constitution. Its last section, dealing with "National Unity and Reconciliation," includes the following statement: "The adoption of this Constitution lays the secure foundation for the people of South Africa to transcend the divisions and strife of the past, which generated gross violations of human rights, the transgression of humanitarian principles in violent conflicts and a legacy of hatred, fear, guilt and revenge. These can now be addressed on the basis that there is a need for understanding but not for vengeance, a need for reparation but not for retaliation."

But, one may ask, what precisely is the role of memory in this process, and how is it to be negotiated so that it avoids two excesses—that of too much dwelling on the past and of too little disclosure—both of which will make reconciliation well nigh impossible? Indeed, one may want to reflect somewhat further on the very possibility and nature of the "reconciliation" that is to be achieved, on its precise relation to remembrance, and on the relation between memory and identity in general.

Memory and Identity

Let me start with the latter. The notion of identity depends on the idea of memory, and vice versa. Any individual or group identity, that is, a sense of sameness over time and space, is sustained by remembering, and what is remembered is defined by the assumed identity.[23] Memories are constantly revised to suit our current identity, and this *memory work* is always embedded in "complex class, gender and power relations that determine what is remembered (or forgotten), by whom, and for what end."[24] Indeed, at this moment, when it is apparent that both identity and memory are political and social constructs,[25] and when we can no longer assign to either the status of a "natural object," we "must take responsibility for their uses and abuses, recognizing that every assertion of identity involves a choice that affects not just ourselves but others."[26]

History avails us a multiplicity of examples of the gravity of that responsibility—here, one only needs to think of the history and historical narratives on the Holocaust—and of widely diverging ways in which memory and identity interact. In situations of "new beginnings," identities are constructed and held together as much by forgetting as by remembering. Such new beginnings sometimes require the eradication of the past and engagement in what Benedict Anderson has called "collective amnesia."[27] This is most evident in the construction of new states in postrevolutionary situations: revolution has to inaugurate an absolute beginning that necessitates the introduction of "new time" and a radical break with the past. Constructing a new Japan and two new Germanys after the Second World War also involved forgetting rather than remembering.[28] It is, moreover, of interest to note that even in the case of the construction of the new state of Israel, the first few years focused more on the present than the past. The concept of the Holocaust only came into existence in the 1950s, after the new state was firmly established and Jews could reflect on the "pastness of the European past." It was only when the memory of those terrible events could no longer be taken for granted that there was a powerful reason to commemorate.[29] Even the need to commemorate then has a history. Gillis argues that commemoration historically has taken roughly three forms: prenational (before the late eighteenth century), national (from the American and French Revolutions to the 1960s), and postnational forms. The early, prenational history of memory shows a sharp divergence between popular and elite memory: whereas the elite classes (the aristocracy, the church, and the monarchical state) had a need for institutionalized memory, ordinary people relied on living memory. National memories, in contrast, tend to focus on the construction of unity and continuity so as to cover over the fragility of new nations.[30]

As our concern is with modern, national memory, it is necessary to reflect further on some of its most central characteristics. National memory is above all archival: it relies on the immediacy of the recording and on the visibility of the image.[31] It is also, however, acutely aware of the efforts of each group to make *its* version *the* basis of national identity. It is thus aware of conflicting accounts of the past. And it is out of this awareness that a different relation to the past emerges in what Gillis calls the *postnational* era, a relation that bears a strong resemblance to the struggles at the time of the Reformation between older Catholic practices of locating the sacred only in certain times and places, and the antiritualistic, iconoclastic Protestants, who demanded that the sacred be brought into everyday life itself. The new iconoclasm attempts to *desacralize* the nation-state, to *democratize* memory, and to retrace a *multiplicity of pasts* better suited to the complexities of a postnational era.[32]

This account provides us with valuable insights into questioning the relation between memory and identity as it is being played out in South Africa today, in the movement toward a postapartheid society. In South Africa, the struggle over the meaning of the past is by no means over, its character by no means settled. Although there is a general agreement on the evil that apartheid represented, that agreement, some argue, has been reached without a thoroughgoing engagement with the past.[33] One only has to think here of the refusal to engage with the work of the TRC evident in the submission of the chief of the South African National Defence Force (SANDF), General G. L. Meiring, to the commission. Instead of focusing on the period under investigation, the submission dealt with the transition period only. The few scant references to the past, moreover, were couched in terms of "acts perpetrated in the context of a war situation." Indeed, this was a characteristic that marked the submissions of all the main parties. It is to these submissions, to the wider discourses informing them, and to the manner in which they relate to and commemorate the past that I turn now.[34]

Identitarian Constructions of the Past

"We are all the children of our times and the product of the cultural and political circumstances into which we were born and with which we grew up," wrote F. W. De Klerk.[35]

We know that during the period of transition in South Africa, many different articulations have been given to the memory of the past. These range from National Party appeals to put the past behind us, to nostalgic demands for a certain resurrection of apartheid, be that in the form of an Afrikaner *Volkstaat* or an independent KwaZulu. National Party discourse, for instance, continuously admonished the people not to be obsessed with past grievances, not to insist on "apologies for everything that has occurred in the past," and to "let bygones be bygones." Indeed, it was argued that one should not "dwell on the real or imagined injustices of the past," but work toward building a future "without mistrust, prejudice, hate and domination."[36]

These themes are echoed throughout the National Party submission to the TRC, which exhibits an exemplary form of "nationalist" history, with all its monuments and archives, its exclusions and denials.[37] National identity, in this reading, is natural, given, and pure, constituted with reference only to the characteristics of the "nation" itself. In denying the fundamentally relational nature of identity, this account attempts to efface the difference at the heart of every identity, and in so doing affirms an essentialist, identitarian, homogeneous, and nonpluralistic conception of nationhood.[38] Young's description of nationalist monuments perfectly encapsulates the account of Afrikaner history presented there. The submission plots "the story of ennobling events, of triumphs over barbarism, and recalls the martyrdom of those who gave their lives in the struggle for national existence."[39]

Much of the submission, then, is taken up by setting out the historical context within which "the conflicts of the past" and "unconventional actions and reactions" should be considered, according to its authors. The emphasis on the plural case here is noteworthy: the conflicts involved many forces, and the commission is constantly reminded that "no single side in the conflict has a monopoly of virtue or should bear responsibility for all the abuses that occurred."[40] Indeed, in judging abuses, de Klerk argues that distinctions should be drawn among those carrying out orders, those carrying out orders "overzealously," and those committing malpractices and serious violations of human rights. But, above all, the context of these actions—working within a state of emergency—had to be considered so as "to explain the historical context in which they occurred."[41] One is struck by the contrast between this narrative and accounts of the Holocaust that, time and again, run up against the sheer inexplicability of its evil. While, in the National Party's case, there is an acknowledgment of the suffering of all those involved in the conflict, the whole submission serves to provide a context that could explain, and so justify, the actions perpetrated.[42] Indeed, this is a feature of all the submissions by political parties, organizations, and state institutions.

Now, in stark contrast to the certainties and clear-cut justifications that have informed the submission of the National Party and of the other main political organizations and official institutions, the whole of the transition process itself was marked indelibly by a series of ambiguities. Because the end of apartheid came about not as a result of a revolutionary break or a complete discontinuity that divided the past from the present and future, it had the character of an impure transition. This raises precise problems for the negotiation of memory, truth, and the institution of a just and democratic society. It both imposes restrictions and opens possibilities for those processes of negotiation. In the first instance, as de Brito notes, because repressors are not defeated, but even given a degree of political legitimacy by their "voluntary withdrawal" from power, successor regimes must avoid a backlash that may endanger the stability of the transition.[43] Second, negotiated democratic transitions set frameworks within which truth and justice have to be pursued: democratic pluralism ensures that voices of victims are heard at the same time as it ensures a continued voice for violators. Third, under these circumstances, there usually are state institutions that survive; institutionalized crimes have to be dealt with, and there must simultaneously be a concern for not entirely destroying state institutions. Fourth, mechanisms and institutions dealing with abuses must be seen to comply with judicial due process so as to strengthen the institutionalization of democratic procedures, even if that means that some of those who are guilty of abuses may not be brought to book as a result of a lack of evidence.[44] In all of these cases, the new regimes are engaged in ambiguous processes of negotiation that are a far cry from demands for clear-cut ethical stances and decisions. It would, therefore, be strange if these ambiguities did not also enter into the processes in and through which past memories and new beginnings are negotiated.

Toward a Different Remembrance

It is in this context that the memory work of the TRC has to be understood. The important investigative work of this commission has brought to light the existence of state structures for identifying targets for elimination, firsthand claims of ministerial-level approval of bombings and killings—all those activities that the National Party submission euphemistically called "unconventional actions"—as well as events known, until now, only to the communities immediately affected by them. Indeed, I would argue that one of the most important effects of the memory work of the TRC is the way it has offered an occasion for survivors to gain recognition of their plight in full public view.[45] In these public hearings, submissions were allowed to contain names of perpetrators of abuses (the TRC's investigative unit sought to check these as carefully as possible beforehand; it warned persons to be named and invited them to respond to allegations) and sought to bring to public attention both well-known events and everyday injustices perpetrated against persons hitherto unnamed.[46] In this focus on the everydayness of injustice, and the reoccupation of memory sites by ordinary citizens, the real significance of the public hearings and the search for justice becomes visible. As one commentator on a similar process elsewhere has put it: It does not bring the dead back to life, but it brings them out from silence; for their families, it means the end to an agonizing, endless search.[47]

The end of those searches, of course, depends on the knowledge obtained during the whole process. As the daughter of an activist argued: "I want to forgive, but I don't know whom to forgive." Steve Biko's mother, shortly before her death last year, said much the same: "Yes, I would forgive my son's killers. I am a Christian, and we Christians do forgive. But first I must know what to forgive, which means I must be told fully what happened and why."[48] The hearings consequently have offered an opportunity not only for survivors, but also for perpetrators of violence to come forward and give full statements of their participation in events. In this manner, reconciliation was sought between the parties participating in and affected by the events.[49] Not only high-ranking officers were brought to book, but low-ranking police officers and ordinary citizens were given the chance to partake in what I would argue is a public memorial exercise that differs from the "standard" nationalist uses of memory and monuments.[50]

Thus, the TRC steered South Africa away from a culture of violence. But it also had several effects that arguably no other form of engagement with the past could have had. It has subverted the ability of national leaders of all persuasions to grasp and represent history in their own image; it has undermined both the possibilities, mentioned earlier, that may make reconciliation impossible: and it helped to avoid too much pastness as well as a covering over of the past. In contrast to the usual constructions of memories of a nation's past, this exercise has brought to light no *singular* past and has commemorated no one *unified* nationhood. The inability to construct such a singular narrative is admitted to in the *Final Report*, which states that in the promotion of national unity and reconciliation, reconciliation cannot be imposed on a diverse society attempting to consolidate a fragile democracy. A healthy democracy requires only respect for common human dignity and shared citizenship, as well as mechanisms for the peaceful handling of unavoidable conflicts. It does not require everyone to agree.[51]

The memory work, therefore, performs a multitude of complicated functions. Through it, all discourses of nationhood and the idea of sacrificing one's life for national existence become problematized, if only as a result of the absence of a singular narrative. Through it, the past is recalled so that it becomes possible to leave the past behind. This memory work is to be supplemented with a public archive where all the materials obtained by the commission will be lodged. This contains the seeds of a relation to past and to memory that may lead South Africa to a *postnational* conception of identity, a conception of identity that takes its character from the distance it takes from that which was exemplary in the identitarian conception of identity that informed apartheid.[52]

On the Possibility of a Postnational Identity

The possibility of a postnational (postapartheid) identity depends on the ability to go beyond apartheid insofar as apartheid functions as a signifier of closure. If apartheid signifies the denial of difference at the heart of identity, a remembrance of apartheid would consist in a remembrance of (the effects of) closure as such. A pluralistic, postapartheid social order will, consequently, be a form of social division in which the constitutive nature of difference is thought. It is this constituting function of difference, the holding-against-an-other, that I would argue becomes visible in the memory work of the TRC. This can further be clarified by analogy to the structure of memory. Remembrance (technically, primary remembrance or retention) serves as the not-now that is constitutive of the possibility of the presence of the Now.[53] Remembrance thus in essence points to the incompleteness of the present. If a postnational order is to be characterized by such a remembrance, it is structurally determined as incomplete. However, this remembering is not to be of just anything. It is to be a remembering of the logic of closure. Thus, we have here a double signification: a remembering as such, which already reminds us of the incompleteness of our present; and a remembrance of something, of a discourse of closure. These two moments reciprocally reinforce one another and serve to show that which cannot be made present. Its marking, paradoxically, can consist only in keeping open the space, the interval between the present and the past, the now and that which preceded the now. In remembering apartheid as a logic of closure, the work of the TRC may open the space for difference that will not immediately be subsumed and transformed into a logic of othering.[54] This remembrance may be able to *encircle*, to mark the space of difference as such constitutive of any already constituted identity.

Beyond the TRC?

"The South African Truth Commission is only one of the structures through which we should hope to dismantle the old regime of truth to replace it with new and multiple narratives. We must remain aware of the dangers of replacing apartheid's false utopian historicism with our own new orthodoxies. As we construct new historical narratives, it will be in the currency of *heterotopias*, multiple idealisms, rather than the single-mindedness of utopia. . . . Our state-sponsored Commission has no monopoly on processes of historical rectification."[55]

Like all narrative structures, the plurality of discourses that, woven together, form the discursive structure of the TRC display certain blind spots. These blind spots have acted as conditions of both possibility and impossibility: they mark the exclusions on which the TRC was set up as an exercise, and they ultimately put into question its parameters. A number of contemporary writings have set out to make visible such blind spots in the discourses of and around the TRC. As a consequence, they open up areas of investigation beyond the remit, and perhaps beyond the conceptual structure of the TRC.

These blind spots may take a variety of forms, ranging from institutional mechanisms and procedures in the actual operation of the TRC to exclusions built into its very remit. To begin with, although much research still needs to be done, a number of writers have begun to question the institutional mechanisms and procedures deployed by the TRC. I focus on only two such areas here, as they impact more directly than other areas on the main concerns under discussion: that of the relation between the TRC and NGOs, and that of the internal procedures deployed to make decisions within substructures of the TRC concerning, for instance, the allocation of "victim status" to applicants. In their study of the relation between the TRC and NGOs, Merwe, Dewhirst, and Hamber point out that the failure of NGOs to "effectively mobilize around the principles and strategic concerns" raised by the TRC could be ascribed, in part, to the structure and process of the TRC.[56] They list four factors that were of significance: the TRC's framework of operation, its political agenda, political tension within the organization that affected the relationship between the TRC and the NGOs, and its internal management structures. For our purposes, the first three are of particular interest.[57] Its framework of operation came in for criticism from NGOs operating outside the human rights sector, arguing that the TRC was based on an overly legalistic framework and that it emphasized investigation and rights-based mechanisms and procedures at the expense of grassroots conflict resolution and social support work. As a result, the TRC failed to engage with the local complexities of particular communities where it held hearings; it underestimated conflicts arising from economic injustices; and its emphasis on gross violations of human rights rather than on the more common violations that "made up the day-to-day experiences of most black people" was seen as potentially marginalizing. The organizations also felt that the TRC's work did not fit in with the national political agendas toward which the work of the TRC was geared. This was also at the root of the internal tensions within the TRC, arising as a result of the need to represent different political persuasions in its composition. Although the TRC, as argued earlier, made great efforts to establish its impartiality, it was reluctant to engage too closely with NGOs for fear of being accused of having too close alliances with political groupings. The NGOs also raised concerns about the simplistic nature of the categorizations into which the TRC divided applicants. The victim/perpetrator dichotomy did not necessarily reflect the experience of the person in the street, just as it probably oversimplified the categorization of major political actors. A disquiet with this categorization and its construction and implementation is also expressed by Lars Buur, based on fieldwork conducted in the Data Processing Unit. Analyzing and problematizing the detailed discussions that lead to persons being attributed "victim" status, Buur draws attention to the contingent decisions, all of which would contribute to the reconstruction of a "new," officially sanctioned history of the past.[58] The TRC has also been exposed to a series of more wide-ranging criticisms. It is to these that I turn in conclusion.

Addressing the very nature of the TRC remit, Steve Robins argues that the TRC has privileged a "modern temporal frame" by taking the whole of its investigation to be delimited by the beginning and end of the apartheid era.[59] One of the consequences of such a framing is that it raises the question of how the histories and collective memories of those "deemed not to have the necessary biological, historical, and cultural background to legitimately speak about 'black experience' under apartheid" will be dealt with.[60] This is not an idle question, but one that goes to the heart of the new national imaginary under construction in contemporary South Africa. Indeed, there is a bias even more narrowly defined than "black experience" that informs this imaginary in the making. One only has to look at the construction of the history of resistance in the writings of some of the prominent government commentators on the TRC. Asmal, Asmal, and Roberts's account of resistance to apartheid, in the context of their discussion of the work of the Truth Commission, crucially limits itself to an account of ANC resistance. Ignoring not only the role of political organizations such as the Pan Africanist Congress and the Black Consciousness movement, it also negates the crucial role of the United Democratic Front (UDF) in the final phase of internal resistance against apartheid. This is no accident, reflecting as it does a very particular history of resistance from the perspective of the ANC in exile. Coupled with the marginalization of UDF and other internal resistance leaders who led democratic opposition inside the country during the crucial years of the 1980s and early 1990s since the return of the exiled leadership, this marginalization appears all the more sinister. Add to that the earlier criticisms of ANC government policies of "affirmative action" by minority groups such as coloured South Africans,[61] and the practical embodiment of the project of nonracialism begins to look all the more flawed. Indeed, one has to question whether what appears at first to be limitations of implementation are not indicators of deeper underlying problems with the vision of nonracialism.[62]

Nevertheless, it could be argued that the fact that the ANC's version of nonracialism is flawed does not necessarily contaminate that propounded by the TRC. The question to be addressed here is whether the practices and viewpoints of the TRC are marked by traces of the closure of identitarian politics—similar to that of the official ideology of nonracialism—even while they are straining to institute a certain pluralism. Indeed, it would be surprising if they were not. These traces could be found, most clearly, in the TRC's representation of the old regime and the entity called the "apartheid state." It is commonplace in the literature on apartheid to question the portrayal of both the project of apartheid and the character of the state in monolithic terms.[63] Yet, the TRC consistently treats "the state" as a homogeneous entity. In the words of the *Final Report*, "The South African state in the period from the late 1970s to [the] early 1990s became involved in activities of a criminal nature when, amongst other things, it knowingly planned, undertook, condoned and covered up the commission of unlawful acts."[64] To question the portrayal of the state as homogeneous entity is not to problematize the main findings of the TRC. It is, however, to draw attention to the problems that such a portrayal may hold for the future. The inability to recognize that different state sectors pursued sometimes markedly different strategies, some arguing from greater repression and others proposing greater liberalization, is to ignore the differences in reforms that may be necessary to construct a truly postapartheid state.

These limitations, however, deal only with exclusions operating "within the present," so to speak. It is now necessary to look more closely at the systematic exclusion of colonial violence in the TRC's reconstruction of the past.[65] The character and complexity of colonial violence and the manner in which it impacts on contemporary South Africa are made visible in a number of contemporary publications. Several new signifiers have emerged as paradigmatic of what is at stake here. They include the figures of Saartje Baartman and Krotoä, as well as the "Miscast" exhibition.[66] While each signifies its own unique singularity, together they act as signs of a new vision of South African identity, one that aims to put into question any homogeneous narrative of nationhood. The struggle for the meaning of Robben Island is a case in point. Harriet Deacon traces the shifts in the symbolization of the island from a repository of "all that was considered negative in society" to acting as "a focus for remembering apartheid and as a spearhead for national revival."[67] Emphasizing the importance of this new symbol in the construction of a new national identity around the observance of human rights, Deacon also draws attention to the negative possibilities of presenting too unitary an account of its significance. She argues that, if it is to be a living monument for the new South Africa, it should also permit diversity "in its opening outwards to other accounts of our past and our future."[68]

In similar vein, Carli Coetzee provides a nuanced discussion of the ways in which Krotoä is remembered today. Through an exploration of the figure of Krotoä (a Khoikhoi woman in Cape Town in the seventeenth century) she addresses both the conditions and implications of the fact that Krotoä, once written out of history, is now reclaimed as *onse ma*, the mother of Afrikaners seeking to reestablish connections with Africa. Coetzee discusses the dangers and advances in such a "return" to Krotoä. Taking her as the founding mother of the Afrikaner people is to reinforce both the urban, Cape Town–based version of South Africa's early history, and to perpetuate the myth of 1652 as its starting point.[69] Moreover, this return to Africa, to Krotoä as mother of the nation, also necessitates amnesia about how and why she was forgotten. In contrast to the writings on Krotoä during the apartheid era, contemporary appropriations offer Afrikaans-speaking South Africans a way to identify with Africa and with a hybrid, instead of a "pure race," identity. However, Coetzee warns against a too easy appropriation that risks "forgetting the conflict and destruction" at the roots of this hybrid identity. Most problematic of this appropriation is "the sense of completeness" of closure that it brings.

The "Miscast" exhibition is an example of the impossibility of maintaining such final closure. "Miscast" functioned, not unlike the Truth Commission, as confessional space, but it had the added advantage of forcing whites "to confront European colonial violence and genocide."[70] It rendered the previously forgotten history of colonialism visible, and in so doing called forth widely divergent responses from different communities. This was the case especially for the design of one of the galleries of the exhibition, constructed so that viewers could not avoid walking on images of the aboriginal KhoiSan people. Angry KhoiSan responses challenged the use of these images and of fragmented body parts as a reenactment, not a critique, of colonial violence. While the "Miscast" exhibition forced whites to confront colonial violence and challenged the exclusionary emphasis on contemporary history in the TRC, it was also used by KhoiSan activists to construct "totalizing ethnic-nationalist narratives that draw upon collective memories of suffering."[71] KhoiSan descendants used the exhibition to advance their current claims to land.[73] In so doing, they invoked discourses of cultural continuity and purity to precolonial KhoiSan ancestors, such as Saartje Baartman and Krotoä.

Conclusion

The meaning and significance of figures such as Krotoä, and the divergent if not clashing appropriations to which they have been subject, attest to the complexity of the processes of the reclaiming of histories. It also throws into sharp relief the fact that contestation of the narratives organizing and framing the TRC does not automatically carry any "subversive" or democratizing connotations. Unitary discourses may be challenged only to be reinvoked at a more particularized level. The apparent opposition between universalism and particularism, between an emphasis on, for instance, "the nation" and "different (national) groups," may thus be misleading. Neither extreme universalist nor deeply particularist views of identity, of necessity, will escape the identitary logic of apartheid. To do so, an emphasis on the noncompletion and interpenetration of both must be maintained. This potentially could be achieved by pluralizing discourses such as that of the TRC. However, as I have argued, this potential will be realized only on condition that more work is done to avoid the closures that a more homogenizing version of nonracialism may bring about.

Notes

I would like to thank Thomas Blom Hansen and Finn Stepputat for their helpful comments on an earlier version of this essay. Some of the arguments were first developed and published elsewhere. I thank Blackwell's for permission to draw on a previously published article (Norval 1998a).

1. The Promotion of National Unity and Reconciliation Bill of 1995 defines gross violations of human rights as the killing, abduction, torture, or severe ill treatment of any person by someone acting with a political objective. It includes the planning of such acts and attempts to commit them.
2. The TRC was constituted by the Promotion of National Unity and Reconciliation Bill, 1995, which combines the requirements of the interim Constitution with those of human rights norms. The significance of this is clear when it is compared to alternative processes through which truth commissions historically have been constituted. In most instances, commissions of this sort are appointed by a president or prime minister of the country concerned, and they have to work out their own procedures, objectives, and methodologies. The benefit of a commission appointed by an Act of Parliament is that a democratically elected group of people participated in the debate and the finalizing of the objectives of the commission (Boraine 1996b). For a detailed discussion of the background on the idea of the TRC in South Africa, see Walt and Walt (1996: 1–21), as well as the information pack published by the TRC (n.d.).
3. For an elaboration of the idea of a postapartheid identity, see Norval (1990: 155–57; 1996: 275–305).
4. I draw here on the distinction as developed by Laclau (1990: 60–68).
5. For an in-depth discussion of this period of South African politics as well as of the various dimensions of the crisis, see Norval (1996: chaps. 5, 6).
6. For a more detailed discussion of these discourses, see Norval (1996: chap. 6; 1998b: 93–110).
7. This criticism was voiced in many quarters, not all of which were "conservative." In their study of the relation between the TRC and NGOs, Merwe, Dewhirst, and Hamber point out that some NGOs were reluctant to work too closely with the TRC, because the TRC was seen as engaged in a national political agenda, of which the Inkatha Freedom Party (IFP) and Pan African Conference (PAC) in particular were suspicious (1999: 68–69).
8. Although there is some evidence that the TRC has experienced difficulties distancing itself from the ANC—particularly visible in its treatment of the now infamous ANC application for

"blanket" amnesty—the TRC in the round has succeeded rather well in not simply echoing what the government wanted to hear.

9. For a discussion of nonracialism, see various contributions to Poley (1988) as well as *Selected Writings on the Freedom Charter* 1955–1985 (1985).
10. For a discussion of the "national question" in the contemporary context, see, for instance, Jordan (1998).
11. This raises the question of whether punishment is always necessary and preferable to other forms of dealing with perpetrators of injustices. De Brito argues that the absence of punishment is admissible only when there has been an official acknowledgment of truth and where a national consensus exists for nonprosecution (1997: 9–10).
12. Ibid.: 3.
13. This is the focus of De Brito's important comparative study of these processes in Uruguay and Chile. A similar focus informs Kaye's study of truth commissions in El Salvador and Honduras; see Kaye (1997: 693–716).
14. Perelli (1993:154, quoted in De Brito 1997: 10).
15. The commission consisted of seventeen full-time commissioners and had three separate committees: a Human Rights Violations Committee, which conducted public hearings for victims/survivors; a Reparation and Rehabilitation Committee, which worked on policies and recommendations arising from those hearings; and an Amnesty Committee, which heard applications for amnesty. The final report of the TRC was published in different forms. I draw on the CD version of the TRC website (November 1998).
16. See Boraine (1996a). The TRC's view of their mandate is discussed in full in volume 1, chapter 4 of the report. See TRC website, file:///D|/final/1chap4.htm.
17. Omar (1995: 2–8); Tutu (1996a: 38–43).
18. Tutu (1996b).
19. There are no general or "blanket" amnesty provisions in South Africa. Amnesty has to be applied for on an individual basis. Applicants must complete a prescribed form, detailing information pertaining to specific human rights violations; such disclosure should be full and complete. A public hearing follows, where offenses fall into the category of "gross violations of human rights." If not, amnesty decisions may be taken in chambers. Several criteria have to be fulfilled for amnesty to be granted. These include the fact that a particular act must be shown to have taken place as part of a wider political event or in the service of a political organization. Actions for personal gain and based on ill will are excluded. It is also important to note that the law does *not* require that applicants should express remorse. They can come to the commission saying, for instance, "that they fought a noble struggle for liberation, but that because they opened themselves to prosecution or civil actions as a result, they are asking for amnesty" (ibid.).
20. "Truth" and "full disclosure" should clearly not be understood in metaphysical terms. The commission can never attain "The Truth." Instead, Krog suggests that one should understand the idea of truth here "as the widest possible compilation of people's perceptions, stories, myths and experiences" (1995: 118).
21. The TRC's power of subpoena aids it in working against the possibility of a "conspiracy of silence."
22. See Boraine (1996).

23. See Gillis (1994: 4).
24. Ibid. 3. For a discussion of the need to introduce a gendered dimension into the work of the TRC, see Goldblatt and Meintjes (1996).
25. This is now an accepted tenet of most social and political theory informed by poststructuralism. It is important to note, however, that the claim that identity is socially produced does not also translate into a claim that it is, consequently, easy to change or challenge such identities. Processes of identity formation are typically subject to deep sedimentation, and identities could prove extremely recalcitrant.
26. See Gillis (1994: 5). This whole process thus is based on a conception of identity as fundamentally relational. Identities are not achieved as self-same and pure, in isolation from other identities, but are always constituted in relation to an other or a series of others.
27. See Anderson (1991: 8, quoted in Gillis 1994:8).
28. Gillis (1994: 12).
29. Ibid.
30. Women, national minorities, and young people were generally admitted to national memories at an even slower pace than to national representative and educational institutions. (ibid.: 10).
31. Pierre Nora (quoted in ibid.: 15).
32. Gillis (1994: 18–20).
33. Although there is general agreement that the work of the TRC is the best possible way to achieve justice and reconciliation, it continues to be challenged from a variety of positions. The National Party continues to warn against the possibility of the TRC's being turned into a witch-hunt; the Freedom Front voices similar objections. The IFP voted against the act and has recently resorted to publishing its objections to the TRC in the national press. These parties were afraid that the TRC may "go too far"; other parties, including the PAC and Azanian People's Organization (AZAPO), argued that it would not "go far enough."
34. It is important to note that there are deep and important differences between submissions by official parties and institutions, and those by individuals. These differences are also reflected in the degree to which positive effects were produced as a result of submissions. Generally speaking, I argue that in the case of official submissions, the exercise was marked by a large degree of cynicism, whereas individual submissions, appearances, and confessions were distinguished by their thoroughgoing and soul-searching nature.
35. See de Klerk (1997).
36. De Klerk (1990: 68). For an in-depth analysis of National Party discourse during the early 1990s, see Altbeker and Steinberg (1998: 49–71).
37. "Submission to the Truth and Reconciliation Commission by Mr. F. W. de Klerk, Leader of the National Party," and "Second Submission of the National Party to the Truth and Reconciliation Commission," 1997, www.truth.org.za/special/party2/np2.htm.
38. I have analyzed the character of apartheid discourse, where I develop the argument that, in addition to its historical specificity, it is exemplary of a generalized identitarian conception of identity (Norval 1996).
39. J. E. Young (1992: 270).
40. "Submission to the Truth and Reconciliation Commission by Mr. F. W. de Klerk, Leader of the National Party."

41. The question of the historical context in which past abuses occurred raises important and difficult practical, ethical, and philosophical issues. It is not possible to treat these issues here. However, it should be noted that although such contextualizations may be used to attempt to explain past abuses, they have not generally been invoked to shirk responsibility for such abuses. Like other organizations, the National Party has gone to great lengths to sketch the context and general aims of apartheid policies. It did, however, recognize that apartheid "led to hardship, suffering and humiliation—to institutionalized discrimination on the basis of race and ethnicity," and that responsibility for actions should be taken by the Cabinet, the State Security Council, individual ministers, and commanding officers for all decisions taken and actions authorized. See "Second Submission by National Party" (23, 26–27).
42. The TRC takes issue with this view for obvious reasons, arguing that "explaining is not excusing, understanding is not forgiving" (TRC website, par. 45, file///D|final/5chap7.htm).
43. De Brito (1997: 6–7).
44. Even though the work of the TRC does not take the form of normal criminal tribunals, it gives great consideration to being seen working within the constraints of due process and the rule of law. This is extremely important, because the names of both victims and perpetrators of human rights violations are made public. An elaborate system has been put into place to ensure that perpetrators to be named are alerted ahead of time and are invited to make representations to hearings. To this end, the TRC has an Investigative Unit that investigates allegations and collects any relevant evidence.
45. This objective is clearly specified in the remit of the work of the TRC as the need to "restore the human and civil dignity of victims by granting them an opportunity to relate their own accounts of the violations of which they are the victims. See Promotion of National Unity and Reconciliation Act: Section 3 (c) (1995).
46. The TRC has, however, been criticized for disregarding "everyday" abuses as a result of their focus on gross violations of human rights. I return to this issue later.
47. Paraphrasing of extract from the Chilean Commission's Report, quoted in Boraine (1996b).
48. Quoted in Woods (1997). The five men who admitted to participating in the killing of Biko in 1977 are Col. H. Snyman, Lt. Col. G. Nieuwaudt, Warrant Officers R. Marx and J. Beneke, and Capt. D. Siebert.
49. In the course of its work, the TRC has widened its investigations to include analysis of the role of the media, the legal and medical professions, and the business community in upholding the institutions of apartheid. It has also arranged for hearings on the question of conscription.
50. For a more detailed discussion of these possibilities, see Norval (1998a: 259–60).
51. See TRC website, par. 45, file///D|final/1chap5.htm, par. 20.
52. Krog, in her discussion of the work of the TRC, raises an important question concerning the trajectory of apartheid and its relation to the fact that British abuses against women and children in concentration camps were never officially acknowledged or condemned by the British: "Wasn't the mere fact that the abuses of the war were never exposed perhaps not a key factor in the character that formulated apartheid's laws? Was the Boer veneration of Emily Hobhouse not a symptom of the desperate need for someone 'from the other side' to recognize the wrongs that had been done?" She argues that the fact that these abuses were

not publicly recognized contributed directly to the possibility that the war "became a folklore supporting the notion of Afrikaners as a threatened group" (1995: 114–15).

53. The theoretical structure of this argument draws strongly on Derrida's deconstructive reading of Husserl's argument on "internal time consciousness." See Derrida (1973).
54. This issue is theorized in Connolly's (1991) excellent study of the paradoxes of identity.
55. Asmal, Asmal, and Roberts (1997: 214).
56. They also discuss factors within the NGO sector and its struggles to redefine its role in the new political context. See Merwe, Dewhirst, and Hamber (1999: 67–77).
57. Ibid.: 67–71.
58. Buur (1998).
59. Robins (1998: 120–40).
60. Ibid: 137. Robins asks, for instance, whether "new public histories" will marginalize the experiences of coloureds "on the grounds that they did not suffer under apartheid as much as black South Africans."
61. I deal with the question of ethnicity in general, and in contemporary South Africa more specifically, in Norval (1999a: 1–22).
62. Indications of this are present in Pallo Jordan's (1998) discussion of the national question in post-1994 South Africa. This is evident, in particular, in his treatment of the question of ethnicity. Ethnicity, for him, is nothing but an artifact imposed by the apartheid regime and an attempt to continue to forge competition with "fellow Blacks" over scarce resources. This hardly is the sort of rhetoric that would make one confident in the depth of the pluralism of the form of nonracialism espoused here.
63. With regard to the former, see Posel (1991); and Norval (1996: chaps. 2, 3). For a discussion of divisions within the state during the 1970s and 1980s, see Sarakinsky (1998: 54); and Swilling and Phillips (1998: 134–48).
64. TRC website CD: par 77, file:///D final/5chap6.htm.
65. Some of the arguments in this section were first developed in a review of literature on the TRC. See Norval (1999b: 499–519).
66. See, for instance, Robins (1998: 120–40); Coetzee (1998: 112–19); and Davidson (1998: 143–60).
67. Deacon (1998: 161–79; 178).
68. Ibid.: 179.
69. Coetzee (1998: 114–15).
70. Robins (1998: 130).
71. Ibid.: 131.
72. Davidson (1998: 159).

RETHINKING CITIZENSHIP Reforming the Law in Postwar Guatemala

Rachel Sieder

This essay addresses the relationships among the state, law, and citizenship in postconflict Guatemala, examining the ways in which struggles to redefine the state and citizenship were fought out on the legal terrain. By definition, processes of political transition following prolonged periods of authoritarian rule or armed conflict involve transformations of the state. Under authoritarian regimes or in situations of internal armed conflict, violations of human rights are a commonplace, either because of deliberate policies toward certain sectors of the population or because of the weakness of the state and the inability of government to protect and enforce basic rights. Any transition to more democratic forms of governance therefore implies the (re)construction of the state as a guarantor of democratic rights and obligations. Through such processes citizenship is reframed as various legal and institutional measures are implemented to benefit and protect those groups and individuals who were marginalized or victimized under the previous regime, that is, those who were effectively excluded from citizenship either de jure or de facto.

Citizenship is often conceived of as a fixed and nonnegotiable set of rights and obligations, such as those embodied in a written constitution. However, it is in fact best understood as a dynamic process rather than a static juridical construct. Both in terms of its legal attributes and its social content, citizenship is contested and constantly renegotiated and reinterpreted. Such contestation is particularly acute during periods of political transition. In considering this phenomenon in postwar Guatemala, I adopt the perspective proposed by Ann Mische, who has argued for a move beyond formalistic conceptions of citizenship "towards a view of citizenship as a historically contingent, interactive vehicle of articulation, conflict and dialogue" (1995: 157–58). Mische's analytical framework is particularly useful for thinking about the changing nature of citizenship during transition processes, as it takes into account the multiple appeals to citizenship from different and often conflicting social sectors and recognizes "the potential dynamism of such appeals in reshaping relationships between state, societal and economic actors" (157–58).

During periods of political transition a range of actors, including domestic elites, international donors, and intergovernmental institutions, and political and social movements attempt to advance different and often competing visions of the state, governance, and citizenship. The state itself can usefully be analyzed as a series of institutions and sites where conflicts over power are constantly negotiated from above and below. One of the primary sites of engagement where such different imaginaries and political projects are contested from the top down and the bottom up is the law. This is because the law is central to claiming rights and enforcing obligations. Nationally and, increasingly, internationally accepted standards are often forged through legal processes in a dynamic of "naming, claiming and blaming" (Felstiner, Abel, and Sarat 1980). In effect, the legal system is converted into a contested site of meaning over state accountability and citizens' rights as the dominant ideas and values that underpin the law provide the framework for advancing alternative understandings (Starr and Collier 1989). As Boaventura de Sousa Santos (1995) has observed, law has become an increasingly globalized or transnational phenomenon. Through the law and legal encounters, different ideas about the appropriate balance between rights and obligations filter among the international, national, and local arenas. Indeed, Santos claims that "the main driving force behind the transformation of the state and its legality is the intensification of transnational practices and global interactions" (119). Certainly, claims by groups and individuals for greater political inclusion, equality of treatment, recognition of minority rights, or punishment of those responsible for gross human rights violations are increasingly framed through appeals to international law. In recent years in Latin America social movements and individuals have used international human rights law to try to secure truth and justice in cases of gross violations of human rights, particularly when local courts fail to enforce accountability (as, for example, in the Pinochet case). In addition, indigenous peoples' claims for special rights are currently being played out through the law across the continent, particularly on the question of whether the increasingly internationally sanctioned rights of indigenous communities should be recognized within national legal systems.[1] Evidently, the ways in which the state and state-society relations develop and change depend on struggles and interactions between hegemonic and counterhegemonic understandings and practices of "rights," "obligations," and "justice" as constituted by different individuals and groups within particular material and historical contexts. An analysis of the ways people resort to and use the law—and the *idea* of law—in periods of rapid political transformation can therefore tell us much about the changing nature of the state and struggles to redefine citizenship in a particular context.

In Guatemala attempts to redefine the state and citizenship centered on the peace negotiations between the government and the combined guerrilla forces of the Unidad Revolucionaria Nacional Guatemalteca (URNG), which were successfully concluded in December 1996. The peace settlement set out a blueprint to overhaul the Guatemalan state, for decades dominated by an anticommunist counterinsurgency logic, and to ensure respect for human rights and the democratic rule of law. The three decades prior to the peace settlement were characterized by gross and systematic violations; over two hundred thousand people perished during this period, including over fifty thousand disappeared. The vast majority of those killed, some 83 percent, were indigenous noncombatants murdered by the military and paramilitary forces (Comisión de Esclaricimiento Histórico [CEH] 1999). Throughout the armed conflict, the judicial system singularly failed to defend even the most elementary of citizens' rights or punish those responsible for gross violations. Throughout the peace negotiations reform of state institutions and practices to ensure protection for basic human rights was therefore seen as central to wider efforts at democratization. The peace settlement also mapped out a radical agenda, which aimed to include Guatemala's 60 percent indigenous population, historically subject to discrimination, socioeconomic exploitation, and political marginalization, in a new nation-building project. In spite of a deep-rooted legacy of racism, by the late 1990s internationalized "rights thinking" had become part of the dominant idiom of political reform in Guatemala. This was evident in the agreement signed by the negotiating parties in March 1995 on the Rights and Identity of Indigenous Peoples, which framed the specific demands of Guatemalan indigenous groups within a wider evolving international discourse and legislation on indigenous peoples' rights. The agreement proposed such measures as a commitment to bilingual education, religious tolerance, and respect for indigenous authorities. It also endorsed the principle of special rights and positive discrimination with the aim of achieving greater social justice.[2] The overall thrust of the agreement aimed to encompass cultural diversity within the unitary framework of a reformed Guatemalan state. This, it was argued, would give historically disadvantaged groups a greater stake in the national polity and articulate different forms of participation in a developing project of multicultural citizenship.[3] Indeed, the successful incorporation of the indigenous population into a democratized body politic was viewed by many as essential to securing a lasting peace.

In the period subsequent to the signing of the peace settlement the law became a key battleground where attempts to redefine citizenship were played out. Efforts to construct the rule of law had to address a legacy of militarization, an ineffectual and corrupt judiciary, entrenched impunity, and the complex challenge of encompassing cultural differences. The 1995 Indigenous Rights Agreement specifically recognized the legitimacy of indigenous "customary law" (*derecho consuetudinario*) and "traditional" community authorities and committed the government to incorporate both into the official state legal system where they did not conflict with national and international legal norms of human rights.[4] This implied the official acceptance of legal pluralism and the right of indigenous communities to resolve conflicts in accordance with their own "customary practices."[5] In effect, it envisaged providing indigenous people with a higher degree of legal autonomy than they had enjoyed for over a century. In the wake of the peace agreement policymakers began to confront the complex challenge of integrating international legal instruments,[6] national law, and indigenous customary law. A number of studies on indigenous legal norms and practices were carried out by national research centers, such as the Latin American Faculty for Social Science (FLACSO) and the Association for Socio-Economic Research (ASIES), a government-sponsored think tank. Research and discussion fora on customary law involving Mayan intellectuals, policymakers, and academics were also sponsored by the United Nations observer mission in Guatemala Misión de Las Naciones Unidos en Guatemala (MINUGUA), set up in 1994 to monitor human rights and verify the implementation of the peace agreements in situ. The debate was heated and often acutely polarized. Indigenous activists and their supporters in international NGOs and the United Nations argued in favor of developing a politico-legal system that could encompass universal human rights and obligations together with the special rights of indigenous communities or ethnolinguistic groups. Such multicultural rule of law construction, they argued, formed part of the wider challenge of building the basis for a multiethnic and multicultural citizenship in Guatemala. However, their opponents, represented in the government, the private sector, the media, and the legal profession, frequently raised the specter of "balkanization," arguing that granting special rights to indigenous people would ultimately lead to ethnic separatism and the breakup of the country. They also claimed that recognition of indigenous customary law would result in "one law for indigenous people and another law for non-Indians," contradicting the constitutional principles of legal equality and universal citizenship. In effect, the battle over multiculturalism and the rule of law in Guatemala illustrated wider political conflicts over the nature of the state, governance, and citizenship.

The following sections situate current debates about citizenship in Guatemala in historical context and analyze transformations in the rule of law that have occurred since the signing of the peace settlement. I conclude by considering the implications of recent developments for the state and citizenship in Guatemala.

Rethinking Citizenship

Following the end of direct military rule in 1984, a constitution was promulgated that enshrined universal principles. However, a history of exclusion, authoritarianism, and racism and, more recently, extreme state-sponsored violence meant that many Guatemalans continued to view the state as an oppressive force rather than a guarantor of their rights as citizens.[7] In addition, until the 1990s, the cold war and the acutely exclusive nature of national politics had engendered an organized opposition that sought to destroy the state rather than to influence or reform it.[8] Beyond highly restricted interelite competition, the state and the law were not perceived by most people as a viable terrain within which to struggle for social change.

The contemporary difficulties involved in constructing a democratic citizenship in postwar Guatemala can be traced back to the constitution of the republic itself. The consolidation of the apparatus of the state during the late nineteenth and twentieth centuries was not followed by the successful construction of an imagined nation-state peopled by an active citizenry. The national project of the country's dominant civil and military elite during the nineteenth century did not include either the indigenous majority or most poor non-Indians as citizens with equal rights, but rather treated them as subject populations to be controlled, disciplined, and "civilized." Following independence, the conservatives proposed a new status for indigenous people, creating a separate, subordinate legal jurisdiction for them, which in effect recreated the colonial *republica de indios*. As Guatemalan historian Arturo Taracena (1995) has observed, although such ethnojuridical exclusion afforded indigenous people a degree of protection, it also meant they did not actively participate in the process of nation-state construction. This did not mean an escape from subjugation; the economic exploitation of the indigenous and poor non-Indian majority was—and remains—central to the constitution of the Guatemalan nation-state. The idea of separate legal regimes for Indians and non-Indians was opposed by nineteenth-century liberals, yet the triumph of the Liberal Revolution of Justo Rufino Barrios in 1871 did not result in the extension of full citizenship status to all Guatemalans. Within the context of the late nineteenth-century agro-export boom, universalist ideals of equality before the law and positivist doctrine constituted the ideological apparatus for the exploitation, expropriation, and assimilation of the indigenous population. Communal lands were increasingly encroached upon, and indigenous men remained legally subject to forced labor requirements until 1944 (McCreery 1994).[9]

During the 1944–1954 period of reformist government, political parties, universal male suffrage, and a program of agrarian reform were introduced throughout rural Guatemala, providing many younger, literate, and Spanish-speaking Mayan men with access to municipal political office (Handy 1994). Although illiterate indigenous women were still denied the vote, these changes stimulated the development of an active civil society and began to lay the basis for the development of a citizenry that included the majority of the population. However, the anticommunist counterrevolution that followed the CIA-backed overthrow of President Jacobo Arbenz in 1954 effectively halted the consolidation of local political power and reasserted the dominance of central government. In subsequent decades municipal and regional government throughout much of the country remained weak, and the majority of the population was politically marginalized and subject to ever greater economic exploitation. This was in part the product of a highly coercive state, but also, paradoxically, of its weakness, which facilitated other forms of domination and exploitation. Indeed, highly centralized government coexisted with the absence of an effective state presence in many parts of the national territory. This was particularly the case in the highland departments of greatest indigenous concentration, such as Huehuetenango, Alta Verapaz, and Quiché, where economic elites relied on coercion and clientelist networks to secure their access to labor and land.

After 1963 the armed forces began to develop a counterinsurgency project to defeat the URNG, which reached its zenith during the early 1980s. The relationship between state and subjects changed dramatically as the army consolidated a highly militarized and authoritarian form of governmental power throughout the rural highlands (Schirmer 1998; R. Wilson 1995b; Kobrak 1997). Extreme and violent repression was combined with institutional mechanisms to incorporate and control the rural, predominantly indigenous population, including forced resettlement in some areas, obligatory participation in paramilitary civil defense patrols, and village-based military commissioners who reported regularly to the army. Existing forms of communal authority and organization were destroyed as thousands of community leaders were murdered or disappeared by the military. Long-standing inter- and intracommunity conflicts over land were often played out through the lethal prism of the counterinsurgency, exacerbating local divisions. Despite the transition to elected civilian government in 1985, the militarization of the countryside and gross violations of human rights persisted throughout the next decade. Only when the peace negotiations between the government of Alvaro Arzú Yrigoyen and the URNG recommenced in earnest in 1994 was the prospect of transforming the militarized, authoritarian state into a guarantor of the rights and obligations of all Guatemalans genuinely raised. The negotiations themselves remained a restricted affair between the belligerents, but social movements did have some limited input to the discussions through the Civil Society Assembly (ASC), a consultative body set up in 1995 through the framework negotiating agreement. The assembly was able to forward discussion documents to the negotiating table, and with the participation of the umbrella Coordination of the Organizations of the Mayan People of Guatemala (COPMAGUA) had an important role in determining the nature of the 1995 agreement on indigenous rights and identity. Civil society participation in the peace agreements was limited,[10] but the contrast to 1984, when civic opposition barely existed and the nature of the political transition was dictated almost entirely by the armed forces, was striking nonetheless.

The principal challenge to dominant liberal, universalist conceptions of citizenship in Guatemala has come from an emergent pan-Mayanism. During the 1990s this diverse social and political movement questioned the existing nation-state, drawing attention to its discriminatory and exclusionary nature (Bastos and Camus 1995; Cojtí 1996; Fischer and Brown 1996; Kay Warren 1998; Nelson 1999). Activists have drawn inspiration and support from the transnationalized indigenous peoples movement in the Americas, but the growing strength of the indigenous movement also reflects the fact that indigenous rights have increasingly occupied the agenda of nongovernmental and intergovernmental organizations in the international arena, not least the United Nations, which after 1994 provided Mayan organizations in Guatemala with a strategic ally in the form of its observer mission. During the 1990s demands for indigenous rights and idealized projections of "Mayan values" came to constitute a new discourse articulated by indigenous leaders and their supporters. This began to affect social relations in Guatemala and helped to frame much of the national debate around judicial reform, democratic consolidation, and citizenship during the peace process (Sieder and Witchell, forthcoming).

A Multicultural Rule of Law?

The ideas of the "rule of law" and "equality in the law" have long been used as a legitimizing discourse of state power. However, they have also provided many groups and individuals with a means to challenge and contest those controlling the apparatus of the state by demanding that certain rights be guaranteed and legally prescribed obligations respected. During the late 1980s and 1990s, NGOs and popular organizations in Guatemala increasingly came to use the law as a site to struggle for citizenship, campaigning for an end to impunity and respect for constitutional and human rights. For example, human rights groups such as the Mutual Support Group (Grupo de Apoyo Mutuo, GAM) and the National Coordination of Guatemalan Widows (Coordinadora Nacional de Viudas de Guatemala) demanded an end to human rights abuses, the observance of due process guarantees such as habeas corpus, and the conviction and punishment of those guilty of violations. The indigenous organization Consejo Etnico Runujel Junam (CERJ) organized after 1988 specifically to lobby state authorities to respect the voluntary nature of the civil patrols prescribed in the 1985 constitution. Struggles over state accountability and citizens' rights were fought out through the legal system as dominant ideas of legality were used by opposition groups to challenge and contest official violations of civil and political rights.

However, the proposal contained in the 1996 peace agreements to incorporate indigenous "customary law" into the norms and institutions of state law represented an even more radical departure. Here, the terrain of the law was being used to contest fundamental assumptions about universal citizenship and the nature and unity of the Guatemalan state. In effect, the proposal can be seen as part of a wider attempt by indigenous activists to secure greater autonomy for indigenous communities and peoples. By recognizing the right of indigenous communities to decide on and apply their own procedures for conflict resolution, the state would no longer maintain a monopoly on the production and regulation of law. This constituted a fundamental challenge to the legal centralist model that had existed since Independence, based on the indivisibility of state, government, and law. Yet the proposal can also be read as an attempt by certain political elites in the state to renew their flagging legitimacy. Santos has pointed to "the way in which the state organizes its own decentering" (1995: 118); the commitment contained in the peace settlement to build a multicultural rule of law by incorporating previously excluded, "nonstate" legal phenomena into state law can also be understood in this light. Concessions to multiculturalism would, it was hoped, secure the support of the indigenous population for a new pact of governance and also convince international donors that the Guatemalan political elite was serious about reform.

In common with other postcolonial nation-states, Guatemala has long been characterized by a situation of legal pluralism where different systems of obligation have coexisted within the same sociopolitical space, albeit in a highly unequal relationship. This stems partly from the spatial and juridical separation of indigenous peoples in the colonial *pueblos de Indios* or their post-independence equivalents, but also from the uneven coverage of the state over national territory, which means that the national legal system remains largely inaccessible for most of the population, who are obliged to develop alternative means to regulate social relations. However, the posited division between "customary law" and "state law" is in fact a legal fiction. As much recent scholarship on legal pluralism has shown, more often than not what are identified as local customary practices are in fact colonial or postcolonial impositions (A. Griffiths 1997; Moore 1986; Starr and Collier 1989). State law and customary law are locked together in a historically asymmetric but mutually constitutive relationship in which state law may be understood as an attempt by the political center to dominate, govern, and administrate indigenous peoples, and local practices seen as a means of adaptation, accommodation, and, occasionally, resistance. In one sense, as Laura Nader (1990) argues in her study of customary law in the Zapotec region of Oaxaca, Mexico, customary law can be understood as a counterhegemonic strategy used by indigenous communities to protect their limited and conditional autonomy from the central state. In Guatemala, central government has never been wholly successful in imposing its authority. Institutions such as the colonial *alcaldías indígenas* or the contemporary *alcaldías auxiliares* and even, according to some recent accounts, the counterinsurgent civil defense patrols instigated by the army were adapted in practice by subject populations to become institutions used to defend a qualified local autonomy (Stoll 1993; Kobrak 1997). However, it is also evident that state law is not something somehow external to indigenous communities; no hermetically sealed spheres of "national state law" and "indigenous customary law" exist, and indigenous people certainly make recourse to all means at their disposal to settle disputes, both official and unofficial.[11] Nevertheless, in the highly contested debates surrounding recognition of indigenous customary law that occurred after the peace settlement, advocates repeatedly emphasized the differences between the two "systems" of law, contrasting what they claimed was the conciliatory and noncoercive nature of customary law with the punitive sanctions imposed by the national judicial system, widely condemned as discriminatory, costly, and ineffective. This revealed the extent to which the moral force of "customary law" rested precisely on its imagined "nonstateness," even while its very nature was partly defined and shaped by national law.[12] Its formal recognition would have meant that something framed largely *in opposition* to the state would in fact have become part of the apparatus of the judicial system. Such a proposal was, in turn, a response to the increasing transnationalization of the Guatemalan legal space, reflected in the influence of international thinking on special rights and multicultural citizenship on the peace settlement.

After mid-1994, the presence of the United Nations verification mission in Guatemala ensured that the discourse of indigenous and human rights reached even the most remote rural areas, even if in some places it was initially received with suspicion or openly rejected by those who maintained close links with the army. During this period the direct presence of the military began to recede. Military commissioners were abolished in 1995 and civil patrols demobilized weeks after the final peace settlement was signed. Combined with the fact that rural inhabitants became aware of the content of the peace agreements and the increased national and international currency of "Mayan rights," this meant many came to question the legitimacy of centralized forms of governance and law. Many Mayan NGOs actively encouraged such reflection, such as the legal rights service Defensoría Maya, which emphasized the importance of the "recovery" of indigenous customary law, or Mayan law, as they preferred to call it. Through this process, unofficial forms of dispute resolution gained a renewed legitimacy in many indigenous communities. In effect, the state was disaggregated and an increasing number of people came to imagine the law as something that could be constructed from the bottom up, not just dispensed from the top down.

Practices varied from place to place, but local dispute resolution was generally characterized by extended dialogue between the parties in conflict to try to arrive at a mutually acceptable solution. The auxiliary mayor, local religious authorities, or other community leaders mediated discussion. Misdemeanors were analyzed in terms of motive and effect, the guilty party usually expected to acknowledge his or her wrongdoing, and the victim given an important role in proceedings—in marked contrast to proceedings in the courts. The sanctions applied were predominantly restitutive and reconciliatory in nature, such as public apologies, replacement of goods damaged or stolen, or community service (Sieder 1996; Esquit and García 1999). This again contrasted with the state legal system, where fines or long prison sentences were the most commonly applied sanctions. Indigenous activists advocated the "recovery" of these practices and "traditional beliefs" as part of an overall strategy to strengthen Mayan identity and improve access to justice for indigenous people. The active reconstruction of a Mayan past involved collective imaginings of foundational myths, traditions, and shared histories, or "imagined communities." In this sense, the essentialist discourse of Mayan activists, which emphasized the harmonious nature of pre-Hispanic Mayan society, is best understood as a strategic resource, what William Roseberry has described as a "language of community and contention," that is, a "social and discursive construction and imagination" (1996: 83) that subaltern groups use as a counterhegemonic mechanism to contest domination.[13]

However, ethnographic research demonstrated that, in practice, indigenous people throughout Guatemala continued to engage in the strategic use of law, resorting alternatively to nonofficial institutions and practices, state law, and, increasingly, to international legal fora to resolve disputes and pursue grievances. Local conflicts, divisions, and factionalism frequently expressed themselves through this strategic resort to different dispute resolution mechanisms, and individuals and groups took their disputes to the courts or other institutions, such as MINUGUA, when they perceived it to be to their advantage to do so.[14] The experiences of conflict, refuge, and resistance during the armed conflict had transformed understandings of law, justice, and rights for many people. Returned refugees, for example, had appropriated and internalized universal discourses and frameworks of human rights as a result of their interaction with NGOs and the United Nations High Commission for Refugees (UNHCR). This highly politicized group lobbied to secure their relative autonomy from the Guatemalan state, securing official commitments through the peace negotiations in 1994 that the military would not enter returnee settlements without prior consultation.[15] Returnees also refused to have civil patrols, local police, or even auxiliary mayors within their resettlements, relying instead on the organizational structures consolidated while in exile in Mexico. The access they had gained to a "transnational political space" (Pritchard 1995: 24) had strengthened their perception of themselves as a population with rights, and they were more willing to appeal to both national law and international human rights law to defend their interests.

Another important change that occurred in "rights understandings" related to gender. During the armed conflict, many indigenous women became widows and were obliged to occupy roles in the family traditionally reserved for men. Some later became important local and national leaders, for example, Rosalina Tuyuc, who became a congressional deputy in 1995 for the left-wing opposition party, the New Guatemalan Democratic Front (FDNG). The protagonism of Rigoberta Menchú, awarded the Nobel peace prize in 1992, also symbolized the growing political importance of Mayan women and their projection onto a global stage. In the wake of the armed conflict, many women increasingly challenged their traditionally subordinate role in local affairs and became less willing to submit to the will of the men in their communities (or customary law). Cases of neglect, abandonment, and domestic violence were taken to the state authorities, where they often received a more sympathetic hearing than before local authorities. Recent experience in Guatemala bears out the observation made by Susan Hirsch that "gender is made, remade, and transformed in fundamental ways through legal institutions and the discourses of disputing," and that "paradoxically, law 'genders' individuals in ways that define their positions both in society and in legal contexts, while also affording space for contesting those positions" (1998: 3, 20). Through recourse to the national courts and also to the international arena, many indigenous women have gained an increased consciousness of themselves as individuals with rights and obligations. In the process, they have, at least potentially, reimagined themselves as citizens of the nation-state.

In general, however, expectations of the national judicial system were paradoxically both extremely low and high at the same time. A growing number of individuals and groups expected the state to guarantee an ever increasing range of rights, yet their everyday expectations of the official justice system remained minimal. Inefficiency, widespread corruption, and impunity continued to prevent the full exercise of rights or the enforcement of obligations, generating a situation for most of the population that approximated what Guillermo O'Donnell has termed "low-intensity citizenship" (1996: 166). In addition, the marked rise in common crime, such as robbery and kidnapping, that occurred in the wake of the peace settlement focused public attention on the question of "law and order." Among some sectors this kindled nostalgia for the time of military rule during the early 1980s, when the militarized state dispensed a highly punitive and summary justice throughout the country. Although a range of judicial reform initiatives were supported by international organizations such as the World Bank and the Inter-American Development Bank, tangible results were slow to materialize. At times, reform efforts were counterproductive; for example, changes introduced to the Criminal Procedures Code in 1994 aimed at guaranteeing the rights of detainees, such as the right of habeas corpus, were accused by many commentators of favoring alleged delinquents. Most dramatic of all was the steady increase in mob lynchings of suspected criminals in rural and urban communities that occurred throughout the country after 1996. As state-orchestrated political violence receded, many instances were reported of residents detaining, beating, and, in the most extreme cases, murdering and burning those suspected of carrying out crimes such as robbery and rape.[16] These lynchings were attributed to a variety of factors, including the failure of state forces to guarantee law and order and the legacy left by the violence of the military counterinsurgency, when a brutal and summary form of "justice" was the order of the day.

Debate continued around the implementation of the commitments on legal pluralism set out in the peace agreements. In effect, the internationalized discourse of indigenous rights and identity contained in the 1995 agreement framed customary law as a localized phenomenon, intrinsically bound up with a particular vision of Mayan identity that derived essentially from rural, agricultural communities.[17] Did recognition, then, mean creating autonomous jurisdictions in Mayan villages? Was indigenous customary law to be incorporated into state law only at this level? And what would the relationship be between local indigenous authorities and the courts? The inherent tensions between ethnic integration and autonomy apparent in the entire peace settlement were played out through this one issue. Some Mayan activists and even some UN personnel argued in favor of separate territorial jurisdictions, where "Mayan law" could be applied to the indigenous population.[18] Other advocates of recognition (myself included) argued that the establishment of "separate but equal" jurisdictions would marginalize indigenous groups even further from the national polity and instead proposed the strengthening of local conflict resolution mechanisms together with the greater incorporation of the general procedural principles of customary law, such as conciliation and mediation, into a unitary judicial system (see Sieder 1998; Esquit and García 1999). In 1998 opposition parties in Congress proposed a reform of the 1985 Constitution to recognize indigenous community authorities as judicial bodies. The congressional formula, endorsed by most indigenous civic organizations, was that these authorities' resolutions and dispositions be mandatory for those individuals who voluntarily opted to accept their jurisdiction as long as they were not in contravention of their constitutional and human rights. In May 1999 the issue came under renewed scrutiny when a national referendum took place to approve a package of fifty constitutional reforms previously approved by Congress designed to institutionalize the commitments set out in the 1996 peace agreements. The proposed reforms aimed to recognize the Guatemalan nation-state as "multiethnic, pluricultural, and multilingual." They also advocated the recognition of customary law as part of the judicial system according to the formulation previously agreed on by the parties in Congress. However, in the end, the majority of Guatemalans were indifferent to the significance of the referendum, and the vote was marred by an abstention rate of 82 percent.[19] Many of those who did turn out to cast their ballot, mainly in the capital city, were alarmed by the strident warnings from far-right and conservative sectors that granting special rights to indigenous people would lead to ethnic division and conflict. Opponents of the reforms had previously obtained legal rulings that prevented the government or the United Nations observer mission from campaigning in favor of a yes vote. In the days prior to the referendum the powerful private-sector association Comité Coordinador de Cámeras Agricolas, Comerciales, Industriales, y Financieras (CACIF) took out full-page advertisements in the national press warning of dire consequences if the package was approved. Numerous newspaper editorials discussed the dangers of giving political rights to "illiterate Indians" and predicted "reverse discrimination" against non-Indians in the future. Although indigenous activists in the cities and the highlands supported the reforms, this proved insufficient to mobilize a skeptical and largely uninformed electorate, and the package was defeated. The possibility that customary law would be formally recognized as part of the state legal system in the short term looked increasingly unlikely. Nonetheless, in the wake of the referendum defeat indigenous activists vowed to continue working to strengthen "Mayan law" in communities throughout the country as an alternative to dispute resolution through the courts.

Conclusions

State formation is a continuous process negotiated both from above and below. I have sought to indicate the ways in which the peace process and the prospect of incorporating indigenous customary law into the legal system changed the possibilities for imagining the Guatemalan state and citizenship. The multiculturalist perspectives embodied in the 1995 agreement on indigenous rights and identity constituted a reframing of citizenship, raising the possibility that the construction of a national citizenry more inclusive of the indigenous majority could take place. However, at the same time as these claims were taken up by sectors of the Mayan movement, resistance from powerful groups to formally recognizing indigenous rights illustrated the highly contested nature of this process. In addition, while certain sectors of the population increasingly called on the government to guarantee certain rights and obligations, expectations of the state in general remained very low. I have indicated here how this is a consequence of historical traditions of state-subject relations in Guatemala and of the current inability of the state to meet even the most basic of its citizens' demands. Although the peace process opened the possibility of constructing an active citizenry of a democratized nation-state, progress toward this goal is far from guaranteed.

However, the contested process of developing a new system of law, rights, and justice in the postwar period has profoundly affected understandings of the state, citizenship, and relations between the state and civil society. In one sense, the proposal to formally recognize indigenous customary law (and, by implication, the autonomy of local indigenous communities) represented a challenge to the legal sovereignty of the Guatemalan state. Indeed, this was one of the principal reasons opponents rallied against it. However, I have argued here that the incorporation of customary law into official legality can also be understood as a new form of governmentality, a way in which the state maps out new territories and communities, extending its control to areas previously beyond its reach. Yet such an exercise cannot be understood merely as an extension of power from the top down; it also signals the manner in which the state becomes increasingly porous as the boundaries between state and society change. If indigenous customary law had been formally recognized as part of the state judiciary, this would have represented the incorporation of unofficial discourses and practices into the realm of a new governmentality. The rejection of the constitutional reform package in May 1999 demonstrated that the idea of a multicultural nation-state is not yet socially and culturally embedded in Guatemalan civil and political society. Nonetheless, irrespective of official recognition, national and international developments in recent years have greatly increased the legitimacy of local forms of conflict resolution for many indigenous people. In addition, the singular inefficiency of the Guatemalan legal system means that many people will continue to resort to "extralegal" practices for dispute resolution. Yet, at the same time, the state will also continue to be a central focus of human rights struggles. The law will therefore remain an important site for the ongoing contestation of the imaginaries and boundaries of the nation-state.

Notes

Parts of this article derive from a previous paper, "Rethinking Citizenship: Legal Pluralism and Institutional Reform in Guatemala," published in *Citizenship Studies* 3, no. 1 (1999). I am greatly indebted to Carlos Flores, James Dunkerley, Maxine Molyneux, Jenny Pearce, Finn Stepputat, and John Watanabe for their feedback on earlier versions. Research in Guatemala was financed by an Economic and Social Research Council postdoctoral award, the British Academy, and the Central Research Fund of the University of London.

1. The 1989 International Labor Organization (ILO) Convention is currently the only statutory international instrument on the rights of indigenous peoples. It establishes indigenous rights to natural resource use, traditional lands, customary law, traditional authorities, bilin-

gual education, and policy decisions over development priorities. Conventions on indigenous peoples' rights are currently being drafted by the United Nations and the Organization of American States. On international law and indigenous rights, see Stavenhagen (1996) and Plant (1998).

2. For example, the agreement proposed specific affirmative action measures, such as the heavier penalization of sexual crimes committed against indigenous women.
3. The settlement as a whole proposed an increase in local autonomy through the decentralization of politico-administrative structures and the strengthening of municipal autonomy. Indigenous claims for greater regional autonomy for specific ethnolinguistic communities were not secured in the negotiations. Efforts by some indigenous activists to secure proportional representation in Congress on the basis of ethnolinguistic identity were similarly unsuccessful. For a discussion of the indigenous movement's position on autonomy during the peace negotiations, see Cojtí (1997); for an earlier position of the Mayan movement on the autonomy question, see Consejo de Organizaciones Mayas de Guatemala (1991).
4. Customary law was not explicitly defined in the peace agreements themselves. It can be understood as the uncodified concepts, beliefs, and norms that, within a given community, define prejudicial actions or crimes; the processes by which these should be resolved; and the sanctions or resolutions decided and applied.
5. On legal pluralism, see J. Griffiths (1986); Hooker (1975); Merry (1988, 1992, 1993); Moore (1986); and Starr and Collier (1989).
6. Recognition of indigenous peoples' right to use traditional legal practices is clearly set out in Articles 8 and 12 of the ILO Convention 169 on indigenous and tribal peoples, which was finally ratified by the government of Guatemala in March 1996 following a protracted political battle. Acceptance of the Convention was made conditional on its subordination to the 1985 Constitution.
7. Gross violations of human rights continued during the late 1980s and 1990s, despite the transition to elected civilian government in 1985.
8. The ideology of armed revolution that posited an alternative, socialist model of the state constituted a vital part of this equation.
9. After the introduction of new vagrancy legislation in 1934 during the regime of Jorge Ubico, poor *ladino* as well as indigenous men became increasingly subject to forced labor requirements.
10. For critical analyses, see Palencia (1997) and Holiday and Stanley (forthcoming).
11. Neither is national or customary law isolated from the changing international legal order; Santos (1987) notes that the legal context is now characterized by interlegality and a mixing of cultural codes, while global discourses are locally vernacularized and constantly acquire new meanings.
12. Customary procedures were conciliatory in nature in part because the threat of punitive sanctions imposed by the state tribunals existed as an alternative if conciliation failed. For a detailed study of the relationship between state law and customary legal mechanisms, see Esquit and García (1999).
13. Roseberry maintains: "As such communities are imagined, symbols of distinctiveness and authenticity are selected and appropriated, within a social field marked by inequality, hier-

archy, and contention. Languages of ethnicity, religion, and nationalism draw upon images of primordial associations and identifications, but they take their specific and practical forms as languages of contention and *opposition*" (1996: 83).

14. As Anne Griffiths has observed, "The administrative and theoretical separation of legal systems does not extend to people's uses of the law in arranging their own lives" (1997: 2).
15. This commitment was tragically broken in September 1995, when an army platoon entered the refugee resettlement of Xamán, Alta Verapaz, and shot dead eleven refugees.
16. A 1998 report by the UN verification mission (MINUGUA) on 119 lynchings carried out between March 1996 and March 1998 found that most had occurred in regions of the country worst hit by counterinsurgency violence during the 1980s, even though these areas had comparatively low levels of criminality (MINUGUA 1998).
17. See Nelson (1999) for an incisive critique of this view of Mayan identity.
18. Many Mayan activists rejected the term "customary law," interpreting it as a colonial imposition that framed indigenous legal practices in terms of "custom." They preferred instead the term "Mayan law."
19. For more on the popular referendum, see Arnson (1999).

GOVERNANCE AND STATE MYTHOLOGIES IN MUMBAI

Thomas Blom Hansen

In all those tasks that need no particular and exceptional efforts, no special courage or endurance, we find no magic and no mythology. But a highly developed magic and connected with it a mythology always occurs if a pursuit is dangerous and its issues uncertain.—Ernst Cassirer, *The Myth of the State*

Shattered Myths

A passage in *The Moor's Last Sigh* by Salman Rushdie captures the gap between the dominant self-images of the nationalist elite and the cultural practices of the popular worlds in Mumbai: Every year during the Ganapati celebrations, when the elephant-headed god Ganesh is celebrated in huge public processions, the modernist painter Aurora Zogoiby dances in her white dress on top of her house at Malabar Hill, displaying her rebellious sophistication as well as her contempt for what she regards as a primitive Hindu mass festival unfolding at the popular beach deep below her. One of the central themes in Rushdie's novel, however, is that beneath this gap in representation, Mumbai's official face and the life of its affluent elite are intimately interwoven with the city's popular worlds as well as its most murky sides: massive corruption, organized crime, and communal politics, personified by the character Raman Fielding, a gangster and populist politician.

This constitutive split in the life and imaginings of the city was highlighted by two rounds of bloody riots between Hindus and Muslims in Mumbai in December 1992 and January 1993 leaving more than one thousand persons dead, many more wounded and more than 150,000 people displaced. The riots dealt a major blow to the images, favored by the middle class, of Mumbai as the epitome of Indian modernity and the site of a pragmatic, enterprising capitalist ethos. The ferocity, the scale, and the political character of the riots made it clear that sectarian violence did not just emanate from residues of irrational beliefs among the ordinary masses, as conventional wisdom had it, but remained central to India's experience of modernity and capitalism. During the riots and their aftermath, these denied but immensely powerful forces and dynamics acquired an unprecedented visibility. Prominent citizens deplored this and bemoaned the demise of public order, tolerance, and cosmopolitanism in Mumbai (e.g., Padgaonkar 1993). Scholars and activists saw the proliferation of crime and sectarian politics as an effect of the "lumpenization" of the city as its industrial economy and its large working class have given way to real estate speculation and small service industries (e.g., Lele 1995).

My basic proposition in this essay, however, is that these concerns can be read as symptoms of a wider anxiety regarding public order. What was at stake during and after the riots in Mumbai was the very "myth of the state," the imagination of the state as a distant but persistent guarantee of a certain social order, a measure of justice and protection from violence. The shattering of this myth obviously appeared in different guises to different groups and communities. To the Muslims in Mumbai (approximately 17 percent of the city's population), who bore the brunt of police brutality and ethnic rage of militant Hindus in both rounds of violence, the riots marked the culmination of a long process of political marginalization and everyday harassment by the city police and Hindu extremist political forces. For more than a decade Muslims had been the targets of a relentless stigmatization by militant Hindu nationalist organizations such as the Shiv Sena (Shivaji's Army). Aided by the police, the dominant Marathi-, Hindi-, and English-language newspapers in Mumbai had consolidated older images of the city's Muslim areas as dens of drug peddling, smuggling, and violence, peopled by clannish, fanatic, and hostile Muslims paying allegiance to dreaded Muslim mafia dons like the Dubai-based gangster king, Dawood Ibrahim.

The anti-Muslim bias of the police force in the city became more obvious than ever during the riots, when police officers issued orders of "shoot to kill" at Muslim demonstrators, while generally milder forms of riot control were administered on Hindu crowds. During one week of riots, killings, and arson in the city—organized and encouraged by Shiv Sena—the police actively assisted Hindus, protected them from Muslim counterattacks, or simply turned a blind eye on the atrocities and plunder by Hindu militants.[1] The presence of leading Congress ministers in Mumbai during the riots and their deployment of the newly formed Rapid Action Force did not curb the sustained attacks on Muslims.

These circumstances gave rise to a range of rumors and conspiracy theories. To most of my informants in the Muslim neighborhoods in central Mumbai, older imaginings of the upper echelons of state and the Congress Party as sites of justice and protection gave way to a radical sense of isolation and betrayal. In March 1993 a group of people, mainly Muslims affiliated with gangster organizations in Mumbai, organized a series of bomb blasts, killing hundreds of civilians on a single day, wrecking bus terminals as well as the stock exchange in the city. A few weeks later, consignments of arms and explosives were recovered at several places along the Maharashtrian coast. Allegations of the involvement of the secret and independent Pakistani intelligence unit Inter-Service Intelligence (ISI) in assisting local underworld networks in Mumbai were immediately raised by the police as well as Hindu nationalist and more moderate public figures.[2]

Regardless of the factual complexities surrounding the bomb blasts, it soon became a well-established popular truth that the blasts constituted a Muslim answer to militant Hindus, a message of "Don't mess with us" sent by the mythological Dawood Ibrahim, now elevated to the status of a stern godfather figure. A Muslim female teacher from Nagpada echoed what I found to be a widespread sentiment when in 1993 she told me, "We all felt horrible during those four months [December 1992 to March 1993]—all over you would hear these derogatory remarks about Muslims, you felt the hostility all over, in the trains, in shops, in my school. I recall riding on a train when a group of Hindu women spotted me and started talking quietly. One said, 'We Hindu women should also do something. Look at that Muslim woman there—one should throw her off the train.' . . . All this stopped after the bomb blasts—not because they accepted us, but because they feared us."

Among the substantial sections of the Hindu middle classes and the slum dwellers who supported militant Hindu nationalism, the shattering of the myth of the state appeared in an altogether different form. Here it was a triumphalist sense of "teaching the Muslims a lesson," of overruling and defying the state, of celebrating an ethnic majoritarian justice opposed to what Hindu nationalist leaders had decried as the state's "pampering" and protection of minorities. During these heated months in Mumbai it was as if earlier, more restrained and guarded modes of naming and talking about Muslims gave way to the most radical xenophobic fears and fantasies that circulated from rickshaw drivers to respectable family doctors.

The supreme dictatorial leader of Shiv Sena, Bal Thackeray, has made a name for himself through colorful and provoking rhetoric, his radical abuse of Muslims and political opponents, and his outspoken contempt for the judiciary and populist attacks on everything associated with *sarkar* (the state/government; see Hansen 1996). Since the riots, the Shiv Sena has consolidated its position year by year. In the elections in 1995 that brought Shiv Sena to power in the state of Maharashtra, the party completely swept the polls in the metropolis. In spite of massive evidence of increasing levels of corruption, open contempt for legal processes and democratic procedures, and Thackeray's celebration of his own "remote control" of the government, the party's popularity was not affected for several years. Amid mounting evidence of corruption at the highest level the party once more swept the polls at the municipal elections in 1997 in Mumbai and several other cities in the state (see Hansen 1998).

Governance and the Imagined State

The state is a name given to various practices and institutions of government, not only as an analytical concept but also as a locus of authority, however elusive, invoked by and reproduced by an endless range of interventions—from validating documents and checking motor vehicles to prohibiting certain substances and encouraging certain forms of behavior that serve the public health or interest. The state, in other words, is an organizing concept through which people in Mumbai, as well as in other modern societies, imagine the cohesion of their own society, its order and its institutions but also its hidden secrets, its sources of violence and evil.

This idea of the state as the site of sovereignty and a symbolic center of political will and power above partial interests, and thus embodying a universality of justice, knowledge, reason, and authority that exceeds any single representation (a party, an ethnic group, a class) is rooted in Western history. According to this idea, the state must govern but it must also reproduce an imaginary dimension that separates the actions of the state from those of any other agency. Whereas the state indeed is made manifest in an amorphous terrain of small arenas and local institutions, governance is not necessarily legitimate. The production of legitimacy, that is, the naturalization of power, requires constant enactment of the state as a symbolic center of society, the source of governance, the arbiter of conflicts, the site of authorization—as delegation of power as well as the right to "write society"—in law, constitution, rules, certificates, and so on.

My argument is that this public and performative dimension of governance and politics is critical to the significance of state spectacles, political rhetoric, and processes of political identification, as well as to the pertinence of "the Law," public legal processes, and so on.

Ernst Kantorowicz (1959) has shown with great subtlety how a legal-political theory of the "king's two bodies" developed in medieval Britain. Here, political authority was constructed as a dual structure: on the one hand, the notion of a sublime, infallible, and eternal body of the king (the law); on the other, the profane, human, and fallible body of the king (the giver of laws). Kantorowicz quotes Blackstone writing on the sublime dimension of royal authority: "[The King] . . . is not only incapable of *doing* wrong, but even of *thinking* wrong: he can never mean to do an improper thing: in him is no folly or weakness" (4).

As Lefort points out, the efficiency of this construction flows precisely from the separation and unity of these two bodies, from the combination of the profane and the sublime in the eyes of the subjects: "It is the image of the natural body, the image of a God made flesh, the image of his marriage, his paternity, his liaisons, his festivals, his amusements and his feasts, but also the images of his weaknesses or even his cruelties, in short, all the images of his humanity, that people their imaginary, that assure them that the people and the king are conjoined" (Lefort 1998: 245).

This union of the two bodies was later reconfigured as the nation, the people, or the leader took the place of the sublime-abstract body and made governance of the empirical and profane people possible in the name of this higher principle (Lefort 1988: 254). Lefort argues that with the advent of democracy this mythical and "original" source of power becomes radically empty, as it can be only temporarily occupied by representatives of the people, or the nation (17). What can be occupied is exactly that which is more permanent and enduring: the central institutions and symbols of the state.[3]

I suggest seeing the imagination of the state as marked by a deep and constitutive split. On the one hand its "profane" dimensions: the incoherence, brutality, partiality, and the banality of the technical sides of governance, as well as the rough-and-tumble of negotiation, compromise, and naked self-interest displayed in local politics. On the other hand, the "sublime" qualities imputed to a more distant state: the opacity of the secrets and knowledge of the higher echelons of the state, its hidden resources, designs, and immense power, and the illusions of higher forms of rationality or justice believed to prevail there. The repertoire of public performatives of the state—from stamps to military parades and imposing architecture—serves to consolidate this imagination of the state as an elevated entity. To paraphrase Durkheim, the celebrations of the rationality and power of the state represent attempts to make a society worship itself and its own social order.

If we keep this duality of the state in mind we may see the full significance of why political forces and agencies of the state felt the need to launch various initiatives in Mumbai to create mechanisms for reconciliation, or at least cohabitation, between Muslims and Hindus after the riots. I argue that these initiatives have been launched to reassert the authority of the state—partly by reorganizing techniques of governance, but also by reconfiguring the legitimacy and authority of the state aiming at retrieving a myth of the state without which a democratic state cannot govern, not even if this state is headed by a government that nurtures the most antidemocratic form of majoritarianism, as in the case of Shiv Sena.

Before proceeding to the complexities of contemporary Mumbai, let me briefly consider whether and how such a line of reasoning derived from medieval Western political thought can be made relevant to contemporary India. Are there any "sublime" dimensions of the state and political authority in modern India? Should one instead adopt a longue durée perspective and inquire into how older registers of kingship and the relations between Brahmins and *khatriyas* (ruling or land-owning castes) are played out today?[4] There is no doubt that notions of honor, patronage, and the appropriate behavior of the landowning aristocracy and dominant castes in various parts of India have shaped the construction of politics there in profound ways.[5] These cultural repertoires seem, however, insufficient to capture the meanings evoked by the term sarkar in contemporary India.

In spite of deeply segmented and competing notions of power, leadership, and legitimacy in postcolonial India, its public culture has produced a large reservoir of shared symbols, languages, and references—from war heroes to politicians and film heroes to sports teams, cultural events, brand names, and styles of consumption shared across the length of India as well as across caste and class. This national, or at least nationwide, culture has systematically been promoted by the state, whose crucial role in producing a national imaginary hardly can be overestimated, as Khilnani (1997: 19) has pointed out.

The political field abounds with religious imagery, and politicians invoke precolonial aristocratic splendor in dress and speech and refer to the wisdom of religious texts when they attempt to represent the authority of the nation-state. However, education, command of English, and competence in science and administration constitute equally, if not more, powerful registers of authority and sublime qualities. The bureaucrat, the planner, and the scientist, the member of the Indian Administrative Service—the heavily mythologized "steel frame" of the state—occupy crucial positions in contemporary political imaginaries, not least of the large middle class. The bureaucrat was until recently the hero of modern India and until the 1970s was depicted in Hindi films as a man of character and insight.

Until quite recently this "modern nationalist aristocracy"—lineages and families of high-ranking bureaucrats, scientists, and politicians—were referred to with awe and respect. The mark of these ideal national citizens that manned the bureaucracy was exactly their combination of moral integrity, commitment to the larger abstract nation, and deep technical insights. The authority of education, especially English education, remains crucial also among ordinary people, where it often generates more respect than wealth. Many ordinary people in India still attribute considerable authority and sublime qualities to institutions such as courts, to judges, to senior bureaucrats, and so on. This testifies to how effectively the modern nationalist elite in India throughout this century has made education, science, the rule of law, and the role of the public sector into core signifiers of the modern nation.

Complementing older registers of public conducts, this nationalist register has evolved into a complex web of public languages and political imaginaries that shape discourses on the state and boost rumors and stories of transgressions of rules, corruption, and abuse of governmental authority. It is the sense of violation of the idealized sublime qualities imputed to the state that makes such stories worth telling. It may well be that ordinary Indians are less in awe of the state than a few decades ago, but the state is still regarded as indispensable in terms of public order and of recognizing communities, leaders, or claims as legitimate and authentic. Bureaucrats, judges, and officers are called on every day to authenticate, inaugurate, and authorize, in brief, to act as transient incarnations of authority and symbols of the state. These manifestations of the authority of the state may well be a structural effect of governance, as Tim Mitchell (1999:9) contends, but they are also important public performances that need to be studied in their own right.[6]

I will illustrate the split representation of the Indian state as both sublime and profane, first, by analyzing the initiatives in the field of the judiciary, especially the construction and impact of the Srikrishna Commission inquiring into the riots and the bomb blasts in 1993 and the proceedings of the special court mandated under the Terrorist and Disruptive Activities Act (TADA) investigating the bomb blasts in March 1993. Second, I discuss how the government maintains public order in central Mumbai and how the so-called *mohalla* (neighborhood) committees were set up by the police and NGOs in these areas in 1994. I look at the trajectory of these initiatives and how they impacted on local perceptions of state and authority in the context of the strained everyday encounters between police and Muslims in the city.

The Srikrishna Commission: Catharsis and the Politics of Truth

A few weeks after the riots in January 1993, the government of Maharashtra decided to set up an Inquiry Commission headed by the high court judge, Justice Srikrishna. The massive evidence of open involvement of Shiv Sena and other political parties in the violence, and of abuse of authority on the part of the police, made it clear that to reestablish its authority in the eyes of the minorities, human rights organizations, and the broader public, the government had to demonstrate its commitment to justice. The commission began its work in June 1993 with the mandate to establish "the circumstances, events and immediate causes of the incidents which occurred in the Bombay Police Commissionerate area in December 1992 on or after the 6th December 1992, and again in January 1993, on or after the 6th January 1993." The commission was further mandated to identify "individuals, or groups of individuals or any other organization" responsible for the riots, as well as to assess the effectiveness of the Bombay Police in handling the situation (Srikrishna 1998: 1).[7]

The commission was supposed to work like a public hearing and initially called "all persons having knowledge about facts touching upon the Terms of

Reference to come forward and file affidavits before the Commission" (Srikrishna 1998: 2) and also called on the police and the government to submit their versions of the events in the city: 2,126 affidavits were filed, 2 from the government, 549 by the police, and 1,575 by various individuals and organizations. After several attempts at obstruction and delay from the state government, the report of the commission finally appeared in August 1998, five and a half years after the riots took place. It was left to the state government to decide whether the massive evidence gathered by the commission should be made available to the advocate-general to allow the state to institute criminal prosecution.

Public inquiries into serious conflagrations, major policy failures, and disasters, such as famines and revolts, have been carried out in India since the 1870s. The inquests of the colonial state were normally carried out by civil servants who interviewed police officers, victims, witnesses, and others to establish the factual circumstances and to apportion responsibility. In the independent postcolonial state, these techniques of governmental self-diagnostics continued but acquired new moral and political dimensions as they became intensely occupied with rooting out harmful practices and with reforming society through reform of the state. As Visvanathan notes in his discussion of corruption inquiries in the 1950s and 1960s, "Public administration was (now) the home science of the modern state. The state was not seen as something gargantuan, a huge organism or a giant machine, but as something tentative" (1998: 15).

With the Shah Commission in 1977 probing into the excesses of the Emergency imposed by Indira Gandhi, a new and more openly "cathartic" mode of inquiry was created. The need was felt to clarify the extent of the damage caused by Gandhi's dictatorship as well as to redeem the apparatus of the state. The Shah Commission was more like a hearing, with submissions from victims of excessive use of state powers, as well as responsible bureaucrats and politicians. Everybody appearing before the commission was allowed to be represented by legal counsel, and the commission sought in its style and proceedings to be as close as possible to those of a courtroom.

The Srikrishna Commission emerged more like a public tribunal: it was decided to make the proceedings public and to call on interested organizations and parties to be represented through legal counsel along with the commission's own official advocate. A number of organizations and parties were represented before the commission. The Shiv Sena, the Bharatiya Janata Party

(BJP; both of which were ruling the state during most of the tenure of the commission), the All-India Milli Council (a coordination group for a number of Muslim organizations), the Jamiyat-E-Ulema (Council of Islamic Scholars), the Communist Party of India (until 1995), and a variety of human rights associations such as the Lawyers' Collective and the Committee for the Protection of Human Rights, from 1993 to 1997 have all been represented at the hearings. The commission could order any public servant to testify before it, whereas ordinary citizens appeared only voluntarily. The same voluntary principle applied to those elected to public office, but given the public nature of the hearings there was pressure on public figures to actually appear and let themselves be cross-examined.

The hearings began as systematic inquiries into the events unfolding in the critical period in the twenty-six affected police districts in the city; later, the focus was on background factors and the role of specific public agencies, especially the police force. Based on independent investigation and affidavits from citizens and police officers, the commission and the counselors representing the interested parties called and cross-examined witnesses of various sorts and loyalties. After the cross-examination of each witness, Justice Srikrishna drew his conclusions concerning the chain of events or cause-effect relationship dealt with, and these brief summaries and conclusions, along with a massive amount of written material, formed the bulk of the material summarized in the final report.

The material the commission dealt with was intensely politicized, just as the form and public nature of the hearings—intensely covered by the press—often made them rhetorical platforms for the counselors of the different parties. The commission openly and self-consciously tried to extract, or approximate, a factual truth from a series of political interpretations. The basic task of establishing positively who did what, when, and how was often exceedingly difficult and had often to rely on inferences rather than clear-cut evidence.

Let me offer a few glimpses into how material was presented before the commission.[8]

Reconstructing "Truth" after the Fact

As the decision to set up a commission of inquiry was taken by the state government in February 1993, Bombay's commissioner of police during the riots, S. Bapat, was transferred and A. S. Samra, a highly respected officer, was brought in to reform the Bombay Police. Samra had been highly successful in preventing the massive riots in Bombay from spreading to Thane, an industrial district north of the city, that had seen the worst rioting in the country in the 1980s, and as a Sikh he was widely assumed to be neutral in the Hindu-Muslim conflict. This move and the wording of the mandate of the commission made it clear to many police officers that the state government was ready to put most of the responsibility on the police force. Hundreds of officers who had been in command at police stations got busy writing lengthy affidavits explaining their actions and perceptions during the riots.

The two handfuls of such affidavits I managed to get access to all ran along similar lines. They began with a long, often rosy account of the career of the officer, his specific distinctions, often pointing to long experience in handling "mobs" or crowds. One officer referred to his long experience at police stations in Bombay's mill district, where on many occasions he had dealt with demonstrators and "violent mobs." Another went through an almost ten-page account of all the demanding postings he had been through—ranging from Dharavi, the biggest slum in Asia, to Agripada, described as one of the most "notorious trouble spots in Bombay"—and rendered a virtual catalogue of situations he had dealt with in these locations: mass meetings, Hindu-Muslim violence after cricket matches between India and Pakistan, religious processions turned into "rampaging mobs," and more.

Armed with these credentials, the officers then turned to descriptions of the areas they were posted in during the riots. One officer described the Muslim-dominated Dongri area in central Bombay as a dangerous and unpredictable place: "This locality has a long history of communal riots [that have] been occurring here at frequent intervals since 1893. . . . Though by and large the residents are peace-loving citizens, incidents of antinational character committed by a few mischief mongers tend to cause sudden escalation of tension. The area has earned such a notorious reputation that the police machinery has to be alert round the year. However, it is not always possible to predict how and to what extent a situation can deteriorate."

The accounts then gave vivid and detailed descriptions of the events and the actions of the officers, the orders issued, the number of rounds fired, and so on. From these accounts a picture of chaos, drama, and confusion emerged: of a city exploding in what the officers described as random and unintelligible violence; of looting, arson, and violence breaking out behind the police as they dealt with one situation, reports arrived of police vehicles being stoned and attacked by rioters in new areas and so forth. These were stories of a force not properly prepared for such situations and of fear of mobs that in the accounts from the Muslim parts of the city seemed intensely hostile to the police force.

In the cross-examinations most officers defended their actions and asserted the need for public order. One maintained that when Hindus were ringing the temple bells on 6 December to celebrate the demolition of the mosque in Ayodhya (the so-called *ghanta naad* [ringing of temple bells] promoted by Shiv Sena), "It was treated as religious activity exempted under the ban order of the Bombay Police Act." A senior inspector from the Nagpada police station admitted that although he was aware that Shiv Sainiks (Shiv Sena activists) made highly provocative speeches in connection with the ghanta naad, "It did not then occur to me to take any action."

An inspector was asked by the counsel for the Milli Council to justify his calling Muslims "aggressors." He replied, "Muslims were aggressors because they came out in large numbers [and] they did resort to violence. The police had to take effective action and the Muslims who were on the streets had to bear the brunt of the police action." According to this officer, the questions of why events took place, who was shot, and so on were not relevant to policing. Their job was to restore public order, and those who got in the way might get shot.

The issue of whether the police used excessive force against especially Muslim rioters was discussed at length at the proceedings. A police officer defended the immediate use of "extreme force" (i.e., shooting directly at rioters to kill): "I do not think that it is always necessary to use graded force when dealing with a situation of violence. If extreme force is resorted to, at the very first stage, to put down firmly the riots, I would consider it justified."

Affidavits from ordinary constables told a less orderly story, full of horror of advancing mobs: "The mob did not respond to our teargas . . . on the contrary, they indulged in heavy stone throwing . . . then someone fired a gun at us." An elderly constable related how he was attacked with a sword and how his colleagues withdrew into the police post: "I was then left alone in the hands of the mob, I was terribly frightened . . . someone attacked my face and neck with a sword."

Most of the accounts by constables seemed to reflect both fear and incomprehension, as if rioters were a sort of natural calamity, displaying an aggression that the policemen did not seem to connect to their own status as police. Instead, many of them depicted themselves as the victims of the riots. Judging from my conversations with policemen, this was not an attempt to exonerate themselves or their actions. None of the policemen I talked to denied he had shot dead or wounded rioters. To them, the shooting was in self-defense, the only way to respond to the mobs they dreaded so much. The sense of being unjustly targeted while doing your job, of being hated by the local people, of detesting those same local people, and of being stabbed in the back by political leaders was a common experience. In some ways it appeared to me to be the strongest bonding, a sort of negative esprit de corps.[9]

The bulk of the evidence presented to the commission was, however, affidavits submitted by victims and bereaved families—mostly Muslim—social workers, local organizations, journalists, and many others who did not share the police's perspective. There were harrowing accounts of the brutality and rage of groups of men attacking Muslims in streets and homes, attacks often led and organized by local Shiv Sainiks; and there were frightening accounts of the anti-Muslim bias of the police in their "cleanup" operations. A young man who worked in a Muslim-owned bakery recounted before the Commission how "commandos in light uniforms and bulletproof vests entered the building. I peeped out from my hiding and saw Samshad standing, two commandos pointing their guns at him. He folded his hands and sat down near the commandos and pleaded that he was a Bhaiya (from Uttar Pradesh). One of the commandos kept saying that Samshad was a Pakistani, the other said that he was Kashmiri. . . . I concealed myself again, then I heard firing and it became quiet. I saw Samshad writhing in pain, blood flowing out. He said his prayers for a minute or two, and then he was quiet."

It was, however, testimonies from leading police officers that elicited most interest from journalists and others interested in the proceedings.[10] V. Deshmukh, former leader of the Special Branch (SB) in Bombay, was the first high-ranking police officer to appear before the commission. A well-spoken man with intellectual inclinations, Deshmukh appeared very humble that day in mid-February 1997 as he stood in his uniform in the dock in the spacious room in the Bombay High Court.

Deshmukh was more frank in his admission of the failures of SB than anyone had anticipated. He explained the lack of intelligence work by the fact that he, as well as many others, "was led to believe that the government would protect the mosque [in Ayodhya, demolished in December 1992 by Hindu nationalists]." He said that he was well aware of Shiv Sena's capacity for violence, that the party "had incited hatred against the minority community," and that "*maha aartis*"[11] were started by Shiv Sena in late December 1992 with the purpose of forcing the minority community to give up their *namaz* [prayer] on the streets." He also stated that SB knew all the central persons of communal organizations in the city, but chose to do nothing, as he and other police officers were reassured that nothing would happen in Ayodhya: "I had assessed that arresting activists and leaders of the Shiv Sena would result in further communal violence. . . . The tension that developed in areas under Shiv Sena influence following a rumor that Bal Thackeray [Shiv Sena leader] would be arrested was not a factor that affected my assessment. It was based on what had happened on previous occasions."

In his cross-examination of Deshmukh, Shiv Sena's counsel, Balakrishna Joshi, followed a course he had pursued throughout the hearings. Instead of challenging the evidence of Shiv Sena's involvement (which would have been a futile exercise), Joshi focused almost exclusively on alleged aggressions and attacks on the police and Hindus by Muslims. During the riots, rumors were rife that Muslims collected arms in mosques and that loudspeakers on mosques were used to incite attacks on Hindus. But Deshmukh stated that SB never recovered any weapon from mosques.

Questioned by the commission's counsel, Vijay Pradhan, Deshmukh admitted that he had not recommended any preventive arrests in early January although it was common knowledge that Shiv Sena was inciting its followers in ever growing maha aartis.

> *Pradhan:* Were you aware of a closed door meeting for the entire Shiv Sena leadership on December 29, 1992? (Alleged to be the time when Shiv Sena's subsequent attack on Muslims was planned.)
>
> *Deshmukh:* Yes Sir, we were aware of that meeting being held.
>
> *Pradhan:* Did you get information about what happened at that meeting?
>
> *Deshmukh:* We were informed that the agenda concerned collection of funds for riot victims.
>
> *Judge Srikrishna:* Would such an agenda in your opinion need closed doors?
>
> *Deshmukh:* No. The SB received reports on December 10 that *masjids* [mosques] maybe were used to instigate violence, but issued no instructions in this regard . . . nor did it act against two Muslims who gave provocative speeches in November 1992.

Deshmukh's reaction here revealed that he subscribed to the widespread notion of communal violence as simple retributive justice, where a killing on each side cancels each and makes the two sides even. The grave failure of the SB to monitor Shiv Sena could, in this view, be counterbalanced by its equally serious leniency toward Muslim communal organizations. One nonaction makes another nonaction plausible and permissible. Shiv Sena's counsel pursued this line in a subsequent attempt to exonerate Hindu policemen by claiming that particular Muslim police officers had acted in a partial and anti-Hindu manner during the riots. No conclusive evidence was produced and the allegations were dismissed by Srikrishna (*Mid-Day*, April 5, 1997).

The perception that Muslim anger or "aggression" justified police brutality and later Hindu "retaliation" also informed the following week's testimony of Shreekant Bapat, who was commissioner of police in Bombay during the riots. Bapat was widely believed to be sympathetic to Shiv Sena and BJP and had submitted a 175-page affidavit. Over a week he was cross-examined by five counselors, among them Mr. Hudlikar, representing the police force. Hudlikar was generous in his questioning and gave Bapat ample time to expand on what he had stated in writing. Bapat was particularly adamant in his rejection of the charge of having an anti-Muslim bias: "According to me the larger number of minority community casualties during December 1992 can be explained on the basis of the much greater aggression of the minority community mobs." Shortly after, Mr. Muchalla, the soft-spoken counsel for the Milli Council, probed further into this, and Bapat said angrily, "It is not true that action against the minority community in December 1992 was wholly unjustified." Muchalla then confronted Bapat with the police's own statistics, which showed that also in January, when Hindus led by Shiv Sainiks were the undisputed aggressors, most of the victims of police firings were Muslims. Bapat replied, "I cannot comment on that."

Then the commission's own counsel took over and asked Bapat why his affidavit never mentioned the by then well-established role in the riots played by the Shiv Sena. Bapat replied, "If there is reference to Shiv Sena, it should be there. If there is no reference, there is none." He continued: "The police are concerned with offense, not with political affiliation."

At this point, Justice Srikrishna lost patience and asked Bapat why the issues of involvement of organizations in the riots were omitted. Visibly disturbed, Bapat assured that the police before the riots "had taken action against organizations known to be violent."

Srikrishna: If this was done, why is there no reference to organizations in your affidavit?

Bapat: We had no material at hand at this point in time indicating that any organization was involved in the riots.

Srikrishna: Were you not aware that Shiv Sena leaders claimed that their volunteers had demolished the Babri Masjid? (A news item splashed across front pages in most of the country a few days after the demolition.)

Bapat: No, I was not aware of such statements being made.

Here the judge sighed, leaned back, and said, "Thank you, sir."

The Politics of Balancing Guilt

The evasiveness and obvious irresponsibility of leading policemen appearing before the commission, as well as the apparent lack of comprehension among ordinary policemen of the social world they were supposed to police testified to how ill-equipped the police were to perform basic tasks of maintaining public order. The interpretations of communal riots in terms of apportioning and "balancing" collective guilt and responsibilities among faceless and abstract communities that emerged from the commission hearings clearly reflected a dominant and widespread modality of politico-moral discourse. But it did not produce material suited for prosecution of actual and concrete crimes committed by individuals. As the former commissioner of police in Mumbai A. S. Samra stated emphatically a few days before he was appointed, "Our penal code and our idea of justice revolves around the idea that individuals commit crimes and are punished, whereas political parties as a whole do politics. There might be individuals within these parties who commit crimes, even leaders, but they must be punished as individuals. . . . What can we do to an organization? Ban it? That is difficult to do more permanently in a democracy" (interview, February 18, 1993).

When appearing before the commission in April 1997, Samra reiterated this point of view, and declined to name particular organizations responsible for violence. When Justice Srikrishna pointed out that a range of organizations such as Shiv Sena, Vishwa Hindu Parishad, and various Muslim organizations were listed in the government of Maharashtra's "Guidelines to Handle Communal Riots" issued in 1986, Samra said, "It is true that they were active in social activities, but it did not come to my notice that they as organizations indulged in illegal acts. Some of their members have done so" (*Mid-Day*, April 12, 1997).

Like other high-ranking police officers, Samra appeared to be rather concerned with protecting the police force. In his deposition, he depicted the police as the protectors of society by conveniently blaming the riots on Dawood Ibrahim and other criminal networks and "land grabbers." These criminals felt threatened after the crackdown on illegal constructions by the municipality and the police force in the preceding year, and "they hit back by exploiting the feelings of the people after the demolition of the Babri Masjid," Samra stated (*Mid-Day*, April 16, 1997).

Yet, the proceedings of the commission inadvertently began to expose the complex links among political parties, the state, and the legal system. This became particularly evident as the main perpetrator of violence, Shiv Sena, assumed office in the government of Maharashtra in 1995. The principal area of contention between the government and the commission concerned the release of documents and files related to the inquiry. The commission had to seek permission from the advocate-general for release or declassification of documents. In some cases, this was refused on the basis of "interest of state" or other compelling reasons, but generally the state could not in principle claim privilege and refuse to hand over the required documents (according to the Public Inquiry Act). Justice Srikrishna could here use powers equivalent to those of a High Court judge and demand the release of certain documents. After the coming to power of the Hindu nationalist coalition government in Maharashtra in March 1995, twelve of more than twenty cases pending against Thackeray for violence-inciting rhetoric were withdrawn or classified (i.e., made a security question and hence neither object for public prosecution nor available for scrutiny by the commission). After a protracted legal tussle, the state government agreed to hand over four cases to the commission.[12] The scrutiny revealed that the cases had been pending for a very long time without any agency daring to take action and that Sena leaders repeatedly had tried to threaten the government to withdraw the cases. Police Commissioner Tyagi stated that if the government decided to withdraw the cases "in the interest of communal peace and social justice," the police force would have no objections (*Times of India*, April 4 1997). It should be added that after his retirement from the police force in 1997, Tyagi was nominated as candidate for Shiv Sena in the 1998 general elections in India but failed to win a seat.

As Shiv Sena and its ally BJP came to power in Maharashtra in 1995 the new government began a process of obstructing the course of the investigation. As mounting evidence pointed to Shiv Sena's crucial role in both rounds of violence as well as to the many links between the party and the police force, it was decided on January 23, 1996, to dissolve the Srikrishna Commission. Although in a strict sense the state had legitimate power to dissolve the commission and Shiv Sena had sworn to do so during the election campaign in 1995, there were few precedents, none of which involved such blatant and transparent bad faith as in this case.

The issue of legitimate authority was at stake here. Could the state actually sustain a credible aura of impartiality if it exercised in such an unmitigated manner a clear ethnic/majoritarian form of justice? In the ensuing debate intellectuals, activists, and political figures argued that the commission had to be reinstated to support the process of consolidating intercommunity peace and harmony, whereas legal questions of justice and prosecution of the perpetrators of violence played a very minor role. Under pressure from the central government it was decided to restore the commission but with an expanded mandate. It was now decided that the commission should include the bomb blasts in March 1993 "to give a clearer and more comprehensive picture of the patterns of violence and civil disturbances in the city," as it was argued by the advocate-general (*Indian Express*, May 29, 1996).[13] The inclusion of the bomb blasts was a rather transparent attempt to deflect the course of the investigation but nonetheless enjoyed considerable support in the public debates following the move. This reflected, once more, that the dominant, and official, interpretation of the riots as irrational excesses spontaneously committed equally by faceless Hindu and Muslim communities (neither as organizations nor as individuals) in extraordinary situations enjoyed widespread currency. The government's decision actually authorized the formula of "balanced and equally apportioned guilt": that every murder by Hindus could be morally neutralized by demonstrating a corresponding atrocity committed by Muslims. The logic of "retributive justice" that Shiv Sena's counsel and the Shiv Sena–led government had been at pains to establish to exonerate itself seemed slowly to impose itself on the commission's work.

There was a glaring contrast between the slow, contested, and in many ways academic character of the work of the Srikrishna Commission, and the simultaneous prosecution of those accused of responsibility for the bomb blasts in March 1993. In the weeks following the blasts hundreds of people, mainly Muslims, were rounded up and detained under the stringent Terrorist and Disruptive Activities Act (TADA, an antiterrorist law passed in the 1980s designed to combat Sikh militants in Punjab). As many as 189 persons were accused of complicity in the conspiracy. Most of these detainees were subjected to the most humiliating and brutal forms of interrogation, and only few of them were granted bail. Even those who were accused of playing minor roles in connection with the arms consignments on the coast of Maharashtra in February 1993 were kept imprisoned for more than two years before they were released because of lack of evidence. A brand new high-security TADA court building was erected in Mumbai, and the police displayed unusual diligence in producing and gathering a massive amount of evidence in the cases. Before the Central Bureau of Investigations in Delhi took over the case, the Bombay Police had charged all the accused with one of the most serious offenses in the Indian Penal Code, "the waging of war against the state." These charges were withdrawn only after a much-delayed intervention of the attorney general (Visvanathan 1998: 127–28). Most of the evidence gathered by the Bombay Police that indicted this large number of people was either irrelevant or of low quality. By contrast, corrupt officials in police and customs departments who had made possible the import of advanced explosives into Mumbai had not even been questioned.[14]

The TADA court proceeded at a brisk pace. It was closed to the public because of the allegedly sensitive character of the evidence presented there.[15] Prosecution targeted individuals and the Shiv Sena government stated explicitly that it wanted to speed up the process against what it called "Muslim gangsters" responsible for the blasts. Some of the accused were sentenced to ten and twenty years of imprisonment. A number of the key accused, in one way or the other supposedly connected with Dawood Ibrahim, are still in hiding. Although the case is not yet fully concluded, it appears unlikely, given the strong political pressure on the TADA court, that those sentenced can expect a new trial or that the government will concede that many have been convicted on questionable grounds.

Diagnostics, Prescriptions, and State Spectacles: The Report of the Srikrishna Commission

The status and authority of a report of a commission of inquiry is always precarious. It is not just an expert's report or a piece of research commissioned by the government. Whether the government agrees with the conclusions or not, it is inevitably an authoritative statement on the matter under scrutiny. However, the government is not compelled by law to implement or even accept the findings and recommendations of the commission. More clearly than in any other commission I know of in India, the complicated and contested trajectory of the Srikrishna Commission had made this inquiry into a spectacular clash of different notions of the state: on one side, the decent high court judge, supported by human rights activists and large sections of the press, defending the idea of the state as impartial, above society, and committed to a universal form of justice; on the other side, the administrative machinery and the police employing their armory of techniques to delay, obstruct, or influence the inquiry to protect their own "secrets" and cover up their failings; and the political forces governing the state, committed to a majoritarian notion of "retributive justice," bending and threatening the administration to serve their ends. Although public in its form, this debate on the authority of state power remained in significant ways internal to the state, in terms of its mandate, resources, methodology, and authority. It was not a citizen's tribunal or an independent investigation putting the state as such on trial.[16]

I argue that both the Srikrishna Commission and the TADA court should be seen as state spectacles, carefully crafted public manifestations of the state as a producer of impartial and universal justice. At the same time, the very simultaneity of the two proceedings, one indicting Hindu organizations and the police, the other "Muslim *goondas* [criminals]," represented in itself the discourse of "retributive justice." Both of these proceedings were marked by the crucial duality inherent in the representation of the state. The Srikrishna Commission revealed numerous examples of the profane sides of state power: the deplorable quality of policing and police intelligence; the partial, biased, and brutal conduct of the police force; and series of blatant attempts on the part of the government to obstruct the proceedings and to prevent powerful political figures such as Bal Thackeray from being prosecuted. At the same time, the very existence of the commission, the tenacity and integrity of Justice Srikrishna, and the public exposure of misconduct, corruption, and liaisons between politicians and the police force also provided a site for a certain process of public catharsis.

In this capacity the commission has become a symbol of the resilience of a higher and more benevolent form of justice, and thus a sign of the permanence of the sublime dimension of the state. This duality was inscribed in the choreography of the proceedings: before the bench a string of counselors who sought to extract their particular and interested, and intensely politicized, truth-claims from the stream of witnesses passing through, while the judge, positioned three feet above the rest, concluded each cross-examination with a summing up supposed to extract the reasonable and the factually plausible—the negotiated truth—from the maze of interpretations before him.

The final report from Justice Srikrishna adopts a medicalized language. As a medical doctor, Srikrishna diagnoses and prescribes a possible cure for what he terms the "communal malady": "Communal riots, the bane of this country, are like incurable epileptic seizures, whose symptoms, though dormant over a period of time, manifest themselves again and again. Measures of various kinds suggested from time to time dealt with symptoms and acted as palliatives without effecting a permanent cure of the malaise." The judge argues further that until a complete change in social outlook and the level of education, "communal riots must be treated, perhaps, as an incurable disease whose prognosis calls for suitable measures to contain its evil effects" (1998: 4).

In keeping with this diagnosis the judge is brief in his examination of the causes behind the riots, admitting that they grow out of complex dynamics of demography, class, and political discourses. Bombay had the unfortunate combination of an increasingly impoverished and isolated Muslim community and a set of very aggressive Hindu organizations (Srikrishna 1998: 25–29). Srikrishna is emphatic in his statement that "[no] known Muslim individuals or organizations were responsible for the riots," and equally emphatic in pointing to the responsibility of Shiv Sena, not as an organization per se, but as "the attitudes of Shiv Sena leaders [as reflected in] its doctrine of 'retaliation' were responsible for the vigilantism of Shiv Sainiks" (30).

Srikrishna regards communal riots as incurable, and he notes in a more poetic vein that because "the beast in man keeps straining at the leash to jump out" (1998: 63), effective measures are of paramount importance. The most interesting part of the report is the judge's diagnosis of the structure and shortcomings of the police force in Mumbai and the string of recommendations he makes to remedy these (31–62). Srikrishna paints a gloomy picture of a complacent, biased, disorganized force where even the most everyday routines of filing cases, physical training, and discipline are incoherent if not absent. Returning to the diagnostic mode, he sums up, "Despite knowledge of the fact that the force had been infected by communal virus, no effective curative steps were taken over a large period of time as a result of which, communal violence became chronic and its virulent symptoms showed up during the two riot periods" (35).

The entire tone of the report maintains this measured distance to the interested parties and gives critical and considered summaries of the events unfolding around each police station. The judge examines the depositions by leading police officers and political leaders, former ministers. Reading through these pages one gets an ever clearer picture of the theory of the state to which Srikrishna subscribes. The tone is not legalistic but moral. He is highly critical of nonadherence to rules and regulations in the police force but even more critical of the ostensible lack of commitment and lack of a moral outlook he detects in leading police officers and in many political figures.

Srikrishna's view is clearly that a sense of duty toward the nation and an ethical view of life must be the basis of the representatives of the state. The formula seems to be "the higher the rank, the deeper the commitment," a formula that resonates with the dominant discourse of the postcolonial nation-state in India. The idea of the state as a moral entity, once again enunciated in an official report, remains exactly its most unattainable and, therefore, most precious and sublime dimension.

In the case of the TADA court, the representation of the state was slightly different. Here, the rhetoric of secrecy and the practices of classifying even the most banal piece of evidence in the supposed interest of the state contributed to create a sense of urgency that something larger threatening the nation was at stake. The Mumbai police eagerly projected the enormous material it had gathered to generate the same illusion of the effectiveness and ubiquity of the state's knowledge and capacity for taking on public enemies. The profane dimensions were equally obvious in the brutality and partiality of the police investigations and in the harshness of their treatment of the detainees. However, the serious character of the crime, the alleged connections of the "Muslim gangsters" to Pakistan, and the secrecy surrounding the case meant that these obvious abuses and human rights violations never generated the kind of public concern and debate that have surrounded the Srikrishna proceedings, especially in the English-language press catering to an educated middle-class audience. In a conversation in 1997, a liberal Hindu businessman expressed quite succinctly to me how the scale of knowledge and violence at the disposal of the state acquire sublime dimensions: "See, many of the accused in this case are well-known criminals. They have committed a terrible crime—even Muslims admit that. We should not be soft on them. . . . Besides, there are so many things we are never told. The government has a lot of information it cannot disclose."

The deep divide between the social worlds of Hindus and Muslims that today traverses the city seems to have affected not only the sense of public justice in rather profound ways but also the public interest in these two proceedings. Many educated people from all communities have taken a keen interest in the Srikrishna Commission. A string of independent reports and documentation of sufferings and abuses have emerged from NGOs and civil rights activists. Many ordinary Hindus, according to my impressions from discussions and interviews over the past four years, seem nonetheless to approve of the formula of balanced apportioning of guilt and responsibility for the riots. It is a convenient nonlegalistic framework that enables the ordinary citizen to bracket these events as events without actors and as an unfortunate aberration from the normal order of things. To most ordinary people I met, the commission of inquiry appeared as a somewhat inconsequential sign of "the state," a manifestation of authority that simply was expected to restore the public order that had been upset by the riots. But the rhetoric of the state as a moral entity, as well as the legal intricacies of the proceedings, were mainly directed at the educated, literate middle class, which always was the primary constituency and concern of the postcolonial state.

Among ordinary Muslims in the parts of central Mumbai I got to know, the commission figured less prominently, although Srikrishna was praised as a "secular person," in the sense of being highly educated, impartial, and critical of Shiv Sena. The Muslim social world in Mumbai is not only spatially separated from that of Hindus, but is also demarcated by the existence of a local Urdu public sphere consisting of newspapers, journals, and local cable TV. To the average Hindu conversant in Marathi and Hindi, this world appears closed and even threatening and the Urdu press is routinely accused of spreading anti-Hindu propaganda. Such accusations were also presented to the Srikrishna Commission but were never substantiated. Rather than being vehicles of sectarian ideology, the Urdu press seems, however, to be strongly introverted and preoccupied by issues internal to the Muslim community. It was unsurprising, therefore, that the TADA case was attributed more importance and concern than the proceedings of the Srikrishna Commission. Muslim organizations documented the harsh treatment of the predominantly Muslim detainees under TADA, which became a symbol of the inherently anti-

Muslim bias of the state. Calls for opposition to the case, and to dismantle the TADA laws altogether, have for some years been high on the agenda of local organizations and of several Urdu newspapers, and are a point often used in campaigns by local Muslim politicians. As we shall see, the TADA proceedings resonate with a long tradition of enmity between Muslims and the police in the popular neighborhoods in central Mumbai.

State Spectacles and Politics in the Mohalla

The position of the Muslim community in Mumbai since Independence has been marked by an increasing level of socioeconomic marginalization (Hansen 1997b). Moreover, Muslim areas have more police stations and *chowkis* (police posts on strategic street corners built of stone and, as in the colonial period, equipped to be barricaded and turned into a bunkerlike structure) than other areas in the city. The Muslim areas are clearly treated as security problems, as dens of crime and mafia activity, in other words, areas where the "police machinery must be alert around the year," as police officers put it before the Srikrishna Commission. In spite of all assurances of the change of mind of the police after the 1992–1993 riots, the infrastructure of the police in these areas expanded considerably after the riots. The practice of making "preventive arrests" of what the police termed "notorious characters" or just "rowdy young men" prior to festivals, elections, and so on was widespread and widely accepted as legitimate.[17] It is no exaggeration to say that for young Muslims in these areas, the police force was an ever present and dreaded representation of a hostile state.

The police force in Mumbai is overwhelmingly Hindu and recruited from the same social environments and caste communities wherein Shiv Sena's masculine Hindu chauvinism has emerged. In the predominantly Muslim areas in Mumbai where I worked, I frequently visited two police stations and met officers and constables there as well as in the chowkis. In each of the compounds of what was supposed to be the strong arm of the secular state, one found two or three small temples devoted to Ganesh or Hanuman (the monkey god associated with courage and fighting spirit). These had been financed by donations from officers and constables and had been constructed within the past decade. "Some of us have questioned whether it is appropriate," an officer from a Christian background told me, "but my superior simply replied that if there were more Christian officers and constables, he wouldn't object to us having an image of Virgin Mary in one corner of the compound."

Talking to the policemen I got a clear sense that the "sociology of the hooligan" that earlier had informed police work in Bombay (Chandavarkar 1998: 180–233) now in the Muslim neighborhoods had evolved into a certain simplified "sociology of Muslims." This matrix of knowledge was based on an admixture of stereotypes, rumors, and circulating stories, many of them modified versions of those circulating in the neighborhoods. Consider the following example based on the stereotype that Muslims divorce their wives all the time. An officer explained, "One reason for the high level of crime is all these young boys who grow up without a proper father—this is because there are so many divorces and the men just leave their families behind." However, anyone with a rudimentary knowledge of Muslim Personal Law will know that according to this legal complex, children belong to the father and even poor fathers would never abandon their sons (though maybe their daughters), who are crucial to their social standing and future life prospects. The following off-the-record statement by a young and inexperienced officer testifies to the enormous gap between the social worlds of the predominantly Hindu police and that of the Muslims in these areas: "In the beginning when I came here, I was nervous when we went on patrol, especially at night. This hostility was something I never experienced before . . . but then after some time I started to look them right in the eyes and pretend that I was indifferent to them. I also learned more of the dirty language they use around here . . . that helped a lot. Now I get answers to my questions and I feel more respected."

Generally, postings at these stations were considered strenuous, full of hard work and dangers but also considerable rewards and bribes from the brisk flesh trade and drug economy in parts of central Mumbai. As a rule, officers are rarely posted more than twelve to eighteen months in one police station, whereas constables typically serve two to three years or more. The police depends vitally, therefore, on its network of informers in the neighborhood, networks created and maintained through flows of *hafta* (literally, "week," i.e., regular bribes or payoffs) and other economic transactions.

The depositions before the commission also revealed some of the many ties between the police force and local political organizations, particularly the Shiv Sena. Officers posted at local stations generally tried to protect the police force by keeping the top political level content and slightly misinformed. It seemed of paramount importance to prevent any disfiguration of the intricate web of hafta and tacit understandings among local operators, builders, and local strongmen politicians (*dadas*), on which the daily working of the police depended. If this web were broken up through massive arrests, the police would have to work much harder, bereft of the local networks of informers and "helpers."

These networks were fluid, multidimensional, interwoven with other networks, cut across lines of caste and religion, and operated on the basis of rumors and gossip. To claim that someone was a police informer or paid by the police was a trivial and well-known part of tacit warfare among networks. The status of "informer" was never positive knowledge, and the claims by policemen that someone "works with us" were often as strategic and fluid as the rumors floating around in the *biraderi* networks.[18] I got to meet only the "public" friends of the police, that is, those who trade openly with policemen, drink with them, "fix" various things for the officers, and walk in and out of the police station. Many of these helpers were "marginal men," at the margins of the powerful networks, small traders, often with criminal records or from low-status families.[19]

In 1994, *mohalla* (neighborhood) committees were set up throughout the areas affected during the riots to promote reconciliation in the city as well as to facilitate the future governance of the urban territories in central Mumbai. After the Bhiwandi-Thane riots in 1984 that also affected large parts of Bombay, peace committees were formed in a number of mixed neighborhoods in Bombay, such as Mahim, Bandra, and Byculla.[20] However, over the years they evolved into platforms for local politicians who saw the committees as an opportunity for forging ties with the police as well as strengthening their position in the neighborhood. None of these committees played any role in preventing violence in 1992–1993, and all were dissolved quickly after.

Police Commissioner Sahani, known for his inclination toward what one officer disapprovingly described to me as "intellectual policing," launched a new reconciliation scheme after a series of unprecedented initiatives: police officers were told to cooperate closely with social activists, to attend long sessions where riot victims gave detailed and moving accounts of their loss of children and spouses at the hands of the police; police officers were made to sit through week-long courses on Islam and Muslim culture conducted by people such as Asghar Ali Engineer, a well-known activist and vocal critic of the police force.

The action plan that was implemented in 1994 entailed that the police initiated the formation of mohalla committees at every police station in the so-called problem areas, which almost exclusively happened to be areas with a substantial Muslim population. The initiatives had many affinities with similar techniques of governance employed over the past century:[21] bodies of concerned and "respectable" citizens from all communities in a neighborhood were called on to assume responsibility, to calm tempers, and to assist the police in taking preventive action. As important, the committees aimed at "recreating confidence in our institutions and in our democracy among the Muslims in this city," as one of the driving forces behind the initiative expressed it.[22] When the mohalla committees were set up in 1994 they mainly recruited members from the Muslim middle classes. Many of the members were known in the locality as respected figures and often were involved in voluntary work and used to being in close contact with institutions of the state. As a young progressive advocate known for her controversial support to divorced Muslim women and active in the committee in Nagpada stated, "The fear of the intentions of the police was the biggest problem, and then the fear of attending meetings inside the police compound itself. Only educated people who knew they enjoyed some respect among constables and officers were willing to do that in 1994. You can imagine how the atmosphere was at that time."[23]

Among police officers it was broadly assumed that the Muslims, especially the poor and the uneducated *badmash* (hooligan), constituted the main problem. In the police analysis, riots started when such people were incited and manipulated by local political leaders and their imams (priests). The police saw the committees as a way to "depoliticize" and contain communalism, that is, to reduce it to occasional outbursts of irrational social behavior and to reduce the element of "political manipulation" that standard common sense among police officers (and many social scientists) in India hold to be the main reason behind riots. Members of political parties and politicians elected in the area were not admitted into the committees. Based on their earlier experience, the police wanted to remain firmly in control of these committees, to keep politics away "in order to curb the divisive effects of partisan interests," as a high-ranking officer put it. The objective was more ambitious this time around, for, as he said, "We want to create a new leadership among Muslims." The police wanted to bypass and exclude the established brokers and dadas (strongmen) in the mohalla and instead create a representation of Muslims by "civilized" citizens, that is, Muslims who, according to the standard assumption so central to governance in India for a century, by virtue of their education had abandoned primitive beliefs and had become amenable to reason and persuasion. Through these representatives the entire community could be addressed and governed, it was assumed.

In their initial phase the meetings were tense and serious, committee members told me. A retired judge who served on a mohalla committee related, "In the beginning, all the top officers from the station were present at the meetings. On Fridays when the streets were full of people assembling for the Friday namaaz, we would all come out with the officers and stand around the crowd, very alert, watching passers-by and making sure that no one made any provoking moves. There were tense moments, but I think we were successful."

As the political attention faded in 1995–1996, the committees were subtly transformed. On the initiative of the new and flamboyant police commissioner, Tyagi, the committees were enlarged from a maximum of fifty members per police station to as many as two hundred. Many of these were the helpers used by the police to gather information in the neighborhoods. They desired some recognition and standing in the community and the police rewarded their loyalty by conferring on them official status as community representatives. This expansion and inclusion of larger groups of people into the committees had several effects. First, the social prestige of sitting on the committees was immediately reduced as people like Y. were included in a mohalla committee. Y. was a rag merchant who had become rich on buying from and exploiting the rag pickers in the area. He was a big, hefty man known for his violent temper and the long whip he carried when ordering his many workers around. He was feared but not respected. Another new face was A., a man known as a supplier of all kinds of goods to the police. He walked in and out of the station, was always excessively servile to commanding officers, and was always joking with the constables. He had a small office in the building opposite the police compound, with nothing but a table, a telephone, and a chair. From there he could fix anything, he boasted: "Just tell me, you are my friend, I will get it for you." S. was another new member. He was a lecturer at a local college and had developed political ambitions. He had been politically active in the Muslim League, later in Congress. "Now, I am a social worker. I work only for the community," he said. S. always moved around with a couple of what he claimed to be "students," muscular young men who answered his cell phone, brought him cold drinks, and drove his car.

As the campaign for the elections for the municipal corporation in Mumbai commenced in January 1997, a large number of those recruited by the police as nonpolitical activists tried to convert their newfound visibility and public standing into a bid for a political career. As a consequence, a large number of committee members had, strictly speaking, to be excluded because of their "pollution" by the political world. This was of little consequence, however, as many political figures already had begun to attend the meetings after the enlargement of the committees. On several occasions prominent political figures not only attended meetings, but even began to preside over functions organized by the mohalla committees. Very few of the politically involved actually left the mohalla committees, and the still more infrequent meetings of the committees at the police stations began to resemble public functions, often lavishly hosted by the helpers and friends of the police.

Another consequence of the expansion of the committees was that certain police stations began to assume new functions of brokerage and "fixing" of local problems, paralleling those of the local politicians they had sought to marginalize. An officer at the Agripada police station told me enthusiastically about his newfound role as "fixer": "Now many people come to us with their usual problems—sewage, water, telephone connections, school admissions. For us it is very easy to solve—we just make a few phone calls. When I present myself to these lazy bureaucrats at the municipal corporation, things start to happen . . . [nodding toward a line of people waiting in the compound]. So, as you can see with your own eyes, people have gained confidence in us. They can see that we actually solve their problems."

The mohalla committees and the new assertive friendliness of the police have indeed reduced the level of tension in these areas, but they have removed neither the mechanisms producing communal enmity nor the organizational structures that perpetrate this violence. It seems as if the mohalla committees have provided the police with a set of new techniques for keeping order in "trouble spots" through a network of underworld operators, liaisons with political figures, direct intervention in the distribution of public services, and more.

Whither the State?

The many continuities in terms of governing the badmash in Mumbai over the past century demonstrate how the dominant governmentality of the postcolonial state in India continues to represent itself as a locus of a higher rationality outside and above the complexities and irrationalities of the lives of the masses. Both the Srikrishna Commission and the mohalla committees were interventions and spectacles that supported this style of governance. In both cases, the "sublime" dimensions of the state—fairness, reasonableness, tolerance, and justice—were represented to the state's preferred audience, the educated middle class.

As relative peace began to prevail in central Mumbai, middle-class society—the high-ranking officers, the educated, and the activists—withdrew from the mohalla committees and more everyday and profane forms of governance and networking were reconstructed. Similarly, the public spectacle of the Srikrishna Commission has come to an end; only the report remains in libraries and in limited circulation among intellectuals and political activists. Ironically, it fell on those most strongly indicted by the report, the Shiv Sena and the Mumbai police, to decide whether and in what form the recommendations of the commission regarding reforms of the police should be implemented. The political world in Mumbai appeared, in other words, to conduct "business as usual." In the elections for the State Legislative Assembly in September 1999, Shiv Sena lost some of its former electoral strength also in Mumbai, and a more centrist coalition formed a new government. However, Shiv Sena remained a force to reckon with in the city and the state. As the new government in July 2000 declared it would prosecute Bal Thackeray for his role in the 1992–1993 riots, Shiv Sena leaders threatened that Mumbai would burn, and the police assessed, as so many times before, that arresting Thackeray would not be in the interest of public order and communal harmony. Shiv Sena remains today the most powerful organization in the city. These events beg the question of whether the "state spectacles" analyzed above had been able to resuscitate the myth of the state. The answer cannot be precise, but let me offer a few reflections by way of conclusion.

The hold of Shiv Sena on Mumbai and its five-year tenure in the state government point to a transformation of the aura of the state as a site of neutrality and a certain predictability based on impersonal rules and technical expertise that both the colonial and postcolonial state painstakingly sought to construct and maintain, not only in terms of practices of government but also in the popular political imaginaries. Listening to the maze of rumors and tales of conspiracy that constitute an important part of the popular debate on government and state, one gets a sense of a widespread understanding of politics as a game and control of government institutions and their resources as the prizes to be won by parties and the communities they are believed to represent. The prevalence of such political imaginaries did make Shiv Sena's style of governance possible to sustain. On the one hand, the party celebrated its conquest of the state government on behalf of the majority of ordinary Hindus and enacted this in grand populist spectacles and equally grand promises of employment or free housing to the slum dwellers. On the other hand, from the top leadership to the local *shakha pramukh* (leader of a local branch) there was at the same time an indulgence in corrupt practices, real estate speculation, and more overt criminal activity unprecedented even in a city like Mumbai. This enabled the party to extend complex networks of patronage, dependence, and alliances at all levels in the city and the state. Moreover, Bal Thackeray's constant assertion of his autonomy and his contempt for the judiciary and the Srikrishna Commission remain central to his popularity and his long-standing efforts to construct himself and his movement as a site of authority that openly defies and challenges the authority of the state. This obviously militates against the desire for social respectability that is equally strong among Shiv Sena's supporters and undoubtedly had a negative impact on Shiv Sena's electoral fortunes in the 1999 elections. But the older myth of the state as the center of society appears nonetheless feebler than before. It is indicative of this weakness of the myth of the state that many Muslims no longer look to the government but to Dawood Ibrahim and the associated myths of the power of the big-time dadas, or the maverick lower-caste Samajwadi Party, for protection (see Hansen 2000).

I suggested above that the attribution of sublime qualities to the state is linked to its capacity for violence. As older myths of the state and its monopoly on violence seem to crumble in Mumbai, competing myths of authority and tales of fear cluster around the actual dispensers of violence in the city: the Shiv Sena, the underworld, and the police. The most profound paradox of this process of segmentation of authority, however, is that each segment remains dependent on the continued existence of the state—as a pool of resources, as a source of legitimate violence, or as an order to be defied and opposed. Even while effective governance crumbles and fragments, the myth of the unity and coherence of the state must be kept alive.

Notes

I am indebted to Véronique Bénéï, Jonathan Spencer, Jonathan Parry, Finn Stepputat, Oskar Verkaaik, Chris Fuller, Vivek Narayanan, Daniel Herwitz, and others who provided useful critiques and comments on earlier drafts of this essay. An earlier and longer version of this essay appears in *The Everyday State and Society in Modern India*, ed. Véronique Bénéï and C. J. Fuller (Delhi: Social Science Press, 2000), 31–67. Unless otherwise noted, all translations are mine.

1. I happened to be present in the city during the riots and on several occasions observed policemen literally protecting arsonists and turning their back on rampaging mobs. Similar incidents all over the city were reported widely by journalists of the English-language press, especially *Times of India.*
2. The official report of the Srikrishna Commission stated that "a grand conspiracy was hatched at the instance of the notorious smuggler Dawood Ibrahim Kaskar, operating from Dubai, to recruit and train young Muslims to vent their anger and wreak revenge by exploding bombs near vital installations and also in Hindu dominated areas so as to engineer a fresh bout of communal riots" (Srikrishna 1998: 60). Justice Srikrishna fails to mention the vital role played by corrupt customs and police authorities in the entire operation. The complicity of high-ranking officials in an operation has recently been documented by Shiv Visvanathan in Sethi and Visvanathan (1998: 118–28).
3. An arresting representation at the level of popular culture of the mythical qualities of this "originary" source of power appeared some years ago in a TV comedy. The protagonist, an African woman who has recently moved to the United States, visits Capitol Hill and stops at the glass montre containing the original American Constitution opened to its famous first page, "We, the people . . ." She reads through the page, returns home, overwhelmed by this revelation, and decides to change her life. Just as the domain of the sacred is fraught with ambivalences, bliss as well as horror, the sublime dimension of the state is dependent on its dark sides. The fascination of spies and secret services, from James Bond to *Nikita* to *Men in Black*, to mention some recent films, is premised on the awe and fear of the brutality and ruthlessness of the state. The state appears sublime because of its inordinate power to condone, redeem, and even purify violence, as René Girard (1977) has pointed out in the context of the pertinence of violence and sacrifice to religious rituals.
4. The literature on kingship in precolonial and colonial India is vast. Landmarks are Dumont (1980), Dirks (1987); see also Cohn (1983) and Price (1996).
5. See a good discussion of continuities and breaks in forms of state on the subcontinent in Kaviraj (1997a).
6. Akhil Gupta's (1995) analysis of corruption as a social practice around which ordinary Indians deliberate the nature of the state and its ideal separation from "the social" is exemplary as a way to grasp the everyday meanings and significance of *sarkar.*
7. The commission was also asked to recommend steps to be taken to improve the performance of the police force and to recommend administrative measures that could reduce the likelihood of such incidents repeating themselves. In other words, the task was daunting and deeply controversial, as it was bound to collide with entrenched political and bureaucratic interests in the government and in the police force.
8. This draws on my own presence at hearings in November 1996 and February–March 1997, as well as written affidavits from a range of police officers and civilians obtained from court officials.
9. Summing up on the low morale of the police, Justice Srikrishna writes: "The police, by their

own conduct, appeared to have lost moral authority over the citizens and appeared to evoke no fear. . . . The criminal elements were emboldened to hurl a crude bomb at the Police Commissioner and hack constables to death without fear. The police developed a psychological fear about attacks on them" (1998: 34).

10. I was fortunate to be able to attend most of these hearings, and the quotes and observations in the following are all from my personal notes and not the official transcript.
11. Mass prayer on streets and footpaths around temples invented and organized by Shiv Sena and other radical Hindu organizations in this period to mobilize Hindus to action against Muslims.
12. The legal intricacies of this unprecedented move are outlined by R. Padmanabhan in *Frontline* (April 18, 1997). An important part of this process was that the High Court in Mumbai actually rejected the government's request for withdrawal and furthermore sentenced Thackeray to a week of "simple imprisonment on the grounds of contempt of court." Thackeray was forced to appear in the magistrates court in the suburb of Bandra on February 17, where he was released on bail. Meanwhile, the court was surrounded by thousands of angry Shiv Sainiks shouting slogans and demanding the immediate release of the *Senapati*, the commander of the army, as he is known among the rank and file (*Mid-Day*, February 18, 1997).
13. The terms of reference of the commission were expanded to include an investigation of "the circumstances and the immediate cause of the incidents commonly known as the serial bomb-blasts of the 12th March 1993, which occurred in the Bombay Police Commissionerate area" and further whether these were linked by common causes or "a common design" to the riots investigated by the commission (Srikrishna 1998: 58).
14. For an overview of the proceedings of the TADA court, see the article "Justice for Whom" in *Humanscape* (December 1995).
15. The secrecy of the TADA proceedings has produced the interesting paradox that the Srikrishna Commission has encountered many difficulties in fulfilling its revised and expanded mandate because it has been impossible to get access to the many classified documents used in the TADA court.
16. Independent human rights group organized the Indian People's Human Rights Commission, which shortly after the riots set up an inquiry headed by two retired judges of the Bombay High Court. Their report, *The People's Verdict*, was published in August 1993 and concluded that the main responsibility for the riots should be laid on Shiv Sena and a partial and incompetent police force.
17. See Dhareshwar and Srivatsan's (1996) excellent piece on police practices concerning arrests of young "rowdies," their subsequent classification as "rowdy-sheeters," and more.
18. In the predominantly Muslim neighborhoods I worked in, most families come from north India, and the structures of the *biraderi*, the clanlike and durable relations of trust between families mostly (but not always) of the same caste, remain of paramount importance when it comes to mutual help, getting jobs, marriage, recruiting new labor from the villages, lending money, and so on. However, in the urban economy, relations and economic networks cut across these structures, and biraderi seems often to function as a last resort in times of crisis or serious decisions.
19. A large number of the residents in these areas are Muslim weavers of north Indian descent,

mostly from the *julaha* community, a low-status and lower-caste community that high-status Muslims did not recognize as proper Muslims. The julahas in this century began to claim recognition by calling themselves *ansaris*, the Arabic word for helper, referring to those who helped the Prophet flee from Mecca to Medina. The contempt for julahas/ansaris still prevails. A high-status Muslim in the neighborhood said about the police informers: "Some of these people call themselves ansaris. But who are they helping? The police! These men are julahas, we know how they are."

20. The 1984 riots in Bhiwandi, Thane, and Bombay are discussed and documented by the Committee for the Protection of Democratic Rights (CPDR) in *The Bombay Bhiwandi Riots* (Bombay: CPDR, 1984).
21. For similar initiatives in conjunction with the riots in Bombay in 1893, see Krishnaswamy (1966: 20–45); for the 1929 riots, see Chandavarkar (1998: 168–76).
22. Sushoba Bharve, activist and self-professed Gandhian social worker (interview, Worli, February 19, 1997).
23. S. Bharve confirmed this view when she said, "Respectable people are not very interested in working with the police. The tout will always come forward, but we did not want that. So we worked really hard to find good people with constructive views. It was very difficult."

III STATE AND COMMUNITY

BEFORE HISTORY AND PRIOR TO POLITICS

Time, Space, and Territory in the Modern Peruvian Nation-State

David Nugent

This essay argues that local people's relation to the nation-state and modernity has distinct spatial and temporal dimensions that shift through time according to complex changes in the organization and orchestration of power. It also identifies three "states of imagination" for the Chachapoyas region of northern Peru. Each "imagined state" is shown to have its own orientation toward the nation and modernity and to be characterized by its own distinct "time and space effects." I also compare the three states of imagination to assess the impact of each on the territorial integrity of the nation-state. At issue are the conditions under which local populations imagine themselves to be a part of or "outside" the historical imaginary of the modern nation-state.

We begin with an analysis of the present, a period when nation-state and modernity are regarded as alien to and contaminating of a local community depicted discursively as remote, pristine, and premodern. We then consider the historical process out of which the present emerged. Particularly noteworthy is the fact that in decades past nation-state and modernity were regarded in *very* different terms than they are at present: in the 1920s as distant but *emancipatory* forces that would liberate people from their oppressors; from 1930 to 1970 as integral to and constitutive of a local citizenry that represented itself as fully modern and national. In other words, we trace the historical process by which modernity and the nation-state "sour" in the local imagination to produce a curious historical inversion, one in which tradition evolves out of modernity. We begin with the traditional present.[1]

Modernity under Siege

In the early afternoon of July 19, 1983, I arrived at the small food store (bodega) in Chachapoyas where I always had my lunch. Upon my arrival six months earlier I had asked Sra. Yolanda, who operated the bodega, to cook for me and had been eating at her store ever since. The arrangement I had with Sra. Yolanda proved to be unusually rewarding. Having lived in Chachapoyas for most of her life, she had at her disposal a wealth of information about the town and its history. She was also an extremely good-natured, open, and friendly person, because of which we quickly became good friends. Indeed, Sra. Yolanda's quick wit, wry sense of humor, and gregarious nature meant that I always looked forward to meal times and to the discussions we had about Chachapoyas.

When I arrived for lunch on this particular day, Sra. Yolanda had just returned from the large store and food supply warehouse of Sr. Lazo, one of the town's wealthy merchants.[2] Lazo was one of perhaps ten other prominent merchants, or comerciantes, each of whom made his living by procuring foodstuffs and other basic necessities in bulk in distant industrial centers, transporting them to Chachapoyas, and selling them in smaller quantities wholesale (and retail) in the town. These men provisioned all of the town's one hundred or so bodega operators (including Sra. Yolanda) and all of the women who had food stalls in the town market with small amounts of cooking oil, salt, noodles, rice, soda crackers, toilet paper, beer, and other articles. The population of the town came either to bodega operators or to the town market to purchase food, making it possible for women like Sra. Yolanda to make a modest living by reselling these items retail to the general populace.

Sra. Yolanda was very angry when she returned from her visit to Sr. Lazo. When I asked what was wrong, she expressed deep frustration about her predicament. With uncharacteristic bitterness and resentment she explained that the comerciantes were making it impossible for her, or any of the other bodega operators, to get along. Beyond that, they were doing real harm to everyone in Chachapoyas. The problem, she explained, was the merchants' greed, their hunger for profits, and the pleasure they took in taking advantage of people like her, who were poor and vulnerable.

Although the merchants rarely left their homes to go anywhere other than their stores, had no friends aside from other merchants, and did nothing but work and work, Sra. Yolanda said, there was one "social occasion" that they never missed. As everyone knew, they had meetings with each other on a regular basis, where they discussed whatever matters they needed to discuss to maintain their control over the town. One of the most important things they did at these meetings, Sra. Yolanda said, was fix prices for the goods they sold. But they also discussed such matters as how to "influence" the police and politicians and how to deal with people who were a threat to them. No one had actually ever witnessed one of these meetings, she admitted, but it was common knowledge that they met late at night in the Camara de Comercio (the Chamber of Commerce), a room in the municipality. It was here, she said, in the dead of night, that they made their plans to take advantage of people and settled on the excessive amounts they would charge the public for their goods.

As a result of this behavior, Sra. Yolanda explained, when bodega operators or market vendors went to a merchant's warehouse to get supplies of oil, noodles, and so on—as she had done that very day—they had to pay far more than should have been the case. And after paying so much for these goods, she and the others were forced to sell them for almost nothing. There were a great many humble people like herself who had small stores or who sold food in the market, and they were all forced to compete with each other to survive. Everyone had to keep their prices as low as possible if they wanted to attract customers. Even so, because of the greed of the merchants, the cost of living kept going up. No one had any choice about the matter, she said, because there were only a few comerciantes like Sr. Lazo, and everyone was forced to go to one of them.

Sra. Yolanda said that she simply couldn't understand what made the comerciantes behave as they did. What she found especially baffling, she said, was that they seemed totally indifferent to the plight of their neighbors. It was obvious, she said, that people were really suffering. Many women didn't have enough to feed their children. All across town people had to cut down on really necessary things, like powdered milk, eggs, cooking oil, and meat. They were eating more of foods like yuca (which she said was filling but not nutritious) and less of rice (which she said was far more nutritious) to make the little money they had go as far as possible. Even people on government salaries were struggling. The government did nothing to control inflation and wouldn't increase salaries, so state employees found that their salaries purchased less and less.[3] Retired government workers, who had fixed pensions, she explained, were becoming desperate. Their monthly payments were based on what they had been earning at retirement, often decades ago, and hadn't gone up in years despite inflation. With the pittance they received from the government, she said, these old people could cover only a small part of their living costs. Many didn't have enough to eat.

According to Sra. Yolanda, however, what made matters worst of all was the fact that the merchants didn't really need to be taking advantage of people in the way they were. After all, she said, they were already millionaires. All you had to do to see this was to walk by their fancy homes, see their shiny new cars parked in their garages, or visit them at work. "Go by one of their stores," she told me, "look inside at all the merchandise they have, and see if they look like people who are struggling. Then, tell me why they are doing this to us."

Sra. Yolanda expressed real bitterness about the situation she and the others were in because of the merchants, a situation she saw herself as powerless to change. I knew that the municipality set official prices for many of the items Sra. Yolanda purchased wholesale from the comerciantes, and thus it was clear that the price-fixing activities of the merchants were illegal. Sra. Yolanda said as much herself. So I asked her why the bodega operators didn't bring this problem to the attention of the local authorities. In response, Sra. Yolanda said, "How can we trust the municipality? It is to that very place that the comerciantes go to make their plans to rob us!"

Sra. Yolanda went on to explain why the government could not be trusted. She told me the story of a bodega operator, a friend of hers, who had protested to the authorities about the comerciantes. Several years earlier, this woman had made a formal complaint to the municipality, but found that the authorities were unwilling to do anything to help her. Much to her dismay, however, this woman discovered that municipal representatives were quite willing to do her harm. Shortly after she made her complaint, she went to the warehouse of one of the merchants to get fresh supplies for her store and to her surprise was told that they were out of everything she needed—even though there were large sacks of these same items in plain sight and other women were purchasing these goods before her very eyes. Thereafter, she was told the same thing at all of the supply warehouses in town. From that day on she found that none of the merchants would sell her any of their goods at any price.

It was obvious to this woman that the municipality had "informed" the merchants about her complaint, and that the merchants had chosen to retaliate as a group—probably settling on this strategy in one of their secret night-time meetings. Despite the boycott, the woman had tried to hang on. First, she had complained to the subprefect's office about the municipality's refusal to enforce its own regulations. Later, she had gone to the prefect when the subprefect proved unresponsive. Ultimately, however, no one in the government was willing to help her. As a result, the comerciantes succeeded in driving the woman out of business. In the end, she had left Chachapoyas.

This story was common knowledge, Sra. Yolanda explained, and no one was willing to risk suffering the same fate as had this unfortunate woman.[4] I then asked why the bodega operators did not organize to present a united front to the comerciantes. She responded by explaining that every effort to do so had been met by either indifference or repression on the part of the authorities.[5] With great bitterness, she explained that the government had never taken any interest in the region or its people, that it did nothing to protect them from the comerciantes. To the contrary: the government actually helped the merchants prey on people. By way of example, she explained that every so often a newcomer would arrive with a truckload of goods that he would sell at prices lower than those offered by the comerciantes. Seeing their monopoly threatened, the merchants would arrange with the police so that the newcomer was falsely accused of and arrested for some serious crime. The individual in question was then given a choice: either he could stay in Chachapoyas and face a jail sentence, or he could leave town and never come back. Several of these falsely accused individuals, she said, had appealed to higher political authorities to free them from the threat of imprisonment so that they could operate a business freely in Chachapoyas. Their appeals, however, had fallen on deaf ears. As a result, all of these would-be food merchants had been forced out of Chachapoyas, and the position of the comerciantes remained unchallenged.

It did no good to turn to the authorities for help, Sra. Yolanda said, because they already knew what was going on. Indeed, they were directly involved in helping the comerciantes take advantage of people. This was undoubtedly because the merchants used the profits they made from local people to bribe the police, the politicians, and anyone else whose cooperation the comerciantes required. In this regard, Sra. Yolanda said, the influence of the merchants extended far beyond Chachapoyas and included the industrial centers where the merchants purchased their wares, renewed their business licenses, and so on. "The comerciantes could never do what they do," she said, "without the help of the government." It was local people like herself and other Chachapoyanos who were left to suffer the consequences.

Sra. Yolanda's angry and articulate outburst was far from the only expression of this kind that I heard in Chachapoyas. To the contrary: laments just like hers dominated public discourse. This discourse, however, was not limited to critical commentary on the disastrous state of affairs then afflicting Chachapoyas. Other themes were equally important, in particular the harmonious, wholesome, and consensual way of life that was said to have predated the contemporary era and the corrupting influence of the forces of modernity and nation-state in bringing about the demise of traditional life.[6]

Implicit in the "discourse of corruption" that dominated the public sphere during this era is a distinct "state of imagination"—a particular way of viewing the institutions and cultural values of the nation-state, and of positioning the region and its people in relation to the nation-state in spatial and temporal terms.[7] "Alien" is an apt term to characterize how the modern nation-state was imagined during this era. Indeed, in public discourse Chachapoyas was represented as a spatially remote, socially pristine, and temporally premodern community only recently subject to the dangerous and corrosive influences of the merchants, modernity, and the nation-state—all of which were closely linked in public discourse.[8] Although these forces were said to have made their presence felt in this remote region for only a short time, they were represented as fundamentally alien to the region and its people and as already having done much to undermine what had traditionally been a simple, harmonious, consensual way of life.

In the local imagination, it was the comerciantes who most clearly embodied the corrupting influences of the outside world, so much so that public discourse depicted people like Sr. Lazo as both dangerous and foreign. Indeed, local people's term for themselves was *naturales* (natives), people naturally and unproblematically of the place of Chachapoyas. Their term for Sr. Lazo and others like him, however, was *forasteros* (outsiders; strangers), people who were "out of place" in Chachapoyas, who did not "belong." Naturales emphasized a fundamental moral schism that separated them from the forasteros and the nation-state, which were construed as entirely distinct and separate from the community of naturales, as belonging at a great "distance" from local life. Indeed, the state was noted primarily for its misuse of or its indifference to the local population. The forasteros were seen as so fundamentally alien to all things truly of Chachapoyas that the naturales felt compelled to generate a theory to account for the forasteros' inexplicable behavior, a theory with time and space effects of its own. The forasteros were said to be descended from one of the ten lost tribes of Israel, who at some time in the remote past crossed the Atlantic Ocean, sailed up the Amazon River, and settled in the town of Celendín (home of the merchant forasteros; see Nugent 1996: 258–61).[9] In other words, the forasteros were thought to belong to a race different from the naturales. The modernity they embodied and the system of state power on which they relied were regarded as being as foreign to the people and place as the forasteros themselves.

It is peculiar indeed that Chachapoyanos represent themselves as naturales, a racially distinct, premodern folk community whose harmonious and consensual way of life has been put at risk by modernity and the nation-state. From the 1920s through the 1970s they depicted themselves as quite the opposite—as members of *el pueblo* (the people), a racially unmarked national community that enthusiastically embraced the institutions and values of the modern nation-state.

Having briefly discussed the "traditional present," we now examine the "state of imagination" that gave birth to this racially unmarked national community, and in the process uncover something of the region's "modern past."

Phase I. 1885 to 1930: The Compromised Nation-State

At the turn of the twentieth century the emerging Peruvian nation-state was rent by contradictions. Although founded as an independent state in the 1820s on liberal principles of democracy, citizenship, private property, and individual rights and protections, the central government was not remotely able to make good on these arrangements even one hundred years later. Although such principles were uniformly invoked in all political ritual and discourse, many parts of the country were organized according to principles diametrically opposed to these precepts of "popular" sovereignty.

Chachapoyas was one such region. Dominating the social and political landscape of Chachapoyas was a group of white, aristocratic families of putatively Spanish descent who saw it as their birthright to rule over the region's multitudinous mestizo and Indian peasant population. These elite families rejected any and all assertions of equality between themselves and the subaltern groups over which they ruled. Rather, the elite regarded and referred to themselves as a separate aristocratic caste, the *casta española*, that was naturally entitled to power and privilege due to its racial purity and cultural superiority. Even social interaction with subaltern groups was kept to a minimum and was structured in such a way as to require public deference and subservience from the subaltern.

Peculiarities of the Peruvian state during this period meant that the central regime in Lima was forced to ally with such aristocratic families if it was to maintain even a semblance of control in the outlying sections of its territory. For the central government lacked the ability to control the national territory directly during this period. Those who controlled the central state apparatus were thus compelled to seek out clients among rural aristocratic families who would rule in the name of the central regime.

In other words, although the independent republic of Peru had been born of armed struggle against absolutist, colonial Spain, and although the central government of Peru embraced precepts that had emerged out of the Enlightenment, the actual operation of the state apparatus depended crucially on maintaining social structures of the ancien régime.

Although elements of the landed class in Chachapoyas enjoyed the backing of the central government, this class was far from unified. Rather, members of the elite saw themselves as having the inherited right to rule that *no one*, neither the central government nor other members of the elite, could legitimately deny them. Furthermore, to exercise these rights the elite did not hesitate to use violence. There was a sense in which elite men regarded themselves as having no true peers, and certainly no masters. Rather, each believed he had the right to use power in defense of prerogatives that were legitimately his because of the elite station in life that he enjoyed by right of birth. No one—not even the state—had the right to interfere with these privileges.

As a result of this state of affairs, in the opening decades of the century the operation of the state apparatus and the imagined community of the nation were "compromised" in two senses. First, the region's landed elite took conscious and systematic steps to publicly contradict what the "state stated" (Corrigan and Sayer 1985): to use state powers and public institutions to subvert the very forms of egalitarian personhood and homogeneous public imagined in national discourse. The elite were compelled to do so for two reasons. On the one hand, national discourse emphasized equality before the law, citizenship, and constitutional rights as the only legitimate basis for national life, principles in blatant contradiction to the racial hierarchy and inherited privilege of the elite and to the violent struggles for power that occurred as different factions of the elite, each with its own extensive clientele of mestizo artisans and "Indian" peasants, battled for regional control. On the other hand, state institutions were designed from the center to support the public sphere imagined in national discourse, one consisting of a mass of formally identical (albeit male) citizens, each jurally indistinguishable from the next, all of whom were united behind the national cause of promoting "progress" and "advancement." This public sphere, and the institutions meant to support it, also offered an explicit critique of a social order in which local aristocratic elites and their clients used unlicensed violence on an endemic scale to defend their privileges, powers, and prerogatives.

To address the threat posed by the institutional and discursive presence of the nation-state, the local ruling elite faction repeatedly and publicly demonstrated its ability to ridicule national injunctions about "proper" behavior—to violate the constitutional protections of the opposing elite-led faction, to do great harm to their persons and property, and to do so with complete impunity. In other words, the ruling faction went to great lengths to compromise state institutions and national discourse, using both to further the aims of social groupings (their own privileged faction), statuses (superordinate racial categories), and forms of interaction (violence and domination) that were "unthinkable" (or deemed "medieval") within the discourse of the nation-state.

It was not just state institutions and national discourse, however, that were compromised by these kinds of actions. The nation-state was compromised in a second way as well. At issue here were the boundaries of the state apparatus. To protect itself from the ruling elite faction, the opposing elite faction organized itself into a set of positions that replicated the state apparatus: a "shadow state" (Nugent 1999).[10] Furthermore, the opposing faction claimed that its rightful position as the local representative of the nation-state had been usurped by the ruling faction through violence and deception, and thus that the ruling faction had no legitimate claim to the position it occupied. As a result, at any given point in time, ruling and opposing factions both sought to occupy the same political space, and both claimed to be "the legally constituted authorities." Neither of these factions, however, could hold onto the state apparatus for more than five to ten years before being deposed by the other. Furthermore, in that the rise of one faction inevitably meant persecution, emiseration, decline, and even demise for the others, each faction fought viciously to protect and promote its own interests. In these conditions it was very difficult for the populace to view the state as a discrete entity above and beyond "society," or the nation as an entity with a general will or interest. Rather, the regional elite subsumed the state apparatus and used it to violate and ridicule the precepts of state and nationhood.

In other words, the attempts of warring elite-led factions to legitimate aristocratic sovereignty, when popular sovereignty represented the sole terms in which political life could be represented, "compromised" the nation-state. Elite efforts to compromise the nation-state, however, were internally contradictory. The more elites "misused" state institutions to undermine the egalitarian forms of personhood and public imagined in national discourse, the more powerfully they generated the image of a state form that was an inversion of their own compromised creation. Indeed, the very fact that the elite devoted such unceasing attention to compromising the nation-state suggested the existence of something of which the elite were deathly afraid, something so powerful and so dangerous to elite power that it had to be compromised and negated at every opportunity. The "thing" in question was a nation-state liberated from the abuses of the local elite, a nation-state that truly did represent justice, equality, and the common good.

There were important spatial and temporal dimensions to these counter-imaginings. The ongoing public demonstrations in which the elite showed their ability to hold the threat of the liberated nation-state at bay—that is, the success of the elite in compromising the operation of the state apparatus regionally—created the illusion (and illusion it was) that a liberated nation-state existed in a different spatial domain, lying beyond the reach of regional power holders. Indeed, because the liberated nation-state had been distanced from local affairs it was possible for the popular classes to conceive of the liberated nation-state not only as a "thing" that could arrive from afar, but also as a thing whose arrival was being thwarted by the elite. And because the liberated nation-state was associated with modernity and the future and the elite self-consciously harkened back to tradition and the past, the spatial plane became a temporal one as well. Not only was the liberated nation-state being held at bay geographically by the elite, so too was the advance of modernity and progress being thwarted by backwardness and tradition.

These mixed messages were implicit in the orchestration of regional political life. We now turn to the social developments that made the messages explicit.

Phase II. The 1930s to the 1970s: The Liberated Nation-State

In 1930 the aristocratic order came undone, as popular classes coalesced into a social movement that mobilized around principles of citizenship and equality, ideals long invoked in political ritual and discourse but that stood in such glaring contradiction to everyday life. Seizing on this radical disjuncture between ritual language and social life, the movement elaborated a telling critique of the existing state of affairs. It did so by affirming the legitimacy of the egalitarian principles invoked by the aristocratic families and by pointing to the elite's consistent betrayal of these principles.

The emergence of this movement in Chachapoyas cannot be understood outside of changes occurring in the national and international arenas. The late nineteenth-century crisis in North Atlantic capitalism resulted in a flood of new laboring people, social doctrines, political ideologies, and investment capital pouring into Peru, which permanently altered Peru's class structure, balance of political power, and state apparatus. Lima, the national capital, saw the emergence of a working-class movement and a form of populist, mass politics that challenged aristocratic control for the first time in the country's history (Burga and Flores Galindo 1979; Stein 1980; Sulmont 1977). Outside of Lima the influx of foreign capital undermined production and exchange relations within and between regions, resulting in movements of secession, civil war, and escalating levels of violence (Collins 1988; Gitlitz 1979; Klarén 1973; Mallon 1983; G. Smith 1989; Taylor 1986). In the absence of any state presence in the countryside, rural elites were left to fight among themselves for control over the new economic opportunities of the era.

In the opening decades of the century the central government also sought to form a solidary national community along three axes: (1) the compression of space, by means of massive investments in road construction, to form a more integrated, national economy; (2) a massive expansion in the state bureaucracy (including the military and the police) and the public sector; and (3) the use of state control over public discourse to promote citizenship, individual rights, and equality before the law as the only legitimate basis of national life (Burga and Flores Galindo 1979). In other words, just as the central government was attempting to form a more cohesive national community based on the rhetoric of popular sovereignty, it was confronted with chaotic conditions that violated these very principles.

In Chachapoyas, nonelite groups responded by embracing the very principles invoked in national discourse as providing the only legitimate basis of national life: a cleansed state apparatus that could help make a reality of the imagined nation-state. Two overlapping political movements, both intent on "democratizing" the aristocratic social order, emerged among popular classes in Chachapoyas: the Partido Laboral Independiente Amazonense (Independent Labor Party of Amazonas) and the Popular American Revolutionary Alliance (APRA). Both seized on state-endorsed notions of equality and the common good and used them to imagine a democratized social order that did away with elite privilege. In addition to extensive political organizing among subaltern groups, one of the movements published a local newspaper, *Amazonas*, which articulated this new image. *Amazonas* asserted that the nation and the people did have a common interest, that they could build an effective future—by rising up against the aristocratic families. The paper asserted that Chachapoyas' elites were not a noble caste, but rather were brutal and rapacious, that they had divided, victimized, and abused the local population for centuries. Nor, the paper argued, were the region's mestizos and Indios uncouth and semicivilized, as the elite asserted. Rather, they were the local embodiment of *el pueblo Peruano* (the Peruvian people), the region's only hope for salvation. El pueblo was deeply committed to democracy, equality, and justice, but the state had neither extended to el pueblo its constitutional rights nor curbed the excesses of the elite. Once rid of the elite el pueblo would be free to become a true part of the Peruvian nation. In the meantime, however, Chachapoyas was best understood as a remote backwater where prenational sentiments and archaic forms of behavior lingered that had long since disappeared from the rest of the civilized world (see, e.g., *Amazonas*, año 1, 15 October 1926; año 2, March–April 1928; año 4, May 1929).

According to *Amazonas*, integrating the region into the nation-state would require a series of major transformations in local life. First, it would mean establishing uncompromised state institutions that were free of elite control, that could safeguard individual rights and protections, and that could guarantee equality before the law. Indeed, according to the paper, this was the most daunting problem facing the region and its populace. Becoming a part of the nation-state would also mean, however, integrating the region into the national economy and culture. With regard to this problem the paper put enormous emphasis on the extension of communication, transportation, and education. *Amazonas* was particularly fascinated with roads and any means of breaking down the physical boundaries that separated the region from the broader national context. All such means of compressing time and space were viewed with a kind of millenarian awe, as capable of ushering in an era of unlimited progress and prosperity (see, e.g., *Amazonas*, año 1, 15 October 1926).

Finally, *Amazonas* argued that profound individual transformations would be required of those who wished to become one with the nation-state. Chachapoyanos would have to forgo the violent and arbitrary displays of power and domination that had characterized local life for so long to transform themselves into a "natural aristocracy" of individuals worthy of region and nation alike.

The characteristics of these worthy individuals were thought to differ significantly by gender. The remade man imagined publicly in the pages of *Amazonas* was the very antithesis of the aggressive, dominating, violent male of the aristocratic order. Rather, he was a peaceful, autonomous, rational, hard-working individual, whose behavior was characterized by moderation, restraint, discipline, and respect for himself and others—an individual who posed no threat to anyone. The actions of such a man did not need to be constantly monitored or controlled by any external body because he policed himself according to generally accepted principles of fair play, truth, and ethics. His motive in doing so was not to gain material rewards or riches. Rather, being this kind of person was depicted as its own reward, knowing that one lived up to the ethical ideals to which all should aspire to live just lives, to be responsible members of community and nation (see, e.g., *Amazonas*, año 1, 15 October 1926).

The newspaper imagined an entire community of such autonomous, hard-working, dignified, ethical, male individuals. These men were to obey the same set of moral principles regardless of race or ancestry, were to identify themselves with the same "common good" and "general interest." They were to live in peace and simplicity, desire not what belonged to others, nor do anyone harm. They were to adhere to general principles of integrity and truth, honesty and humility. And they were to free themselves of any and all feelings of fear, admiration, or envy toward the powerful. In other words, they were to become disciplined, principled individuals who were neither abusive of nor obsequious to others, who possessed the "inner strength" to be fully self-reliant, independent, and autonomous. Furthermore, they were to evaluate the worth of all, regardless of social position, in terms of the same ethical standards of behavior (see, e.g., *Amazonas*, año 1, 1 February 1927).

The remade woman depicted in the paper differed profoundly from the rational, hard-working, principled individual into which men were to mold themselves. The ideal woman was one whose moral purity, natural simplicity, and emotive empathy made her worthy of inclusion in the national community. The most important obligation of a woman, asserted *Amazonas*, was to devote herself to the domestic sphere, where she was entrusted with the heavy responsibility of providing the proper environment for turning boys into the proper kind of responsible, disciplined men. Indeed, mothers were depicted as local embodiments of the national community in *Amazonas*, for it is they who inculcate in their sons the kinds of values and orientations that will make them "useful elements to community and nation" (see, e.g., *Amazonas*, año 1, 1 February 1927; April 1927).

Given this faith in the key role played by women and the home in the process of nation building, it is not surprising that every issue of *Amazonas* included special sections—a "Woman's Column" and a "Children's Column"—devoted specifically to these topics. The "Woman's Column" went into considerable detail about how women were to order and maintain their domestic space (focusing on cleanliness and hygiene) if they wished it to be truly "proper," if it was to be the kind of environment most conducive to turning their sons into men suitable for membership in the modern nation-state. The column was particularly helpful in alerting mothers to the existence of hidden dangers lurking within and around the home that threatened the integrity and order of the all-important domestic sphere. In this way the paper proved that maintaining the home was anything but a simple task, and that *Amazonas* had an important part to play in educating mothers as to how it could best be done (see, e.g., *Amazonas*, año 1, April 1927; año 4, May 1929).

It was the region's laboring poor, el pueblo Chachapoyano, who were regarded as having the most potential for becoming the remade men and women of which the new social order was to be composed. Even these remade individuals, however, would have to take one additional step if they were to overcome the divisive political affiliations of the past. They would have to join forces with all other hard-working, disciplined, and committed individuals. Only by acting with the strength that came from unity could even these remade individuals be sure that the elite did not subvert the process of national integration and regional regeneration (see, e.g., *Amazonas*, año 1, 1 March 1927).

In identifying who was most likely to transform themselves into the remade women and men of which region and nation were so much in need, *Amazonas* worked with existing social distinctions but gave them a transformed significance. Specifically, *Amazonas* used the disdain of elite groups for manual labor as the basis for identifying the "superior man," but inverted the terms of moral legitimacy associated with manual labor, making it into a virtue rather than a vice. On this basis, the paper attempted to erase distinctions between Indio and mestizo and to make common cause among all those who labored. For, according to the newspaper, it was the region's laborers who exemplified the superior man, who could make society over in a new form (see, e.g., *Amazonas*, año 1, 1 March 1927).

This appeal for a "liberated" nation-state, in which el pueblo could reap all the benefits of modern state and nationhood, attracted large numbers of the laboring population. In August 1930, at a moment of crisis in the national political order, these marginalized middle sectors risked their lives in an armed "revolution" that overthrew the region's aristocratic power holders. Elderly individuals who participated in the uprising liken their assault on the prefecture, decisive in bringing them to power, to the storming of the Bastille in revolutionary France. The local newspaper was renamed *Redemption*. In it, the calendar was set at "year one": "year one of the redemption" was 1930, year two was 1931, and so on.

Within a few years of the 1930 "revolution" the elite-based political order, with its congeries of material, behavioral, and symbolic markers of privilege and distinction, disintegrated. With the breakdown of the aristocratic order, "the people" became actively involved in the region's most vital social activities, assumed control over its key political positions, and reorganized its most basic forms of religious practice.[11] Furthermore, under the protection of liberated state institutions, el pueblo elaborated a range of new sociocultural forms. These "horizontal associations" (Wolf 1966) strengthened "the people" as a group, and also celebrated the principles of equality and justice around which the middle sectors had mobilized as a political community.[12]

The ascent of el pueblo into these multiple arenas of social, political, and religious life enabled people who had recently risked their lives to bring about a transformed social world to broadcast the legitimacy of the principles for which they had fought—and to do so in myriad domains of social life that until then had remained the exclusive preserve of the regional elite. The combined effect of these changes was twofold. On the one hand, they resulted in the emergence of a new kind of public culture in Chachapoyas, one in which the constant assertion and celebration of equality replaced the host of material, behavioral, and symbolic markers of hierarchy previously acted out on a daily basis in the reproduction of aristocratic sovereignty. On the other hand, these changes created a situation in which the principles of popular sovereignty took on a transformed significance in public life. For the first time in the region's history these principles came to define the standards to which individuals who occupied positions of public trust could be held accountable. This marked a radical change from the status of these principles during the period of elite rule, when they had acted as nothing more than empty phrases uttered mechanically in political ritual and discourse by elite groups who publicly flaunted their ability to disregard the most fundamental aspects of these principles.

There was also an important material dimension to the ascent of el pueblo. Beginning in 1930, successive regimes in Lima provided crucial material support to Chachapoyas's middle sectors. The government bureaucracy expanded in size and scope in the form of a growing number of separate ministries, offices, and financial institutions, and in the process absorbed growing numbers of the local populace (Nugent 1988: chaps. 4, 5). As early as 1950 employment in this bureaucracy had absorbed as much as 40 percent of the working, male population of the town (up from 13 percent in 1930; see 69–70). And because the real wages of those employed by the state rose steadily throughout the 1940s, 1950s, 1960s, and the first half of the 1970s (69–70), the growth of the bureaucratic sector was able to support the expansion of artisanal production of many kinds (Nugent 1995) as well as a whole array of ancillary "service industry" activities (Nugent 1988).

Changes in economic, social, political, and cultural life following the revolution of 1930 thus led to a significant expansion in the size of the town's middle sectors, the very social group of which el pueblo was composed. At the same time government investment in communication, transportation, education, health care, the judiciary, and the police force—all of which expanded steadily beginning in the 1930s—acted to strengthen the autonomy and security of the growing middle sectors of regional society and to make superfluous the group-based protections and coercions that had characterized the earlier period of elite rule. In this way the central government replaced the elite as the source of patronage and protection for the local community, and in the process established direct dependencies with an emergent, national citizenry that it helped to create and whose rights it protected.

As part of the same process that "liberated" el pueblo and the state, the central government also established the conditions in which national commodity circuits could penetrate the region free from the encumbrances of elite politics. For with the dismantling of elite factions, in which the personnel and the property of opposing factions had not been safe from the predations of the ruling faction, the state underwrote the safety of individuals, the security of their possessions, and their ability to move through the regional space unmolested. In 1960 the first major highway was completed that linked Chachapoyas to the coast. From this point onward the goods and labor of the Chachapoyas region were "free" to enter markets of more national scope, and foodstuffs and manufactured goods of all kinds from outside the region could likewise participate in what had formerly been the rather limited, regional markets of Chachapoyas (Nugent 1988: chap. 6). As the region became progressively more integrated into national commodity circuits, local people (and products) were increasingly drawn into a national, exchange-based economy that provided them with most of the material necessities of life.

By the 1960s, then, the local populace had succeeded in realizing most aspects of the vision that had first inspired them to political action in the 1920s. Integration with the nation-state had, in the words of *Amazonas*, libergated the region from the "claustrophobic insularity," the "boorish provincialism," and the "remote backwardness" that characterized the period of aristocratic rule. State institutions had been liberated from elite influence, local life had been democratized and modernized in virtually all ways, and the rights and responsibilities of citizenship were realities for most townspeople. Furthermore, el pueblo dominated the region's major social activities, controlled its key political positions, and organized its central forms of religious practice.

Phase III. 1980 to the Present: The Alien Nation-State

From the 1930s until the early 1970s the institutions of the nation-state did much to support the citizenship-based public sphere imagined in national discourse, the very public sphere that el pueblo had helped bring into being as a result of the movements of democratization of the 1920s and 1930s. By the 1980s, however, the local populace came to regard the modern nation-state as a "foreign body": an entity wholly separate from, alien to, and dangerous for a way of life depicted as simple, natural, and harmonious. So foreign were the nation-state and modernity perceived to be by this time that local people sought to distance themselves from everything associated with the nation-state—including the very public sphere that they had helped bring into being with the assistance of the nation-state, and the discourse of popular sovereignty that had formerly acted as the ideological expression of their political mobilization. In other words, by the 1980s local people were no longer willing to depict the public sphere as the contingent achievement of an emergent social group (el pueblo) with an explicitly modern orientation working directly in concert with the nation-state. Rather, by this time the representation of both the public sphere and the local populace itself had undergone a discursive inversion. Both were imagined as prepolitical and ahistorical, as having timeless features that were inherent in the people and place. So alien did the nation-state and modernity appear to local people by the 1980s that they reimagined their own history in such a way as to excise both from their past. Indeed, in this regard, the naturalizing dimension of contemporary public discourse is very effective; one would never know of el pueblo's previous "romance" with forces now regarded as dangerous and foreign, would never suspect that the nation-state and modernity were once regarded as powerful forces of emancipation. The very fact that Chachapoyas's "modern" history is a hidden history thus says much about how alien the nation-state has come to be in the local imagination. We now turn to a consideration of the forces that led to the emergence of this most recent "state of imagination," that of the alien nation-state.

In 1968 severe economic problems occurring at the national level, related to Peru's dependent position in the global capitalist economy, accompanied by widespread peasant land invasions and social unrest led to a military coup, which was followed by twelve years of military rule. The discourse of the military regime can be characterized as "radical populist." The military critiqued not only an unjust international economic order that exploited Peru and robbed it of its resources, but also the country's highly unequal class structure, in which an entrenched landed elite held power over the masses of peasants and workers. The military government promised to address these problems, to involve the masses in the political process, and to bring to an end the marginalization of the country's majority (Booth and Sorj 1983; Lowenthall 1975).

Although the discourse of the military regime stressed democracy, popular participation, and rule by the people, the actual structure of power established by the regime was the antithesis. Military rulers set up a highly centralized form of governance in which their own appointees (prefects) were given virtual monopoly control over the state political apparatus for the sections of the national territory (departments) entrusted to them. Prefects, and those they appointed to lesser administrative posts, were given free rein to govern according to their own prerogatives, without "interference" from elected politicians (Congress had been dissolved), political parties (parties had been outlawed), or the host of other formal and informal mechanisms that had evolved during previous decades by which people had made their influence felt in local affairs.

The military government's imposition of autocratic rule in Chachapoyas established conditions in which the democratized public sphere that el pueblo had helped bring into being was increasingly undermined. In alliance with the Guardia Civil (the national police) and a dependent judiciary, prefects and their appointees were free to coerce wealth out of the local population and to persecute and harass those who did not acquiesce to their demands, whether for wealth, labor, subservience, sexual favors, or other.

The military government thus introduced a form of rule that was autocratic and centralized, both nationally and locally. It imposed its will arbitrarily on the populace and subverted democratic process, even as it proclaimed the importance of popular rule. This contradiction between the discursive representation of the nation and the actions of the state apparatus in some respects resembled the contradictions of pre-1930 aristocratic rule. There were important differences, however, between the two periods. As of the 1970s it was no longer the case that the national community could be conceived of as being compromised at the regional level by a backward-looking local elite, as had been true in the 1920s. In the 1970s the national community was being compromised at the national level—and by a state apparatus that claimed to be oriented squarely toward the future.

Faced with these circumstances, local people could no longer look to a liberated nation-state as an alternative to a locally compromised state of affairs, as they had in the 1920s. Rather, in terms of spatial imaginings, the local populace was compelled to "distance" itself from the broader, national context. Local people were compelled to look inward, to themselves, for an alternative to a nationally compromised state of affairs. The danger was no longer internal, as it had been in the 1920s, but rather external, embodied in the state itself, and made manifest in the state's behavior nationally.

Although the military state was compromised in one sense (it violated the principles of popular sovereignty on which legitimate rule was based), in another it was quite whole and intact. Unlike the compromised nation-state of the 1920s, in the 1970s the boundaries of the state apparatus were anything but compromised or unclear. Local people knew exactly what "the state" was, and it was not they! In the 1970s it was not an element of the local population (an aristocratic elite) that could be blamed for compromising a state of affairs (popular sovereignty) deemed legitimate and normal beyond the confines of the locality (as was the case in the 1920s). Instead, it was a group of "foreign" individuals (prefects, judges, police), imposed on the populace from beyond the locality by the military state, who were compromising the national community regionally and nationally.

These conditions continued into the 1980s. Although military rule ended in 1980, and thus government institutions lost their overtly dictatorial character, in the context of economic disintegration and the brutal war with Sendero Luminoso, political parties ruled from the center in an increasingly autocratic manner. Even so, they proved themselves incapable of managing national affairs and eventually delegitimized themselves due to revelations of massive fraud and graft. All across the country there was mass disaffection from institutionalized political parties and processes, as people looked for alternatives to a system that had obviously gone bad. In the second half of the 1980s, as the Peruvian economy disintegrated in the context of triple- and even quadruple-digit inflation, and as the government wrestled unsuccessfully with a huge foreign debt and the censure of the "international economic community," state institutions of virtually all kinds ceased to operate and even collapsed.[13] This was especially true in outlying sections of the national space like Chachapoyas. As the citizenship-based public sphere once maintained by the state apparatus continued to weaken, Chachapoyanos perceived themselves to be a small island in a vast sea of insecurity. It was as if the national community itself was disintegrating.[14]

Compounding local people's sense of "external threat," heightening their sense of betrayal and isolation—but adding a temporal dimension to their sense of spatial remoteness—were changes in the exchange economy. The disintegration of the elite order, and the integration of the Chachapoyas region into the national economy, had profound and unanticipated effects on regional social relations. From the 1930s onward el pueblo differentiated into two distinct subgroups, one mercantile and the other bureaucratic/artisanal. The bureaucratic/artisanal sector can be characterized as "nonaccumulating"; people within it were unable to accumulate surplus. To the extent that the institutions of the nation-state continued to provide material and political support, however, the subgroup maintained itself quite well.

Those involved in the mercantile sector, on the other hand, were able to accumulate surplus, and in considerable quantities. Some of these merchants were based in Chachapoyas, others just to the west in the town of Celendín. Merchants from both areas had long been involved in regional and interregional commerce, but always on terms set by the local elite (see Nugent 1996, 1997). Merchants from both areas had also been centrally involved in the movements of democratization and thus in the 1930s were able to harvest the fruit of their own political efforts. After 1930, however, the Celendino merchants (who in the 1980s and 1990s came to be referred to as the "Jews" of Celendín) were able to draw on their deeper involvement in and greater familiarity with more all-embracing national circuits of exchange to gradually eliminate their Chachapoyas-based competitors.

As the Celendino merchants increasingly monopolized interregional trade, they began to import a wide range of manufactured goods (and later mass-produced food staples) into Chachapoyas on a scale never before possible. Seeing little possibility for profit by exporting agrarian products or handicraft production from the region, however, the merchants never became involved in the ownership of land or the exploitation of local labor. Rather, they remained a true merchant class, one whose interests were restricted exclusively to the realm of exchange. The national, exchange-based economy on which most Chachapoyanos became increasingly dependent for their livelihoods after 1930 was thus brought to them by this small group of merchants who were focused on commercial affairs to an unusual degree. They and their descendants thus became the mediators between the Chachapoyas region and the national economy.

As the town's middle class differentiated into accumulating (merchant) and nonaccumulating (bureaucratic/artisanal) sectors, those involved in each were thus confronted with a distinct set of life possibilities and limitations. As this occurred, the formerly unitary vision of social justice that had provided the cultural basis for the entire middle class's struggle with the elite order in the 1920s underwent a similar differentiation. Those involved in each middle-class sector selectively appropriated those dimensions of the original moral vision that best corresponded with their new life circumstances and pushed the remaining ones from view.

For those in the nonaccumulating sectors economic livelihoods were secure but also modest and more or less fixed, regardless of individual effort. Despite their vision of prosperity coming from hard work and individual merit, their actual life possibilities in this regard were limited. Those in this sector therefore expressed their newfound strength by seizing control of the political, social, and cultural arenas from which they had been excluded by the elite, by "democratizing" these practices and opening them up to "the citizenry" as a whole. Involvement in these democratized public activities became an important indicator of this sector's new solidarity and social ascendancy, of their triumph over the elite families.

Because of the possibilities for accumulation available to them, on the other hand, the small handful of merchants who monopolized long-distance exchange were able to realize precisely those dimensions of el pueblo's original vision of social justice that were closed off to the nonaccumulating sectors: growing prosperity through hard work and individual effort. And they emphasized precisely those dimensions of el pueblo's original vision that the nonaccumulating sectors "forgot": hard work, savings, thrift, sobriety, individual merit, and so on.

To distance themselves from the social obligations and entanglements that posed a threat to commercial accumulation, the merchants began to shun the very social and cultural practices so recently democratized by their nonaccumulating peers, those that expressed the new collective identity of the nonaccumulating sectors. The merchants went so far as to ridicule these explicitly social practices as "backward customs" and to identify themselves with "modern," national culture. The merchants attribute their own prosperity to their "modern" work habits and orientations. And they explain their nonaccumulating neighbors' inability to prosper by pointing to their "backward customs" and their "laziness."

Because merchants have come to occupy the key role of commercial mediator between region and state, local people's most direct, lived experience with national integration has come to be embodied by their experiences with the merchant sector. And because of the way that relations of exchange came to be structured in the region—as clearly differentiated from the social and material life of those in the nonaccumulating sectors—these people's interactions with the merchants have been characterized by impersonality and even hostility.

With the disintegration of the national economy that began in the late 1970s, itself heavily conditioned by the crisis in international capitalism, much of the local populace faced seriously deteriorating living conditions. In these circumstances it appeared to local people that the merchants were willing to put their hunger for profit before even the survival of the local community—before the ability of their neighbors to feed their children. That they could do so was a function of their control over the distribution and sale of food staples. That they would do so was something local people had no easy way of understanding.

As the local populace sought some way to comprehend the inhuman behavior of the merchants all the cultural differences and social distances that had characterized Chachapoyano-merchant interactions over the years came together in the local imagination to form a logical, ordered "explanation," one that attributed to the merchants an inherently different human nature. Nothing short of this, it seemed, could explain their indifference to the suffering of others, their willingness to take advantage of the misfortune of others for private gain.

In these circumstances the superior attitudes and modern pretensions of those who mediated between the local and national community were cast in a new light. Local people felt compelled to resist the exploitative behavior of these forasteros and to distinguish themselves as clearly as possible from everything associated with the merchant realm—not only accumulation, "greed," and impersonality, but also the corrupt political system that was so directly involved in unleashing these forces on the local population. In so distancing themselves, local people seized on the very "backward customs" that the merchants had used to ridicule them, but in the process were able to invert the terms of moral legitimacy normally associated with "things backward" and "things modern." For in light of the highly negative attributes that came to be associated with the merchant realm and beyond, the sociality, interactiveness, and also the innocence and naïveté of simpler folk who embodied a simpler way of life could easily hold the moral high ground. The modern world did indeed threaten this simpler way of life, these more primary and enduring identifications (of family, community, and friend), as the merchants themselves had taught them. For this very reason the modern world had to be contained, controlled, and carefully monitored.[15]

Conclusion

The forgoing analysis underscores the fact that states of imagination have distinct "time and space effects," distinct ways of conceiving of and organizing temporal and spatial realms. In closing, I would like to compare the time and space effects of the three states of imagination discussed above to assess the impact of each on the territorial integrity of the nation-state. Two points are at issue: the conditions under which local populations imagine themselves to be a part of or "outside" the historical imaginary of the modern nation-state; and the centrality of "modernity" in understanding contemporary social processes.

The compromised nation-state of the pre-1930 period was in essence preterritorial, its population prenational. That is, central rulers in the national capital had little if any direct control over everyday life in regions like Chachapoyas, had virtually no ability to impose a truly national order of social classification. Instead, local elite rulers oversaw a social order that classified people according to nonnational criteria; insisted on their "right" to control the movements of goods and people within the regions they monitored; and refused to relinquish these "rights" to the central regime. Symptomatic of the preterritorial, prenational character of the compromised nation-state was the following. When leaders in the national capital truly threatened the ability of local elites to monitor local affairs (or when national leaders were especially weak), it was not uncommon for local elites to seek to secede, to establish their own territorially distinct, independent polities (as occurred in Chachapoyas in the 1880s and in the 1920s, for example).[16] Neither national nor local leaders approached the territory of the nation as a foregone conclusion. Rather, the issue of territory was a "problem" to which there were many possible "solutions."

As a result of the "cultural revolution" of the 1920s, however, and the emergence of the liberated nation-state, these conditions changed. The nation-state became truly national and territorial for the first time, as the local populace vested in central rulers the moral authority and the political right to classify social persons (as citizens) and to regulate their activities and movements within state boundaries. Symptomatic of the newly territorial nature of the nation-state was the following. In political struggle, the territory of the nation did indeed become a foregone conclusion, as did the integrity of the state apparatus. Political warfare came to be waged only over who would control the state apparatus and the given territory of the nation. Efforts to reconfigure territorial boundaries or to redefine the national polity (through secession) ceased.

By 1980 national and global economic crises undermined the state's ability to maintain and order a viable national economy. As the state lost its territorial integrity in economic terms it lost the ability to sustain el pueblo. Chachapoyanos' response verged on the "postnational." They attempted to withdraw from the broader national context, if only in cultural terms—to erect spatial and temporal boundaries between themselves and a modern nation-state perceived as "alien." The fact that the local populace looked to themselves as a moral alternative to a nationally compromised state of affairs, and in the process sought to inscribe their identity into space, reflects their effort to "correct" the failure of the nation-state. Chachapoyanos attempted to divest the state not only of moral authority (to classify social persons) but also of territorial integrity (to regulate the movements and activities of these persons).

It is important to recognize, however, that Chachapoyanos' spatial and temporal retreat from the modern nation-state, though in one sense explicitly antimodern, is in another sense anything but that. It is true that Chachapoyanos naturalize their connection to a distinct and autonomous place that is said to be a moral alternative to, as well as to lie beyond the reaches of, the nation-state. It is also the case that Chachapoyanos essentialize their membership in a community that is said to be premodern, unchanging, and timeless, one that represents a moral alternative to the corrosive and alienating forces of modernity. It is revealing, however, that the equality, commonality, and consensuality, said to embody the essence of this remote, premodern community only emerged (discursively) with the breakdown of the elite order, which divided the population into mutually antagonistic and warring groups whose members would acknowledge having nothing in common with each other. In other words, the very qualities said to exemplify the timeless, natural community of Chachapoyanos emerged in the context of the citizenship-based public sphere brought into being by el pueblo during the modern era of the liberated nation-state. What the naturales of Chachapoyas call tradition is modernity. Thus, even as it appears to recede, modernity continues to define the parameters of contemporary social processes.

Notes

This essay was prepared for States of Imagination, a conference hosted by the Centre for Development Research, Copenhagen, Denmark, February 13–15, 1998. I would like to express my gratitude to conference organizers Finn Stepputat and Thomas Blom Hansen for inviting me to participate, and to conference participants for their valuable questions and comments. In addition, I would like to thank Catherine Besteman, Tom Biolsi, Constantine Hriskos, and Mary Beth Mills for their insightful comments on an earlier version of the essay. The research on which this essay is based was generously funded by the Henry L. and Grace Doherty Charitable Foundation, Sigma XI, the Scientific Research Society, the

MacArthur Foundation Pre-Doctoral Fellowship Program, the Fulbright-Hays Pre-Doctoral Program Abroad, the National Endowment for the Humanities, the Colby College Social Science Grants Committee, the Colby College Interdisciplinary Studies Grant Program, the Program in Agrarian Studies at Yale University, and the Wenner Gren Foundation for Anthropological Research. I gratefully acknowledge the generous support of all these institutions. Unless otherwise noted, all translations are mine.

1. The discourse of corruption concerning merchants, modernity, and nation-state discussed in the pages that follow, and the analysis of the conditions out of which this discourse emerged, pertains to the 1980s. There were, of course, positive and negative attitudes toward past and present expressed during this time. The overwhelming emphasis, however, was as described in the text. Beginning in 1990, the rise of a new governmental and political-economic regime in the national capital resulted in a transformation in the relationship between region and nation-state. A discussion of this more recent period is beyond the scope of the present essay.
2. Lazo is not the actual name of the person in question.
3. This was a period of rising prices and rapidly falling real wages for most people in Chachapoyas.
4. Several women market vendors told me virtually identical stories during this period.
5. Several years after my discussion with Sra. Yolanda the police used tear gas to break up a local protest march led by market women and small bodega operators who were protesting wholesale price fixing by the merchants (see Nugent 1996).
6. Considerations of space preclude anything but the most cursory examination of these aspects of public discourse.
7. Discourses of corruption have long been of interest to social scientists (see Douglas 1966). In recent decades, efforts have been made to address the explicitly political dimension to these discourses (see Chatterjee 1986, 1993; Gupta 1995).
8. Modernity was associated with the merchant realm in the local imagination in large part because the merchants went to great lengths to affiliate themselves with what they characterized as "modern" work habits and cultural orientations (see below).
9. A discussion of why it is specifically "Jews" who have come to symbolize what is regarded as the alien nature of commerce is beyond the scope of this essay.
10. This alternative structure of governance included individuals whose positions mirrored those of the departmental prefect, provincial subprefects, and district governors, and thus replicated the posts of the executive branch of government. It included as well individuals and corporate bodies (mayors and municipal councils), chosen by means of election, who replicated the structure of municipal government (complete with councilors for each of the areas distinguished herein). It even included senators and congressional deputies, chosen by means of election, who traveled to Lima and presented themselves to Congress as the legitimate representatives for the Department of Amazonas (see Nugent 1999).
11. Key in this regard were: (1) el pueblo's domination of municipal councils, juntas de pro-desocupadas (which made federal money available to localities for infrastructural improvement), newspaper publication, and school board membership; (2) el pueblo's ability to elect "their own" to Congress, initiating what people refer to jokingly as the era of "cholo politicians"; and (3) el pueblo's democratization of religious practice, in particular the substitution

of the two patron saints that had formerly been recognized in the town (San Juan de los Caballeros and San Juan de los Indios) by a single *patrona* (the Virgin de Asunta), celebrated by all Chachapoyanos regardless of background (see Nugent 1997).

12. These new sociocultural forms included (1) the Fraternal Assembly of Artisans and Laborers of Amazonas, a mutual aid society that established strong bonds among the town's many artisans; (2) rotating credit associations; (3) sport-culture clubs for young men and women alike, which established an arena in which the new forms of democratized personhood imagined discursively in the newspaper *Amazonas* could be enacted publicly; (4) neighborhood associations; (5) social clubs; (6) a chamber of commerce; and (7) a teachers union (see Nugent 1997, chap. 8). It is important to emphasize that this new public sphere was a highly contested domain. The movements of democratization sought to form cooperative organizations that could establish community control over the public sphere. The central government, on the other hand, sought to block the formation of these organizations and to make the public sphere a highly *individualized* domain. The government did not hesitate to use violence to pursue its ends. A more detailed analysis of this struggle to define the nature of the public sphere is the subject of a work in progress (see Nugent n.d.).

13. As mentioned above (see n. 12), since the 1930s there has been an ongoing struggle between local social elements and the central government to define the nature of the public sphere. Most of the local population has favored group controls over economic and political processes, while the government has favored a highly individualized public sphere. The implementation of structural adjustment–type policies beginning in the mid-1970s has settled this matter definitively in favor of the government (and the merchant forasteros). The consequences have been devastating for most Chachapoyanos.

14. This perception that Chachapoyas was endangered by the broader national context was aggravated by the emergence of revolutionary movements like Sendero Luminoso and the Movimiento Revolucionario Tupac Amaro (*MRTA*), and by the government's brutal response to these movements.

15. Alan García, leader of the APRA political party, was elected president of Peru in 1985. Immediately after the election some people in Chachapoyas were hopeful that García's election would result in positive changes for their region. The policies of the García government, however, did nothing to alter the commercial monopoly enjoyed by the large-scale merchants from Celendín, and therefore did nothing to improve the living conditions of the majority of the local population. Nor did García's government succeed in preventing the deterioration of state institutions in the context of the war with Shining Path and the censure of the international economic community. As a result, the García regime did little if anything to change Chachapoyanos' view of the nation-state as alien.

16. Individuals now in their seventies and eighties inherited a view of the movement of the 1880s as one whose intent was to form an independent polity. The documentation from the 1880s concerning this event (much of which has disappeared) simply records the fact that the prefect was forced to flee Chachapoyas in the face of a regional uprising. After a month or so, during which he marshaled military forces in the neighboring department of Cajamarca, the prefect returned to Chachapoyas with a large contingent of soldiers, canon, and so on. From this vantage point he was able to regain control of the region.

URBANIZING THE COUNTRYSIDE

Armed Conflict, State Formation, and the Politics of Place in Contemporary Guatemala

Finn Stepputat

An incident experienced by a former colleague of mine from the UN human rights mission in Guatemala brought home to me the point which is at the center of my argument in this essay. While sitting outdoors in a village in the Cuchumatán Mountains, my colleague was chatting with a villager about the armed conflict, peace negotiations, and human rights. "Rights?" the man said. "Oh yes, I've heard about rights. Over there they've got rights, I've heard them once, there," and he nodded across the deep valley in the direction of the town, la Concepción, the administrative center of the area since colonial times. "But I am not sure whether we could bring them here [*traerlos hasta acá*]."[1]

The universality of the rights of the citizen wherever he or she may roam is one of the hallmarks of the modern nation-state. Against this background, the above depiction of rights as being place-bound stands out as being somewhat particular. It points toward a broader perception of the modern state as located in cities and towns, while the population in the rest of the national territory is represented as living under a different set of conditions. The spatially differentiated representation of state and citizenship poses the question of how the state is territorialized and how different segments of the population relate to the state as an idea and a set of institutions (Abrams 1988). To approach these questions, the present essay explores processes of state formation during thirty-five years of armed conflict in Guatemala, a conflict that formally ended in 1996 when the government and the guerrilla organization Unidad Revolucionaria Nacional Guatemalteca (URNG) signed the accords for a "firm and lasting peace."

State formation has been theorized in a number of different ways. Very crudely, I distinguish among three different approaches that have emerged from non–political science disciplines. One is the "penetration" approach, which emphasizes the infrastructural and administrative aspects of state formation. They depict the process as an often violent penetration of the territory by army, bureaucracy, and capital. The penetration establishes networks and nodes that (in principle) facilitate the centralized control of flows of goods, people, capital, information, and images (e.g., Lefebvre 1991; Giddens 1985; M. Mann 1988). Social and physical landscapes are organized, leveled, and straightened out so as to permit the state to "see" what is going on within its territorial boundaries (Scott 1998), thus constructing an "abstract space" (Lefebvre 1991). Here we could also include Marx's idea of the "urbanization of the countryside." Marx focused on the commodification of space, that is, the creation of a (national) market for land, but he also linked this process to the effects of "enclosures" of private property, the concept of vagrancy, and the disciplining of the labor force (see also Giddens 1985).[2]

A different approach focuses on the cultural aspects of state formation, that is, the production of new subject identities through the categorization, regulation, and routinization of everyday life and encounters between citizens-subjects and state institutions. The central question addressed through these theories is how the state is rendered natural, taken for granted, or even legitimate to the subject-citizens, and how the state monopolizes the power to categorize people and to make categories stick (Corrigan and Sayer 1985). Thus, while the state is associated with the generation and sanctioning of certain, more or less naturalized orders, "the secret of state power is the way it works within us" (200).

There are many different answers to the question of how this "internalization" of state power comes about, but the answers tend to adhere to a "diffusion" model of power, in which people are reduced to objects of centralized power: the only option left for those who are subjected to state power is to reproduce or resist the power (Latour 1986). Foucault's analysis of the disciplinary techniques employed in the garrison, the school, the clinic, the church, and the family is a good case in point. However, his later work on government gives more scope for the active involvement and even complicity of subjects in processes of state formation, in particular in relation to liberal and developmental states (Foucault 1991). Techniques of government—counting, taxing, mapping, reporting, naming—are not necessarily monopolized by state institutions. They may circulate in different regional, national, or transnational networks and be employed for government in sites outside the state institutions. This is particularly so under the neoliberal regimes where citizens and groups of citizens (including "indigenous people") are encouraged to develop autonomy and self-government. But still, state institutions seek to monopolize the power to authorize and coordinate the use of these techniques, as discussed in the introduction to this volume.

Although the idea of government or governance opens a theoretical space for subject-citizens as agents of state formation, it is hard to get beyond the "iron cage" image of modern power, to actually grant them an effectivity as subjects of power, in particular when they do not directly challenge or resist state power (van Krieken 1996). In this regard, it is important to analyze how techniques of government and images of state articulate with techniques and ideas of self-reflexivity and emancipation. Embedded in processes of modernization, this latter set of techniques, practices, and ideas is not directly linked to state formation, but they may produce "projects of change" that contribute to the formation of state-centered orders (Asad 1993).

The third approach focuses theoretically on agency and projects of change in processes of state formation. This approach has developed through studies of state formation in localized and historical contexts, of what we may call state formation through the "politics of place." These processes have been explored by anthropologists who have discovered the state as part of their localized fields of research. Peter Sahlins (1989) and David Nugent (1997) are but two examples of studies that show how people at the margins of existing jurisdictions have contributed to the extension, territorialization, and centralization of the state by producing or supporting state order in specific localities.

One underlying assumption is that the territorial nation-state, at least during the twentieth century, has been contingent on the containment and fixation of the population in visible and governable places, and that these places have been formed, in part, in relation to a centralized state. I suggest that the approach of the politics of place will give us an idea of the ways in which projects of change have emerged in specific struggles over resources, entitlement, and political control in the making of localities. Such struggles over the definition of "the context of localities" (Appadurai 1996) are to some extent structured by existing cleavages of, for example, class, region, ethnicity, and gender, and the relations between centralizing elites and those deemed "locals" by the central elites.

Rather than being different approaches as such, the ways of studying state formation are distinguished by the kinds of processes and subject matter they scrutinize, which leads to certain limitations in their analytical perspective. Whereas the first tends to fetishize the state as an actor, it shares with the second approach a tendency to regard state formation as a top-down, from-the-center-outward process. I suggest that by combining the three approaches, we may be able to go beyond some of their limitations. In the following I explore how processes of state formation have articulated with localized struggles and emergent projects of change in the north of Guatemala, at the border with Mexico. Based on several field studies from 1994 to 1996, the essay focuses on the period of the armed conflict in Guatemala from the early 1960s to 1996, arguing that the Mayan villages in this region and in this period have been increasingly urbanized in the sense that they have been turned into "sites of governance." Different actors, including the villagers themselves, have contributed to this development, which also has placed the villages within an extending field of politics in Guatemala.

State Formation and Armed Conflict in Guatemala

The armed conflict in Guatemala may be seen as three to four decades of rapid change, occasional outbursts of armed resistance, and the steady development of a counterinsurgency state, as Carol Smith (1990) has named it. The key moment of this conflict is the quasi-revolution and the subsequent counterinsurgency campaign in 1981–1983. In 1981, a coalition of guerrilla movements had achieved momentary support from a substantial number of Mayans in the Guatemalan countryside who backed a counterhegemonic project of "the poor"—peasants, workers, and students—against "the rich"—basically the landed elite, "their" army, and "their" state. The military government reacted by establishing a disproportionately fierce counterinsurgency program, which brought about numerous selected killings of community leaders and organizers, massacres of entire village populations, and the organization of the rural population in armed "civil patrols for self-defense," the PACs, with close to one million members in the Guatemalan countryside.

Discussing how the conflict may be interpreted in a historical perspective of Guatemalan state formation, Smith (1990) presents the view that political life in Guatemala is constituted by a struggle between "Indians and the State," a struggle that has formed both the state and the Indian communities. Thus, the army's counterinsurgency campaign was carried out by "a weak but despotic state that attempted to eradicate the bases for the autonomous Indian community once and for all" (21). Smith explains the autonomy of the Indian community[3] by way of this historical opposition in which the Indian communities emerged as corporate units engaged in political struggles with the state since the conquest. A basic premise for the apparent unity of the Indian communities is the establishment of territorial administrative control along previous territorial divisions through the church and the missions, rather than through an alliance with an indigenous elite engaged in the indirect rule of the conquered (21).

In spite of its weak "infrastructural power" over territory and population, the colonial state managed to establish a hegemony through the church (Smith 1990; Van Oss 1986). The postcolonial state did not. The infrastructural power of the postcolonial state, that is, the capacity of the state to "actually penetrate civil society and to implement logistically political decisions throughout the realm" (M. Mann 1988: 5), developed considerably as Guatemala was inserted into the expanding world market from the late eighteenth to the early twentieth century. The nineteenth-century liberal onslaught on the Catholic Church provided means for the formation of a national army, which took over the Church's role as representative of the government in the countryside. Revenues from coffee exports made it possible to extend the modern infrastructure to larger parts of the territory, not least the telegraph, which was essential for the military control. In northern Huehuetenango, schools, town halls, and water supplies reached the towns—the capitals of the municipalities—between 1890 and 1910 (Recinos 1913).

However, according to Smith (1990), the state never achieved legitimacy within the Indian communities. Only through coercive means could the state control the communities, and attempts to impose new institutions on them were not successful. Smith concludes: "The fact that all such attempts to assimilate or incorporate the Indians into the nation in the postcolonial period have been forced rather than urged on them, has led to further loss of state legitimacy in Indian communities" (17). Below, I return to this discussion in relation to the army's civil patrols, the PACs.

Smith's position points to two problems. Epistemologically, she (with many others) tends to project the modern concepts of state and civil society into the past as if established by the conquest (Rønsbo 1997: 59). Thereby, she disregards how this duality developed in the political thinking in the region from the late eighteenth century, when the state emerged as an entity to secure wealth through the free acts of individual subjects, and society emerged as an independent process to be disciplined and framed through politics (65). In the same period, political elites conceived of the project of extending the "order of the city" to the totality of the territory in the form of an "infinite network" (Foucault 1984) akin to Lefebvres's (1991)"abstract space" through which society could be seen and ordered.

The state/society duality was enforced through the use of different technologies of government, in particular in the late nineteenth century. The liberal land reforms, which privatized and individualized land, together with the conceptualization of vagrancy, the laws of forced labor for those who did not possess (enough) land to be considered productive, and the regulation and surveillance of the towns, became instrumental in the territorialization of the state and the construction of state, society, economy, and politics as separate spheres.

Together, the labor and land reforms produced a dualized society: on one side, property owners with political rights; on the other side, "docile bodies" who were subjected to forced labor on private properties in the developing plantation economy. In other words, society was divided between citizens and subjects. The citizens were the "white" landowners and the local "non-Indian" (ladino) elites in the towns who mediated relations between the (Indian) subjects and the state. The dual society also had effects in terms of identity. As McCreery (1994) has shown, the well-known hierarchical and dichotomous identity construction of ladino-Indio (as superior-inferior) was a particular product of the epoch of the liberal reforms and the positioning of ladinos as intermediaries between Indian laborers and white landowners in the coffee export economy.

Returning to Smith's position, there may be a problem of interpretation as well. She insists that the state, given the autonomy of the Indian communities, could impose institutions only by force, whereby the state became even less legitimate. However, she ignores that "state" may be perceived in different ways in different contexts and moments, and that people may hold seemingly contradictory ideas of the state as "sublime" and "profane" at the same time (see Hansen, this volume). To many Mayans, tata Presidente (grandfather President) has been an ally in the struggle against exploitation and abuse by landowners and local representatives of the government. Also, Smith's position tends to ignore that in many cases Mayans have striven without success to become full-fledged members of the national society.

Thus, we may conclude that the exclusion of "Indian subjects" coincides with the construction of state and society as distinct entities, and that this exclusion should be seen against the background of the relative inclusion and protection of Indians in the colonial forms of government (Van Oss 1986).

The rest of the story, from the liberal land reforms to the 1990s, may be interpreted as a story of how the Mayans and others have negotiated the conditions of their exclusion and their possible reinclusion. And it is the story of how the projects of individualizing land property and of establishing an "infinite network" that facilitates the institutional gaze of the state have been carried out. Still, in the wake of the armed conflict, development agencies lament the continuing importance of communal forms of land tenure and the ambiguities of documents and existing land registers that cause permanent communal and intercommunal conflicts over land.[4]

The structures for state formation were in place with the liberal reforms of the late nineteenth century. But it was still a project. The effects of the land reforms in terms of individualization of communal land have been gradual (Watanabe 1992; McCreery 1994). The capacity for surveillance (Dandeker 1990) has been limited by the central state's dependency on alliances with local elites and/or the subaltern opposition to local elites. As Watanabe (1997) mentions, the province of Huehuetenango employed three policemen in the late nineteenth century; otherwise, "public" order depended on ladino militias, privately employed armed men at the private estates, and locally appointed volunteers taking turns during one year of service, a system that still, in the 1990s, functions in the highland villages (and in some towns).

The dictatorship of General Ubico from 1930 to 1944 represented a new move toward the strengthening and centralization of the state apparatus. Ubico engaged heavily in road construction, and the better part of the roads connecting the towns in Huehuetenango were built due to the *vialidad*, the law of forced labor in road construction. During the Ubico regime, the representatives of the central state in the towns, the *intendentes*, were appointed among nonresidents and sent to the towns by the president. This opened up the possibility of new negotiations and alliances between the central state and the Mayan elite of the towns against the local ladino elite. Among older Mayans, the image of Ubico is not as negative as the one constructed by historians. He is seen as *muy stricto* (very strict) and a just man who did not differentiate between Indians and ladinos (see Carmack 1995: 218); his laws (the vagrancy laws and the vialidad) applied to both groups (K. B. Warren 1978: 149). This image of order, justice, and state authority was no doubt something that the army tried to resuscitate during the counterinsurgency campaign.

Whereas towns increasingly have come under the institutional gaze of the central state since the liberal reforms, the space beyond the towns has been controlled only to a limited extent, despite the fact that the codification of a level of administration below the town took place in the nineteenth century. In an act regarding municipalities from 1879, the Barrios government gave the order that deputy mayors in *fincas* (private properties, haciendas) and hamlets must be appointed by the municipality on the basis of suggestions from "owners and possessors." Thus, reflecting the dual society of the liberal reforms, the act refers to two groups of population: the white or ladino owners of land at the fincas, where their tenants (*mozos-colonos*) were living and working beyond the reach of the state, and the Indian "possessors" (not owners) of communal land in the hamlets (quoted in Ochoa Garcia 1993: 34).

Although the number of villages increased slowly over the decades, the presence and control of the central state apparatus remained episodic and dependent on the goodwill of the deputy mayor to give information. In most outlying villages, occasional visits by land surveyors or the treasury police were the only direct contact with state institutions before the armed conflict of the 1980s. Usually, direct encounters with state institutions took place in the towns or the cities, and the compulsory obligations of villagers to participate in work turnouts in the public works, to work as voluntary policemen, and to supply firewood to teachers and authorities were directed at service in the town rather than in the villages.

This, however, has changed since the 1970s, and in particular during the armed conflict. There has been an increasing contradiction between the exclusive definition of nation-state and citizenship and the gradual acquisition of land on the part of Mayans, in particular from the 1940s on. Also, their engagement in export crop production, in the commercial sector, and in the textile industry has contributed to increasing contradictions between their position as producers of wealth for the nation and the narrow de facto definition of citizenship. These contradictions fed into the armed conflict as the attempts in the 1960s and 1970s to acquire political influence at local levels through formal, democratic procedures were blocked by the elites.

Agents of Village-ization

In this section I consider some of the contemporary agents who have sought to put villages and hamlets onto the political map of modern Guatemala. Although their goals have been different, they have all engaged in the noble art of forging or resisting change by means of engaging people in an abstract community with a common cause, whether modern Catholicism, armed revolution, or national security and development. Before these, other projects articulated cleavages and identities that contributed to the production of villages, most notably the liberal land reforms (Davis 1997) and the political and agrarian reforms of the populist interlude 1944–1954. Regional variations are huge, both in terms of the timing of the process and in terms of the agents who have been active in changing the conditions and positions of villages and hamlets. Since the 1960s, however, the combination of the growth of the rural population, local conflicts, and the intervention of national actors has turned villages and hamlets into increasingly visible and discrete loci of development and "governance."[5]

The following sections focus on the development in the municipality of Nentón, a poor area on the northern side of the Cuchumatán Mountains as they slope down into Mexico. The area is dominated by cattle farms and corn-producing communities from where the inhabitants routinely migrate to Mexico for agricultural wage labor. The capital, Nentón, was connected to the national network of roads in 1980, which was extended into the hinterland by the army's construction company, and under armed protection during the 1980s. Half of the population was displaced at some point in the early 1980s, and the last armed encounter took place in 1995.

The Catholic Church

One of the first agents to move beyond the towns was the Catholic renovation movement Acción Católica (AC) and related foreign missions that founded centers and built chapels for the indoctrinization and "awakening" of the population at village level. This process, baptized as "village-ization" (*aldeización*) by Ricardo Falla (1978: 518), may be seen as a decentering tactic in the context of the struggle against the syncretic, popular Catholicism that became "tradition" (*costumbre*) as the reform movement managed to hegemonize the practices and beliefs of modern Catholicism, known as "the religion." Struggling against the existing hegemony of the elders who were locked in patron-client relationships with powerful town ladinos, the reform movement gathered young potential leaders at week-long seminars in the departmental capitals or other central towns and sent them back with new visions and new capabilities in the areas of health, education, organization, and pastoral practices. Apart from involving converted villagers in a translocal institutional network that provided an abstract authorization of new modes of being human, the AC activists and communal lay priests employed and spread new "techniques of the self" (Foucault 1984) to develop a new set of ethical practices around the notion of human dignity and equality.

Although Catholic Action was formed as an anticommunist movement that supported the military governments of the 1950s, it turned to a more critical position as parts of the clergy approached the program of liberation theology. The movement became very involved in politics of place, articulating generational as well as ethnic struggles over a communal hegemony embedded in the liberal construction of state and citizenship, and in the spatial hierarchy of city–town–village. In Nentón, the North American Maryknoll mission encouraged young leaders from the villages to present petitions for land and other resources at the offices of the central administration in the capital, thus circumventing existing patron-client relationships. In other regions, the activists of modern Catholicism engaged in issues of communal socioeconomic development, in particular by forming cooperatives or creating village markets that bypassed the control of the ladinos. Only the latter was the case in Nentón.

The Guerrillas

In the 1970s, the new guerrilla movements started to work in villages in certain areas in their attempt to organize the population against the government. Moving from the periphery toward the center, as prescribed in their strategy, the guerrillas sought to gather military strength and establish their "rear party"—their social and logistical basis—in areas with weak presence of the state, and of the army in particular (Payeras 1991: 18). In the case of Nentón, recognized as a ladino town (although many old people still speak Mayan languages), the guerrilla strategy produced a spatialized image of the resurrection as taking place "in the villages" and threatening the town.

The guerrillas entered and to a large extent used the modernizing structures established previously by the Church, for example, by taking over the category of the "responsible," the leader of the village group of activists, and by establishing corresponding local clandestine committees (CCLs) that organized the collection and transport of food, metal, money, and young men for the "fighters in the wilderness." According to narratives recorded in Nentón, the guerrillas tore down the characteristic barred wooden doors to the village jails: "We used to have a jail with bars but they tore it down: [The guerrilla said] 'He who commits a crime will meet this one, and he pointed to his rifle. Now there is no jail, only arms'" (field notes 1996). They also discouraged any attempt of the Mayans to purchase land, although this had been a major aspiration and struggle in which many Mayans had been engaged during the late 1970s: "'The land belongs to everybody,' they said." Also, they put pressure on the village mayors (*auxilliares*) to make them stop collaborating with the town mayor. In sum, they attacked those structures and symbols that connected the villagers to the state apparatus. At the same time, the guerrillas sought to construct an alternative state by installing "people's tribunals" and themselves as surveyors of order and justice; by wearing uniforms, the symbol of armed men's loyalty to a state (see Dandeker 1990); by registering births and deaths; by installing a comprehensive intelligence service; and by imposing taxes, drafting young men, and engaging adult men in modern bodily exercise (drills). As noted by Wagner (1994), disciplinary techniques are not an exclusive property of modernization offensives "from above"; they are as often appropriated by agents of modernization offensives "from below."

Unlike the "real" state, the guerrilla state was a portable, partly invisible state with a minimum of physical infrastructure and an unlocatable center somewhere in the wilderness, from where authorization of representatives, rituals, actions, and ideas emanated. This state was legitimized as a redistributive state in favor of the poor, a state that represented popular sovereignty. But as the conflict intensified, the practices of the guerrillas became increasingly authoritarian. In Nentón, at least, they never engaged in the fields of education or health. Meetings, tribunals, organization, and the daily drills were the only techniques with a bearing on the formation of new subjectivities in which the guerrillas engaged. In these other fields they rested on the involvement of associated agents of modernization, such as progressive teachers, missionaries, peasant unions, and the cooperative movement. But in Nentón most of these left the region when fighting got fierce in 1981.

The Army

The next village-izing actor to appear in the villages was the army, which, faced with massive subversion, had to reconceptualize its military strategy and organization. Following the experience of the French army in the Algerian war,[6] the Guatemalan army mimicked several aspects of the guerrillas' strategy, including the establishment of a presence at the village level, the attempt to win the hearts and minds of the population by recognizing social and economic inequality, and promises of substantial changes in rural living conditions. Organized civil defense patrols and "local development committees"[7] were the means for establishing security and development, respectively, at the subtown level. As a decree from 1983 says: "It is convenient to establish a system of coordination at the national, municipal and local level to make the actions of the state's institutions—aimed at realizing a program of reconstruction and development—reach the smallest communities in the rural areas" (Linares 1988: 235).

This turn became an important element of the army's identity as the only truly nationalist and effective sector of the state, different from the corrupt police, the corrupt politicians, and the lazy state employees in offices, and different as well from the unpatriotic oligarchy. A civil affairs officer in Huehuetenango explained to me, "We are Guatemalans, we belong to the people. The majority of us are indigenous—the general is indigenous, and I walked barefoot as a kid. Look! I have the hair of an indigenous! . . . If there is a conflict in the countryside, it's our duty to enter as mediators to make peace. The National Police are not well structured for this, they don't reach the villages. They stay in the cities. The soldier, on the other hand, leaves his garrison. He only stays there for three or four days after having been on patrol. He provides security" (field notes 1994, 1995). Thus, the army leaves the bounded "power containers" (Giddens 1985)— the cities and the garrisons—and accompanies the real (indigenous) people in their villages and hamlets and, beyond that, in the wilderness (*la montaña*).

The army represented itself as an egalitarian, nationalist force of change and development. In Nentón, people tell stories about the strict colonel who brought order to the town, organized the population, and saw to it that everybody had equal shares of the relief provisions. No favoritism was accepted. The teachers from the town were sent with the army to the villages, where the population was ordered to (re)build schools. Although the presence of the army has been disastrous to many villages, it should not be neglected that the very fact that urban authorities, landowners, developers, and others make themselves present in the villages may legitimize existing power differentials in the eyes of many rural dwellers. It takes some suffering to overcome the hardships of travel in the countryside.

Apart from organizing state penetration, the army employed a repertoire of different techniques (known as "psy-ops"), which aimed at transforming the Indian subjects. As a civil affairs officer in Cobán explained: "Our obligation [is] to make them see the situation. Indians are very susceptible, they are easy to ply, just like clay" (R. Wilson 1991: 47). Some of the techniques did not differ from those employed by the Church and the guerrillas, such as confession, ritualized conversion, education, physical training, and drills. From the villagers' point of view, some of these interventions are seen as civilizing, as expressed, for example, by a village leader in Trinidad: "Nowadays we are somewhat refined/tanned (*curtido*) by all the advice we have had from the Church and from the army" (field notes 1995). The notions of "advice" and "ideas" are uniformly used to conceptualize a specific (pastoral) relationship between the modernizing agents and the Mayans. In this respect, the receivers do not distinguish among different agents.

In terms of surveillance, the civil patrols extended considerably the army's capacity. As I have argued elsewhere (Stepputat 1999b), the effect of the massacres was to produce displacement and a spatial dichotomization of the rural population between the network of villages, which became organized and armed, and the "wilderness," a space beyond control in which the people encountered were defined as subversives. Anybody who was not from your village was "unknown" and should be detained. Thus, the villages were constructed as discrete spaces, isolated from one another. Even known persons were unknown: a lay priest from a village in Nentón told me that he had once been detained in another village on his way to Nentón, "with pass and ID card and everything." He knew the head of the patrol in Chaquial because they had attended the same courses for lay priests in Huehuetenango and asked: "But why, Juán? You know me. 'Yes,' he said, 'but we don't know what you think.'"

Inside the villages, surveillance worked as well. Because of the danger of being accused of being subversive by fellow villagers, everybody tended to act in unison: "What one did, everybody did. Nothing was done in secret [*a escondidos*]," as a patroller explained (field notes 1996). This village was in principle turned into a disciplinary space, a human panopticon where the villagers themselves undertook the disciplining. One could argue that small face-to-face communities always have an element of strong (normalizing) mutual surveillance, but the new element of the armed villages was the installation of an exterior authority among the patrollers themselves. When people returned to their village from exile or displacement, they were taught the lesson: "Here you have to follow the custom [*el costumbre*]," that is, Here you have to patrol like everybody else. The patrol could also work as a "buffer institution" between the villagers and the army, which allowed the former a good measure of autonomy, provided that everybody in the village agreed. The communal authority reigned over individual members, and dissidence was always dangerous for the individual as well as for the community.

The violence had an explicitly disciplining effect: "Before [when they worked with the guerrillas], people thought of themselves as being very brave, but suddenly they became very humble," a village representative explained to me. But the patrols may also be interpreted as an inclusion of the villagers in the state, as a kind of recognition. After all, the state armed the civil population, which is an exceptional and potentially counterproductive measure. McCreery (1994) mentions that the Indians in most cases were excluded from the nineteenth-century ladino militias in the highland, but during the armed conflict of the 1980s, ladinos left the zones of conflict in large numbers. Beyond the towns, only Mayans, *grosso modo*, were present.

Although the regular, physical presence of the army alongside the villagers—no matter how far from the roads—often took the form of threatening intrusions and measures of control, the patrollers also received training, "advice," and direct linkages to a range of civil state institutions that were all under army control. Although the notion of citizenship would be misleading in this context, as the patrollers did not have any individual, constitutional rights, we may perhaps coin the subject formation as "corporate patriotship." This formed the basis of the hegemonic "army-peasant partnership" in which the patrols may be seen as forming both part of the counterinsurgency apparatus and the communal hegemony of the villages (Kobrak 1997: 17), which enabled the patrollers to embody the state at the frontier.[8] They produced surveillance among themselves and were collectively rewarded with symbolic inclusion in the nation-state, with certain liberties that gave them material benefits as well.

Development Agencies

Development agencies have operated in Guatemala since the 1950s, and since the early 1970s, they have increasingly targeted the rural Mayan areas. Depending on the accessibility, the potential for production, and the actions of other agents of village-ization, there are huge regional differences in the degree to which communities have received attention from development agencies. Thus, a growing guerrilla presence in particular areas in the late 1970s elicited development action from the government and USAid, and after 1984 the counterinsurgency program (e.g., "beans and rifles") was accompanied by some, although limited, development initiatives.

Before the 1990s, Guatemala was not a significant receiver of aid as compared to other Central American countries. However, as the peace process has gained momentum, the armed conflict has dwindled, and refugees and displaced people have resettled in the former areas of conflict, governmental and nongovernmental agencies have focused their actions in these areas. In Nentón, a well-known focus of armed conflict, a former patrol commander and lay priest (and supporter of the present neoliberal government) made the following observation: "Before, the governments were only a saying [*de dicho*]. We learned who won the elections but nothing else. The governments never gave their part to the people. It was not like the Mexican government that gave people their roads, their water, and their electricity.[9] Now it's different, the [public] workers come here to serve. Before, they were only scolding us; they came to kill people, it was the slavery. Now a person has value, there is respect. Now they take us into account" (field notes 1996).

In this account, the exclusive predatory state has been substituted by a more benign, apparently inclusive one, for which the provision of security and welfare to the citizens is its reason to be. The employees of the state have always acted with contempt toward the Maya; they have acted as superiors to them. In the vernacular, the exclusive governmentality is conceptualized as lack of "respect" or lack of "recognition" (*no nos reconoce* or *no nos toma en cuenta*). Phenomenologically, this governmentality is embodied in the occasional face-to-face encounters in which the Mayans have had to carry the state employees on their backs across the mountain ranges; have had to bring them food and firewood; have had to take off their hat, bow their head, and look to the ground when talking to ladinos in general and state employees in particular; have had to put up with arbitrary taxation and humiliating violence, although they have had some space for negotiation with superior (central) authorities (see McCreery 1994).

Now, however, the villagers note a change in the attitudes of state employees and modern state substitutes, such as NGO workers and employees of international development agencies. In the villages of Nentón, I met few Mayans who made the distinction between governmental and nongovernmental. To the villagers, the agencies and their people were all "employees," *licenciados*, and "institutions," which is the indigenous term to designate external entities with resources to be solicited. Institutions are explicitly contrasted to organizations, which are "something among ourselves" and potentially dangerous to get mixed up with. Now, the employees "come here to serve." The previously excluded subjects in the villages have become entitled to public services, which in general terms are defined as "development." If the villagers embark on the national development project, they are included on a collective basis as "community," while their codified representatives become "civil society." If we take a look at the practices of development agencies, it appears that the "community" is given priority in relation to villagers as individuals.

First of all, according to the unwritten criteria of several NGOs in the area, most agencies "do not work with private fincas, but only with *comunidades*," a notion that in this context refers to villages or hamlets.[10] Second, agencies organize the communities for collective appropriation of the development projects through publicly registered committees and representatives. This is not only a technique for the formalization of the interface between the rural population and the development agencies; it is also a technique for the unification of a (temporarily) divided communal subject: "The most important thing is to strengthen the unity of the community, to create a communal spirit," which is based on "tradition, the culture of cooperation, and communal work." In the postconflict context, the development discourse presents the divisions of community caused by war, displacement, and mixed resettlements as the most important problem to solve. The villages of Nentón are considered to be "the worst in terms of communal cohesion," and the model village of Chacaj, designed and reconstructed by the army, is "an artificial community."[11]

Development projects target entire communities or formalized groups within them. An interesting counterexample is the case of the scheme of individual credits for "the productive reintegration of repatriates" (FORELAP). Each household was offered a credit of U.S.$1,500 (1,000 daily wages in agriculture). After two years, the rates of reimbursement in three villages in Nentón were so poor that new repatriates returning to these villages were denied credits until their fellow villagers had paid their due reimbursements. As an angry and disappointed repatriate said, "They only offered us other projects such as latrines, vegetables, and reforestation. It is not just. Everyone [should have] his own account, everyone [should have] his own life." In this case, the recurrence to the "community spirit" was seen as an imposition.

According to the representative of the E.U.'s integrated rural development project in Huehuetenango, the (re)construction of the community spirit constituted the first step in the creation of a "municipal spirit" and, eventually, a spirit of nation. In the mid-1990s, the new line of thinking among transnational NGOs and intergovernmental agencies involved in the area was to increase sustainability by developing townshipwide associations of communal committees and representatives that managed communal credit schemes, health promoters, dispensaries, barefoot vets, and so on. The institutions envisioned self-sustaining region- and nationwide networks of communal organizations. As coined by Michael Woost (1994) in the case of Sri Lanka, the agencies wanted to develop a "nation of villages." But unlike Woost's description, in which governmental agencies produce (ideal) villages as the basis of the nation-state, postconflict rural Guatemala is characterized by a multiplicity of governmentally and nongovernmentally induced networks of villages.

Forming "Sites of Governance"

Very briefly, here I attempt to characterize the composite effects of the actions of different agents of village-ization, including the villagers themselves, as the stabilization of the village-community as a "site of governance." Heuristically, we may describe the stabilization effects as spatial, social and symbolic.

The *spatial stabilization* consists in the unambiguous delimitation, measurement, and registration of landed property or possession in relation to authorized communities with a well-defined group of members (*vecinos*). The proliferation of land conflicts indicates that the boundaries between individual as well as communal properties are poorly defined and registered, and in many cases double residence strategies, migration, and shifting alliances make it difficult for the agencies involved to establish an unambiguous body of knowledge about membership of communities involved in conflicts. In a situation where entitlement to land is negotiated rather than defined through property relations, the agencies involved take "historical and social factors" into account. Thus, belonging, identity, and conflict trajectories of displacement and suffering become resources for the negotiation of entitlement. Furthermore, the issue of unambiguous definition of land has importance beyond the land itself. In practice, only settled communities that are not engaged in conflicts are eligible for the development projects, in particular for the development infrastructure (schools, clinics, roads, water, etc.). As a representative of a group of presumably displaced people declared after the ritual measurement and circumscription of their new "urban zone": "Today we are happy, because now we can work with the institutions."

The *social stabilization* consists in the tendency toward a definition of membership not only by birth but also by participating in communal labor obligations in the public works and by accepting appointments for communal offices (*cargos;* literally, burdens) in the struggle for, and organization of, communal development projects. This is indicated by a conflict between the village of Aguacate and the settlement of returned refugees in Chaculá, in Nentón. In this case, returned descendants from Aguacate who held inherited deeds to ideal parts of the communal land were denied access to land on the grounds that they, unlike the resident adolescent men, had failed to contribute to the communal development projects. As suggested by Cancian (1965), one reason behind the downfall of the political-religious hierarchies (of the costumbre) is that they could not accommodate and give status to the increasing number of young men in the communities. The committees, representations, and promoterships required by development projects serve this function, as I have shown in the case of the Guatemalan refugee settlements in Mexico (Stepputat 1992). Thus, it seems that the flows induced by development projects and public works push toward a sharper and less inclusive definition of membership, and make it meaningful to reinvent the hierarchies of rotating offices of the *costumbre.* The internal struggle to become representative of a group or a community is also intensified, and apparently a "community career" is an asset for further ascendance in the greater society, as, for example, an employee in a development agency, a politician, or an entrepreneur.

The *symbolic stabilization* takes the form of a remolding of the settlements in the image of the town (and the city). As the infrastructure of the public services is installed, the ideas of center, public space;[12] and public order materialize, if at all possible, around a central park or plaza, *el parque.* Sometimes, the central park is even provided with a fountainlike construction when the water supply is installed. This urbanization is not necessarily imposed, as in the case of some model villages (e.g., Chacaj in Nentón). The design expresses the striving of the village elite to become full-blown members of national society. When talking with representatives, the image of a checklist of symbolically loaded public works emerges: "The development committee has struggled for five years now. We've achieved the new school, the clinic, and the new 'deputy mayor building' [*auxiliatura*] with an office and a hall for meetings. The only thing missing now is the [covered] market."[13]

Often, the checklist also includes a concrete basketball field in the central park, not to mention electricity/public lighting and the pavement of emerging streets. These latter features mark the present in the town of Nentón, but they belong to the (vision of the) future in the villages. A significant absence from the checklist is the Church, the key symbol of early colonial governmentality in the Indian towns. Religion has become a contested issue with the proliferation of non-Catholic missions and churches, in particular during the armed conflict, and it is no longer to be taken for granted that the Church is centering settlements.

Borrowing from Karen Fog Olwig's (1997) notion of "cultural sites," we suggest approaching this process of stabilization as a production of "sites of governance."[14] Olwig defines cultural sites as "cultural institutions which have developed in the interrelationship between global and local ties" (17), such as the localized but ever changing family land and house that are reimagined and recreated by otherwise migrating people in the Caribbean. A "site of governance," then, is a spatial, social, and cultural matrix that orders the interface between citizens-subjects and translocal institutions. This is where subject-citizens must position themselves to claim rights or entitlement. It is also one of the sites where images of state and citizens are produced and consumed. In comparison with Gupta's (1995) notion of the "necessarily localized instantiations" of the translocal state, sites of governance do not necessarily comprise representatives/offices of state institutions. A certain order and governability is sufficient.

Furthermore, we may notice that the communities as sites of governance are mutually exclusive in the sense that citizen-subjects in principle must belong to one community only, the community through which they can claim their entitlement/rights. Many of the problems encountered and generated by the intervention of the development agencies in postconflict dynamics are related to the murky business of defining unambiguous belonging. In the cases of conflict that I have followed in Nentón, the agencies were not able to generate precise and reliable knowledge of who people "really" were and to which community they belonged. Communities emerged and disappeared as alliances and conditions changed over time; people moved in and out of categories (displaced, local, repatriates) and communities.

State Formation and Politics

In 1988, a former lay priest and cooperative leader from northern Huehuetenango who had sought refuge in Mexico told me about the experience he had gained through conflict and exile. He depicted "politics" as one important element of this experience: "Little by little we have learned what politics are about. . . . Is your country a socialist country?" Obviously, he was talking about national and international politics—and in general, the refugees' curiosity and willingness to learn about politics and named political systems around the world were impressive—but his depiction of politics as a specific field of knowledge and practice that "they" had entered and were exploring more or less collectively seems to offer a fruitful approach to the analysis of political forms and dynamics in relation to localized processes of state formation and conflict.

As we have seen, the process of state formation in Guatemala has been contested, far from linear, and not always centered in the institutions of the governing elite in the capital. The process has articulated various visions and versions of how individuals and communities should relate to the state, which form the state should take, which elements of modernization state institutions should further and which they should curb. Hence, political struggles have developed. In the Foucauldian sense, the techniques and rationalities that produce the state as an effect do so by simultaneously producing economy and society as fields to be governed and framed through politics. As an increasing number of subjects, places, and everyday practices are brought within the purview of state institutions, the points for potential disagreement and contestation multiply. The central questions are, however: Who are included and formed as political subjects? Which kind of processes and problems are defined as political? What means of power do those excluded from the political process command, and what is their relation to politics?

During most of the history of the Guatemalan state, politics as well as state institutions have been the turf of the ladinos. As mentioned above, the liberal land reforms and other techniques involved in the formation of the coffee export state excluded the Indians from the emerging political domain, and those regarded and defined as Indians have been able to enter the political field only by crossing certain boundaries, that is, by leaving their communities and "redressing"—literally and symbolically—as ladinos. These ethnic boundaries and the ambivalence they have engendered have left their mark on the form of political struggles in general and on the struggle of the "Indians" for reinclusion and recognition as more than cheap sources of labor in particular.

On one side of the divide, the national elite has been ambivalent in its dealings with the Mayans. In spite of a liberal project of extending the order of the city to the totality of the territory, of individualizing and privatizing landholding in the name and spirit of the modern nation-state, the national elite has continuously contributed to the reproduction of a system in which the Mayans existed only as corporate subjects with communal landholding, if any. When Mayans finally began to engage in politics, they were excluded by all means if they were not strongly controlled through clientelist networks of the elite. In the late 1970s, when the army systematically began to persecute community leaders, organizers, and other organic intellectuals, "politics" was a central element of the complex of labels used for identifying those who transgressed the boundaries. Thus, their abilities to read and write, to speak Spanish, and hence, to engage in politics were the criteria stated for persecuting them. One refugee remembered how an army officer had interrogated him and other cooperative leaders, asking them, " 'Do you read and write?' ('No!') 'Of course you do. We don't want you to be experienced. You have a lot of experience, you speak Spanish, you know how to write, you have politics in your heads.' The colonel was very angry: 'It's your fault that we have to come here.' "

As the power struggles left behind the subtleties of decades of a "war of position" and moved into the terrains of the "war of maneuver," it became outright dangerous to be associated with "politics" if you were poor and/or Maya. When the refugees returned from exile, the army warned the villagers in the areas of conflict: "Be careful. They bring their organization, they bring politics." As an army officer told me in 1994, the refugees had been "ideologized" after having spent many years abroad. In general, the army identified politics with foreigners or foreign influence that had polluted the Guatemalan countryside, and in particular with "organization," the hallmark of the popular movements of the 1970s that defined *organización* as the universal means of forging political change.

The dangers of being associated with "organization" and "politics" have left their marks on political life in the former areas of conflict. When the national labor union, Unsitragua, in 1996 began to operate in the villages of northern Huehuetenango, after international and nongovernmental organizations had paved the way for more traditional political organizations, a community leader consulted me about the identity of this entity: "Do you know if this union is an institution or an organization? We are preparing a group of the union. Let's see if it brings something good. It seems to have some foundation. [The village of] Yuxquén solicited grains, and soon after, eight sacks of maize and beans arrived. They have offices they are not working secretly. It is not some politics but [about] necessities [*no es ninguna política sino necesidades*]." Under the polarized and dangerous conditions of political conflict it has been vital for the population to be able to distinguish between institutions and organizations, between necessities and politics.

At the other side of the national divide, Mayans have had an equally ambivalent relationship to their inclusion in the nation-state through politics and to the city, the paradigmatic place of politics and the nation-state. Mayans have identified these with the ideas and ways of the ladinos, who were positioned as intermediaries between the state and the Indians in the countryside of the postcolonial state. Since then, politics and the state have been the turf of ladinos. To engage in politics has been delegitimizing for most Mayans, who saw politics as opposed to sincerity, honesty, and humility, the attributes of the real Christian, that is, the ideal Indian as invoked by the colonial missions. In the countryside, the *politiqueros* (a derogative term for those who engage in politics and negotiate with the representatives of the central state) are powerful but godless ladinos, the heirs of the Jews (the Spaniards) who killed (the Indian) Christ (see Bricker 1981). To give but one example, a representative of a village where the inhabitants negotiated the conditions of return from Mexico with a group of refugees characterized his opponents in the following way: "They are very politicianlike, they are not sincere. We like honesty, sincerity, this is the most important thing; but they are not straight [*reales*]. They want to take advantage of us."

Owing to this combination of the power/culture constructions of the nineteenth-century nation-state and the conditions and stigmas introduced by counterinsurgency, politics was still, in the 1990s, considered a dubious affair in the villages. With the policy of decentralization and the distribution of 10 percent of the state budget to the municipalities, however, the intensity and interests in municipal elections have increased to a degree that by far outdoes national politics. The national political parties are involved in municipal elections for practical, not ideological, matters. They are means of playing out the competition for leadership within communities and the scramble for access to public resources and symbols among villages. Thus, the stabilization of village-communities through public works is very much a part of this political field.

The Politics of Place

Although municipal elections, associations, and translocal identities are gaining importance, the village-community has been at the center of political action during the 1990s. With the governmentalization of the Guatemalan state in the former areas of conflict, village-communities are increasingly engaging in relations with state or other resourceful institutions without defining these relations as political. "I don't want to make politics, I just want to improve this place" is a very common expression of individuals who engage as community organizers and intermediaries between the community and the mayor, development funds, NGOs, credit schemes, ministries, international agencies, and other institutions. They become registered and authorized as representatives, promoters, and committees; they receive credentials and ID cards from the institutions; and they often use their connections with one institution to further the interests of their community (and themselves) in relation to other institutions or communities.

Apart from this kind of "new clientelism" (Palmer 1998), communities engage in a number of other ways in communication with state institutions. One of these is (threats of) violence. Within a postconflict conjuncture, when the eradication of political violence becomes a marker of transition, violence is an efficient means of getting the attention of governmental and intergovernmental institutions.[15] Occupation of land or government offices, kidnappings, roadblocks, and threats of communal violence may be interpreted as ways of achieving access to resources or to negotiations over rights and entitlement. In the case of Guatemala, many such actions are coached in a language of rights, equality, and order. One incident of threatening behavior in Nentón, for example, was legitimized as an attempt to halt what the perpetrators considered a disorderly resettlement of former refugees: "They are about to build their houses on this land, without due demarcation, without landmarks, without documents. . . . We need to see a map, we have to have *licenciados* and engineers measure the land." The action and its framing is, of course, situational, but these are nevertheless calls for the kind of order states provide.

In other cases, this kind of order is rejected, either in a political language—exemplified by the former refugees who have returned from Mexico with an explicitly antistatist ideology (Stepputat 1999b)—or by way of roadblocks, threats to government officials, rumors, or conspiracies of silence that are used to seal off communities from the gaze and control of state or other institutions. Ideas of local sovereignty, backed, for example, by narratives of the heroic struggle of the civil patrol against the guerrillas while the army was absent, may be invoked to legitimize resistance to institutional intervention in what is considered to be communal affairs. In one case in Nentón, an NGO worker was denied access to a village and accused of being Anti-Christ as he was trying to make a list of children for a vaccination campaign. Likewise, during the 1990s, rumors identified certain institutions (such as the UN mission MINUGUA) with "the sign of the beast—666,"[16] or warned villagers against human vampires, *choleros*, in the shape of unknown foreigners.

To the degree that politics has become a meaningful field of action for villagers, the reversal of ethnic and spatial hierarchies tends to legitimize political engagement in and for the villages. In particular, two features have marked a break with prior clientelistic relations: the civic committees and the villages-against-the-town alliances. The civic committees are presented as exponents of a legitimate "politics from here" that contrasts the usual "politics from there," that is, the politics of the national political parties that are dominated by ladinos and based in the capital. In northern Huehuetenango, for example, civic committees have been promoted from the town of Jacaltenango in an attempt to create a regional, pluriethnic identity based on a village-centered, sustainable, and culturally sensitive development in las Huistas, comprising five municipalities at the Mexican frontier.

Within municipalities, the town/village divide was often decisive for the outcome of municipal elections during the 1990s. Given the limited funds of the mayor, he has to make a choice between, for example, paving more streets in the town or supporting the construction of schools and clinics in some of the villages. In the (numerous) cases in which ladinos have been in control of the town and the public services while the Maya-speaking population in the hinterland have worked in the construction of public works in the town, the town-village contradiction has been framed in the idiom of ethnicity. In 1992, in Nentón, the first Chuj mayor was elected by an antitown coalition of villages that protested against the previous "all-for-the-town" policy of public works. In the municipality, Chuj-speaking villagers held: "Now the mayor is natural like us, he supports the indigenous people. He fulfills [his promises] while the Spanish let us down." At the time of this interview (1995), the explicit Mayan identity had not yet reached this region to any significant degree,[17] but the ethnically informed political engagement was evident.

State Formation and the Urbanization of the Countryside

Postconflict Guatemala, much like postapartheid South Africa, has been turned into a laboratory for social and political science. Competing theoretical and methodological approaches are brought together in the same arena in an attempt to unravel the meaning of the conflict. What happened? How and why did it happen? And what are the effects of the conflict for the future of Guatemala in general and the rural areas in particular? As Arturo Arias remarked, a review of books on the conflict reveals that the discussion therein of the transformation of Mayan subjectivities during the conflict tells us more about the positioning and theories of the writers than about how the Mayans position themselves (Arias in Hale 1997: 825). The present essay, informed by theoretical debates over the intersections of power, space, and culture, runs the same risk. However, the theoretical debates do not take place in a vacuum. In the late 1990s the population of Guatemala passed through a moment of "intense need to remember" (Hale 1997), and among scholars who have taken part in this moment of remembrance and interpretation of the armed conflict, there is an explicit sense that "the state" in Guatemala is a seriously underexplored phenomenon. There is an acute need to understand the state.

The present contribution argues that processes of state formation may fruitfully be explored from the vantage point of the politics of place, of the ways in which, in specific locations, populations become recognizable and governable and states imaginable and effective. This approach helps us get beyond the state-centric analysis by addressing the question of how a range of actors contributes to the formation of state as they articulate national, transnational, and regional flows in processes of place making.

The empirical exploration of state formation in a former area of conflict in Guatemala suggests that three important changes have taken place during the 1980s and 1990s:

1. The reach of state institutions has been expanded territorially from the towns to the level of villages and hamlets, not least through the presence of the army.

2. State practices have become increasingly governmentalized since the moment the army succeeded in imposing control over the armed insurgence: "Now the employees come to serve us," as villagers noted in the mid-1990s, thus observing the change in governmental rationality.

3. Social spaces, which are defined or authorized by state institutions, constitute sites of negotiation and struggle for segments of the population who were marginalized or excluded from effective citizenship before the armed conflict. In contrast to the strategies of the guerrillas and their followers, who basically sought to destroy or turn away the existing state, and to the civil patrollers in the 1980s who tried to defend themselves by allying themselves

with the army, villagers in the 1990s engaged in the definition of the conditions and forms of services that the state should provide and the negotiation of limits to state control and surveillance.

We may suggest two elements behind the apparent change in the villagers' position *vis-à-vis* state and nonstate institutions in the area. On the one hand, the increased engagement of state institutions in the villages has multiplied the points of contact and possible contestation and negotiation. On the other hand, if we regard the resistance toward the state as an exception from a more consistent, longue durée effort on behalf of the Mayans to become recognized and included as full-fledged members of the nation, the current embrace of the state appears as a continuation of a process that was initiated by the exclusions of the liberal reforms in the nineteenth century and interrupted by the armed conflict. In this perspective, the armed conflict and the struggle against the state may be explained by the frustrated attempts to become full members of the nation in previous decades. As people in Santa Eulalia told Shelton Davis around 1970: "Yes, we are *naturales*, but we are also Guatemalatecos."

The exploration also shows that nonstate actors have been instrumental in bringing about preconditions for the villagers' creative engagement with state institutions. The modernizing movements of the Catholic Church and the guerrillas, who gave explicit attention to the village level, provided organizational capacities, languages, and forms of reflection that in the present juncture of state formation have enabled the villagers to align, to some degree at least, with "the institutions." We are talking about the modern forms of governance embedded in committees, meetings, negotiations, representations, planning, projects, and other practices that have not been developed through the curriculum of the national education system. Through their engagement in the modernizing movements, villagers have also developed a modern language for the critical assessment of the kind of order installed by state institutions.

Although in principle this language permits them to enter formalized political fields, "politics" is almost exclusively focused on issues related to the "urbanization" of the villages: provision of public services (education, health, transport), symbols of urban life and order (fountains, parks, plaques, monuments, sports facilities, markets), access to financial institutions, and an embryonic industrialization.[18] The scramble for attention from the "institutions" articulates identifications and cleavages between Maya and ladino, town and village, between villages, between competing leaders, and between individuals and village-communities. The prime objective of the villagers is not necessarily to order life in the localities according to the order of the state, yet the ensuing politics of place tends to have the effect of stabilizing the villages as sites of governance. The process, however, is marked by the continuing weaknesses of state institutions in rural Guatemala, the ambivalence of the village population *vis-à-vis* the order of the state, and, not least, the ambivalence of the white elite and the urban ladinos toward the Mayans. As Rachel Sieder notes in her contribution to this volume, the urban population in Guatemala rejected proposals for the devolution of certain judicial powers to village-level authorities.[19]

If we are to judge from the experience in the former areas of conflict in the most isolated parts of Guatemala, the village-level population have increasingly become members of the nation-state. However, for many practical purposes, such as access to credit, social infrastructure, and development projects, they are being incorporated as a kind of corporate citizen, as members of a territorial community that has been authorized as a site of governance. Thus, their recognition as citizens depends on their neighbors. As stated by a villager who was giving one of his days of work to the construction of the village school: "Some people don't understand that their children need the school, or they think they'll have it for free. They don't understand that we have to give our labor to become recognized as persons."

Striving to become recognized as persons, to bring the rights across the valley from the town to the village, seems to be a recurring theme that may give us an idea of the current state of imagination. We get the image of villagers striving to make the state present, to become included. This image is difficult to accommodate within a penetration approach to the state; it presupposes decades of nonrecognition and exclusion produced by violent forms of state penetration of the territory. But the discourse of recognition and rights also presupposes the appropriation of ideas of human dignity and equality as predicated by the Catholic reform movement, as well as the idea of the state as the ultimate authorizing entity. Thus, the patterns, processes, and subject matters of state formation change over time and space. Processes of state formation are always working in and through politics of place. But whereas state formation at some junctures is driven from singular centers, other junctures, such as the current one, are characterized by decentered and diffuse dynamics. These changes are also reflected in our theories of state formation.

Notes

I appreciate the constructive comments from Thomas Blom Hansen, Sudipta Kaviraj, Henrik Rønsbo, Rachel Sieder, Carol A. Smith, Ninna Nyberg Sørensen, and Fiona Wilson. Unless otherwise noted, all translations are mine.

1. Anthropologist John Tinella, MINUGUA, personal communication, 1996.
2. While Giddens and Foucault focus on the institutional aspects of state formation (i.e., the development of the administrative apparatus and the capacity for surveillance), Paul James (1996), drawing on Marx, emphasizes how the abstractions involved in the commodification of space and time (land and labor) precondition the emergence of a new subjectivity: nationalism.
3. Unlike the South Asian studies tradition, "community" in the Latin American studies tradition is usually understood as organized at the level of the colonial "Indian towns" or, after independence, the municipality.
4. For example, the E.U. development project in Huehuetenango, ALA/91, could invest only 10 percent of the funds designated for irrigation because of irregular land tenure during the mid-1990s.
5. Only in the 1950s did the population of the highlands surpass the estimated number of preconquest inhabitants of these areas. The population growth and local conflicts have sparked a process of duplication of authorized settlements.
6. See Trinquier (1964) for an analysis of the experience by a French officer who participated in the counterinsurgency in Algeria. The architect of the Guatemalan counterinsurgency program, Benedicto Lucas Garcia, was trained in the French army and participated in the Algerian war.
7. According to Gustavo Porras, the army even mimicked the name of the village-level guerrilla organization, CCL, Comité de Coordinación Local, later the Comité de Desarollo Local (personal communication, November 1994).
8. See also Alonso (1995) and Stepputat (2000) for a similar interpretation of frontier dynamics.
9. During the 1980s the Mexican government gave priority to social investment at the frontier to stabilize the boundary between the revolutionary, poor Central America and Mexico.
10. Interview with employees in the Centre Canadien D'etude et de Cooperation Internationale (CECI), September 1994. The distinction was blurred, though, because some private estates had been abandoned by the owner/administrator during the conflict, leaving it to the tenants to work the land on their own. The E.U., UNHCR, and others did carry out communal projects here, such as schools and water projects, but only after negotiating with the owner, who afterwards told the tenants, "This school is mine, this water tank is mine," etc.
11. Interview with the representative of the E.U. ALA/91 project, April 1995.
12. Public space is understood as a historically specific construction of common space, as discussed, for example, by Sudipta Kaviraj (1998). It is a space that is connected to the abstract authority of the state with increasingly codified notions of appropriate behavior/public order. In the villages of Nentón, for example, the idea that drunkenness is unsuitable in public space is emerging as an index of civic conduct and respectability: "If I drink, I drink at home, *tranquilamente*, without making trouble [*bulla*]." The missions, the Protestant in particular, have been promoting these codes of public behavior.

13. Interview with the committee secretary in Aguacate, November 17, 1996.
14. The concept is being codeveloped by the author and Henrik Rønsbo.
15. The efficiency of violence as a means of access to resources is conditioned by the public attention to the given area and the presence of resourceful institutions with a peace agenda.
16. Referring to biblical notions of the devil.
17. Villagers referred to themselves as *naturales*, a colonial category, *indigenous*, a postcolonial category related to the 1944–1954 reform period, or as *Mateanos* or *Sebastianos*, the highland towns to where the Chuj-speaking inhabitants belonged in the colonial period. The linguistic term *Chuj* was used in the same way as *Mateano*.
18. Struggles over access to land is another field of primary importance.
19. The proposal formed part of a major package of proposals for changes in the constitution—many of them coming out of the peace accord—which was rejected in the referendum in 1999, mainly due to the negative votes in the capital.

IN THE NAME OF THE STATE? Schools and Teachers in an Andean Province

Fiona Wilson

I want to explore a case study from Andean Peru to reflect on the ways in which images and practices of the state are forwarded and communicated, countered and opposed between central government and provincial periphery. By envisaging state policy and practice as involving specific kinds of spatial flows, I wish to discuss the changing forms taken by state intervention in the provinces, and pay particular attention to confrontations with regard to education and the extent to which schoolteachers, the largest group in provincial society employed by the state, have been bearers of the designs of the state in different historical periods.

For the bureaucracy of the modern state, the school has become an emblem that demarcates the territory effectively governed by the state, an institution that relays ideas about state, nation, and citizen. Nearing the frontiers of the modern state, the school has taken over functions of the military outpost. It is the place where symbols of nation are kept and regularly displayed. Here, children are taught to become citizens by saluting the flag, standing at attention at hearing the national anthem, marching on civic occasions, and learning about national history, geography, and ceremonial events. This aspect of the school has long been appreciated in Peru: in the 1960s Vásquez noted that it was "la unica agencia estatal de la cultura nacional" (the only state agency of national culture; 1965: 133). The school has become a focal point through which the state enters local public culture in a more benign guise than, say, the police. The mission of the school is to produce citizens not only by educating the young but also by drawing parents into multiple social activities, including observance of national commemorations. Not surprisingly, then, schools and institutes of higher education have also had symbolic and practical significance for antistate and revolutionary groups.

In the provinces, schoolteachers work at the outer fringes of the state; they can be envisaged as the fingers of the state's long arms reaching down to the people, embodying and negotiating the blurred meeting point between state and society. However, teachers are more than state employees. They are also local intellectuals, recognized as having the authority and responsibility to defend and promote their community, town, and province. This means teachers may take up political causes that bring them into sharp conflict with the state and its agents. Teachers localize and translate different kinds of cultural flow that open up new worlds and ways of imagining for the local community. They are placed in mediating positions, often intensely ambiguous ones, on two counts: they act between state and local society and they also link town and countryside. Rural communities have at times perceived teachers as dubious emissaries, a double-edged blessing that could be beneficial but also potentially harmful and costly.[1]

In Peru up to the 1970s, most teachers were drawn from the dominant urban-mestizo class. When put in charge of the new alien, intrusive school in the rural community, they tended to act as *mistis*, as mestizos with a strong belief in their own racial and cultural superiority, constantly mindful of the unbridgeable gulf between themselves and their Indian charges. According to one reading of Peruvian history, schooling and teaching were channels through which a deeply racist social order was reproduced. However, expansion of higher education and the greater access of social groups subordinated in the Andean race-class hierarchy to the teaching profession could destabilize and totally transform this relationship. Educational institutions became sites of new struggles against prejudice and injustice waged in the name of nationalism and a new moral order, and against the broken promises and betrayal of white governments in the distant capital, Lima.

This essay explores the conflictive relations between the Peruvian state and an Andean province at different periods during the twentieth century as seen through the lens of education. The discussion is framed by recent debates on the nature of state power and how states extend their power over space. The Peruvian state's changing spatial practices and the reactions these provoked in Tarma, a province in the department of Junín in the central highlands, is then examined. In the final section, I explore contemporary state spatial practice and local reaction by focusing on interpretations and actions in response to a key event in the school and national calendar, the celebration of Fiestas Patrias, Peru's national Independence Day.

Transmission or Translation? Extending State Power over Space

Much theoretical work on the state, as Allen (1999) has pointed out, rests on the idea of the state as an impersonal organism with inherent authority whose attributes can be transmitted over space. It is a straightforward matter. From this it follows that the outcomes of state control in national territory are relatively easy to discern. Strong states are considered to possess the power to impose state rule at a distance. This necessitates direct force (or the threat of it) to extend sovereignty over space as well as a more insidious fostering of structures of feeling to spread ideas of national community and national imagination. Subject-citizens enrolled in a nationalist project become involved in multiple forms of allegiance to the state. The space of state territory in the modern state is seen as constituting a planning frame in which the state bureaucracy can count, measure, and map and can institute policies to educate, improve, and develop the national population. Weak states, in contrast, are defined as unable to extend sovereignty over space, drum up nationalist sentiments, or bring progress or development to the population.

There are many reasons why models of state power that stress the dominating, coercive properties of states have been emphasized in official histories; for one, they record the state's triumphalist view of its past. But models that define state power as located in and contained by the apparatus of the central state overlook the interplay between central state and provincial political/cultural narratives and histories and dismiss the notion a priori that state formation is a process that also takes place "from below." Here the state's rhetoric as to the orderliness of its administrative structure, clear-cut hierarchic division of territory, and top-down lines of command paper over the complex, mutating arrangements and relationships that weld province and state together. The model is encapsulated in a particular ideal-type typology that, as in the case of Peru, produces particular attitudes among ruling groups that totally misread and misrepresent subterranean counterdiscourses at work in the provinces.

How and through what discourses and techniques, channels and networks, intermediaries and brokers are images and understandings of state, nation, and citizen relayed? Until recently, few attempts have been made theoretically to inquire into the dynamic processes through which states achieve a presence in space. To move away from reified, instrumentalist notions of the state, one needs to think through the connections between state power and territoriality and explore a different set of metaphors. How—and through whom—does the state *flow* over space so that it can reach its outer provinces, filling national territory with practices and symbolic sites? How does the state take on—and how is it given—the authority to coerce, persuade, and seduce spatially dispersed populations so that they act as subject-citizens and accept as legitimate forms of governance and relations of ruling imposed from the outside? As Gupta (1995) usefully suggests, there are two processes at work. One is the production of the state as a translocal presence, a shared imagination of the state spreading like a color wash across the map and distinguishing one national homogenizing space from others beyond its borders. The other process involves the implanting of institutions and agents that constitute networks through which messages and directives can flow between central state and province. Color washes and flows need to be conceived as potentially involving two-way exchange, though these may be blocked or ineffective under reigning constellations of power.

Taking a historical view, I suggest that in Peru one can discern three periods distinguished by the form and intensity of state intervention in the Andean provinces. In each of these, the state has been represented, imagined, and contested in different ways. Starting in the late nineteenth century, some seventy years after the end of colonial rule, the Republican state began to extend authority and sovereignty over the territory claimed. It did so partly by dispossessing provinces of their governing capacities. This marked a first phase in the spatial extension of state power. But in practice the state did little in the way of implementing postcolonial ideals or spearheading policies to bring modernity and progress to the Andean provinces. Postcolonial Peru gave birth to an "aristocratic state" whose seat of government was on the coast, not to a "developmentalist state" concerned with the well-being of its citizens. Up to the late 1960s, Peru was considered "one of South America's weakest states" (see Lowenthal 1975: 7). When social unrest was deepening in the Andean highlands and a broad consensus had emerged among professionals and intellectuals that the country needed a strong state, one capable of planning and executing structural reform, the military took power in 1968 and established the Revolutionary Government of the Armed Forces. Years of neglect gave way to enforced, structural reform, heralding a new, greatly intensified phase of state intervention in the provinces.

But the turbulence provoked by structural reform and influx of state agencies tended to sharpen opposition to the state. This found expression in the growing appeal of Marxism-Maoism in the 1970s and eventually to the emergence of a hard-line, ultra-left Maoist party, Sendero Luminoso (full title, the Communist Party of Peru, the Shining Path), which promoted a strategy of violence and terror to bring down the state. Subversion in the Andes was not taken seriously by the government in Lima until it had a revolution on its hands. In the words of Sendero ideologues, the party applied a Maoist strategy to separate the nation from the state, relentlessly attacking the state's spinal column to remove its presence by liquidating its agents. It was hoped that the convulsions produced in provincial society would eventually weaken the head, that is, the government, which would need only a little push for it to drop off of its own accord. Sendero's onslaught provoked a third phase in state intervention: a greatly expanded military presence in the Andean provinces to stamp out terrorism and the survival of a centralist, autocratic government that has made very little concession to the demand for a greater decentralization of political power.

By focusing on the analytic space between state and province, one discards the assumption that states can reckon on ready-made agents or representatives. They have to be produced. One important site is the school, another the military. In the business of ruling at a distance, states need to adopt, co-opt, work through, and rely on hierarchies of intermediaries, emissaries, officials, employees, and underlings. Some are socialized and disciplined to act more or less on behalf of the state in military and bureaucratic orders that are stretched out over national space (often with particular concentrations on the frontiers). But a great many others are not enrolled by the state so directly or formally, such as schoolteachers, minor officials, and *técnicos*. These actors are capable of changing face, of moving across and blurring the notional divide between state and society, of being tricksters who challenge in myriad ways the extent and nature of state power. What happens to these relations on the borders is integral to processes of state formation.

One needs to envisage those carrying out the work of the state as possessing some degree of latitude and choice, a capacity to translate—as opposed to transmit—ideas about the state and the state's directives, practices, and messages, or "tokens" to use Latour's (1986) terminology. The translation model as proposed by Latour differs in several important respects from the commonly held diffusion model of state power. In the latter, messages issued by powerful states are assumed to be transmitted largely intact through networks of agents. Though losing force due to the friction of space, the content of the messages has not been altered significantly. What counts most in the diffusion model is "the initial force of those who *have* power" (267). Following a Foucauldian line of argument, Latour rejects this static concept on the grounds that power is not something that can be held or possessed. Successful transmission over space does not reflect the power of the initial impulse: "The spread in time and space of anything—claims, orders, artifacts, goods—is in the hands of people; each of these people may act in many different ways, letting the token drop, or modifying it, or deflecting it, or betraying it, or adding to it, or appropriating it. The faithful transmission of, for instance, an order by a large number of people is a rarity in such a model and if it occurs, it requires explanation" (267). Latour goes further. Because the token is in everyone's hands in turn, everyone shapes it according to his or her different projects: "Instead of the *transmission* of the same token—simply deflected or slowed down by friction—you get . . . the continuous *transformation* of the token" (268).

This is a logical and appealing reformulation of the concept of power, but to what extent is a poststructuralist interpretation relevant to a discussion of relations existing between state and province in Peru? The concept of translation builds on the notion of flow in which messages are both propelled and altered as they pass through networks of actors, themselves mobile and changing. In Peru, teachers are generally physically mobile, and as local intellectuals and cultural brokers they capture, channel, and localize new ideas and practices. But given that they are employed and controlled (at least in theory) by officials in local branches of the Ministry of Education, teachers have not had unlimited scope to transform "tokens" that the state directs through the education system. So where and in what do powers of translation lie?

For state bureaucracies, not only has the school been considered a fixed site of state presence, but constant attempts have been made to also "fix" the teacher. As trainees in teacher training colleges, teachers are exposed to a particular rationality, vision of modernity, and concept of pedagogy that are markedly different from ideas and cosmovisions held in the rural community. It would not count as education otherwise. But the state is not the only, nor necessarily the most effective, institution that has engaged in producing new rationalities among the literate population. In Peru, proselytizing, catechizing Protestant churches have done so; so too have forceful, left-wing political movements and parties. Teachers may have been through a number of socializing experiences in their lives that have instilled different mental frameworks, ideologies, ideas of personhood that interact in a multiplicity of ways. The extension of the state over space as borne by schoolteachers therefore involves the state in networks and interactions that it cannot hope to control, and that modify, and may even reverse, the state's messages and demands.

If we look at the translation model of power in relation to Peru's Maoist opposition, especially the cold, claustrophobic ideology of Sendero in its attempt to produce a mirror, mimic state, we can see that messages pronounced by leaders, the Ayacucho *cupola*, have not been open to much mutation or transformation. Indeed, enormous efforts were expended by Sendero ideologues to implant a dogmatic, unchanging, untranslatable doctrine, as firm as a religious faith. This can be seen as one reason for the party's failure to keep its early support. But in everyday contacts, there had to be some flexibility and openness if militants were to hope to win recruits and pursue the strategy of separating the nation from the state. Whether Sendero leaders liked it or not, militants were taking part in processes of translation, the outcomes and effects of which they were unable to predict—though they might try to control them through expulsion or assassination.

The perspective adopted here, therefore, is that neither the Peruvian state nor its quasi-religious Maoist opponent could impose or carry out policies and designs in an unmediated way. They could not transmit commands or messages over space; instead, they have had to accept and allow for some level of translation. The scope of this translation, what it entailed and its consequences for provincial society, is the subject under discussion here. I begin the story by looking at the context of postcoloniality and events taking place in the early twentieth century, when state encroachment started in earnest. This period is not only of historical interest for certain ideas as to the purpose of education; its control and the proper relations between teacher and community were worked out then and have continued to frame perceptions to the present day.

State Territorializing and Provincial Reactions

Producing a National Education

In the decades after Independence from Spanish rule in the 1820s, liberalism as a political philosophy shaped the mutual recognition and intelligibility of messages exchanged between state and province. Liberalism had been introduced at the very end of the colonial period and had prompted the Spanish Crown to grant Indians the same civil rights as Creoles (Spanish settlers who, due to the taint of being born in the colonies, were barred from holding office in the colonial administration and church). But liberalism proved unsettling, for it fired Creole patriots to wage revolution to liberate America from Spanish rule. Following Independence, liberal ideas guided the new nation builders and underpinned Republican constitutions and legislation. However, as Hale comments, this European political philosophy was applied "in countries which were highly stratified socially and racially, and economically underdeveloped, and in which the tradition of centralized state authority ran deep" (1996: 368).

In Peru, at the start of the Republic, the liberators declared that all Indians or naturals would be known as Peruvians. Like all other citizens, they would be recognized as possessing individual rights to land, that is, to the land granted to Indian communities by the Spanish Crown. They were also liberated from the obligation of providing tribute in cash, labor, and goods on the grounds of their race. But in practice, it proved far from easy to carry out the emancipatory legislation; tribute was in effect retained and Indian communities were under great threat as a result of the change from corporate to individual ownership. By the end of the nineteenth century, liberalism had been transformed from an ideology of opposition to the old colonial order to an ideology that coupled progress with social control and new "scientific" ideas of racism and positivism. In the process, the initial emancipatory vision of citizenship rights was dropped. Seen from the perspective of the national elite, the mass of the indigenous population of the highlands was immersed in a backward subsistence economy, not reached by flows of modernity, lacking all vestiges of civic culture, and too humble, ignorant, and uncivilized to be capable of exercising rights of citizenship.[2] The Constitution adopted at the turn of the century included literacy as an essential attribute of citizenship, and this move effectively barred the majority of the indigenous population. National and provincial elites alike then came to see education as a national crusade, as the route through which ignorant Indians would, eventually, be civilized and integrated into the new nation.

In his discussion of imagined communities, Anderson has put forward the argument that the nationalism espoused by the Creole pioneers of Spanish America was characterized by a "well-known doubleness . . . its alternating grand stretch and particularistic localism" (1991: 62). One can go a step further to suggest that neither the local nor the continental expression of nationalism corresponded to the spatial scale required for the formation of Latin American states after the 1820s. The spatiality of the independent state, a former administrative unit of the Spanish empire, was not particularly meaningful to Creole elites, who identified more with the spatially circumscribed provinces that resembled city-states run by white or multiethnic ruling groups with powers of government over the surrounding indigenous population. Nor was the spatiality of the new states meaningful to indigenous populations. The old ethnic polities had been broken up under colonial rule and Indians had suffered both spatial enclosure and deterritorialization, pushed around by colonial administrators to provide tribute and workers and goods for the mining economy.

The effective scale of government inherited from colonial times was the province. Provincial elites, euphoric at the end of colonial rule, were expanding and diversifying through the incorporation of waves of immigrants of largely European origin who looked for adventure and fortune in the New World. Tarma, a prosperous Andean province relatively close to Lima, had long provisioned the mining centers in the central highlands with workers, pack animals, and foodstuffs and was actively promoting the recolonization of the tropical lowlands on its eastern margins and benefiting from the vastly expanded production of cane alcohol, *aguardiente* (F. Wilson 1982). During the nineteenth century, the province attracted ripples of foreign immigrants who came directly from Europe or via Argentina or Chile as well as from China. These men (and a small number of women) preferred to settle in the flourishing Andean town, located not too far from the still unruly Lima. Some hoped to make their fortunes in mining or from properties in the recolonized lowlands; others offered professional services or were master craftsmen much in demand by property-owning families resident in the town. Others were merchants and traders, muleteers and transporters, the largest concerns setting up import-export houses from the Tarma base. Newcomers, one could argue, would tend to have less-ingrained prejudices as to the place of an Indian peasantry in postcolonial Peru. Indeed, for a short period in the mid–nineteenth century, family histories retold in hushed voices reveal that a number of European men married women from indigenous families and gained access to resources.

In Tarma, as in other Andean provinces, property owners and professionals (though rarely the Italian or Chinese merchants) were forming a provincial elite eager to govern and even more eager to engage in local politicking. There was an unusual enthusiasm in Tarma for transforming the *cabildo* (council) of colonial times into a modern governing institution. This was signaled by the remarkable decision in the mid-1860s to keep copies of the mayor's correspondence and the minutes (*actas*) of provincial council debates, bind them into leather volumes, and deposit them in the municipal archive. With a degree of autonomy that included the right to collect taxes levied on movement and the consumption of luxury goods as well as commandeer Indian labor, provincial elites could actively govern and take steps to improve infrastructure and establish schools.

The tradition of centralism, though, bit hard. As the correspondence of the Tarma mayors shows, the provincial elite insisted on imagining the state as a superior juridical body and constantly asked for advice and guidance. Although at the start, the embryonic central government headquartered in Lima possessed neither the capacity nor the imagination to intervene directly in what was going on in the provinces, the activity of the provincial councils was partly responsible for forcing presidents to finance the expansion of the central state administration. In terms of political ideas, there had been much common ground between modernizing provincial and national elites. Sharing class and race identifications, a horizontal affinity existed among the clusters of white/mestizo elites dispersed over space, but there was not yet much general acceptance that a vertical, hierarchic relationship bound province to state.

By the 1870s, after a messy period of rule by *caudillos* (military strongmen), the central state was stabilizing and growing stronger (Gootenberg 1989, 1993; Klarén 1986, 2000). State revenues expanded greatly due to levies raised on the windfall profits earned during the guano bonanza (when nitrate-rich bird shit was exported as fertilizer to Europe). These revenues financed an expanded state bureaucracy, public works, and wild schemes to throw railway lines across the Andes with the aim of linking Pacific and Atlantic Oceans. But Peru suffered ignominious defeat in the War of the Pacific (1879–1884) when Chilean troops rampaged through the country. The coastal nitrate fields were lost to Chile, and the state was bankrupted and forced to take costly loans from Britain. The shock of the defeat was salutary. A general view emerged among intellectuals debating the causes of the catastrophe and possibilities for future reconstruction that the country was plagued by racial, cultural, and geographic fragmentation. The gap between coast and highlands, between modern Peru and backward regions still steeped in the colonial past needed to be bridged. This heightened the importance given to education and generated a view that only a national education project under state control could integrate the Andean provinces. Let us look at the emerging conflict between province and state from the perspective of Tarma.

In 1870, the state had declared that free primary education was to be made available in the capital of every district in the country and in 1873 handed over responsibility for education to the provincial councils. The Lima ministry in charge of education (along with justice, culture, and welfare) relayed limited state subsidies to the provincial councils to pay for schools and teachers, but after Peru's bankruptcy following the War of the Pacific, the provinces had to find their own revenues to make up for the loss of state subsidies. In Tarma, the provincial council recommended that teachers of the seventeen primary schools in the province try to collect small sums from parents, but the measure was unpopular, especially in the rural areas.[3] Circulars sent by the Ministry urged the opening of more schools and that the physical condition of the boys should be improved: "Nothing contributes so much to physical education as military exercises."[4] This indicates the connection being made between schooling and military recruitment.

Tarma's municipal archive reveals that during the 1890s, 40 percent to 50 percent of total municipal income (raised largely from consumption taxes on aguardiente) was devoted to education. The Tarma mayors wrote frequently to the Lima Ministry to try to secure funding from the state, but the Ministry replied that the province was wealthy enough to manage without a state subsidy, given that Tarma's municipal income was known to have doubled since the war. The mayor continued to complain that other, pressing expenditures had to be postponed due to the burden of education and threatened to close schools to redirect funds to public works.[5] But members of the provincial council were deeply divided in their views as to the proportion of funds that ought to be devoted to education compared to public works. Despite the wrangling, the mayor made the claim that forty schools were functioning in the province in 1892; the vast majority were to be found in rural hamlets where teachers from Tarma town attempted to teach Quechua-speaking children to read and write in Spanish.[6] This claim, however, sounds like an exaggeration.

A radical group of intellectuals and educationalists in Tarma, under the intellectual leadership of Adolfo Vienrich, were inspired by the challenge of bringing citizenship within reach of the indigenous population.[7] They developed attractive teaching materials that drew on local natural history and myths and legends for use in rural schools, produced the first newspaper in Peru in Quechua as well as Spanish, and opened a night school for the education of artisans and their children. Not only was the Quechua language valued, but Indian cultural traditions in the present were respected as well as Inca achievements in the past. The radical group (supported by artisans and traders) had won the municipal elections on two occasions (in 1897 and 1903) and installed Vienrich as mayor. Thus, attempts had been made at an early date in Tarma to define and implement an alternative form of education and pedagogy and to translate the content of education so as to inspire a less racist, less unjust vision of postcolonial society. There had been deep criticism in the provinces of the state's view of education; in Vienrich's words, "There does not exist in the Republic, even in embryo, a form of national teaching that is truly Peruvian in spirit and direction."[8]

Attempts by the central state to intervene in provincial matters and extend its authority were not considered by Tarma's citizens as efficient or beneficial. How, then, in practice, did the central state manage to subdue the proudly independent provinces? Here Tarma's municipal archive provides a vivid, day-by-day account of the erosion of provincial autonomy.

During the 1890s, the Education Ministry wrote in an increasingly peremptory tone demanding that provincial councils furnish statistical information on the exact numbers of schools, teachers, and pupils. At the start of the decade, demands for information were sporadic, but in 1896 Tarma received a visit from an official inspector sent by the Ministry of the Interior to report on local government in the central Andean departments. In his assignment he would also review what support was being given to education and conditions in the schools. The inspector was not well received in Tarma. He failed to gain an audience with the mayor, and when trying to collect a list of the children enrolled in provincial schools was fobbed off with the excuse that the municipal authority had no representatives who could collect this information in the rural areas.[9] Tarma paid the price for its high-handed treatment of the inspector, for he published "most unfavorable" comments in the Lima press that, according to the mayor, were full of "grave inaccuracies."[10]

In line with the crusading spirit now found in Lima, a massive effort was made to collect national educational statistics for the year 1901–1902, notwithstanding the noncooperative provincial authorities. The Directorate of Primary Education in Lima sent out a stream of official letters, and finally resorted to the threat of fining the provincial councils who did not comply with the request for information. Adolfo Vienrich, who had just been elected mayor, wrote at length explaining the difficulties of collecting accurate statistics from far-flung districts whose authorities were themselves barely literate and who kept no records.[11] In Tarma, as elsewhere, difficulties of data collection probably meant there was substantial underreporting. The result of the 1902 census shocked the Lima Ministry, for it revealed that despite the national crusade, only 29 percent of children between the ages of six and fourteen years were receiving instruction (Contreras 1996: 11). The Lima Ministry decided to intervene.

In 1904, the Directorate of Primary Education sent out a circular to inform the provincial councils that the state would now take over the responsibility of guaranteeing the provision of primary education throughout the Republic. To do this, better and more regular statistical information was imperative as to the numbers of schools in operation, their condition, and their location. Provincial authorities were told they could reduce the salaries of teachers who failed to send data to the district and provincial authorities.[12] Mayor Leon wrote unceasingly to Lima excusing the delays and reiterating his predicament. In 1905 the government passed a resolution imposing fines on the mayors of the provinces and districts who did not send data on time. Members of Tarma's provincial council were both incensed and bemused. This treatment at the hands of minions of the state was thoroughly disconcerting to the men who ran provincial affairs. The Tarma mayors no longer responded to Lima's demands with long letters, written in a familiar, man-to-man style. They now wrote more cautiously. After receiving a particularly sharp telegram that threatened to remove Mayor Leon from office unless the statistics were dispatched immediately, Leon wrote: "There must be some mistake."[13] The orders and threats from the state bureaucracy ridiculed local democracy, undermined the dignity and respect of the provincial authorities, and gave them very little room for negotiation, let alone translation, of state demands. Peremptory demands created an image of the state as being all-powerful. The provinces' age-old tactic of noncompliance no longer sufficed, for there were serious shocks in store.

The state's efforts to make government rational and efficient were increasingly depicted in the Lima press as blocked and aborted due to slow, cumbersome, anachronistic, noncompliant provincial government. The image implanted was of a backward, lethargic, rural elite that ought not to remain in charge. The way was being cleared for the state to crush locally elected government and remove its capacities and responsibilities. Finally, in 1906, the control, planning, and financing of primary education was taken out of the hands of the provincial councils and shifted to a state ministry. Thus, the launching of a national education project was accompanied by the bypassing, discrediting, and disempowering of provincial government, and a new subservient relationship between province and state was born.

Peru's national education project in the early twentieth century depicted the Indian as ignorant, defective, uncivilized. To integrate the Indian, Contreras notes: "Armies of teachers and personnel were sent off to the countryside, accompanied by packs of books, pencils and maps, while poor but diligent peasant communities built classrooms and school yards to receive them. The task involved not only teaching reading, writing and simple arithmetic, but above all, to transmit the 'national language,' which was Spanish, . . . and national history and geography, and to inculcate nutritional habits, as well as notions of hygiene and of 'urban living' that would improve the physical condition of the indigenous race" (1996: 9). The missionary view of education was fostered by the local as well as the national press. In 1910 and 1911, almost every issue of Tarma's newspaper, *El Imparcial*, carried an article on the imperative need to civilize the Indian through education: "For the future prosperity of the nation, education is essential for the indigenous race still living in semi-savagery" (10 January 1910). The signs were hopeful: "We have seen that those from their race who know how to read and write have formed families according to civilized custom" (7 November 1910). Numbers of schools in the province rose slowly, but opposition was voiced by the property owners. Local *hacendados* (families resident on the hacienda) had no interest in extending education to their *gente* and chased the schoolteachers away from their properties.

Schooling was closely bound up with an authoritarian form of pedagogy, military ethos, and militarized regulation of the body through drilling, marching, and sitting still. There also developed a preoccupation with hygiene and cleanliness, with checking the bodies of Indian children. One can question the extent to which these ideas reflected the power of the state to transmit and impose a common regulatory framework, for these ideas also emanated from the dominant class in Andean society. But one also needs to question the extent to which the practices revealed purely the microphysics of disciplinary power, for in a postcolonial situation (one never addressed by Foucault), they could also be seen as carrying liberatory potentials. It should be remembered that an important objective was to transform the body and body language of the bent, despised, humble, servile Indian into the upright body of the citizen, a citizen who in the Latin American context was expected to be male and prove his patriotism by bearing arms.

The state's erosion of provincial powers of government and absorption of education had come at a time when countercurrents were surfacing in the Andean region that rejected the state's crude civilizing mission. In Tarma, this incipient indigenista line of thought had been pioneered in the pedagogic and political work of Vienrich and his group from the Radical Party. Vienrich had been an exceptional example of a local intellectual who in the early 1900s had adopted a socialist perspective to analyze postcolonial society and to guide his political actions as mayor. His critique of the state (and its representative, the prefect) cost him his life and also his reputation as a socialist.[14] But although much of his political work was expediently "forgotten," some of his ideas lived on among later generations of local intellectuals. Opposition to the integrationist educational project of the state came to the fore briefly in the 1940s and with greater force in the 1970s.

Structural Reform and the New Philosophy of Education

From the first phase of state expansion in the 1900s up to the 1960s, the form of state intervention in the Andean provinces changed little.[15] But the Revolutionary Government of the Armed Forces under Juan Velasco Alvarado, aided by professionals and intellectuals from the "left," was intent on imposing a series of structural reforms in the 1970s to modernize the country. Of particular relevance for the Andean provinces was a sweeping agrarian reform that aimed to dispossess the hacendado class and transform their large properties into cooperatives, along with a series of measures to reorganize education. But the military government got off to a bad start. Two events in the late 1960s were later singled out as symptomatic of the underlying violent clash between an authoritarian state and citizens with their own interests and agendas. One was the overturning of a locally directed agrarian reform in the department of Andahuaylas and its enforced return to state control (Sanchez 1981). The other was the violent suppression of protests by parents in the department of Ayacucho who rejected the government's plan to levy charges on schoolchildren having to resit exams (Degregori 1990). In both cases, the military was sent to restore order, deaths occurred, and the confrontations generated support for revolutionary parties, hardening the view that the brutal imposition of state power should be opposed with violence if need be. Leaders of both movements were later to join Sendero.

With respect to education, the military government inherited a heavy financial commitment from the previous government (under Belaunde) that had promised to introduce free education at the secondary level and to increase teachers' salaries. To this, the military government added a political commitment. Education was to be a cornerstone of the revolution. Velasco, in well-publicized speeches, criticized the state education system and, inspired by the teachings of Brazilian Paulo Freire, stated that his government "aspires to create an educational system that satisfies the necessities of the whole nation, that reaches the great mass of peasants, up to now exploited and deliberately maintained in ignorance, that creates a new consciousness among all Peruvians of our basic problems and that attempts to forge a new kind of man within a new morality that emphasizes solidarity, labor, authentic liberty, social justice, and the responsibilities and rights of every Peruvian man and woman."[16]

An Education Reform Commission (on which some 120 specialists labored for a year) delivered a long report with many recommendations for comprehensive reform. Despite the widespread criticism this report provoked, it formed the basis of the new Law on Education (Decree Law 19326) of 1972. The new Peruvian education was to build on three ideological pillars—humanism, nationalism, and democracy—tied together by the central idea of *concientización* (awareness raising) that would lead to liberation and participation in the historic process of removing the old structures of dependence and domination (Drysdale and Myers 1975). But many schoolteachers remained unimpressed. They were openly critical of the government for reneging on promises made by the Belaunde government for salary increases.

Through the reforms, secondary and higher education was expanded in the highlands and a new national policy for bilingual education inaugurated. For the first time the teaching profession was put within reach of youngsters from poor rural, indigenous, and *cholo* backgrounds, for teaching was the only profession where trainees could work (and earn a salary) while studying for their qualifications in vacation times. Now young men and women from the subordinate groups in the Andean race-class hierarchy could hope for social mobility through education. Mediating and keeping a watchful eye on the turbulence provoked by the changes was the state-sponsored, nationwide organization for "popular participation" whose well-chosen acronym, SINAMOS, meant "without masters."[17]

The agrarian reform led to the implanting of new state offices in the provinces and brought greatly increased numbers of *técnicos* and *ingenieros*. This represented an era of more intense state presence and intervention. On national territory a set of technical reforms had been mapped out and was being strenuously implemented with the aim of creating a homogeneous economy and society. But the military government did not succeed in selling a new popular image of the state nor in replacing the old racist social order and discourse with visions, models, and possibilities that corresponded to popular needs or demands. In Tarma, the new state functionaries were often given disparaging names, such as *yanagringos*, pseudo- or cholo gringos, who assumed authority and were protected by the state but who were judged incompetent impostors. Jokes about the new state agents abounded, told on journeys by an increasingly mobile population. The state was being experienced as dominating and authoritarian and was being reimagined through laughter. But it was black humor.

The contradictory processes of structural reform and the complexity of the outcomes had not been foreseen by members of state planning agencies, many of whom were Peruvian and foreign academics of Marxist persuasion laudably working to end feudalism and dependency and launch Andean society on a modernizing track. But the reforms could not be transmitted down through the state's administrative hierarchy in a direct or systematic way. Instead, certain groups, such as the ubiquitous ingenieros, were seen in the provinces to be the main beneficiaries, for they were in a position to take hold of and translate particular aspects of state policy in the light of their own interests. Now, instead of blaming the state for its neglect, there was plentiful evidence at hand to accuse the state of bringing chaos and misfortune. A new translocal discourse of state corruption was gaining ground while the localization of state institutions sharpened perceptions of inherent contradictions between the state planners and the people's desires, demands, and place-making practices. Agrarian reform had not given peasants control of their land, nor could rapid training programs compensate for their lack of preparation. Instead, the reform had substituted state-employed administrators, few of whom knew anything about agriculture in the Andes, for the old *patrones* and had failed to make sufficient resources available to manage the transformation. The state's cooperative adventure started to crumble, and poverty and disillusion came in the wake.

Violent Responses to State Presence

State-led structural reform inevitably failed to meet popular aspirations and expectations. When the central state discovered it could not control outcomes and feared ungovernability, it put a stop to the top-down process of change.[18]

Yet, in the postreform phase, the expansion of schooling and higher education and the new language of concientización and empowerment continued to politicize perceptions of racism, social exclusion, and patterns of privilege. The state's expansion of education was linked with the development of a new language of dissent. This was a strident, belligerent form of political speech, behavior, and body language that crystallized in centers of higher education. As Portocarrero and Oliarte (1989) note, the new political discourse of the schoolteachers rested on the "critical idea." This Portocarrero defines as "the vehement opposition to a hated order . . . a discourse which is presented as a jolt to the conscience, as a revelation about something the dominant classes had previously hidden" (1998: 124). The critical discourse provided a simple set of schema and methods of analysis that could transpose painful lived realities into standardized conceptual and categorical forms.

The state's efforts to incorporate schoolteachers into its new national education initiative and use them to convey its messages were far from successful. The schoolteachers were no transmission belt, and by the 1970s increasing numbers became classroom Maoists (Angell 1982). The Ministry of Education fought to take greater control over what was taught in schools through a reform of the curriculum, but the educational content could be communicated and translated in a variety of ways. The government was caught out in its own rhetoric. People had been pressed to become aware and to criticize the old order as a prelude to giving their support to structural reform. But they were not supposed to critique the state or the inroads the military government had made into local political processes and aspirations.

At an organizational level, the critical idea was brought into play in the mounting political opposition to military government. The teachers' union, Sindicato Unico de Trabajadores de la Educación Peruana (SUTEP; Union of Peruvian Education Workers) founded in 1972 had a membership of over one hundred thousand by the end of the decade and was the largest union in the country. But declared illegal by the military government, it was not permitted to act as a channel through which grievances and demands could be brought before or negotiated with the state. The union denounced the government as a military dictatorship and organized strikes and popular actions to influence public opinion into taking an antigovernment stand (Hinojosa 1998). In response to mounting national strike action in the late 1970s, the government turned to repression. Union leaders were murdered, jailed (some fourteen, in the case of Tarma province), hounded, and denied employment in state schools. The confrontation generated a greater susceptibility, especially among younger teachers and secondary school pupils, to consider a politics of violence as legitimate.

The reform and rapid expansion of education had drawn on poorly prepared teachers without much access to teaching materials other than cheap editions of Marxist manuals (available in marketplaces throughout the highlands) and crude political pamphlets (some of which came from the state's own organization, SINAMOS). Students who poured into the provincial universities, teacher training colleges, and institutes of higher learning were presented with an education glued to Marxist principles (Degregori 1991). Yet, although it was critical of the state in terms of its underlying philosophy, some of the premises of the state's civilizing mission were retained under the guise of producing the "new socialist man." The "good" teacher tried to interest pupils in politics and current events, but the preoccupation with hygiene and cleanliness, and with disciplining and regulating the body, continued.

From out of an alphabet soup of Maoist factions, the political and ideological lead was captured by force in the 1970s by a group of intellectuals and teachers from the University of Huamanga, Ayacucho. Sendero Luminoso proclaimed a hard-line, highly simplified, and thus more accessible version of Maoism that was presented as "scientific truth" (Degregori 1991: 239). The dogmatic ideology and visions of destruction and bloody revolution caught the imagination of some of the young who looked for a way to confront the racism, injustice, and economic and social hardships they had known from childhood. The school became Sendero's most important gathering point and target. Paradoxically, Sendero declared the start of its armed insurrection in 1980, the year Peru returned to constitutional rule after a decade of military government. The transition had marked an unprecedented opening up of channels of legal political action, and most Marxist parties opted to participate in the national election (Manrique 1995b). Not so Sendero. The Party remained clandestine and pledged itself to bring down the bourgeois state by wiping out its agents in the provinces and sweeping away revisionists by liquidating all instances of popular action not under Sendero control. Sendero strategy involved militarizing society in preparation for a long war. But the kind of future state envisaged by the Party was only vaguely indicated. Under the New Power or New Democracy, people were told they would live in great harmony, free from all contradiction, in which divisions of class, race, gender, and generation would be erased, the project kept on track through obedience to an absolute philosopher-leader.[19]

In Tarma, most teachers had been exposed to the critical discourse of

Marxist-Maoist politics in centers of higher education during the 1970s and 1980s. Some had attended Sendero-inspired *escuelas populares* (clandestine night schools) offering a political education that ranged from reading Maoist texts to dynamiting police stations. Sendero militants worked secretively and left characteristically cryptic codes and messages in the landscape (as in the sudden appearance of crude slogans painted in red on walls, or the communist flag, or unexpected attacks) to suggest they were everywhere and nowhere. In the schools they tried to turn state nationalism and militarism inside out by substituting the communist flag, hymns to Sendero's leader (Abimael Guzman under his nom de guerre, President Gonzalo), and a new calendar of heroic events. Most schoolteachers now found themselves caught in the middle, having to translate between the opposing demands of state and Sendero. This involved a dangerous mix of symbolic practices. They might hoist the red flag in public while singing the national anthem in secret, or vice versa. All the while, they had to persuade local officials of the Ministry of Education that schools were functioning as normal, for no one knew for sure which side these officials were on. After Sendero had dominated extensive areas in the Andes and numbers of deaths, physical destruction, and terror were mounting, the state gave full power to the military to crush the subversion and bring the "regions of emergency" back to the state government.

Sendero had gained effective control of the more sparsely populated regions at a distance from Tarma town and transformed them into support bases for the armed groups. The party had also won some popular sympathy by organizing the redistribution of land and livestock, symbolically showing it was capable of putting into effect what the state's agrarian reform had failed to accomplish. The entry of Sendero, especially into the northern perimeter of the province, provoked population displacement, the conflict tending to enhance patterns of movement already underway. Ironically, Muruhuay, an important place of religious pilgrimage in the central Andes, became a place of rest and recreation for Sendero militants. When fighting the subversion, the military came to employ such brutal tactics that they became more feared than Sendero, and Indian-looking people were singled out for exceptional mistreatment. But people caught up in the conflict came to make a distinction between the hated military units sent up from the coast and the units of *serranos* (men from the highlands) who more easily gained people's trust. Rural communities were more likely to throw in their lot with the state when they could ask *paisanos* for arms and help in setting up peasant militias *(rondas campesinas)* to fight both the *terrucos* (terrorists) and the murderous spirits, the *pishtacos*, who now roamed at large on the community borders.

The military mode of state power had to change to mark the passage from war to peace. The transition, taking place during the years 1992–1995, demanded that the military stand up as a moral force, exact retribution by punishing those accused of terrorism, but also reprieve those who offered information (through the Law of Repentance) and safeguard an orderly return to a state of government. The military defeat of Sendero was not accompanied by an attempt to initiate a process of reconciliation or national healing. Instead, the Ministry of the Presidency that took charge of donor funds sought to reestablish state presence by instigating a vast program of public works in which building schools lay at the center. Now the smallest, most remote communities are being provided with school buildings of standard design and color whose inauguration may bring the president on a lightning visit. The school building has become the reminder in the landscape of a return to state government. But most schools still stand as an empty shell, without books, furniture, or equipment, and staffed by an increasingly despairing body of teachers to whom the Fujimori government consistently refused to pay a living wage. One suspects that the teaching profession is being punished for its oppositional politics and sympathy for revolutionary action that has lasted nearly thirty years (F. Wilson 2000).

Celebrating Fiestas Patrias

In Peru, the national myth of origin celebrated in Fiestas Patrias on July 28 carries a fractured meaning. On the one hand, the eviction of Spain and achievement of independence are seen as resulting from a popular struggle for liberation. On the other, the state is celebrated as extending its power and sovereignty through two lines of transmission: the military and the school. In Fiestas Patrias, as Gose (1994) argues, an ideological image of the nation is built up through a militarized presentation of the local school system, where *la patria* (the Mother-Fatherland) is treated as "a school writ large." From this metaphorical representation, education is seen to provide "the fundamental medium of social relations within the Fatherland" and in so doing demarcates the reach of state territoriality. This ideology, though, is contested and undermined during the celebration (70–71).

Fiestas Patrias has been celebrated since the early nineteenth century with parades of schoolchildren accompanied by military bands playing martial music; they file past local dignitaries, sing the national anthem, and salute the national flag. In later years, Independence Day has been marked by a parade of Peru's armed forces in Lima, a celebration of military might subsequently brought to the notice of increasing numbers of Peruvians through television. It was hardly surprising that Sendero prohibited this celebration in the Andean regions they dominated. Nor was it surprising, given its connotations of liberation, that in postconflict times, towns and communities have wanted to register the end of civil war by returning to their celebratory calendar, including the parades of schoolchildren at Fiestas Patrias.

In this final section, I want to suggest that the celebration of Fiestas Patrias in recent years can provide a window through which to observe how the uneasy relations between state and province are now being played out. The parades of schoolchildren traditionally held on July 28 mark a contested site of public spectacle, the time-space slot where both state and locality seek representation and where, in postwar times, new rules of the game are imposed, played out, and opposed. I look at events relating to Fiestas Patrias from two perspectives: first, by commenting on a story told by a rural schoolteacher about his role in reestablishing the parades in a community of returnees; second, by presenting my observations of the effects produced by the government's decision in 1999 to reorganize the celebration to give greater prominence to the armed forces.

Fiestas Patrias and Popular Nationalism

The narrative I discuss describes with particular clarity the teller's careful formulation of an antistate stance. It belongs to a genre of mobile popular culture, of convivial storytelling in bars and on journeys.[20] It articulates a discourse that few teachers dare to express openly in the tense postconflict situation where agents of the state's intelligence service are suspected of having taken over from the military in keeping a watchful eye on the activities of schoolteachers. The ideas expressed can be seen as belonging to an oppositional, subterranean discourse that flows among teachers. Through stories such as this one, patriotic events can be vested with oppositional meanings and subject to endless improvisation.

In 1996, the local office of the Ministry of Education offered a contract to the narrator to reopen the primary school in a small hamlet in the northern highland fringes of the province. The population had fled on account of Sendero and later military occupation and had been branded as accomplices of the terrorists. For the narrator, this post gave him the chance to return to the community bordering his mother's home. Belonging to a family from the region, he claimed to be both *paisano* (fellow countryman) and educated outsider. At one level, his story weaves together ideas about state and antistate, citizen and subversive, teacher and community. At another, the story is used to justify, both to himself and the listener, how he assesses and maneuvers in postconflict society, where the danger of mistaken identity abounds. Extracts from the narrative are followed by my commentary.

> There are some experiences that are well worth talking about, and recording, that can serve to promote the identity of the peasant, the identity of indigenous people about their reality, about their pueblo. I should like to talk about last year, about the month of July, when, as you know, Peru celebrates Fiestas Patrias on July 28 and when we in Tarma celebrate the feast of our patron saint, Santa Ana, on July 26.

With these opening remarks, the presentation of the national holiday is downplayed by being linked to an event in the provincial ceremonial calendar. This suggests that the national will be viewed and framed by the regional, rather than considered a manifestation of state power.

> At the time of Sendero's occupation, many of the customs of the citizen were prohibited. It was prohibited that children take part in parades. It was prohibited that in indigenous peasant society, they could sing the national anthem of Peru, or have a military escort raise the Peruvian flag. As educators and teachers, though we are not in agreement with the political system of the government in office, nevertheless we believe in a state, in a nation, in an identity, and that the teacher has to also understand that there are ancestral customs in the pueblos, which cannot be changed from one day to the next. On the contrary, one must respect their customs. One of these is that the people are accustomed to organize parades to celebrate Fiestas Patrias. The mothers and fathers feel that they are somebody in their community when they see their children, the pupils, participate in a civic-patriotic ceremony, *even though there has come no legal order from the state that obliges them to hold a parade* [emphasis added].

The narrator suggests that the peasantry had embraced and made their own the customs and rituals concerning patriotism and nationalism, practices brought to the countryside by earlier generations of schoolteachers. These rituals have become integral to the claims of the indigenous peasantry to identity and citizenship. Sendero is blamed for failing to understand the context and meaning of these "customs" or that this popular form of nationalism indeed expressed a separation of the nation from the state. The narrator believes that teachers guiding the communities represent a superior, transcendental nationalism. It is the teacher rather than the government who is the true patriot and works toward the realization of a better state, one that listens to and acts on the needs of the people.

> For the people who want to carry out this kind of event, they see it as a kind of distraction, for this is a pueblo that suffers from the lack of many indispensable services. For example, it does not have public lighting, or electricity; it does not have a road that is passable by vehicles; it does not have drinking water; it does not have a sewage system; it does not have a medical post. In reality, the peasantry of this community has very little of anything.

The transcendental nationalism of the teacher and strength of popular nationalism is juxtaposed with the failure of government to fulfill its obligations of bringing modernity to the countryside. But in this part of the narrative, the teller is clearly interweaving an older political discourse that is now out of step with the change in government policy. The Fujimori government won popular support with its emphasis on *obras publicas* (public works), although "government by public works" is providing only shoddy, empty symbols of modernity.

> In the community, the only entertainment for the men is sports, sporting events, but the mothers do not participate for it is mainly soccer. . . . But the mothers really like parades, they like to see their children take part, parade, dress up and take part in the customary dances of the region. It is the mothers who enjoy the parades most. I understand this reality. Therefore at an assembly we held, we agreed we would celebrate the July holidays with a parade, to celebrate not only the anniversary of independent Peru but since the community belongs to the province of Tarma, also Tarma's anniversary. In this way the people would have a little distraction, entertainment, a little happiness, and feel hope that one day their sons would become professionals and do something to serve their communities.

The narrator positions himself as an active sponsor of popular nationalism in the community, where he expresses support for the wishes of the mothers in particular. Not only does the parade involve the active participation of children, but the social status of parents is reflected in how clean and well-turned-out the children appear. The choice of which children are allowed to march and carry flags, pennants, batons, or swords is a social issue, for not all in the community have the resources allowing them to present their children in a suitable way. The choice of who marches is partly up to the teacher, and it is his duty to drill and instruct the children selected. In the community celebrations, soccer tournaments have now taken the place of an older tradition, *corridas de toro* (bull runs). The substitution is indicative of modernizing tendencies and changing social relations. But these activities of the men lie outside the sphere of the teacher, as they have nothing to do with the school. Instead, the narrator concentrates his energies on planning a parade for the children. The final comment encapsulates a familiar trick of magnification: a tiny event, in this case a parade of schoolchildren, is linked with a vast panorama, an overturning of the social order whereby poor peasant children can hope to enter the professions and serve their community.

In the end, the parade was not realized, for the plans were interrupted by the appearance of unknown, threatening strangers who dressed as peasants but who did not have the faces of peasants. The narrator records that they had asked: "How is it possible that you are going to hold a parade for Fiestas Patrias when in Peru there are enormous economic and social problems? How is it possible that the flag flying will not be the flag of the people?" The Sendero militants threatened to kill the teacher if he did not "take care."

> I was not going to "take care," as I believe that man is born one day and then has to die. If we are going to live, then it must be with dignity. It seems to me that if we cannot live with dignity, then life is worthless. And whether one dies today or tomorrow is immaterial. The styles and forms are of no interest to me. Thus, when one is able to work honestly on behalf of the people, trying to stimulate the development of the pueblo, one's death would be received as a great message for the children, who in future would see that one has to live with dignity and that nobody should push them around.

The beginning of a new narrative theme is indicated by a shift in tone and style. Its purpose is to elaborate on the image of the heroic teacher, prepared to sacrifice himself for the sake of the people. In this interlude, we find another example of the trick of magnification: the teacher's martyrdom in the service of the people seen as a great message for the children. The implication of this passage is that teachers in the postconflict phase need to redefine their political identity through a renewed commitment to the people and that the Sendero militants still at large have no contact with the popular base.

> Sadly, teachers in the peasant communities are caught in the middle, between on the one side a state that pays miserable wages and issues laws that teachers must follow, and on the other side, groups that still survive and wish to impose new laws in the style and custom of the reality and ideology they stand for. The teacher is in the center. For the state, teachers are members of the other side, and for the others, let us call them Sendero, teachers are state informers. So when the Peruvian military is on its way, the teacher is threatened, and when the other group comes, he is also threatened.

The narrator's presentation of the heroic teacher is juxtaposed by a description of the fraught position of all teachers caught between Sendero and the military. While living in the community, the narrator had been indefatigable. He had kept in contact with other teachers and sought out those he thought were behind the threat to his life. On two occasions, he had visited *arrepentidos* (those accused of terrorism but released through the Law of Repentance after providing information to the military). He had "hard dialogues" with them, noting that although they were of greater physical stature, he possessed greater "character." But the day before the parade, more strangers arrived and caused alarm in the community. The narrator resolved to lead his colleague to safety. Retreat was not a heroic act, but was explained by the narrator's concern for the young teacher, and the story of the nighttime walk and their reception by teachers in a district capital constitutes a healthy antidote to earlier references to sacrifice.

Although the main message of the narrative lies in the claim being made of a separation between the nationalism sponsored by the state and the nationalism espoused by the people, there is much room for improvisation and border play. Depending on audience and circumstance, the narrative can be more or less explicit as to the narrator's own identification with the community as well as with the oppositional politics of Sendero. Teachers like the cholo narrator can develop a quite different level of empathy with the community than could earlier generations of mestizos, ever conscious of their social and cultural superiority. Although ideas and practices associated with school may appear relatively unchanged, they acquire new meanings and significance. In this case, we are no longer witnessing enforced, state-directed integration. Rather, education is recognized as the route out of *desprecio* (disdain). In this, the ideas of the narrator come close to those expressed nearly a century earlier by Adolfo Vienrich, for whom the school was "democracy in action." Through the narrator's eyes, one sees dislocation; the parade, flags, trappings of nationalism have become abstracted from the state. Fiestas Patrias has been translated into local, oppositional nationalism. This reversal, however, must also be seen as an integral part of state formation "from below," in that images of state and citizen are being opened up for scrutiny and reformulation.

Fiestas Patrias and Locality

The Peruvian state has not been unaware of the dislocation, nor of the potential offered by Fiestas Patrias to rally opposition in the provinces. In 1999, the format for its celebration was changed by government decree in a move that aimed to give greater prominence to the armed forces and police. In Tarma town, as in all provincial and departmental capitals, parades of schoolchildren had to start earlier than July 28, in Tarma's case, ten days earlier, on July 18. The reason for shifting the date was to allow the state to orchestrate a nationwide marching competition in which military judges would adjudicate which schools produced the best-turned-out, best-marching children. The winning schools at the provincial level would then compete in parades held in the department capitals, and these winners would have the honor of going to Lima to take part in the march on the day of Fiestas Patrias itself. In Tarma, responses to the changes decreed in Lima were critical. Some interpreted the staggering of the parades and increased military presence as a sign of nervousness on the part of the government and fear of retaliatory action by remnants of Sendero. Others were annoyed at the government's move to take over what they considered a locally organized event in the hands of local schoolteachers. But on the day, many people came along to cheer.

On July 18, educational institutions from Tarma province—from primary and secondary schools to teacher and nursing training colleges and branches of university departments—participated in a parade that lasted over five hours. Music was provided (as usual) by bands of the police and the boys' secondary school. High stands had been erected in the central square where spectators could sit, and a podium was built, covered by an awning, for members of the municipal authority, visiting dignitaries, police chiefs, and military guests. In front of the podium were three tables where gold-braided military judges sat, and keeping the parade route clear were armed soldiers. Holding the event together was a commentator, who shouted into the public address system introducing the schools and reminding the crowd of the civic-patriotic nature of the event and of Tarma's support for President Fujimori. The parade was broadcast live by the local television station.

The parade over, at supposedly its crowning moment, the commentator read out the names of the winning schools selected by the military judges. Immediately the festive mood evaporated. The crowd began to boo and whistle, people muttered among themselves that the wrong decision had been reached. This reaction brought consternation on the podium, reevaluation by the military judges, and a welcome silencing of the commentator. After considerable delay, when many spectators had drifted away, a new decision was announced. Declared as winners were the leading boys and girls secondary schools in the town, a decision that accorded with the opinion of the diminished group of spectators. The event was significant. Local ideas as to the hierarchic ranking of provincial schools could not be overturned, even by high-ranking military judges. On this occasion, the desire of the crowd won out. The state's effort to stage-manage the public spectacle of Fiestas Patrias had met with limited success. The allure of a national competition was far less important than the local parade. But because this had been held ten days before national Independence Day, there was not much happening in Tarma town on the day itself.

Rural districts and communities in the province were much less affected by the change in dates or practice or by the greater military presence decreed by the government. District schools had sent few children to march in Tarma on July 18 and were far more occupied with organizing their festivities for July 28. In the district capital one hour away from Tarma town where I spent the day, weeks of preparation had gone into the parade that gathered children and teachers from all the district's schools. Children were well-turned-out, wearing clean school uniforms or fancy dress. At the podium were members of the municipal authority, all schoolteachers; representatives of the district living in Lima, who were presented with a gift of live sheep; and a single uniformed policeman. The festivities in the district were enjoyed as reinforcing the bonds of community by celebrating the work of the local schools and their teachers. Through a loudspeaker, the commentator repeated the community's aspirations for the future and pledged that the youngsters of the district would make a patriotic contribution to Peru. The hopes of the community, said the commentator, rested on these children, who would one day enter the professions and return to serve their community, thus giving voice to the same trick of magnification employed in the narrative discussed above. Schoolchildren came up to the podium to recite poems and speeches about the need to fight poverty and the exclusion suffered by most of Peru's citizens. But no mention was made of Fujimori or of the government in Lima.

Fiestas Patrias has become a contested political site. Taking place in 1999 was an attempt to reinsert a stronger military presence and substitute a national agenda for the popular celebration of community. Although the state had managed to affect the staging of the event in departmental and provincial capitals with mixed success, it had been unable to reach down to districts or communities. The greater involvement of the armed forces in Fiestas Patrias can be seen as an instance of the way the Peruvian government has tried to reintroduce a military presence, but it is uncertain to what extent this will set a new pattern for years to come. The celebration of Fiestas Patrias in the year 2000 was overshadowed by reactions to President Alberto Fujimori's assumption on that day of his much-disputed third term of office.

Conclusion

This essay started by raising questions about the techniques and mechanisms through which states make their presence felt in the provinces. A conceptual framework was suggested through which relations at the meeting point between state and province could be analyzed in terms of the flows and spatialities of state power and the possibilities for mediators to translate rather than transmit orders and directives of the state. By way of conclusion, we should look again at the kind of state that has been described and the kind of political reactions it has induced. An initial focus on flow and translation has been a useful way of conceiving of state-province relations; this must now be set in context.

In the periods under review, the state has appeared in the Andean provinces in various guises. We have seen how the increasingly impersonal and authoritarian bureaucratic apparatus of the central state took away the capacity for government from the provinces in the early twentieth century, and in the process squashed the fragile local democracy at the provincial level as well as ideas generated locally about education. Following a long period of state neglect, a reformist military government in the 1970s strove to apply much-needed structural reform. But although well-intentioned, it did so by fiat and force, and this served to fuel resistance that turned to Marxism and Maoism for its oppositional political models and strategies. In response to subversion in the Andes, the state first unleashed violent military repression and then tried to alter the image of the military to fit better with times of peace. During the 1990s, an autocratic presidency centralized state power and took direct charge of processes of recuperation within a framework of neoliberal economic order. In sum, one can see that although there have been swings between direct intervention and neglect by the state, few openings have appeared for alliance building or negotiation with the provinces.

In response to a generally intransigent and peremptory state, reactions in the Andean provinces have taken an increasingly confrontational and violent form. The silencing of the early expression of oppositional politics pushed resentment and hopes for political change underground, the subterranean political discourse surfacing now and again. With turmoil and instability brought about by top-down structural reform with all its unintended consequences, a new violent phase of confrontational politics made headway. The spread of a belligerent Marxist-Maoist discourse in centers of education paved the way for the attempt by a small, highly disciplined group of militants to bring down the state. Once again, after their military defeat, a period of silencing has ensued. Political opposition, however, remains latent, just under the surface, finding expression in the contests over meanings, as exemplified in the question of whose liberation is being celebrated in Fiestas Patrias.

The schoolteachers caught in the middle have led a double life, moving between state and opposition. Dealing with this doubleness has generated not an ironic distancing but a propensity to adopt a politics of violence. Emerging from this history is an overall view that the scope for translation by teachers as mediating agents between state and province has been quite limited. It is inconceivable to consider social and political action taking place without some element of translation; nevertheless, in view of the intransigence of both the state and its revolutionary opposition, there has not been much room for mediation.

If we look again at this history, and at the nature of the political alternatives that emerged in the Andean provinces, then the period when most was at stake and most was lost, I believe, can be dated to the turn of the century. The undermining of local government cut short an experiment in postcolonial democracy and institution building at the provincial level. Absorption of the provinces by an ineffective state led to the worst of all possible worlds. This does not mean that I harbor a sentimental attachment to Tarma's provincial council or the work of the radical indigenistas. The viewpoint reflects my awareness of the verve and dynamism, the contests and conflicts, the ample evidence of an understanding of locality, which is to be found in the letters of the Tarma mayors as matters of the day were reviewed and commented on at length during the 1860s to 1900s. With the expansion of the scope and power of the central state, this local debate was stifled, and there was no other recognized political channel where it could be redirected.

Notes

This essay owes a great deal to colleagues in the research program Livelihood: Identity and Organization in Situations of Instability. In particular, I want to thank Finn Stepputat for his inspiring comments on a very preliminary draft. Unless otherwise noted, all translations are mine.

1. See, for example, discussions of the uneasy relationship between teacher and community in Primov (1980); Ansion (1989); Montero (1990); Contreras (1996).
2. See Mallon (1995) for a discussion of the emergence of this discourse of citizenship in the central highlands, especially in the context of the War of the Pacific and its aftermath.
3. Tarma Municipal Archive (TMA) Actas, 1886, October 29. The number of schools (seventeen) exceeded the number of districts (ten) at the time.
4. TMA Letters, 1886, Mayor Piedra to Inspector of Schools, Tarma.
5. TMA Actas, 1891, December 21.
6. TMA Letters, 1892, April 13, Mayor Carranza to Director General de Gobierno, Lima.
7. Politically, they belonged to the Radical Party. In his student days in Lima, Vienrich had been a disciple of the iconoclastic liberal, Manuel Gonzalez Prada.
8. Quoted in the introduction to Vienrich's compilation, *Fabulas Quechuas* (1906; reprinted 1961).
9. TMA Letters, 1896, March 14, Mayor Philipps to Subprefect, Tarma.
10. TMA Letters, 1896, September 8, Mayor Cantella to the Official Inspector, Lima.
11. TMA Letters 1903, July 21, Mayor Vienrich to Prefect of Junín.
12. TMA Letters 1904, April 30, Mayor Leon to district mayors.
13. TMA Letters 1905, April 4, Mayor Leon to the Directorate of Primary Education, Lima.
14. Vienrich, along with another member of the Radical Party, were hounded to death in 1908; posthumously, he won fame as a "folklorist."

15. There was a short turbulent period in the 1940s when the state changed character. An indigenista challenge to the state's education project in the 1940s was associated with critiques launched by novelist and educator José María Arguedas and by Luis Valcarel and José Antonio Encinas. For a brief period these men were able to influence state policy under the presidency of Luis Bustamante (1945–1948).
16. From a speech given by Velasco in 1971, quoted in Drysdale and Myers (1975).
17. SINAMOS is Sistema Nacional de Apoyo a la Movilización Social (National System for the Support of Social Mobilization).
18. This was marked by a change of president, when in 1975 General Velasco stepped down and General Morales Bermudez took over.
19. Important discussions of Sendero's political thinking and agenda include the following works. Gorriti (1990, 1999) provides the most comprehensive chronological account of Sendero's strategy and actions, and Poole and Renique (1992) also give a useful overview; Arce (1989) reproduces versions of texts by leader Abimael Guzman for foreign audiences; Harding (1987) examines the work of Sendero intellectual Diaz Martinez; Tapia (1997) discusses Sendero strategy from Guzman's notes captured by the military; Taylor (1998) explores their military strategy; Ansion et al. (1993) look at Sendero and education; and Manrique (1995a) covers the later story from Guzman's arrest to the division of the Party. Insightful commentaries on Sendero's politics, their appeal, and representation are found in Degregori (1991); Poole and Renique (1991); Starn (1991); Palmer (1994); Portocarrero (1998); Stern (1998); and Beasley-Murray (1999).
20. I first heard the narrative while on a journey in 1997 and agreed with the teller that we could later record it, though it lost wit and spontaneity in the retelling under more formal circumstances.

THE CAPTIVE STATE Corruption, Intelligence Agencies, and Ethnicity in Pakistan

Oskar Verkaaik

The term PIA stands for Pakistan International Airlines, but not according to many Muhajirs, a term widely used in Pakistan for those whose families migrated from India in the years after independence in 1947. Most live in the two big cities of Karachi and Hyderabad in the southern province of Sindh. Since the 1980s, they massively support a political party called the Muhajir Qaumi Movement (MQM; Muhajir National/Ethnic Movement) that has given shape to a collective and political Muhajir identity. In 1996 and 1997 I did fieldwork in one Muhajir neighborhood in Hyderabad, an area of shoemakers, blacksmiths, shopkeepers, street vendors, bangle makers, rickshaw drivers, and their families. In this area, most people say that the official meaning of PIA is merely a promising veil of national solidarity that conceals a rather disgusting face of ethnic exclusivism. The real but hidden meaning of PIA, they say, is *Punjabi* International Airlines.

The airline offers its white-collar employees the safety of employment, good educational facilities, excellent medical care, housing in quiet, clean, and safe enclaves separated from the dusty and often dangerous city areas that surround them, possibilities for cheap foreign travel, and high social status. Apart from the army, PIA may be the most attractive state-owned employer in Pakistan. But many of my Muhajir acquaintances say that they would never stand a chance if they applied for a position in PIA. That, they insist, has nothing to do with merit. On the contrary, they maintain that Muhajirs are well-known to be the most educated and patriotic people of Pakistan. Yet PIA has been captured by Punjabis, and Punjabis will never allow a stranger to enter their stronghold.

This is typical, they say, for the way Punjabis control *all* state institutions. They do this through family ties. A typical Punjabi extended family consists of brothers, cousins, and uncles, who among themselves divide the strategically important posts. One is sent into the army, another develops a network among bureaucrats, a third takes care of the landed property, a fourth does the dirty work in the Punjabi Muslim League, a fifth works himself up into the rank and file of the rival Pakistan People's Party, a sixth may become a judge, a seventh starts a family branch in the United States, an eighth joins PIA, and so on. If one branch suffers, the others make up for the losses. As a whole, the Punjabi family prospers.

When my informants talk like this, it is not always clear what they mean by "the Punjabi family." Do they allude to several families who happen to be Punjabi? Or do they talk about all Pakistani Punjabis who live as one extended family? The question appears irrelevant to them. What matters is that Punjabis arrange things according to the wrong sense of loyalty. The Pakistani state, after all, is a creation for all South Asian Muslims. Its fruits belong to all Pakistani citizens. Muhajirs too have the right to a share of the profits of PIA. Any true Muslim would recognize that. Yet Punjabis, like Westerners—sorry, my friend, don't take it personally—care only about money. They would sell Pakistan, a state created in the name of Islam, to American capitalists. Such an unpatriotic attitude is in their blood. Did they not form the backbone of the British colonial army? A typical Punjabi would sell even his own mother if it would benefit his interests. Small wonder, then, that Pakistan is in such a sorry state today, captured as it is by unpatriotic hypocrites who only use Islam for their own purposes.

I have to admit that I have not quoted anyone in particular in this introduction. It is instead a loose compilation of many casual conversations. Perhaps none of my informants would endorse this view entirely—certainly not when presented to them by a foreigner or on paper. Yet the text contains a basic idea that I have heard often in Hyderabad, namely, that the Pakistani state is made in the name of Islam and belongs to the whole of the Pakistani nation, but is captured by one ethnic group. This essay is meant to examine more fully this interrelatedness among Islam, ethnicity, and images of the state in popular discourse among Muhajir residents of Hyderabad and Karachi.

To do this, I relate Dale Eickelman and James Piscatori's (1996) remarks on the character of Muslim politics to an approach for studying the state as proposed by Philip Abrams (1988) and put to practice by Akhil Gupta (1995) in the case of South Asia. The aim is to show how people in Pakistan can talk about the state. I argue that the modern nation-state is collectively imagined as a space of legitimate power, relatively unconnected to and untouched by real power struggles that are going on within society, and that this is done by depicting the state as an expression, or even the guardian, of true Islamic principles of loyalty and authority. State functionaries, government leaders, and others associated with the process of nation building and state formation in Pakistan have promoted an image of the state as being opposed to, and aimed to reform, prevailing "un-Islamic" tendencies within society, such as ethnic or kinship loyalty and "feudalism." At present, societal groups and emancipatory movements appropriate and use this discourse for their own purposes. Continuing to reify the ideal of the state as the potential promoter of a just society, they also accuse the elites associated with state power of polluting this ideal by using it as a veil to conceal the very particularistic loyalties the state is supposed to reform. This has added to an increasing crisis of state authority, as, for instance, indicated by extremely low turnouts during national elections, a growing sense of displacement among certain societal groups, and a growing polarization within Pakistani society, manifested in, for instance, the rise of ethnic and sectarian movements. I end with some remarks on why the widely held assumption that the rise of social unrest and social/political violence is caused by a collapse of state authority is too simplistic, as it focuses solely on changes that occur within state institutions and ignores possibly more important transformations in society at large.

Muslim Politics and the Reification of the State

To a large extent, the contention of Eickelman and Piscatori (1996) that Islam constitutes the moral-symbolic language of Muslim politics is also true for Pakistan. Eickelman and Piscatori argue that most political debating, bargaining, and cajoling in Muslim societies contain explicit references or more implicit allusions to Islamic notions of loyalty, authority, respect, justice, solidarity, and so on. Of course, despite claims to the contrary, Islam leaves much room for disagreement over such issues. In modern societies, Islam may serve many goals and objectives, as no person or institution enjoys a monopoly on the interpretation of Islamic traditions. However, as is clear, for instance, in the case of women's movements, it is practically impossible, or at least unwise, to reject Islam altogether as a common ground for social-political discourse.

Apart from and in addition to Islam, the state constitutes another legitimizing principle in the name of which people claim to say or do things. It is probably true that for a long time states were built and maintained in the name of something else, such as the monarch, the emperor, or a religion; all the same, the idea that the state itself constitutes an autonomous principle of authority seems to be at least several centuries old. This idea is based on what Philip Abrams (1988) calls the reification of the state into an almost sacred entity in the name of which order must be restored or people can be asked to make sacrifices—an idea of order that to a large extent helps shape people's perception of social reality. Because Abrams himself formulates what he has in mind more accurately than I can, it is best to quote him somewhat extensively:

> The state is not the reality that stands behind the mask of political practice. It is itself the mask, which prevents our seeing political practice as it is. . . . There is a state-system . . . a palpable nexus of practice and institutional structure centered in government and more or less extensive, unified and dominant in any given society. . . . There is, too, a state-idea, projected, purveyed and variously believed in in different societies at different times. . . . The state comes into being as a structuration within political practice; it starts its life as an implicit construct; it is then reified . . . and acquires an overt symbolic identity progressively divorced from practice as an illusory account of practice. The ideological function is extended to a point where conservatives and radicals alike believe that their practice is not directed at each other but at the state; the world of illusion prevails. The task of the sociologist is to demystify; and in this context that means attending to the senses in which the state does not exist rather than to those in which it does. (82)

It is of some importance to see that the reification of the state can be reached only by separating the state from society, and that this separation is a discursive or imaginary practice. Concretely, state functionaries are seldom, if ever, not part of society. They may belong to a particular ethnic community or an income group, they are men or women, and so on; yet they derive their power from the negation of their social identities and the claim that they, as state functionaries, stand outside or above society, act impartially, and are not directed by any prejudice or self-interest. It is therefore important to study how this idea of impartiality and authority is being constructed and reproduced by people associated with state power. This includes the study of the symbolism of state rituals and processions, state monuments, military uniforms, and bureaucratic new speech.

Building on these insights, Akhil Gupta (1995) has shown that popular images of the state hinge on the same separation of the state from society. In an article on popular debates about state corruption in a northern Indian village, Gupta argues that the very theme of corruption enables the villagers to maintain a division between themselves and local state representatives. State functionaries enter local power struggles, but they also deny this by claiming to act in the name of an impartial and translocal state. Not surprisingly, the villagers evaluate this discrepancy as hypocrisy or corruption. The villagers thus subscribe to the ideal of an impartial and translocal state and then condemn the activities of local state functionaries on the basis of these high expectations. The ideal of an impartial state is maintained; in contrast, the state as it is experienced locally is talked about as a pool of moral decay that pervades the state but has little effect on society. The separation between state and society is thus maintained to confront the power abuse of local state functionaries with the moral superiority the villagers ascribe to themselves. The idea of a state that exists relatively independently of society may thus become the basis for rebellion, resistance, or other forms of subversive action.

In the case Gupta (1995) describes, the theme of corruption is the most important argument through which the villagers construct the image of a polluted state or a besieged ideal of impartiality and justice. Although corruption serves a similar goal in Pakistan, I also think that Muhajirs in Hyderabad have more strategies at their disposal to make a similar argument about a besieged and conquered state. Ethnicity, or the argument that other ethnic groups have captured the state, is one of them. Apart from corruption and ethnicity, I also pay attention to a discourse revolving around secret intelligence agencies. Seen as the hidden, true power players operating behind the bureaucratic façade of the democratic state, intelligence agencies are said to corrupt the original ideals of the Pakistan Movement. I furthermore discuss the presence of rumors and the production of a quasi-secret atmosphere in which to distribute such rumors that help construct the image of the captive state.

In this essay, then, I am most concerned with the myth of the state rather than with the doings of the state. Rather than focusing on the production of the state myth by state officials themselves, an issue someone like Timothy Mitchell (1991) has paid attention to, I limit myself mainly to the popular appropriation of this myth as it is linked to the themes of corruption, ethnicity, and the works of intelligence agencies, all of which are "hot issues" in popular debates in Pakistan today. To put these popular images of the state into perspective, however, I first say a few things about state formation in Pakistan and how the idea of state authority has been linked to a modernist interpretation of Islam.

Islam and Nationalism in Pakistan

State formation in Pakistan, as nation building, is closely related to modernist trends in the interpretation of Islam as they were being developed throughout the nineteenth and early twentieth century. Perhaps more than anybody else, the poet-philosopher Muhammad Iqbal has linked Islamic modernization to Pakistani Muslim nationalism. His ideas have been very influential in Pakistan, so much so that he is generally considered the national thinker of Pakistan. The most prestigious university of the country is named after him, and his grave in Lahore, located next to the Badshahi Mosque and other monuments of the Moghul Empire, has become a place of secular pilgrimage for many Pakistani citizens. Iqbal argued that the future of an independent Muslim state in South Asia would rise or fall depending on the extent to which South Asian Muslims would be able to modernize Islam and free themselves from what he saw as erroneous innovations and regional pre-Islamic traditions that had come to pervert the original revelations of the Prophet. The new state of Pakistan was thus not simply based on Islam, or the ideal of Muslim unity, but, more precisely, on a particular interpretation of Islam that stressed the importance of modern education leading to an individual *Bildung* into modern citizens and the ability of independent reasoning concerning religious matters (*ijtehad*). In nationalist ideology, particular practices were rejected as being traditional, backward, syncretic, a remainder of Hindu or colonial influence, and therefore un- or not-quite-Islamic.

Three sets of practices and mentalities were considered especially unworthy of a modern Pakistani citizen. The one that has been given most attention in academic writing is popular Sufism, especially saint worship, which is dismissed by many Pakistani as either a sign of backward mentality or a Hindu perversion (e.g., Ewing 1983, 1997; Gilmartin 1988; Werbner and Basu 1998). Two others have been less noticed thus far. "Feudalism" has been identified as being in contradiction with the Islamic ideal of social equality (*musawat*).

In Pakistan today, words for different types of landlords, such as *jagirdar*, *zamindar*, and especially *wadera*, are widely used as insults in public conversation. In speeches, politicians accuse each other of wishing to rule Pakistan as "their private *jagir*" (landed property). In TV series, the wadera persona is almost by definition the evil genius. This rather recent type of landlord who cannot flaunt an aristocratic background, as he is usually from a family who used to produce the village headman, who worked as the representative of the more traditional jagirdar or zamindar, is typically portrayed as driving around his vast lands in a four-wheel-drive Pajero jeep with tinted windows, exploiting his bonded laborers (*haris*), raping their daughters and sons, drinking whiskey, and terrorizing the countryside with the help of a private army of armed strongmen (*dacoits*). This talk probably has its roots in the power struggle that has been going on in Pakistan between the city-based bureaucracy and military, and regional elites of landlords (Jalal 1995).

Further, several forms of exclusivist solidarity that may divide the Muslim community have come under attack as being un-Islamic. This is most profoundly the case with the concept of caste (*zat*), which is widely condemned as being part of a Brahmin ideology. As a result, many Pakistani have dropped their indigenous family names, most of which refer to a caste-specific occupation, such as *mochi* (cobbler) or *qasai* (butcher), and have adopted a so-called *ashraf* (noble) name with an origin in Islamic territories such as Arabia, Persia, or Central Asia. To a lesser extent, kinship solidarity, as in so-called *biradaris* (endogamous groups), are condemned as being in violation of the ideal of Muslim unity, as symbolized by the *hajj* as well as the *hijra*, the exodus that marks the leaving behind of tribal ties in favor of a new religious community. Finally, regional solidarities, commonly labeled "ethnic," are often said to endanger the all-Muslim unity.

In the early decades of Pakistan independence, cultural and political elites depicted the state as a major initiator of social and cultural reform—literally as a set of parents (*ma-bap*) educating their children (Ahmad 1964: 103–20). Modernization was seen as a liberating gift presented by a social avant-garde to a backward society steeped in tradition. Modernization was a mixture of, on the one hand, a mimicry of things Western, including ideas of military discipline and economic development, a bureaucratic style of clothing, a knowledge of British philosophy and poetry (at a minimum, one was expected to be able to quote from Russell and Wordsworth), and on the other hand, a training in a *sharif* or noble, mostly urban culture, centered around the Urdu language as it had been developed in the nineteenth century in northern India. Condemning saint worship, "feudalism," and particularistic loyalties as traditional and un-Islamic, members of urban elites tried to compete with established regional and rural political networks centered around powerful landlords and spiritual leaders. The effort to make the state of Pakistan prosper, as well as the attempt to purify Islam from Hindu and colonial influences, were their claims to legitimacy.

From the late 1960s onwards, a counterdiscourse emerged that developed and promoted regional or "ethnic" identities. With some exceptions, regionalists have not rejected the idea of Muslim nationalism as such, but have tried to give a new meaning to the concept through a much more positive evaluation of regional syncretic Islamic traditions. Especially Sufism or *tasawwuf*, as the mystical, less *shari'at*-oriented branch of Islam, has been reevaluated as a form of Islam that is more at home in the various provinces of Pakistan than the reformist notions of the urban modernist elite. There has been more attention to ecstatic practices, as well as more physical expressions of faith—music, dancing, crying—which in the 1960s and 1970s especially attracted the urban, vaguely left-wing students, intellectuals, artists, and others, who found in these passionate and swinging practices of devotion more opportunities for social rebellion, fun, and identity construction than in the modernist emphasis on the importance of reason (*'aql*) and discipline (*nazm*). In the province of Sindh, which together with former East Pakistan became the most rebellious province in the late 1960s, the shrines of two local saints, Lal Shahbaz Qalandar and Shah Abdul Latif, became important centers of regional resistance and the construction of a separate Sindhi religious and political identity.

The rediscovery of syncretic traditions and Sufism was taken up by the Pakistan People's Party (PPP), which in 1970 won the first democratic elections in the history of Pakistan. During the administration of the PPP, ethnic or regional identities were promoted as intrinsically part of the complex identity of a Pakistani citizen. Whereas a Pakistani identity had always had a national and religious component, an ethnic one was now added. Four ethnic groups were more or less officially recognized; these coincided with provincial boundaries, so that a Pakistani was required to identify as either Punjabi, Sindhi, Pakhtun, or Baluchi. Moreover, a *quota system*, which distributed positions in the civil service as well as places in educational institutions on the basis of ethnic background, allotted certain rights to members of these various ethnic groups.

Partly in this context, young Muhajirs in Karachi and Hyderabad mobilized themselves on the basis of a new Muhajir identity from the late 1970s onwards. They became the most vocal of those groups that have not been willing to identify with one of the four recognized ethnic groups. In 1978, the All-Pakistan Muhajir Student Organization (APMSO) was formed, followed in 1984 by the Muhajir Qaumi Movement (MQM). The MQM has since then made headlines in both the Pakistani and international press as it has been a major player in the dramatic increase of ethnic polarization and violence in urban Sindh. It is a movement with many different faces. From an academic standpoint, it is movement of remarkable social mobilization based on a rare perception of ethnicity, as the MQM does not claim a separate ethnic identity for Muhajirs on the basis of a shared homeland but rather on the basis of a shared experience in exodus and migration. For many of its supporters, the MQM is a revolutionary movement that has given voice to large sections of the underprivileged population of Karachi and Hyderabad. Its critics associate the Party mainly with armed terror, ethnic discrimination, nepotism, and crime. The Party, which has won elections in urban Sindh with large margins since 1987, has seriously suffered from an internal split in 1991 and even more from attempts of various governments to break the back of the party's street power in a series of so-called Operations Clean-up, which have been criticized by human rights commissions for the extrajudicial methods that reportedly were being employed.

Corruption and Violence

In the neighborhood where I did fieldwork, the experiences people have with state functionaries clearly do not meet their expectations. Expectations are based on the ideal of an impartial, transparent, autonomous state, which, as a benevolent and just parent, rules over society. That is the standard—the way things should be. In practice, however, that ideal is felt to be constantly corrupted by dishonest and insincere state functionaries with whom the people of the neighborhood have to deal daily. As Gupta (1995) also observes in his northern Indian village, there is a profound discrepancy between expectations of the state and everyday experiences with local state functionaries, a discrepancy that serves as the basis of a discourse of popular protest and resistance.

Most residents of my neighborhood—all of them are Muhajirs—subscribe to the legitimacy of state authority. In this respect, they consider themselves different from, for instance, the Pathans in the mountainous north, who, as a tribal people, are said to be an unruly, unpredictable lot who do not recognize the authority of the state. Notwithstanding the fact that Pathans are to some extent admired for their proverbial sense of independence, they are also condemned for their tribal laws, especially the custom of blood feud, which are seen as evidence of an un-Islamic and backward mentality and a violation of both the shari'at and the Constitution. Very often, the discourse of modernity is being used in this respect: the tribal laws are said to belong to a past that educated people have left behind. These traditional laws, based on exclusivist loyalties of tribe and family, should now be replaced by the impartiality of the shari'at and the bureaucratic laws of the modern nation-state. Moreover, as Muhajirs who claim to have left their homelands in India for the ideal of Pakistan, the residents of the neighborhood feel that they have profoundly contributed to the establishment of Pakistan, which was expected to make real the ideals of Muslim unity and social equality and put an end to particularistic solidarities and traditional law systems. Generally speaking, the residents identify the state as an agent of modernity and reform and hold that Muhajirs—as an educated people and a people who went through the chastening, if not purifying, experience of exodus—are especially equipped to understand and promote the ideals of Islam and modernity. Their everyday talk is full of condemnations of the identified antipodes of modernity, not only tribal laws, but also Sufism, feudalism, and caste and kinship loyalties.

Although always softened by an ideology of Muslim unity and national solidarity, the idea that Muhajirs are the champions, if not the chosen people, of Pakistan regularly pops up and most often comes with a feeling of solitude and displacement, of having been betrayed and left in the cold by the other peoples of Pakistan, who have bartered away the ideals of Pakistan for their regional or ethnic interests. The personal experience of migration and the stories that are told about this in the family and the neighborhood have always been linked to the national experience of independence and, subsequently, the building up from scratch of Pakistan. The sacrifices that are said to have been made by Muhajirs have never been properly appreciated. On the contrary, the state, once established, has been conquered and barricaded by others who are less receptive to the liberating ideals of Islamic modernism.

With such arguments, people in the neighborhood evaluate and talk about their daily dealings with local state officials. Very few of them work in state institutions, although some work as policemen or other low-grade civil servants, and most look at state institutions as impenetrable bastions. It is generally considered a waste of time and energy to apply for a job in the civil service unless you are willing and able to pay a bribe as high as one year's salary. Further, the implementation of governmental development schemes (legalization of illegal housing, construction of sewage systems, etc.) depends on personal contacts or high bribes and takes a frustratingly long time. The police in particular are considered untrustworthy, hostile, and humiliating: when in trouble, stay away from the police if you do not want more problems. Nevertheless, it is not always possible to avoid the police, who regularly set up checkpoints to relieve passers-by of their money and valuables.

Over the past few years, corruption has become a major theme in political debates—not only on a popular level, but also in newspapers, on TV, and in the National Assembly. Prime ministers are usually dismissed on the charge of corruption: Muhammad Khan Junejo in 1988, Benazir Bhutto in 1990 and 1996, Nawaz Sharif in 1993 and 1999. In November 1996, after Bhutto had been dismissed, a major operation was launched by the interim government to overcome corruption. With great fanfare, an Accountability (Ehtasab) Commission was installed that would check the bank accounts of every major politician and bureaucrat. During the same period, Pakistan appeared second on some international list of most-corrupt countries, which became a popular topic of public debates and jokes. Some said that it was to be Pakistan's tragic fate never to be the first in anything; others countered that Pakistan had initially been on the top of the list, but then some government official had bribed the makers of the list to persuade them to put some African state first. Meanwhile, the national television network daily reported on the findings of the Ehtasab Commission, showing the commissioner behind a huge pile of documents on his desk, or solemnly talking with the president of high court judges against the background of high-ranking uniformed soldiers. It created the illusion that corruption and nepotism were not an intrinsic part of state power but, on the contrary, a foreign, if contagious and dangerous, disease that had affected many a state body and that was now being fought with all the power the state could muster. Interestingly, the Ehtasab Commission itself has since become a subject of controversy and allegations of political intrigue, but although this has affected the accountability of yet another state institution, it has hardly damaged the belief in the possibility of a transparent and impartial state as such. It has, however, seriously added to a general public distrust of politicians and bureaucrats, who are commonly believed to "eat your brain" (*dimag khana*) with hollow phrases of Islam and national solidarity while ruthlessly exploiting the common or poor people (*am log, gharib log*).

The popular perception of the state is shaped not only by corruption, but also by violence and humiliation. According to the neighborhood residents, state violence has become salient and more brutal since the 1970s. This includes everyday instances of harassment by the police, but also more violent state persecution of potential militants of the MQM. Backed by massive propaganda that depicts the series of Operations Clean-up as battles against "terrorists" funded by foreign enemies such as India, state forces have killed a large number of MQM militants in what the press commonly defines as "police encounters." At times, the army has proudly, almost as a trophy, published the monthly number of *dacoits* (bandits) it has shot dead. Several newspapers and magazines have published critical stories about these practices together with pictures of maimed bodies. Further, the youth of the neighborhood tell each other stories about peers who have been arrested and put in jail, where they are reportedly raped, urinated upon, made to squat for prolonged periods of time, and otherwise humiliated.

Despite these experiences and rumors, the people in the neighborhood have not altogether lost their belief in the ideal of a just and impartial state. Rather, they have found explanations that ascribe the moral rot to particular groups of people who are said to corrupt the ideal in a concealed manner, according to secret deals and hidden loyalties. One of these explanations hinges on the presence of intelligence agencies. A second builds on the notion of ethnic exclusivism.

Popular Explanations of Corruption: Intelligence Agencies and Ethnicity

A great deal of political rumor in Hyderabad is about *agencies*. Intelligence agencies are believed to be the real rulers of Pakistan, the secret manipulators of politics. They are believed to be omnipresent, and to some extent that seems true. This was brought home to me one day when a friend told me that a man who had identified himself as an agent of the Inter-Service Intelligence (ISI), the army's intelligence agency, had visited him. The agent had asked about my doings in Hyderabad. The best way to get rid of him, my friend suggested, was to casually inform the right persons about the harmless character of my research. The way to do this was to make a tour around the city to visit anybody likely to be an ISI informer, to drink a cup of tea, have a chat, and leave a good impression. It took us a couple of days inside travel agencies, petrol stations, post offices, tea stalls and restaurants, shrines, offices of lawyers and NGOs, the Press Club, and several shops and workshops in the bazaar. Most intriguing of this limited study was to find out that the identity of intelligence agents was known to, or at least suspected by, a large number of people. When I returned to the neighborhood of my fieldwork with the exciting idea that I had qualified information to tell, it appeared that most informers I had been drinking tea with were already known there.

I do not want to suggest that Pakistan is at par with the state of Rumania prior to the 1989 revolution in which, as Katherine Verdery (1996) describes, an astonishingly large percentage of the population was involved in secret intelligence work. But I am convinced that intelligence agencies are an established aspect of Pakistani politics and that the ISI is not the only such agency operating in Pakistan. In fact, several law-and-order forces run their own agency and often appear to be interested in each other as much as in anybody else. This also means that the state cannot be regarded as Big Brother, spying on its subjects through secret activities penetrating private places and thereby effectively keeping society under its thumb. It instead resembles a troubled, fragmented family of several brothers who are deeply distrustful of each other and cannot rely too much on each other in their dealings with the outside world. Partly for this reason I think that the influence of the intelligence agencies should not be exaggerated, even though there is little doubt that the ISI in particular is an important player in Pakistani politics.

Nevertheless, many wild speculations can be heard about their supposedly far-reaching power. Almost all major political developments are regularly ascribed to the secret manipulation of "the agencies," a category that usually remains unspecified. Large-scale riots are often believed to be masterminded by "the agencies." This also goes for remarkable election results. It is commonly believed that "the agencies" work for particular economic, political, and military elites who try to defend their "vested interests" through a policy of divide and rule. The idea is that the ideals of Pakistan—social equality, Muslim unity, the abolition of feudalism, and so on—would harm their position, but because they cannot openly declare their unpatriotic conservatism, they need secret agencies to spread hatred and distrust among the common people of Pakistan. In this way, the problems that pester Pakistan—poverty, corruption, ethnic polarization—are seen to be the result of the wheelings and dealings of a happy few who are in control of the secret niches of the Pakistani state, rather than of inequalities in social relations or ethnic or religious prejudices, which are deeply ingrained in society at large.

Comparatively speaking, this discourse on intelligence agencies is rather optimistic and less dangerous than the other explanation for state corruption, which revolves around ethnic competition. Compared to the ethnic discourse, arguments about the prevailing power of intelligence agencies put the blame on an almost invisible and unidentifiable enemy. According to this talk, different social groups within Pakistani society would live peacefully together if it were not for the dividing scheming of unknown intelligence agents. In contrast, the argument of ethnic differences potentially blames anyone who belongs to the rival ethnic group.

In the beginning of this essay I sketched the contents of the argument about Punjabi biradari solidarity. Punjabis, however, are not the only ethnic group said to have captured and polluted the state by unpatriotic and un-Islamic means. In a slightly different argument, Muhajirs also accuse Sindhis of dominating the state through traditional and backward forms of loyalty that damage national solidarity. If Punjabis are condemned for their exclusivist kinship mentality, Sindhis are considered an inveterately feudal people. The Sindhi way to domination is through the vertical networks of feudal patronage headed by either a landlord (wadera) or a spiritual leader (*pir*). These rural big men are primarily blamed for the prevailing feudalism that is said to continue to dominate Pakistani politics and that is especially believed to characterize the PPP, which is led by the Sindhi landlord family of the Bhuttos. The ordinary Sindhi, however, is not considered free of guilt either. He is said to be of a lazy, unmanly, submissive, and superstitious disposition, which does not befit a modern Pakistani citizen. In a gesture of welcome, he puts his hands before his chest like a Hindu instead of offering a fellow Muslim his right hand. He bows in front of his master. He begs rather than demands. Some residents in my neighborhood also said that the Sindhi prefers fish for dinner rather than meat and that this disputable taste symbolizes his fishy, unreliable, deeply feudal character.

It would be an interesting study to trace down the genealogy of such ideas. I am not in a position to do this, but it is clear that negative images of the backward Sindhi Muslim (the Sindhi Hindu, in contrast, has the reputation of an energetic and efficient moneylender and trader) were already circulating in northern India during colonial times. From cities like Delhi, Lucknow, and

Agra, the Sindh looked like an uncivilized backwater and an unhealthy wilderness of extreme heat, dangerous animals, strange diseases, mad mullahs, and fanatical fakirs. Such notions were also promoted in colonial writings. There are many examples of this, but the most well-known is probably Sir Richard Burton's travel accounts. In an early work, Burton wrote, "The dark complexion of the Sindhi points him out as an instance of arrested development. . . . He is idle and apathetic, unclean in his person, and addicted to toxication; notoriously cowardly in times of danger, and proportionally insolent when he has nothing to fear; he has no idea of truth or probity, and only wants more talent to be a model of treachery" (1988: 283–84). To be fair, Burton did make an exception for the Sindhi woman. In a later work, which also contains a chapter entitled "The Sindi Man: His Character, and Especially What He Drinks" and that was recently reprinted by the Department of Culture and Tourism of the Government of Sindh, Burton describes the Sindhi woman's attitude as "not ungraceful, she carries herself well, she never stoops and, observe, she has high but not round shoulders" (1993: 328).

Although informed by older, pre-Independence traditions of prejudice, it is clear that popular images of a state captured by a backward ethnic group to a large extent follow the discourse of modernity and tradition as it has been promoted by the mostly urban elites, who have considerably shaped the process of state formation and nation building in Pakistan. In the popular imagination, we see a similar notion of a reforming state fighting the evils of traditions, such as feudalism, superstition, or, in the case of the anti-Punjabi argument, a too exclusivist kinship solidarity. From a national perspective, such traditional mentalities have always been depicted as the trait of particular ethnic groups. In the hands of underprivileged social groups, such as the Muhajir shoemakers and rickshaw drivers in the neighborhood of my fieldwork, such ideas are appropriated to lay bare the hypocrisy of the privileged strata of society. These notions feed into a sense of betrayal and displacement so pivotal to present-day Muhajir identity.

A Geography of Secret State Power

The captive state, then, is seen as the true, but hidden, image of power that is concealed by empty words about bureaucratic transparency, Muslim fraternity, and self-effacing patriotism. It is important to realize that the hypocrisy that is considered self-evident and for everyone to see is at the same time said to take place within a domain of secrecy that cannot bear the light of day. It is in this sense that the image of the captive state contributes to the reproduction of a separate Muhajir identity. It is not simply the fact that corruption, nepotism, and abuse of power have rendered talk about the impartiality of the state meaningless—a development that has been going on for several years and is now accepted as a fact by probably most Pakistani citizens and, for that matter, most foreign observers. More important, such practices are said to take place in an atmosphere of secrecy and conspiracy of which the common people (*am log*) are excluded. This sense of exclusion from what actually and rightfully belongs to the nation—a notion that, in the hands of Muhajirs, has an ethnic as well as a class component—is an important theme in present-day Muhajir identity.

It is, of course, well-known that secrets, rumors, and gossip can be important means of communication through which to establish a sense of community or loyalty. From the theoretical works of Simmel (1950) and Goffman (1959) to, for instance, a recent study of ethnic conflict in south Senegal (De Jong 2000), we find the notion that secrets must first be identified as secrets to become secrets at all. Second, secrecy creates a community of people who are "in the know," as opposed to the ignorant, who are therefore outsiders. In this way, a secret, regardless of its contents, may become the glue that binds a group together. But secrecy can also generate insiders and outsiders in a different way, by creating the fiction of a secret syndicate that controls and penetrates society through covert means. Rumors about Freemasonry and a worldwide Jewish conspiracy are historical examples.

In Hyderabad, secrecy and the communication of rumors worked both ways. On the one hand, rumors about intelligence agencies or invisible biradari or feudal networks depicted opponents as scheming conspirators connected through traditional and less than transparent networks that are anathema to the ideals of a free, democratic, Muslim nation-state. On the other hand, however, such rumors were seldom communicated openly. Although everyone was aware of the existence of such rumors to the point that they can rightly be called public secrets, most of my informants took care to contribute to the notion of secrecy by first creating a conspirational atmosphere before telling me what I had already been told a thousand times. At a minimum, the person would lower his voice, take me by the arm, and look at me significantly to indicate that the words to come were both valuable and dangerous. Other people were not content with this and would propose to retreat into unlikely places, such as air-conditioned restaurants, which had the additional advantages of coolness and expensive beverages, to put me in the know. Two places were especially favored for this purpose. One was a poorly lit restaurant on one of Hyderabad's main streets, owned by a well-known man who himself had a reputation of being close to the secret center of things. He had been a candidate in local elections in the 1970s and had spent brief periods in jail for his political activities. In those days, the restaurant had been a meeting place of politically active students. Since his retreat from active politics, the owner usually sat outside the restaurant, mostly accompanied by one of his former friends and comrades. Inside, the fans on the ceiling were ramshackle enough to make plenty of noise so that private conversations could not be overheard.

The other place was a coffee house, equally centrally located and also known as a place where radical politicians, students, journalists, and, also, intelligence agents met. Like the air-conditioned restaurant, it maintained a reputation as a place of rumors and secret knowledge. Amazingly, then, to exchange secrets, my informants would often propose going to places that made one suspect by just being there. These places served as identified hotbeds of classified information; being seen there to some extent made one feel involved in the secret center of local politics. It made these places, which also included certain shrines of Sufi saints, the Press Club compounds, and student hostels, awe-inspiring. In addition, they were characterized by an anonymity that went well with the rumors that were being exchanged. These were typically without an author; they came from nowhere in particular but were believed by everybody.

These places, then, formed a geography of power complementary to the prestigious and often colonial architecture of official state buildings, such as the court buildings, the head office of the police, and the army bungalows in the lush Cantonment area. Considered the dark workshops of local politics, they were seen as places not only where conspirators would meet, but also where the secret bodies of the state gathered information, bribed informants, and hired people for illegal activities. If conspiracies were masterminded within the drawing rooms of Punjabi biradaris or the residences of Sindhi feudal lords, they were believed to be carried out in the workshops of covert state power where one could find the people willing to do the dirty work. On visits to such places, my informants would never fail to point out to me the men who had been involved in spying activities.

It is not my intention to argue that rumors about covert networks of power and illegal state activities stem from collective fantasies that have no basis in actual fact. On the contrary, intelligence agencies do play an important role in Pakistani politics, just as biradari and patronage networks continue to be important. However, the atmosphere of secrecy in which such activities are discussed makes it possible to overestimate their influence. Probably the most well-known example of this is the contention that the army, through the illegal and hidden activities of the ISI, is responsible for the rise of the MQM. This is a rumor that has become a widely accepted fact among the critics of the MQM. The idea is that in the mid-1980s the military regime needed a popular political party in the province of Sindh to curb the power of the PPP, the regime's main opponent. Although it is possible that the ISI had some dealings with the MQM in its early years, it seems rather farfetched to make the army responsible for the massive popular support the Party subsequently received. The argument contributes to the notion of an omnipresent, all-powerful state that may produce popular movements wherever it wishes. Such rumors thus reinforce the notion of a state that is both separated from society as well as capable of manipulating society totally. Without wishing to belittle the force that state officials can mobilize through both overt and covert means, it is also clear that the rise of such popular movements as headed by the MQM are, among other things, forms of protest against state crime and corruption rather than the planned outcome of state manipulation. Rumors that make the ISI responsible for the movement, however, enable one to close one's eyes to the complex changes that are going on in society at large and that offer much more plausible, if alarming, explanations for ethnic conflict. Instead, they enable one to interpret the crisis as a crisis of the state alone.

By way of conclusion, I will say a few words about this tendency to explain complex social transformations solely in terms of a crisis of governability.

Conclusion

A very influential, almost commonsensical, theory of the state explains the recent rise of political violence and social unrest in Pakistan in terms of a "crisis of governability" or a "collapse of state power" (e.g., Nasr 1992). According to widely held public opinion, the trouble is caused by a decay of political institutions and an erosion of state authority. When the state loses its grip on society, the subjects, according to an almost Hobbesian logic, will take care of their interests in a chaotic and opportunistic manner. In Pakistan, it is often recalled that the most violent episodes in the history of the country occurred during the collapse of an authoritarian military regime, in the late 1960s and the late 1980s. Democratic regimes, it is argued, are weaker and less willing or able to maintain law and order through violent means.

I have difficulties with these assumptions. Surely it is difficult to maintain that the Pakistani state has become a weak state in the 1990s. A large number of heavily armed military, paramilitary, and police forces have been brought out into the streets of Karachi and Hyderabad since the late 1980s. I am not so sure that the transition to democracy since 1988, an arrested process since the coup of 1999, lowered the readiness of government leaders to use force against civilians. All the same, it is possible to argue that the state is increasingly characterized by fragmentation. Various state institutions are constantly in competition with each other. The most dramatic expression of this is the violent confrontations between police forces and the military in a number of incidents (Verkaaik 1999: chap. 7). Much of this is the result of the fact that new administrations often establish new governmental bodies and law-and-order forces and staff them with known allies, rather than work with, or try to rearrange, existing institutions staffed by civil servants whose loyalty is doubtful. In this way, social and political rivalry is firmly established within the state apparatus, but that in no way implies that these various state institutions are less willing or able to use effective force.

Rather than look at the state as an autonomous, unified, and monitoring agency, then, it appears more fruitful to study the state as a particular part of society that is characterized by a relatively high degree of political activities, including competition over resources, exchange of information, ideological debates, and the use of physical coercion. One should not look for causes of this increasing fragmentation of the state merely in the state apparatus itself, but rather take it as a reflection of a more far-reaching transition of society at large. To quote Sandria Freitag, who has made a similar argument in the case of India, present-day social unrest and political violence are symptoms of "a much larger and more challenging process under way: the redefinition of Indian civil social space and who will be allowed to participate publicly inside that discursive space" (1996: 232). The same applies to present-day Pakistan. In other words, the argument that social unrest is caused by a collapse of state authority fails to acknowledge two important facts. First, it accepts the idea of a separation between state and society, though there is no evidence that such a strict separation exists outside the domain of the political imagination. Second, it reduces social unrest to a crisis of the state, whereas it is an expression of changes that are taking place in a much larger part of society.

In this essay, then, I have tried to initiate a more integrated approach of studying present-day relations between state and society in Pakistan by looking at the state "from below," that is, by examining popular perceptions of the state within an "ethnic" group that has been at the heart of social transitions and political unrest in urban Sindh since the mid-1980s. Building on the work of Eickelman and Piscatori (1996), I have argued that the popular imagination of the state is linked to a modernist concept of Islamic nationalism so that the state came to be regarded as the leading agent of religious and social reform. This notion of the state as a benevolent parent was itself based on the myth of the state as separated from and impartial to society. In turn, this ideal of the state has become the basis for a popular critique of state practice. Expecting the impossible, namely, a truly transparent and democratic state sincerely devoted to the ideals of Muslim fraternity, Muhajirs have grown deeply disappointed with and distrustful of the state, which they feel fails to live up to its own high standards. Instead of reforming a backward tradition, the state has been captured by social groups who, through secret and invisible means, hold on to their particularistic sense of loyalty and use state power to enhance their self-interests. The growing attention of the theme of corruption in Pakistan must therefore be seen primarily as a sign of emancipation rather than an increase of immoral behavior among state officials. The practices now increasingly labeled as corruption are not new. What is new is the growing sense of indignation about these practices in Pakistani society.

Note

This study was part of a dissertation project, which has resulted in a dissertation entitled "Inside the Citadel: Fun, Violence, and Religious Nationalism in Hyderabad, Pakistan." The research was financed by the Netherlands Foundation for the Advancement of Tropical Research (WOTRO) and was carried out at the Amsterdam School for Social Science Research (ASSR).

PUBLIC SECRETS, CONSCIOUS AMNESIA, AND THE CELEBRATION OF AUTONOMY FOR LADAKH

Martijn van Beek

Die Welt ist einmalig. Das bloße Nachsprechen der Momente, die immer und immer wieder als dasselbe sich aufdrängen, gleicht eher einer vergeblichen und zwangshaften Litanei als dem erlösenden Wort. Klassifikation ist Bedingung von Erkenntnis, nicht sie selbst, und Erkenntnis löst die Klassifikation wiederum auf.—Horkheimer and Adorno, *Dialektik der Aufklärung*

Bureaucrats work on the categories of social existence much the same way as sorcerers are supposed to work on the hair or nail clippings of their intended victims. —Herzfeld, *The Social Production of Indifference*

Paradoxes of Recognition

On a sunny morning in September 1995, one of Ladakh's political leaders and I were sitting in his garden, sipping tea. A week earlier, he had been among the twenty-six elected and four nominated members of the new Ladakh Autonomous Hill Development Council in Leh (LAHDC), who were sworn in during a ceremony presided over by the governor of the State of Jammu and Kashmir (J&K), General K. V. Krishna Rao, PVSM (Retd). Congratulating the people on their use of "peaceful and democratic means," the governor said, "This is a shining example for everyone in our democratic country, that one can achieve one's legitimate demands through constitutional means."[1] That morning the young political leader and I shared a sense of closure: for me, the creation of the Hill Council coincided nicely with the end of several years of research on the movement that led to its constitution. I could hardly have wished for a better conclusion to my doctoral project. For him, autonomy signaled the end of a long struggle whose final, successful phase he had been instrumental in planning and implementing. The Hill Council signified an opportunity to finally take charge and show the people, the state government, the world, that Ladakh could develop toward greater prosperity while protecting its cultural heritage. Even communal harmony among the dominant religious communities of the region, which had suffered during the agitation, could be restored, he was sure, as Muslims had been given adequate representation on the council. Where generations of previous political leaders had failed, his associates and he had succeeded. I asked him whether he regretted anything about the agitation. He expressed regret over some of the "arm twisting" that had been necessary, "but we couldn't have done it any better way. Even at the risk of blowing our own horn: we did it well."

Although the atmosphere among the spectators and invited guests at the swearing-in ceremony on the polo ground was one of celebration, the governor's escort of "Black Cat" commandos, constantly scanning the crowds, fingers on the trigger of their automatic weapons, provided a reminder of the fact that elsewhere in J&K there was considerable resistance to India's claims of "Unity in Diversity" and secularism. Yet, while sections of the population of Kashmir had been fighting for decades to break away from India, Ladakhis had for an even longer period been struggling to "Free Ladakh from Kashmir." The Ladakh region covers an area of about sixty thousand square kilometers in the rain shadow of the Himalayas to the northeast of the Kashmir Valley.[2] The estimated two hundred thousand people who inhabit the region constitute almost equal shares of Muslims and Buddhists, yet the region is commonly characterized as Tibetan in terms of culture, religion, and language. Muslims predominate in Kargil District, and Buddhists constitute the overwhelming majority of the population in Leh District. At least since the 1930s Ladakhi grievances had been expressed in terms of the "unique conditions" of the region. As Secretary to the Government, Jammu and Kashmir Affairs, K. Padmanabhaiah wrote in the "Reasons for Enactment" for the Ladakh Hill Councils Act: "Ladakh region is geographically isolated with a sparse population, a vast area and inhospitable terrain, which remains landlocked for nearly six months in a year. Consequently, the people of the area have had a distinct identity and special problems distinct from those of the other areas of the State of Jammu and Kashmir."[3] The granting of a Hill Council was the outcome of an agitation launched in 1989 under the leadership of the Ladakh Buddhist Association.[4] This movement, not quite so peaceful and democratic as the governor made out, relied on a communalist strategy, arguing that Buddhist Ladakh could prosper only if it were liberated from the yoke of Muslim Kashmir.[5] Ladakh, then, was Buddhist; Buddhists are patriots; logically, Muslims are not proper Ladakhis, and—as the separatist violence in the Valley testified—they were not patriots and could not be trusted.

The purpose of the present essay is to explore ethnographically the ways in which official and illegitimate hegemonic grammars of identification, based on reifying and often fetishized imaginings of community and identity, do not necessarily evoke either compliance or resistance, but more complex practices of representation, performance, and belonging. The celebration of autonomy for Ladakh is premised on the public recognition of a unique identity, which must remain unspecified and fuzzy to be recognizable to bureaucrats, politicians, scientists, and ordinary people. The unambiguous specificity of Ladakh's officially recognized eight tribes is singularly unsuited for the kind of shared notion of Ladakhi identity that is purportedly being celebrated, and has no basis in local understandings of identity and belonging. At the same time, the dark reality of the communalist strategy that, as Ladakhi political leaders and many others are convinced, at last led to the recognition of the legitimacy of Ladakhi demands for autonomy is regarded as illegitimate and unsuited to public recognition and certainly celebration. Both the public recognition of the tribes in the straight-faced application of a sociologically impossible set of criteria, and the denial of communalism as a real and effective strategic resource in Indian politics as expressed in the celebration of Ladakhi identity and the granting of autonomy, illustrate the salience of everyday dissimulations that make the impossible purity of exclusivist categorizations practicable. Neither communalism nor tribalism captures the "reality" of social identification in Ladakh, but their reality as sources of empowerment—a reality premised on the shared imaginings of bureaucrats, politicians, activists, and scientists—requires dissimulations that make them appear as such expressions of the "truths" of Ladakhi social life and Indian politics. The following is intended to show how such dissimulations are necessary to live with the irresolvable incommensurabilities of communalism and exclusive official systems of classification, and the fluidity, multiplicity, and indeed "disorder" of social practices of identification.

I first discuss the "tribalization" of Ladakh. With communalism out of the question, officially, as a basis for recognition and empowerment, other legal classifications were explored, in particular Scheduled Tribes legislation. Second, I briefly trace the historical production of communalist imaginings and representations of Ladakh. The links of communalism with colonial and nationalist imaginings of religious "identity" as central to Indian society and culture have been the subject of many excellent studies, and the story in Ladakh follows a similar pattern.[6] Communalism, of course, is an officially illegitimate discourse, at odds with the Republic's secular, democratic principles, and could not be used as a formal justification for affirmative action for Ladakh after Independence. Ladakhi political leaders, however, perceived communalism to be the nature of the Indian political system and hence ultimately adopted a communal strategy to demand autonomy. And it worked, they say.

Both the formulation and implementation of the Scheduled Tribes scheme—publicly and officially—and the recognition and empowerment of religious community—mostly "secretly"—are possible only through the complicity of bureaucrats, scientists, politicians, and ordinary people. Their survival and effectiveness as principles of organization of Ladakhi identities rests on the willingness of these different actors to ignore, in the case of tribal identities, the impossibility of their existence in most aspects of everyday social life and, in the case of communal identities, their reality and effectivity. However, also in the case of communalism, the efficacy of the strategy was premised in large part on the *perceived* reality of communalism. While communalism was performed effectively in Ladakh, it had to be policed and imposed with sanctions on a reluctant population. There was, as I have argued elsewhere, no natural and lasting mobilization of the general Buddhist population in communalist opposition to Muslims in Ladakh (van Beek 1996).[7] In particular, I take up examples of the ways in which not only "ordinary" citizens, but also the state, political leaders, and bureaucrats ignore, violate, or creatively interpret in their daily practices the various demands of order placed on them.

Interstices

> Might it turn out, then, that not the basic truths, not the Being or the ideologies of the center, but the fantasies of the margined concerning the secret of the center are what is most politically important to the state idea and hence state fetishism. (Taussig 1993a: 23)

In a recent article, Michael Herzfeld notes that today "it becomes increasingly difficult to sustain the idea that facts exist independently of the social world" (1998: 80). Indeed, in the wake of the onslaught by hermeneuticists, deconstructionists, and "other invading hordes" (Skinner 1985: 6), the "facticity of facts" (Herzfeld 1998) is no longer a heretic proposition. As Taussig points out, this means that we live, all of us, in a space between fact and fiction, between the real and the really made up (1993b: xviii). The ways people negotiate this irreducible gap, then, is the substance of culture; it is these acts of classification, the production of their logics, and the filling of the spaces of the matrices thus devised, as well as the ways in which the objects of classification engage them. Anthropologists and other social scientists have studied the classificatory practices of colonial and metropolitan states, focusing on the transformations of space and identities through technologies of governmentality such as statistics, mapping, and census taking.[8] The contrast between lived practices of community—multiple, fluid, overlapping—and the formal seriality of communities in state and bureaucratic representations—singular, exclusive, fixed—has been the subject of many illuminating studies. With respect to India, Chatterjee (1986, 1995) and Kaviraj (1992) stress the qualitative change in conceptions of identity and belonging that occurs in the formation of the modern nation-state.[9]

Governmentality is often treated primarily or exclusively as a technical issue, and one imposed by the state. The technologies of state agents and institutions threaten to become treated as hegemonic in a narrow sense, the metaphor of the panopticon is literalized, and the objects of governmental technologies are confined to live within ineluctable "iron cages." This, of course, is far removed from Foucault's (1991) understanding of governmentality. O'Malley et al. have noted that resistance and contestation as constitutive dimensions are rarely given serious attention in the literature: "The separation of contestation from rule," they argue, "leaves little space for theorizing the *productive engagement* between them" (1997: 511). They call for more attention to the "messy implementation" of programs and recognition that these are not "written by one hand" but "multivocal, internally contested and thus, in a sense, always in change and often internally contradictory" (512–13). This multivocality and lack of internal coherence is particularly clearly illustrated by the process of constructing official identities for the people of Ladakh, applying different conceptions of race, caste, tribe, and community. At the same time, specific forms of governmentality, through the production of practical political rationalities in Weber's sense, contribute to the constitution of specific forms of political practice: in this case, "tribalism" and communalism.[10]

The Importance of Being Tribal

When the British government sold Kashmir in 1846 to the Dogra Maharaja Gulab Singh, this marked the emergence of a new kind of state in the region. Ladakh, the trans-Himalayan region between Himalaya and Karakoram broadly comprising the upper valleys of Shyok and Nubra, Zangskar, Suru, Dras, and Indus, had been conquered by the Dogras several years earlier. The British were keen to determine and demarcate the boundaries of not only their own new possessions (e.g., Lahaul, Spiti, and Kinnaur), but also those of the lands now under control of the maharajah. The British also developed an interest in long-distance trade through the region with Central Asia, and in a commercial treaty of 1870 gained joint control over the main trade route through Ladakh, while ensuring tax exemption on certain goods to be carried along these roads. The growth of trade and other colonial effects, such as the travel of officials, sportsmen, and adventurers, had an impact on the lives of some Ladakhis, especially those living along the roads who were subject to obligatory labor requisitions (Grist 1994), but official interest in the region was largely limited to the imposition and collection of taxes. The explorations of the Boundary Commission did lead to a number of publications, such as Cunningham's encyclopedic *Ladak: Physical, Statistical, and Historical* (1854). Another Englishman, Frederic Drew, produced a comprehensive survey of the realm, published in 1875 as *The Jummoo and Kashmir Territories*. Drew had joined the services of the maharajah in 1862 as a geologist, and ended his career a decade later as wazir (governor) of Ladakh. Drew's book included some tables from the first census of Kashmir published in 1873 and an attempt to categorize the population of Kashmir and Ladakh according to race. Drew admitted race turned out rather like nationality in his proposed scheme, but he suggested that his book contains "ample illustration of the principles of Ethnological Science" for one "who would work it out in detail" (1976: 6).

The spate of publications describing, mapping, and quantifying the facts about the region reflects the emergence of a modern concern with population and economy, with governmentality. With the growing desire to know the country and its population, cartographic *horror vacui* accompanied the fear of embarrassment of ambiguity of the census takers: the population needed to be classified precisely. The classification of Ladakh's population reflected changes in colonial and scientific discourse, as central organizing categories such as race were substituted with religion, caste, tribe, community, and finally, once again, tribe (van Beek 1997b). The collection of information, of facts about the country was, of course, "sternly practical," as the geographer Hugh Robert Mill put it (quoted in Livingstone 1992: 213). And its adoption by the Kashmir government, arguably with considerable British complicity, reflects a process of change in the reason of state, initially colonial, then national developmental, toward the kind of modern governmentality described by Foucault.

As Gupta has argued, "To be a national subject in an 'underdeveloped country'—for example, to be a citizen of India—is to occupy an overdetermined subject position interpellated by discourses of the nation *and* by discourses of development to which that nation is subjected" (1998: 34). The notion of backwardness, isolation, and cultural difference expressed in Ladakhi representations, well before Independence, was already the product of a reimagining of Ladakh according to new, colonial/national perceptions of normalcy and development derived from a selective reading of European history.[11] A central element in the legitimizing strategies of the late colonial and postcolonial Indian state has been the "upliftment" of "backward" sections of the population. Groups deemed to be characterized by particular disadvantages, such as so-called Scheduled Castes and Scheduled Tribes (SC/ST), were singled out for different forms of affirmative action and protection. Once this principle was accepted, the identification of castes and their enumeration became an important object of governmental technologies. In accordance with British colonial perceptions of the nature of Indian society, standardized lists of tribes and castes were drawn up, each assigned specific characteristics, and for each district the number of people belonging to each determined.[12] Certain castes and tribes were designated as "scheduled" groups, eligible for certain kinds of protections and benefits. Areas with a significant share of tribal populations were "excluded," both as a strategy of control and out of a paternalistic desire to protect the "primitive and backward" tribal populations (Metcalf 1994; Sonntag 1999). After Independence, this colonial practice was continued and expanded. The Constitution of India contains provisions for, among other things, reservations in education and government service, and a host of national and state-level programs exist to funnel additional resources into the development of SC/ST. The links among data collection, bureaucratic operation, and the national project are clearly illustrated by Home Minister C. Rajagopalachari's exhortation to the census takers in the first enumeration after Independence:

> Yours is not an isolated local inquiry. You are one of about six hundred thousand patriots, all of whom will be engaged on an identical task at the same time. All of you are jointly responsible for enumerating all the people. Collectively you will prepare a record of basic facts relating to the life and livelihood of all the citizens and families in our Republic. If this record is to be correct and complete, the part that you contribute should, in itself, be correct and complete. You should master the simple instructions you have received, and apply them uniformly and conscientiously. These instructions are based on a common plan for the country as a whole. Like a swarm of bees that build a beautiful hive according to the laws of geometry, each doing its part in obedience to a mystic urge, you should do your part according to conscience and the sense of truth inherent in us all. (Census of India 1951: vi).

Ladakh and its people, too, were mapped, measured, counted, and classified to enable the central planners and administrators to devise and implement the correct measures to bring Ladakh into the mainstream. As Nehru himself had told the Ladakhis in 1949, "In Ladakh you are backward and unless you learn and train yourselves you cannot run the affairs of your country" (*Amrita Bazar Patrika*, 8 July 1949), and so the task had been entrusted, as in colonial days, to others more advanced. Ladakh would be guided along the path to progress and prosperity by other sympathetic members of the nation. Although the practice of reservations for SC/ST populations has come under increasing criticism, it continues to be a central element in central and state government policy, and given the benefits that come with it, it was a long-standing goal of Ladakh's political leaders to have the population classified as ST.[13]

Since 1931, when Ladakhi representatives first presented demands to an official Commission of Inquiry, there has been a steady flow of petitions, memoranda, and reports in which local leaders sought to present Ladakh's condition in such a way that it might be recognized as entitled to special treatment. The situation of Ladakh was routinely described as "extremely deplorable" (Buddhists 1932: 127) and "most underdeveloped, poor and backward,"[14] and its people were dubbed "ignorant, illiterate, addicted to drinks"

(Wattal 1948) and "dumb driven cattle" (Kashmir Raj Bodhi Maha Sabha [KRBMS] 1935). As Nehru wrote in 1951 to Karan Singh, son of the last maharaja of Kashmir: "The real difficulty about Ladakh is its terrible economic backwardness" (Singh 1982: 141). The forms of demands and their justifications have varied, but the content of the demands, the concrete measures sought, have been basically the same: more resources, faster development, and greater control over decision making.

With Ladakh's difference from other parts of the state generally recognized and well established in both academic and official texts, its backwardness and isolation widely accepted as an accurate designation of its condition, it would seem reasonable that Ladakhi political leaders expected that special provisions would be made to promote education and development in the region. A number of measures were taken, including the creation of a special office for Ladakh Affairs headed by Kushok Bakula Rinpoche, and several development schemes were introduced. However, none of this was deemed adequate by Ladakh's leadership, and by the early 1960s a local opposition was forming that accused Bakula Rinpoche and his associates of corruption and a general lack of initiative in promoting the interests of Ladakh. The office for Ladakh Affairs was, according to one former Ladakhi civil servant, little more than a "post office" where files passed through but no action was taken. Over the next years, local resentment grew, and in early 1969 a large-scale agitation was launched for local autonomy along the lines of the Northeast Frontier Administration that existed on the other extremity of the Himalayan range. It was in the context of this agitation that the demand for recognition as ST was first voiced.

It may seem odd that it took Ladakh's leaders twenty years to raise this demand, which, as mentioned earlier, could provide such a range of benefits, including possibly greater autonomy. According to several people who were active at the time, Nehru had actually offered ST status for Ladakh to Bakula Rinpoche shortly after Independence. There is no documentation or independent corroboration of this story, but it is said that he declined it because he thought it would be degrading to be ranked with savages and untouchables and in general was unaware of the potential benefits flowing from ST status. In any case, the demand was rejected in 1969 and only occasionally raised in the course of the next decade until in 1980 an All-Ladakh Action Committee for Declaring Ladakh a Scheduled Tribe was formed. The goal of this movement was to achieve greater autonomy through Scheduled Tribe Area status.

In the wake of a bloody clash between protestors and security forces in 1981, the demand was reported to have been accepted by the state government, but no action was taken until several years later, and ST declaration did not take place until 1989.

Identifying Tribes

Although there may have been many political and other reasons for the slow process of recognition of Ladakhi claims to tribal status, there were a number of issues to resolve that followed from the ways tribes are conceived in the ST legislation. To qualify, Ladakh's population would need to meet a set of criteria of tribality, which were derived from colonial and nationalist imaginings of subcontinental tribals. Here the identification of tribes and their distinction from castes was fraught with difficulty: "The only safe criterion to distinguish the tribes from the castes is the former's territorial affiliation" (Majumdar 1961: 390). Despite the absence of clear-cut criteria, there were a number of more or less explicit assumptions tied to an evolutionary vision. As a formerly independent kingdom with considerable literary and religious tradition and involvement in long-distance trade and diplomatic relations, Ladakh hardly matched popular, official, and scientific imaginings of tribality. Despite the considerable creativity in identifying tribes, because of the absence of a fixed set of criteria there were limits to the possible. For one, it was soon evident that "Ladakhi" was an unsuitably inclusive category, as it included Shia and Sunni Muslims as well as Buddhists, sedentary farmers, traders, and businesspeople, as well as nomads and sections of the population who were treated as lower-status groups. Some kind of subdivision of the population was necessary.

Finally, in the mid-1980s the process of recognition gained pace and the registrar general, responsible for census operations, was charged with the task of ascertaining how many people belonging to which tribes were worthy of ST status. Ladakhi representatives drew up a list of proposed tribes to be recognized, which was presented to the government (see Table 1).[15] Social scientists were dispatched to Ladakh to investigate the conditions of these tribes and found eight of them worthy of recognition. One category, Shamma, was rejected on the grounds that these were basically identical with the Bot/Boto tribe, which was said to constitute the bulk of the population of Leh district.[16] The other tribes recognized were Balti, Beda, Brokpa/Drokpa/

Table 1 Scheduled Tribes by Religion

	Balti	Beda	Bot/ Boto	Brokpa, etc.	Changpa	Garra	Mon	Purigpa
Buddhist		319	76,493	2,000	3,511	827	873	
Muslim	10,272		11,265	24,386				54,017

Dard/Shin, Changpa, Garra, Mon, Purigpa. The three smallest tribes—Beda, Garra, and Mon, each with fewer than a thousand members—are groups of "gypsies," blacksmiths, and musicians, which are regarded as more or less polluted groups of low status. Changpa are mostly semisedentary sheep, goat, and yak herders concentrated in Rupshu and Changthang areas on the border with Tibet. Balti is used to designate Shia Muslims settled around Leh in parts of Kargil and those living in the Batalik area bordering on Baltistan; by contrast, Shia Muslims of Kargil and the Suru Valley are classified as Purigpa, after one of the names for the region. Brokpa and so on are the labels for a number of different groups of people, some Muslims, some Buddhists, generally referred to as Dards in some of the literature.

Although the identification of these tribes is surprising given the lack of substance of their tribality in Ladakhi identifications, their fabrication is not the main concern here. Rather, the creatively selective identification and application of criteria to classify the population is what is strikingly clear—despite the fact that both the report of the minicensus of 1986 and 1987 and the social scientists' report on the tribes remain classified information. Whereas the formal creation on paper of these tribal identities was, after all, an academic and bureaucratic matter, the implementation of The Constitution (Jammu and Kashmir) Scheduled Tribes Order, 1989 requires even greater creativity, as many of these identities have little or no grounding in social practice in Ladakh and were not recorded anywhere as formal identities prior to the Act.

With regard to identification of the population, the first obstacle was to ensure that the Indian scientists sent to investigate the proposed list of tribes would find a reality matching those claims. As the experience of census takers prior to Independence had shown, when caste, class, tribe, and community were still enumerated, self-identification led to a bewildering proliferation of identities. The 1911 census, which allowed self-identification, produced literally thousands of caste names and more than twenty thousand subcaste names for the frontier region as a whole (including Leh, Kargil, and present-day Pakistani-controlled Baltistan).[17] Ladakhi activists were also only too aware of the fact that people were liable to identify themselves inappropriately when asked what they were. Although I have heard different stories about the process, it is clear that both people to be surveyed and the interpreters on whom the scientists were dependent were instructed on appropriate answers and findings. Villages and households included in the supposedly random samples were also cautioned not to display too much wealth and "modernity." Two groups in particular feared to be excluded in view of the management of the process of identification and recognition: the small community of Christians at Leh, and the larger, powerful group known as Argons.

The "chairman" of the Christian community, S. S. Hischey, wrote to the deputy commissioner of Leh to express his concerns. His primary complaint was the organization of the survey "performa" (*sic*), which restricted the possible choices for Buddhists and Muslims. Certain categories, in other words, were apparently reserved for either one. Mon, Beda, and Garra were wrongly limited to Buddhists: "Such possibilities can also be under the Muslims and Christians." He concluded his letter with a plea for an entirely new category to be added: "My submission to you is to kindly broaden the scope of admissibility of *Ladakhis* into the Schedule Tribe and not *religion* as the latter might produce the fruits of bitterness in the soil of peace and brotherhood."[18]

In the end, Christians were encouraged to identify themselves as Bot/Boto, the most "generic" category available, and so there is no Christian tribe today. The fate of the Argons was less easily settled. When the tribes were declared in 1989, 89.71 percent of the population was said to have been included. Hindus and Sikhs were among the excluded, but also Argons, said by their leaders to constitute up to 7 percent of the population of Leh. The official, public reason for their exclusion was, as Leh member of the Legislative Assembly (MLA) Tsering Samphel wrote in a letter to the editor published in the Jammu-based newspaper *The Daily Excelsior*, "technical." The term Argon is used to designate families of mixed Ladakhi-Kashmiri or Ladakhi-Yarkandi ancestry. Leh, as an important entrepôt on the trade routes connecting Central Asia with Kashmir and beyond, attracted many foreign settlers, often members of the large trading families of Central Asia.[19] The trade was ended by the closing of borders in the 1940s and 1950s, and Argons shifted to other forms of business, including contracting. As we shall see below in the discussion of communalism, their success in cornering a substantial share of the profitable modern economy, as well as their identification, rightly or wrongly, with conversion and the Sunni population of the Kashmir Valley, made them a primary target of Buddhist activist ire. Thus, although the "technical" reason used to exclude them was, apparently, that they were not a stable community but one that anyone who was of mixed descent would automatically belong to, it is clear that other political considerations played a part in their exclusion.

Although Argons were thus formally excluded (their case continues to be appealed at various central and state levels), the operationalization of the ST order proved to require creativity of a different order and to invite yet more bending of rules and regulations. Because tribal membership was not registered previously, the documentation of belonging was an obvious challenge. This problem was resolved, on paper, by taking the records of the Land Settlement of 1908 as a basis. Hence, if one could show ancestry in the 1908 records in, say, Karnak, one would automatically be Changpa, whereas if one's house was recorded in, say, Batalik and one were a Shia Muslim, one would be Balti. In principle, then, things were clear. In practice, however, this posed several problems arising from people's shifting identifications and locations. A striking example is the case of a Muslim who converted to Buddhism upon marriage in the 1920s. This person's ancestry were Argons, as was he himself in 1908. Therefore, his offspring, although Buddhist, were technically ineligible for recognition as ST. To resolve this dilemma, the president of the Ladakh Buddhist Association issued a statement to the effect that X, upon his marriage and conversion, had "fully adopted the way of life, customs and traditions of the Bot/Boto tribe. Thereafter, all the children born out of the marriage and the grandchildren have followed the Bot/Boto way of life and have been following all the Customs and Traditions of the tribe in the exact manner that any other member of the tribe would do. Consequent upon their complete assimilation into the Bot/Boto tribe, all the descendants of X and Y have been accepted by the Bot/Boto tribe as members of the said tribe and have been and are being treated as such members of the tribe."[20]

Hence, for all practical purposes, the Ladakh Buddhist Association (LBA)—a religious, social organization, according to its statutes—certified the authenticity of the tribal identity of these applicants by referring to a set of apparently well-defined "customs and traditions" of the equally substantial social entity of the Bot/Boto tribe. Again, although the mode of existence of the Bot/Boto tribe would be a topic worth exploring, the point here is to illustrate the creativity with which the reality of the tribe, its customs, and the notion of membership are dissimulated, and how the case is then cemented by reference to other cases of creative interpretation. The impossibility of Bot/Boto tribality, or at least of unambiguous notions of membership, custom, and tradition, is overcome by creative action.

Creativity of a different sort is also said to characterize the issue of ST certificates, which are necessary to gain access to the benefits of ST status, such as loans against advantageous conditions and quotas for jobs and education. As explained, it is the Tehsildar's (district revenue officer) Office that issues these certificates, and given the benefits of ST status, it is not surprising that there are numerous stories about corruption. People complain that it is almost impossible for villagers to get the certificate, as they do not know the system and are confronted with demands for bribes. Some Buddhist activists are now convinced that the Argon issue is no longer acute, because most Argons have obtained ST certificates anyway—presumably as Bot/Boto tribe members, who can be either Muslim or Buddhist. With larger percentages of the population of J&K now in possession of the coveted I.D., for example, as Gujjar have now also been recognized as ST, the benefits in gaining access to quotas are in any case now limited.

Although ST was granted in 1989 and Ladakh's two districts have been eligible for a range of affirmative action programs, their impact has been limited. To be sure, individual opportunities such as cheap loans have encouraged hundreds of people to take out loans to buy taxis or to open telecommunications businesses, many of which are likely to go bankrupt in the coming years. Yet several people who had been in the forefront of the agitation for ST status argue that too little has been done to attract larger amounts of central resources through, for example, the Tribal Subplans and other special funds. Hence, dependence on state programs and development initiatives remains high, and the state government's performance continues to be regarded as insufficient. Among factors contributing to the relative lack of action on the part of the state government may have been Ladakh's very marginality in economic, geographic, and electoral terms, but for many Ladakhi leaders the explanation was simple: communalism. Ladakh's Buddhist and Shia Muslim populations were discriminated against by the Sunni Muslim–dominated Kashmir government. This complaint was voiced time and again in the course of the past seventy years, and Ladakh's political leaders consistently strove for some form of autonomy from Kashmir, with either Union

Territory status—implying direct rule from New Delhi—or outright statehood as ultimate goals. Autonomy, in whatever form, proved to be an elusive goal until the compromise of the Hill Development Council was reached in the wake of the 1989 agitation.

The Secret of Communalism

"It would be a tragedy if . . . the people of Ladakh remain unhappy and discontented, and thus an easy prey to all sorts of exploitation, both communalist and communist" (Karan Singh, letter to Nehru, 1951; cited in Singh 1982: 141).

The All-Ladakh Action Committee in the 1980s reflects local traditions of noncommunal activism in the region. This all-Ladakh ethos is exemplified also by the fact that Kargil's majority Shia voters have commonly supported the Buddhist candidate from Leh in elections to national parliament, while sending a Muslim to represent the district in the J&K Legislative Assembly.[21] Parallel to this broad identification with *Ladakhi* interests, there has also been a tradition of political activism along communal lines, pitching Buddhist Ladakh as the oppressed victim of Muslim Kashmiri discrimination. Communalism is widely believed to be the true character of Indian politics in general. Always controversial, and certainly after Independence publicly illegitimate, communalism was commonly regarded as the motivating force of J&K policy toward Ladakh.

Whereas ST status was reluctantly and belatedly put on the agenda in Ladakh, communalist diagnoses of the plight of the region were introduced as early as the 1930s around the time of the Glancy Commission of Inquiry into Grievances and Complaints. This commission was instituted by the government in the wake of severe unrest in the Kashmir Valley targeting the Hindu maharaja. Glancy's brief was specifically to solicit representations on the basis of community, and hence the composition of his commission reflected the officially recognized communal arithmetic of the state. Buddhists, however, were not invited to sit on the committee, and to ensure that their voice would be heard, a group of Kashmiri Pandits (Hindus), some of whom had converted to Buddhism, founded the Kashmir-Raj Bodhi Maha Sabha (KRBMS) and asked to be allowed to make a representation on behalf of all Buddhists in the state, almost all of whom, of course, were Ladakhis. This was granted and on 21 November 1931, three Kashmiris and a young Ladakhi student,

Sonam Norbu, presented the Buddhist community's submission to the commission, emphasizing the backwardness of the region and demanding suitable measures.

Among the initiatives proposed by the KRBMS was a ban on polyandry, the practice of several brothers marrying the same wife. Polyandry, in the view of the Pandits, was a major factor in the low growth rate of the Buddhist population. Its practice would lead to the demise of this last remaining stronghold of Buddhism in the state, as Muslims not only were deemed to be reproducing at a higher rate, but also to be actively converting Buddhists, for example, through marriage of "surplus" Buddhist women. The focus on polyandry, although certainly also reflecting a general disapproval of such immoral practices, powerfully illustrates the "general scramble for percentages that characterized the politics of the State at that time" (Ganhar and Ganhar 1956: 216). In 1934, as a consequence of the Glancy Commission's work, a legislative assembly, the Praja Sabha, was constituted with nominated members for Ladakh, as elections were deemed impossible in view of the geographic and educational situation of the region.[22] Around this time, a local Buddhist Education Society was founded, succeeded a few years later by the Young Men's Buddhist Association, which later changed its name to the Ladakh Buddhist Association. Both were established very much at the encouragement of local Pandits and KRBMS members.[23] Hence, by the late 1930s Leh's developmental and political landscape was already thoroughly communalized.

While communalist motives were routinely attributed to the state government, local and regional relations between Muslims and Buddhists were generally cordial. During Partition, although Pakistani "raiders" came to within a few miles of Leh, tensions between Muslims and Buddhists in Central Ladakh remained relatively low.[24] In the subsequent period, one of the arguments commonly used by Ladakhi political leaders in justifying their claims for autonomy or other kinds of special treatment was precisely the population's patriotism and noncommunalist ethos (van Beek 1998). It is only in 1969 and especially in 1989 that sustained communalist strategies were used in agitations for regional autonomy. The 1989 agitation for Union Territory status, which culminated in the granting of a Hill Council in 1995, was led by the Ladakh Buddhist Association (LBA) and involved a social boycott of the Muslim community for three years. The agitation was presented by the LBA and the media, both domestic and international, as a natural uprising of the discriminated Buddhist community. But for this image to stick, creative representation, image management, and arm twisting, as one agitation leader called it, were necessary. As in the case of the ST identification, a series of contradictions and inconsistencies needed to be "forgotten," while the publicly illicit character of communalism posed important restrictions on its use as a political strategy.

A first obstacle to be overcome was the absence of a cohesive Buddhist community in Ladakh. To be sure, a distinction is routinely made between Buddhists (referred to as *nang.pa* or "insiders") and non-Buddhists (*phyi.pa* or "outsiders"), but there are a host of socially, economically, politically, and geographically significant differentiations that militate against any easy all-Buddhist identification beyond this immediate, coarse dichotomization. Ladakhi society, like most Tibetan societies, is historically characterized by a strong hierarchical division of the population. There continue to be strong antagonisms among different sections of the nobility, who are also commonly affiliated with monastic establishments of different Tibetan Buddhist sects. Although doctrinal differences between sects and arguably sectarianism in general are generally not as important in Tibetan societies as they are in Christianity, the intersection of economic and political power with monastic establishments—for example, through landholdings, taxation, and religious patronage—sustains rivalries among households. The political salience of the clergy is also evident in the central role of religious authorities such as Kushok Bakula Rinpoche and his longstanding rivals Khanpo Rinpoche and Togdan Rinpoche.[25]

Many villages in Leh District have no or very few Muslim inhabitants, but several thousand Shia Muslims are settled along the Indus River near Leh, and there is a sizable Sunni community in the town itself. As intermarriage, especially with Sunnis, had not been uncommon, many people had kinship ties across "communities," and social and economic ties between households similarly crosscut religious divisions. In addition, there were rather banal realities to consider, such as that all butchers and bakers were local Muslims, and the vegetable market was an exclusively Kashmiri affair. There were, in other words, social as well as economic relationships that made mobilization on the basis of religious difference difficult.

There was also much difference in perception between village farmers and urban professionals of the state government's policies. Whereas those with modern education or business interests would lament the lack of government jobs, infrastructural development, or differential treatment, villagers commonly applauded the government as a provider of services, roads, canals, fertilizers, cheap rations, and other developmental boons. In the villages, there was no feeling of discrimination, and in the absence of Muslims in many villages, the issue of communalism simply did not stir up much emotion. Hence, the LBA leaders first built up a network of youth organizations and cultural associations in the villages to prepare the ground for the agitation, and in 1988–1989 leadership and Youth Wing activists toured the villages to "educate the people," as one activist put it, about the fact that Buddhists were, in fact, victims of discrimination. Despite these efforts, there was a real danger that a communal agitation would not be sustainable over time. Popular support could not be taken for granted, and a strong unified leadership was crucial, as the 1969 example had shown when the coalition of Bakula and his opponents fell apart within months.

Hence, two broad tasks lay before the LBA: first, to ensure and maintain popular compliance with the communal agitation, or at least to ensure that such broad support appeared to exist; second, to ensure that outside Ladakh public and political perceptions of the agitation were that the movement was noncommunal and democratic. Although communalism was seen as necessary in getting the attention and support of the central government, LBA leaders were well aware that communalism could not be officially rewarded with recognition of their demands. Or, to push the point a little further: although communalism was not much of a reality in daily life of most people in Ladakh, it must be represented as such, and although communalism needed to be represented as central to Ladakh's plight, it must be represented as involuntary, passive, imposed. Ladakh's Buddhists needed to argue like communalists and behave like communalists to fit the dominant discourse of Indian politics as they understood it, while simultaneously deploring communalism and insisting on the "age-old traditions of communal harmony."

Identifying the Buddhist Community

Soon after the agitation for Union Territory status was launched in June 1989 in the wake of clashes between Buddhist and Muslim youths, the LBA came out as the driving force behind the agitation. Initially, care had been taken to distinguish between (Ladakhi) Shia Muslims on the one hand, and "Pakistani agents" (Kashmiris) and their supporters (Sunni Muslims, Argons) on the other. A publication documenting the grievances and demands claimed to be the manifest of a Ladakh People's Movement for Union Territory Status, but soon this pretense was dropped and a social boycott was imposed on all Muslims in Ladakh. Officially, this move was said to have been necessary because of the reluctance or refusal of Shias to join the LBA-led movement, but there are indications that the communal strategy targeting all Muslims may have been planned from the start.[26] Within a short time, Buddhist bakers and butchers set up shops in Leh, and vegetable sellers appeared along the newly opened road from Manali in Himachal Pradesh. After three Buddhists were shot during a demonstration in Leh's main bazaar on 27 August 1989, an ultimatum was given to all Kashmiris to leave the district.[27] Efforts were made to mark Buddhist and Muslim spaces, structures, speech, and bodies unambiguously. Painters went to non-Muslim-owned shops to write the names in Tibetan script, helping shoppers to know where to go and which establishments to avoid. Radical youths started sporting earrings to signal their Buddhistness, while many Muslims stopped using the local greeting, "Julley," and instead offered a "Salaam." And on religious holidays loudspeakers on the main temple in Leh rang with the tape-recorded recitations of monks.[28]

At the swearing-in ceremony of the LAHDC in 1995, Governor Krishna Rao echoed Indian news reports and many academics' assessment of the agitation: "I am happy to note that your struggle has been peaceful and democratic means were used towards this end."[29] John Crook noted that "incidents of violence have been few, and have been denounced by the leadership" (1991: 238). This perception bears witness to the success with which the LBA managed the public image of the agitation, rather than the practice of the agitation. The LBA imposed a strict code of behavior on all Buddhists, with sanctions enforced by young vigilantes ranging from a fine to beatings and social boycott.[30] Signs of public support, such as the groups of volunteers—mostly women—who demonstrated daily in Leh Bazaar during 1989–1990 or who went on relay hunger strikes, or the thousands of people who showed up at mass rallies, were also realized through "arm twisting" such as the demand that each (Buddhist) household send a representative for such occasions. Noncompliance would incur a fine of several hundred rupees.

Having thus ensured some stability at home, the LBA sought to ensure that the correct view of Ladakh's predicament and aspirations were reported in India. Hence, they carefully groomed certain journalists from national newspapers, sometimes flying them in to Ladakh at their expense, ensuring they met with the desired spokespersons, witnesses, and politicians, and keeping them away from others. Consequently, the LBA rarely received negative press, not even during the explicitly communal phase of the agitation between 1989 and 1992. To add pressure on the central government and perhaps to exploit the escalating secessionist violence in the Kashmir Valley, the LBA also sought support from Hindu nationalist organizations such as the Vishwa Hindu Parishad (VHP) and Bharatiya Janata Party (BJP). Contacts with these organizations dated back to at least 1988, when the LBA had received support from the VHP in its campaign against the alleged abduction of Buddhist children by Christian missionaries in Srinagar. Overt political support from the BJP for the Union Territory demand was extended by Atal Behari Vajpayee at the BJP congress at Jammu in September 1990. However, in the wake of the demolition of the Babri Mosque in Ayodhya in December 1992 and the return to power of the Congress, the LBA leadership no longer maintained these contacts intensively.[31]

Neither subsequent opposition-led governments, such as those of V. P. Singh, nor the Congress regime of Narasimha Rao would want to be seen to reward communalist campaigns, and so the LBA was told that it should lift the boycott of the Muslim community and that negotiations over the future status of Ladakh would need to be conducted also with Muslim representatives. Although the boycott remained in force until late 1992, the political leaderships of LBA and Muslim organizations[32] gradually began to cooperate more closely and eventually a Coordination Committee was formed that also included a representative of the small Christian community in Leh. It was this joint Ladakhi representation that negotiated the final compromise solution of an Autonomous District Council, giving everyone the possibility to ignore or at least downplay any communalist element in the process or outcome of the agitation. Thus, the president, the prime minister, the governor, and the celebrants gathered on Leh's polo ground could all congratulate themselves and one another on the democratic and peaceful way in which India's pluralist, secular democracy had once again prevailed, allowing Ladakh's Hill Councilors to "bring out the full potential of this unique part of the J&K State and the Union of India."[33]

Conclusion: The Impossibility of Being a Ladakhi

There is a profound irony in the fact that each discursive strategy used to state Ladakh's "legitimate" case must rest on the exclusivist categorizations of bureaucratic and scientific formalism: ethnicization and communalization as the price for entry into the liberal democratic system, to join the world of nations on the march to freedom and prosperity. The official recognition of the series of specific tribal identities in Ladakh has had the paradoxical effect that *the* Ladakhis no longer exist. The recognition of the eight Scheduled Tribes has meant that almost all people in Ladakh now possess a picture I.D. stating unambiguously their identity: Bot/Boto, Balti, Changpa, and so on. At the same time, the success of the agitation for regional autonomy has been at the cost of a thorough communalization of Ladakhi society, dividing the population into Buddhists and Muslims. While the LBA leadership consciously chose a communal strategy in 1989 to get the attention of the government (because communalism was seen as the secret, because illegitimate, but real character of the Indian political system), a younger generation has come of age who are unfamiliar with the historical all-Ladakh antecedents of the struggle for Ladakh. Communalism for them is a way of life in accordance with reality. Yet, as I have sought to illustrate here, it would be a mistake to think that local identifications—the ways activists, politicians, bureaucrats, lawyers, and common people live their lives—are reducible to either "tribal" or "communal" identities. Nor can these two discourses of identity be differentiated by their degree of spuriousness, as both are products of imaginings with specific historical, scientific, and legal-bureaucratic antecedents.

In a recent article, Arjun Appadurai (1998) examines some of the consequences of "new frameworks of identity, entitlement, and spatial sovereignty." Echoing Anderson (1992), he argues that globalization has produced a new order of uncertainty in life, which is expressed, among other ways, in ethnic violence. Joining a host of anthropologists who draw on Mary Douglas's discussions of "matter out of place" to analyze ethnic violence, he uses Malkki's work on the genocide in Rwanda, in particular the problem of ambiguity of ethnic bodies, that cannot in the real world be consistent with the cosmologies they are meant to encode: "It is this reversal of Douglas' cosmologic that might best explain macabre patterns of violence directed against the body of the ethnic other; to eliminate the flux introduced by somatic variation, by mixture and intermarriage; and to evict the possibility of further somatic change or slippage" (Appadurai 1998: 232): ethnic violence, in short, as a means of eliminating uncertainty.

There are, in my opinion, two issues here. First, as Appadurai allows in a footnote, "Of course, not all forms of abstraction in social life conduce to violence, nor have such potentially violent forms of abstraction as the map, the census, and models of economic development always led to coercion or conflict" (1998: 240). Mindful of the facticity of all facts, classification and cosmologic are pervasive aspects of human existence, although the modes of their justification may differ (e.g., divine order, rationality, nature). Second, as Herzfeld reminds us, "Cultural identity is the material of national rhetoric, social variation that of everyday experience" (1992: 108). We all live in this "silly if not desperate place between the real and the really made-up" (Taussig 1993b: xviii). There is, in other words, little reason to treat complexity, disorder, and insecurity as experiences or conditions that are particularly new, or to assume that human beings are ill-equipped to handle them. As is well-known, corruption, turning a blind eye, and other forms of creative interpretation of rules are integral parts of the functioning of any bureaucratic order.[34]

Chatterjee's conclusion that the modern state "cannot recognize within its jurisdiction any form of community except the single, determinate, demographically enumerable form of the nation" (Chatterjee 1993: 238) is rather too pessimistic, I believe, for two reasons. First, although nationalism frequently tends toward ethnic/culturalist exclusivism, this is, as Anderson (1992) reminds us, not an inevitable movement.[35] Inclusivist conceptions of nations, even fuzzy ones are possible (Kaviraj 1992). Second, as I have sought to demonstrate through experiences from Ladakh, it is important to bear in mind that bureaucrats and politicians also must dissimulate. The purity demanded by legal and other formal systems of classification of populations cannot exist on the ground. To be sure, as Appadurai and others have argued, that impossibility may lead to ethnic cleansing and genocide, but it may also, as is rather more commonly the case, lead to a constant violation, creative interpretation, and experiential moderation of the hard, sharp rules of imagined orders. It may no longer be possible to be *a* Ladakhi, but there is no reason to think that therefore Ladakhis can no longer exist. Indeed, the absence of a formal-legal Ladakhi identity and the varied practices of identification that temper the officially sanctioned as well as unofficially practiced exclusions and inclusions may provide the space for the kind of social engagement that only too often is now located in romantic longings for primordial, original, authentic, cultural identity.

Notes

This essay draws on research conducted in Ladakh since 1985. I particularly want to thank current and previous leaders and activists of Buddhist and Muslim organizations, as well as many other individuals in Ladakh for their courage and openness in sharing documents and personal reflections. In view of the sensitivity of some of the matters discussed here, I have generally refrained from identifying the source of specific materials and information. Research in 1994–1995 was made possible by a Jennings Randolph Peace Scholar Award from the United States Institute of Peace, and supplemental support was provided by the Peace Studies Program, International Political Economy Program, and South Asia Program at Cornell University. Responsibility for what is presented here is solely mine.

1. Address by General K. V. Krishna Rao, PVSM (Retd), His Excellency the Governor of Jammu and Kashmir State to Ladakh Autonomous Hill Development Council, Leh, 3 September 1995; typescript.
2. Officially, the size of the region is 97,782 sq km, but this figure includes territories effectively under Pakistani and Chinese administration. Recent population figures, and hence precise relative shares of the different religious communities, are unavailable, as no regular census has been held in J&K since 1981.
3. *The Gazette of India*, extrapart II, section 1, 9 May 1995, p. 19.
4. Kargil District declined the offer of a Hill Council for the time being, although the Act provides for it, as people here feel that their greater proximity to and dependence on the Valley makes it less politic to risk antagonizing the Kashmiris. Regular shelling of Kargil town and the border area in recent years and the incursion that took place from across the line of control in 1999 are understood by people in Kargil to be retribution for their lack of support for the militant secessionists in Kashmir proper.
5. In South Asia, the term "communalism" refers to the evils of religious community partisanship.
6. See, e.g., Chandra (1984); Hansen (1999); Jaffrelot (1996); Kaviraj (1997a); Pandey (1990); Tambiah (1996); van der Veer (1994); Vanaik (1997).
7. I realize that this is a tricky proposition. I do not mean to suggest that only politicians think communalism is the name of the game, but I question the universality of the communalist logic implied by its recognition as a potent force in Indian political practice. My experience in Ladakh and elsewhere suggests that "identity fetishism" is especially a vice of scientists and politicians, of the national(ist) elites in general, perhaps.
8. The literature is vast, but important examples are Abraham (1996); Anderson (1991, 1998); Appadurai (1993); Cohn (1991); Hacking (1990); Jones (1981); Herzfeld (1992); Mitchell (1988); Pedersen (1986); Visvanathan (1988). For a review of the anthropological literature with reference to colonial states, see Pels (1997).
9. In Ladakh, it is possible to trace the same "ethnicizing" or "communalizing." Thanks to the encyclopedic urges of its administrators, students, and missionaries, this process can be traced in great detail. See, e.g., van Beek (1996, 1997a).
10. I take this point from Hindess (1997).
11. For genealogies of development, see, e.g., Escobar (1995); Esteva (1992); McMichael (1996).
12. An excellent historical discussion is offered by Metcalf (1994). Anthropology and sociology were not only instrumental in the designing and filling of the matrices, but also in the formulation and implementation of policies targeting these populations. Discussing academic anthropology in India, D. N. Majumdar noted in 1944 that "the training of personnel for manning the welfare services and feeding the research institutes has been given priority, for obvious reasons" (1961: xiv). To be sure, the racial interpretation of caste and tribe exempli-

fied by Risley's influential work (e.g., 1969) lost influence after independence, but its traces, particularly its essentializing of such "identities," continue to have considerable influence on Indian ethnographies, also those of Ladakh (e.g., Mann, 1986; and Bhasin, 1992).

13. In particular, the Mandal Commission report in the late 1980s triggered massive violence, including self-immolations by upper-middle-class youth on the streets of New Delhi. The controversy over reservations was one of the elements that led to the downfall of the Janata Dal–led coalition government of V. P. Singh. See, e.g., Hansen (1999: 140–45).
14. The quote is from a speech by Kushok Bakula Rinpoche, the representative of Ladakh's Buddhists in the Kashmir Legislative Assembly during the budget session on 12 May 1952. The late Sonam Stobdan Lachumir provided me with a manuscript version of the text, and Javed Mir Qasim helped to translate this from Urdu.
15. These data from the classified report on the Special Census conducted in 1986 and 1987 were published by Ladakhi Member of the Legislative Assembly of J&K Tsering Samphel in a letter to the editor of *The Daily Excelsior* newspaper, 16 March 1991.
16. Sham (*gsham*) is the name of the region of the lower Indus Valley roughly between the towns of Basgo and Khalatse.
17. The mess was "resolved" by drafting a limited list of sixty-odd categories, which was further reduced to about a dozen in the next few decades. By the time of Independence, the enumeration was abandoned altogether, except for SC and ST—which did not exist in Ladakh—and religion. For religion, census takers were instructed not to ask "What is your religion?" but "Are you a Hindu, Muslim, Sikh, Jain, Buddhist, or Christian?" These, too, are good examples of the creativity with which impossible purities are put into practice and made real. For a detailed discussion of the census classification process in Ladakh before Independence, see van Beek (1997a).
18. Both quotes from a letter from S. S. Hischey to the D.C., Leh, dated 20 August 1986; emphasis in the original.
19. For a discussion of aspects of these trading networks, see the autobiographical account of Abdul Wahid Radhu (1981), only recently published in English with an excellent introduction by José Cabezón (Henry 1997). On trade in Ladakh in general, see, e.g., Rizvi (1994, 1997, 1999); Warikoo (1985, 1990, 1995); Grist (1985).
20. The statement was issued in June 1993. Attached to it is an affidavit prepared by a lawyer, who offers the genealogical pedigree of the family, as well as citations of legal precedents from other parts of India. I have, of course, left out the names of the people concerned.
21. This is no longer the case. Since 1989, Congress has only once, in 1996, managed to win the Lok Sabha seat, but lost control again by a landslide in 1998. Most recently, in 1999, the National Conference Party candidate from Kargil defeated former LBA supreme Thupstan Chhewang. See van Beek (1999) for a discussion of this and other political developments in Ladakh since the granting of regional autonomy.
22. The commission of inquiry was followed by a Constitutional Reform Conference, also chaired by Glancy, and a Franchise Committee, which recommended the constitution of this parliament. For the recommendations, see Jammu and Kashmir (1932a; 1932b; 1934).
23. See, e.g., Bertelsen (1997) for a discussion of the role of Kashmiri Pandits in Buddhist organization in Ladakh in this period.
24. Local accounts vary, but apparently there was agreement to remain with India. A local militia

was raised to help defend the region and Muslims joined, albeit after initial hesitation or exclusion, depending on whose account one follows. There is as yet no thorough historical account of the Partition period in Ladakh. Kaul and Kaul (1992) offer an overview, albeit from a partisan perspective.

25. These three continue to play a prominent role on the political stage in Ladakh. In recent years Bakula Rinpoche has been serving as Indian Ambassador to Mongolia; presently, Thikse Rinpoche is a member of the Rajya Sabha and Togdan Rinpoche is a Minister of State for Ladakh Affairs in the J&K government of Farooq Abdullah. The impossibility of entirely reducing rivalries to sectarian differences is exemplified by the fact that Thikse Rinpoche has been an ardent opponent of Bakula Rinpoche since the early 1960s, although both belong to the same Tibetan Buddhist school, the Gelugpa (*dge.lugs.pa*).
26. There is no "hard" evidence of this in the form of documents, but personal accounts of Buddhist activists show that ostracization of all Muslims was intended from the start, particularly by the urban Buddhist youth. During secret meetings in the winter of 1988–1989, for example, several youths swore oaths never to have social contact with Muslims again. Today, these oaths are the subject of some amusement among activists who did not go so far and see some of their friends vainly struggling to keep them.
27. As a convoy, including buses carrying tourists, leaving the region was attacked near Khaltse, the news of the Buddhist uprising even made the international press.
28. In 1995 this practice escalated into a competition between the muezzin of the Leh Sunni mosque and the taped monks of the Chokhang, just across the street from one another. Whenever the Muslims were called to prayer, the sound of the monks rang out as well. A Buddhist activist joked that Buddhists also were now called to prayer five times a day. This still continued in the summer of 1999, despite much popular resentment.
29. Address by General K. V. Krishna Rao to LAHDC, 3 September 1995, p. 7.
30. Each offense carried a specific penalty, increasing with repeat offenders. Of course, such measures were kept secret, and even a document for internal use listing these sanctions merely stipulates "if transacts with X" as an offense, carefully avoiding naming the community. There is no such shyness about penalties; "transaction with X" is punishable with a fine up to Rs 500, and a "beating" is added in case of repetition. Other forms of punishment include *chhags* (prostrations), beating, and "sound beating." The unrepenting offender would ultimately face social boycott.
31. Historically, Ladakh has had close links with the Congress Party, but many Buddhists, especially youths, resigned their membership in 1989. Prior to the elections for the Hill Council, most rejoined Congress and only two seats were contested by non-Congress candidates. All seats on the first Hill Council were initially held by Congress members. Links with the BJP and other Hindu nationalist organizations have been revived in recent years, particularly since the rise to power of the BJP at the center (van Beek 1999).
32. Although in times of crisis statements are made on behalf of a Ladakh Muslim Organization, the LMA is no equivalent of the LBA, lacking as it does any formal status, membership, or statutes. There are two main Muslim organizations in Leh: the Anjuman-e Mu"in-e Islam is the main Sunni social organization; the Anjuman-e Imamia is its Shia counterpart. See Pinault (1999) for more detail.
33. Krishna Rao, address to the Hill Council.

34. This is not to deny the salience of the links between semantic purity and social action, but to question the rather easy causal linking of such orders with ethnic violence. Indeed, "new forms of identity, entitlement, and territorial sovereignty" are crucial in the mediation of this connection, as I have argued elsewhere (1997a).
35. See also the excellent collection edited by Cheah and Robbins (1998).

BIBLIOGRAPHY

Abraham, Itty. 1996. Science and power in the postcolonial state. *Alternatives* 21(4): 321–39.

Abrams, P. 1988. Notes on the difficulty of studying the state. *Journal of Historical Sociology* 1(1): 58–89.

Abu-Lughod, Lila. 1990. The romance of resistance: Tracing transformations of power through Bedouin women. *American Ethnologist* 17(1): 41–55.

Act (South Africa). 1995. *Statutes of the Republic of South Africa: Constitutional law. Promotion of national unity and reconciliation. Government Gazette.* Act no. 34 of 1995 as amended by Act no. 87 of 1995. South Africa.

African National Congress (ANC). 1996. *Resolution of ANC peace and security summit.* August–September.

———. 1997. *Strategies and tactics: Resolution adopted at 50th national congress in Mafekeng.* December. Available from www.anc.org.za/ancdocs/history/conf/conference50/strategyamend.html.

Afrikanerbond forges ties with ANC. 1999. *Electronic Mail and Guardian,* 27 August. www.mg.co.za.

Agamben, Giorgio. 1998. *Homo sacer: Sovereign power and bare life.* Stanford, CA: Stanford University Press.

Agnew, John. 1999. The new geopolitics of power. In *Human geography today,* ed. D. Massey, J. Allen, and P. Sarre. Cambridge, England: Polity Press.

Agnew, John, and Stuart Corbridge. 1995. *Mastering space: Hegemony, territory and international political economy.* London: Routledge.

Ahmad, Muneer. 1964. *The civil servant in Pakistan: A study of the background and attitudes of public servants in Lahore.* Karachi, India: Oxford University Press.

Albán Gómez, E., A. Andrango, and T. Bustamente, eds. 1993. *Los indios y el estado-pais: Pluriculturalidad y multi-etnicidad en el Ecuador.* Quito, Ecuador: Abya-Yala.

Allen, J. 1999. Spatial assemblages of power: From dominance to empowerment. In *Human geography today,* ed. D. Massey, J. Allen, and P. Sarre. Cambridge, England: Polity Press.

Almeida, I., ed. 1991. *Indios: Reflexiones sobre el levantamiento indígena.* Quito, Ecuador: ILDIS.

Alonso, Ana Maria. 1994. The politics of space, time and substance: State formation, nationalism, and ethnicity. *Annual Review of Anthropology* 23: 379–405.

———. 1995. *Thread of blood: Colonialism, revolution and gender on Mexico's northern frontier*. Tucson: University of Arizona Press.

Altbeker, A., and J. Steinberg. 1998. Reason and representation in National Party discourse, 1990–92. In *South Africa in Transition: New Theoretical Perspectives*, ed. D. Howarth and A. J. Norval. London: Macmillan.

The ANC triumphs at Mafekeng. 1997. *Electronic Mail and Guardian*, 23 December. www.mg.co.za.

Anderson, Benedict. 1991 (1983). *Imagined communities: Reflections on the origin and spread of nationalism*. London: Verso.

———. 1992. The new world disorder. *New Left Review* (193): 3–13.

———. 1998. Nationalism, identity, and the logic of seriality. In *The spectre of comparisons: Nationalism, Southeast Asia and the world*. London: Verso.

Andolina, Robert. 1999. *Colonial legacies and plurinational imaginaries: Indigenous movement politics in Ecuador and Bolivia*. Ph.D. diss. Minneapolis: University of Minnesota.

Angell, A. 1982. Classroom Maoists: The politics of Peruvian schoolteachers under military government. *Bulletin of Latin American Research* 1(2): 1–20.

Ansión, J. 1989. *La escuela an la comunidad campesina*. Lima: Proyecto Escuela, Ecología y Comunidad Campesina.

Ansion, J., D. del Castillo, M. Piqueras, and I. Zegarra. 1993. *La escuela en tiempos de Guerra: Una mirada a la educación desde la crisis y la violencia*. Lima, Peru: Tarea, Asociación de Publicaciones Educativas.

Appadurai, Arjun. 1993. Number in the colonial imagination. In *Orientalism and the postcolonial predicament: Perspectives on South Asia*, ed. Carol A. Breckenridge and Peter van der Veer. Philadelphia: University of Pennsylvania Press.

———. 1996. *Modernity at large: Cultural dimensions of globalization*. Minneapolis: University of Minnesota Press.

———. 1998. Dead certainty: Ethnic violence in the era of globalization. *Public Culture* 10(2): 225–47.

Arce Borja, L., ed. 1989. *Guerra popular en el Peru: El pensamiento Gonzalo*. Brussels: El Diario.

Arendt, Hannah. 1958. *The origins of totalitarianism*. London: Allen and Unwin.

Arnson, Cynthia L., ed. 1999. *The popular referendum and the future of the peace process in Guatemala*. Latin American Program, working paper no. 241. Washington, DC: Woodrow Wilson International Center for Scholars.

Asad, Talal. 1993. *Genealogies of religion: Discipline and reason of power in Christianity and Islam*. Baltimore: Johns Hopkins University Press.

Asmal, K., L. Asmal, and R. S. Roberts. 1997. *Reconciliation through truth: A reckoning of apartheid's criminal governance*. Cape Town, South Africa: David Phillip.

Baig, Tara Ali. 1979. *Our children*. New Delhi: Government of India, Ministry of Information and Broadcasting, Publications Division.

Bastos, Santiago, and Manuela Camus. 1995. *Abriendo Caminos: Las organizaciones mayas desde el Norel hasta el Acuerdo de derechos indigenas*. Ciudad de Guatemala, Guatemala: Flasco.

Bauman, Zugmunt. 1989. *Modernity and the Holocaust*. Ithaca, NY: Cornell University Press.

———. 1995. *Life in fragments: Essays in postmodern morality*. Oxford: Blackwell.
Bayart, J. F. 1991. Finishing with the idea of the third world: The concept of political trajectory. In *Rethinking third world politics*, ed. James Manor. London: Orient Longman.
Bayart, J. F., S. Ellis, and B. Hibou, eds. 1998. *The criminalization of the state in Africa*. London: James Currey.
Beasley-Murray, J. 1999. Learning from Sendero: Civil society theory and fundamentalism. *Journal of Latin American Cultural Studies* 8(1): 75–88.
Bertelsen, Kristoffer Brix. 1997. Protestant Buddhism and social identification in Ladakh. *Archives de sciences sociales des religions* 99 July–September: 129–51.
Bhasin, M. K. 1992. *Cold desert: Ladakh. Ecology and development*. Delhi: Kamla-Raj Enterprises.
Billig, Michael. 1995. *Banal nationalism*. London: Routledge.
Blasting a hole in crime stats. 1997. *Electronic Mail and Guardian*, 19 September. www.mg.co.za.
Booth, David, and Bernardo Sorj. 1983. *Military reformism and social classes: The Peruvian experience, 1968–80*. New York: St. Martin's Press.
Boraine, Alex. 1996a. *Alternatives and adjuncts to criminal prosecutions*. Paper presented at seminar Justice in cataclysm: Criminal tribunals in the wake of mass violence. Brussels, Belgium, 20–21 July.
———. 1996b. *Justice in cataclysm: Criminal tribunals in the wake of mass violence*. Paper delivered in Brussels, Belgium, 20–21 July.
Boraine, Alex, and Janet Levy. 1995. *The healing of a nation*. Cape Town, South Africa: Justice in Transition.
Boraine, Alex, Janet Levy, and Ronel Scheffer. 1994. *Dealing with the past: Truth and reconciliation in South Africa*. Cape Town, South Africa: IDASA.
Bourdieu, Pierre. 1977. *Outline of a theory of practice*. Cambridge, England: Cambridge University Press.
———. 1990. *The logic of practice*. Cambridge, England: Polity Press.
———. 1999. Rethinking the state: Genesis and structure of the bureaucratic field. In *State/Culture: State-formation after the cultural turn*, ed. G. Steinmetz. Ithaca, NY: Cornell University Press.
Breuilly, J. 1993. 2d ed. *Nationalism and the state*. Manchester, England: Manchester University Press.
Bricker, Victoria R. 1981. *The Indian Christ, the Indian king: The historical substrate of Maya myth and ritual*. Austin: University of Texas Press.
Brito, Alexandra Barahona de. 1997. *Human rights and democratization in Latin America: Uruguay and Chile*. Oxford: Oxford University Press.
Buddhists, Representatives of Kashmir. 1932. Memorandum of the Kashmir Buddhists. *The Mahabodhi* 40(3): 127–31.
Burga, Manuel, and Alberto Flores Galindo. 1979. *Apogeo y crisis de la república aristocrática*. Lima, Peru: Instituto de Estudios Peruanos.
Burton, Richard F. 1988 (1851). *Sindh and the races that inhabit the valley of the Indus*. Karachi, India: Indus Publishers.
———. 1993 (1877). *Sindh revisited: Government of Sindh*. Karachi, India: Department of Culture and Tourism.

Buur, Lars. 1998. *Processes of state formation: The South African Truth and Reconciliation Commission and the practices constituting the modern nation-state.* Paper delivered at the international seminar States of Imagination, Copenhagen: Denmark, 13–15 February.

———. 1999. *Monumental history: Visibility and invisibility in the work of the South African Truth and Reconciliation Commission.* Paper presented at the international conference "The TRC: Commissioning the past." Johannesburg, University of the Witwatersrand, 11–14 June.

Cancian, Frank. 1965. *Economics and prestige in a Mayan community: A study of the religious cargo system in Zinancatan.* Stanford, CA: Stanford University Press.

Can new leadership heal the ANC? 1997. *Electronic Mail and Guardian*, 12 December. www.mg.co.za.

Cape activists resist truth hearing. 1996. *Electronic Mail and Guardian*, 26 April. www.mg.co.za.

Carmack, R. M. 1995. *Rebels of highland Guatemala: The Quiché-Mayas of Momostenango.* Norman: University of Oklahoma Press.

Cassirer, Ernst. 1946. *The myth of the state.* New York: Doubleday Anchor.

Cawthra, G. 1993. Policing South Africa: The SAP and the transition from apartheid. Cape Town, South Africa: David Philips.

Census of India. 1951. New Delhi: Government of India Publications.

Chandavarkar, R. 1994. *The origins of industrial capitalism in India.* Cambridge, England: Cambridge University Press.

———. 1998. *Imperial power and popular politics.* Cambridge, England: Cambridge University Press.

Chandra, Bipan. 1984. *Communalism in modern India.* New Delhi: Vikas.

Chatterjee, Partha. 1986. *Nationalist thought and the colonial world: A derivative discourse?* London: Zed Books.

———. 1993. *The nation and its fragments: Colonial and postcolonial histories.* Princeton, NJ: Princeton University Press.

———. 1995. Religious minorities and the secular state: Reflections on an Indian impasse. *Public Culture* 8:11–39.

———. 1998. Beyond the nation? Or within? *Social Text* 16(39): 57–69.

Cheah, Pheng, and Bruce Robbins, eds. 1998. *Cosmopolitics: Thinking and feeling beyond the nation.* Minneapolis: University of Minnesota Press.

Cliquet, Robert, and Kristiaan Thienpont. 1995. *Population and development: A message from the Cairo conference.* Boston: Kluiwer Academic Publishers.

Coetzee, C. 1998. Krotoä remembered: A mother of unity, a mother of sorrows? In *Negotiating the past: The making of memory in South Africa*, ed. S. Nuttall and C. Coetzee. Cape Town, South Africa: Oxford University Press.

Cohn, Bernard. 1983. Representing authority in victorian India. In *The invention of tradition*, ed. Eric Hobsbawm and Terence Ranger. Cambridge, England: Cambridge University Press.

Cohn, Bernard S. 1987a. *An anthropologist among the historians and other essays.* Delhi: Oxford University Press.

———. 1987b. The census, social structure, and objectification in South Asia. In *An anthropologist among the historians and other essays*, ed. B. S. Cohn. New Delhi: Oxford University Press.

Cotjf Cuxil, Demetrio. 1996. The politics of Maya revindication. In *Maya cultural activism in Guatemala*, ed. Edward F. Fischer and R. McKenna Brown. Austin: Texas University Press.

———. 1997. Unidad del estastado y regiones autónomas mayas. In *Guatemala: Oprimida, pobre o princesa embrujada? Discusiones abiertas sobre economía y sociedad*, ed. Fridolin Birk. Ciudad de Guatemala, Guatemala: Friedrich Ebert Stiftung.

Collins, Jane L. 1988. *Unseasonal migrations: Rural labor scarcity in Peru*. Princeton, NJ: Princeton University Press.

Comisión de Esclaricimiento Histórica (CEH). 1999. *Memoria del silencio*. Available at http://hrdata.aaas.org/ceh/report/spanish/toc.html.

Connolly, W. E. 1991. *Identity/Difference*. London: Cornell University Press.

Consejo de Organizaciones Mayas de Guatemala (COMG). 1991. *Derechos especificos del pueblo maya*. Cuidad de Guatemala, Guatemala: COMG.

Consejo de Planificación Nacional para Indígenas y Negros (CONPLADEIN). 1997. *Comite de Gestión del PRODEPINE: Documento de trabajo*. Manuscript. Quito, Ecuador: CONPLADEIN.

Contreras, C. 1996. *Maestros, mistis y campesinos en el Perú rural del siglo XX*. Lima, Peru: Documento de Trabajo, Instituto de Estudios Peruanos.

Coronil, Fernando. 1997. *The magical state: Nature, money and modernity in Venezuela*. Chicago: University of Chicago Press.

Coronil, Fernando, and Julie Skurski. 1991. Dismembering and remembering the nation: The semantics of political violence in Venezuela. *Comparative Studies in Society and Culture* 33(2): 289–337.

Corrigan, Philip. 1994. State formation. In *Everyday forms of state formation: Revolution and the negotiation of rule in modern Mexico*, ed. Gilbert Joseph, and Daniel Nugent. Durham, NC: Duke University Press.

Corrigan, P., and D. Sayer. 1985. *The great arch: English state formation as cultural revolution*. Oxford: Basil Blackwell.

Cortés, S. 1960. Breve reseña histórica del instituto geográfico militar. In *Instituto Geográfico Militar 1928–1960*. Quito, Ecuador: IGM.

Crain, M. 1990. The social construction of national identity in highland Ecuador. *Anthropological Quarterly* 15(3): 43–59.

Crook, John Hurrell. 1991. Buddhist ethics and the problem of ethnic minorities: The case of Ladakh. In *Buddhist ethics and modern society*, ed. C. Wei-Hsun Fu and S. A. Wawrytko. New York: Greenwood Press.

Dandeker, C. 1990. *Surveillance, power and modernity*. Cambridge, England: Polity Press.

Dasgupta, Shahana. 1990. Child welfare legislation in India: Will Indian children benefit from the United Nations convention on the rights of the child? *Michigan Journal of International Law* 11: 1301–16.

Davidson, P. 1998. Museums and the reshaping of memory. In *Negotiating the past: The making of memory in South Africa*, ed. S. Nuttall and C. Coetzee. Cape Town, South Africa: Oxford University Press.

Davis, Shelton H. 1997. *La tierra de nuestros antepasados: Estudio de la herencia de tierra en el altiplano de Guatemala*. Antigua, VT: CIRMA and Plumsock Mesoamerican Studies.

Deacon, H. 1998. Remembering tragedy, constructing modernity: Robben Island as a national monument. In *Negotiating the past: The making of memory in South Africa*, ed. S. Nuttall and C. Coetzee. Cape Town, South Africa: Oxford University Press.

Dean, Mitchell. 1999. *Governmentality: Power and rule in modern society.* Thousand Oaks, CA: Sage Publications.

Dean, Mitchell, and Barry Hindess, eds. 1998. *Governing Australia: Studies in contemporary rationalities of government.* New York: Cambridge University Press.

Death and drudgery on the beat. 1997. *Electronic Mail and Guardian,* 20 June. www.mg.co.za.

De Brito, A. B. 1997. *Human rights and democratization in Latin America: Uruguay and Chile.* Oxford: Oxford University Press.

de Certeau, Michel. 1984. *The practice of everyday life.* Berkeley: University of California Press.

Degregori, C. I. 1990. *Ayacucho 1969–1979: El surgimiento de Sendero Luminoso.* Lima, Peru: Instituto de Estudios Peruanos.

———. 1991. How difficult it is to be God: Ideology and political violence in Sendero Luminoso. *Critique of Anthropology* 2(3): 233–50.

De Jong, Ferdinand. 2000. *The power of secrecy: Performance and the politics of locality in Casamance, Senegal.* Ph.D. diss., University of Amsterdam.

De Klerk, F. W. 1997. *Submission to the Truth and Reconciliation Commission.* http://www.truth.org.za/np-truth.htm.

———. 1990. Eensgesindheid binne bereik. *RSA Beleidsoorsig* (7).

Derrida, J. 1973. *Speech and phenomena.* Evanston, IL: Northwestern University Press.

de Sardan, Olivier. 1999. A moral economy of corruption in Africa. *Journal of Modern African Studies* 37(1): 25–52.

Dhareshwar, V., and R. Srivatsan. 1996. Rowdy sheeters: An essay on subalternity and politics. Subaltern Studies 9. Delhi: Oxford University Press.

Dijkink, G. 1996. *National identity and geopolitical visions.* London: Routledge.

Dillon, Michael. 1995. Sovereignty and governmentality: From the problematics of the "New World Order" to the ethical problematic of the world order. *Alternatives* 20: 323–68.

Dirks, Nicholas. 1987. *The hollow crown: Ethnohistory of an Indian kingdom.* Cambridge, England: Cambridge University Press.

Douglas, Mary. 1966. *Purity and danger: An analysis of concepts of pollution and taboo.* London: Routledge and Kegan Paul.

Drew, Frederic. 1976 (1875). *The Jummoo and Kashmir territories.* New Delhi: Cosmo Publications.

Drysdale, R., and R. Myers. 1975. Continuity and change: Peruvian education. In *The Peruvian experiment,* ed. Abraham Lowenthal. Princeton, NJ: Princeton University Press.

Duffield, Mark. 1998. *Aid policy and post-modern conflict: A critical policy review.* School of Public Policy, discussion paper no. 19. Birmingham, England: University of Birmingham.

———. 2001. *Global governance and the new wars: The merging of development and security.* London: Zed Books.

Dumont, Louis. 1980. *Homo hierarchicus.* Chicago: University of Chicago Press.

Eickelman, F. Dale, and J. Piscatori. 1996. *Muslim politics.* Princeton, NJ: University Press.

Ellis, Stephen. 1998. The historical significance of South Africa's Third Force. *Journal of Southern African Studies,* vol. 24(2): 261–99.

Escobar, Arturo. 1995. *Encountering development.* Princeton, NJ: Princeton University Press.

Escolar, M., S. Quintero, and C. Reboratti. 1994. Geographical identity and patriotic representation in Argentina. In *Geography and national identity,* ed. D. Hooson. Oxford: Blackwell.

Esquit, Edgar, and Iván García. 1999. *El derecho consuetudinario y la reforma legal en Guatemala*. Ciudad de Guatemala, Guatemala: Flasco.

Esteva, Gustavo. 1992. Development. In *The development dictionary: A guide to knowledge and power*, ed. Wolfgang Sachs. London: Zed Books.

Evans, P., D. Ruschemeyer, and T. Skocpol, eds. 1985. *Bringing the state back in*. Cambridge, England: Cambridge University Press.

Ewing, Katherine P. 1983. The politics of Sufism: Redefining the saints of Pakistan. *Journal of Asian Studies* 42(2): 251–68.

———. 1997. *Arguing sainthood: Modernity, psychoanalysis, and Islam*. Durham, NC: Duke University Press.

Ex-spy Williamson clashes with Pik. 1995. *Electronic Mail and Guardian*, 27 December. www.mg.co.za.

Falla, R. 1978. *Quiché rebelde*. Cd. de Guatemala: Editorial Universitaria de Guatemala.

Feldman, Allan. 1991. *Formations of violence*. Chicago: University of Chicago Press.

Felstiner, W., R. Abel, and A. Sarat. 1980. The emergence and transformation of disputes: Naming, blaming, claiming. *Law and Society Review* 15(3–4): 631–54.

Ferguson, James. 1990. *The anti-politics machine: "Development," depoliticization, and bureaucratic power in Lesotho*. Minneapolis: University of Minnesota Press.

Fernandez, Lovell. 1991. *Police abuses of non-political criminal suspects: A survey of practices in the Cape Peninsula*. Cape Town, South Africa: University of Cape Town, Institute of Criminology.

Fischer, Edwin F., and R. McKenna Brown, eds. 1996. *Maya cultural activism in Guatemala*. Austin: University of Texas Press.

Fivaz takes on Mbeki Police Squad. 1997. *Electronic Mail and Guardian*, 1 October. www.mg.co.za.

Fog Olwig, Karen. 1997. Cultural sites: Sustaining home in a deterritorialized world. In *Siting culture: The shifting anthopological object*, ed. Karen Fog Olwig and Kirsten Hastrup. London: Routledge.

Foucault, Michel. 1977. *Discipline and punish: The birth of the prison*. London: Allan Lane.

———. 1978. *The History of Sexuality*. Vol. 1. New York: Random House.

———. 1979a. *Discipline and punish: The birth of the prison*. New York: Vintage Books.

———. 1979b. *The History of Sexuality*. Vol. 1. London: Allen Lane.

———. 1980. *Power/Knowledge*, ed. Colin Gordon. Brighton, England: Harvester Wheatsheaf.

———. 1982. Afterword: The subject and power. In *Beyond structuralism and hermeneutics*, ed. Hubert Dreyfuss and Paul Rabinow. Chicago: University of Chicago Press.

———. 1984. On the genealogy of ethic. In *The Foucault reader*, ed. Paul Rabinow. Harmondsworth, England: Penguin.

———. 1984. Space, knowledge and power. In *The Foucault reader*, ed. Paul Rabinow. Harmondsworth, England: Penguin.

———. 1988a. The ethic of the care of the self as a practice of freedom. In *The Final Foucault*, ed. J. Bernauer and D. Rasmussen. Cambridge, MA: MIT Press.

———. 1988b: The political technology of individuals. In *Technologies of the self: A seminar with Michel Foucault*, ed. L. H. Martin, H. Gutman, and P. H. Hutton. London: Tavistock.

———. 1988c. Politics and reason. In *Politics, philosophy, culture: Interviews and other writings 1977–1984*, ed. L. D. Kritzman. New York: Routledge.

———. 1991. Governmentality. In *The Foucault effect: Studies in governmentality*, ed. Graham Burchell, Colin Gordon, and Peter Miller. London: Harvester Wheatsheaf.

———. 1997a. *The essential works 1954–1984*, vol. 1, *Ethics, subjectivity and truth*, ed. Paul Rabinow. New York: New Press.

———. 1997b. *'Il faut défendre la société'*. Paris: Gallimard/Seuil.

Freitag, Sandria. 1996. Contesting in public: Colonial legacies and contemporary communalism. In *Contesting the nation: Religion, community, and the politics of democracy in India*, ed. David Ludden. Philadelphia: University of Pennsylvania Press.

Friedman, J. 1992. Myth, history and political identity. *Cultural Anthropology* 7(2): 194–210.

Ganhar, J. N., and P. N. Ganhar. 1956. *Buddhism in Kashmir and Ladakh*. New Delhi: Authors.

García González, G. 1992. *Resumen de geografía, historia y cívica*. Ciclo básico, 1. curso. Quito, Ecuador: Editora Andina.

Geertz, Clifford. 1980. *Negara: The theatre state in nineteenth-century Bali*. Princeton, NJ: Princeton University Press.

Giddens, Anthony. 1985. *The nation-state and violence*. Cambridge, England: Polity Press.

———. 1992. *The consequences of modernity*. Stanford, CA: Stanford University Press.

Gillis, J. R. 1994a. Memory and identity: The history of a relationship. In *Commemorations: The politics of national identity*, ed. J. R. Gillis. Princeton, NJ: Princeton University Press.

Gilmartin, David. 1988. *Empire and Islam: Punjab and the making of Pakistan*. Berkeley: University of California Press.

Girard, René. 1977. *Violence and the sacred*. Baltimore: Johns Hopkins University Press.

Gitlitz, John. 1979. Conflictos políticos en la sierra norte del Perú: La montonera Benel contra Leguía, 1924. *Estudios Andinos* 9(16).

Gledhill, John, 1994. *Power and its disguises: Anthropological perspectives on politics*. Boulder, CO: Pluto Press.

Goffman, Erving. 1959. *The presentation of self in everyday life*. Harmondsworth, England: Penguin Books.

Goldblatt, B., and S. Meintjes. 1996. *Gender and the Truth and Reconciliation Commission*. A submission to the Truth and Reconciliation Commission. May. http://www.truth.org.za/submit/gender.htm.

Goodenough, Cheryl. 1999a. Richmond: One man's war? *Crime and Conflict* 15, autumn.

———. 1999b. Who killed Sifiso Nkabinde? In *Helen Suzman Foundation, Kwa-zula natal briefing* 14. Helen Suzman Dunbar: Helen Suzman Foundation.

Gootenberg, P. 1989. *Between silver and guano: Commercial policy and the state in post-independence Peru*. Princeton, NJ: Princeton University Press.

———. 1993. *Imagining development: Economic ideas in Peru's "fictitious prosperity."* Berkeley: University of California Press.

Gorriti, G. 1990. *Sendero: Historia de la guerra milenaria en el Peru*. Lima: Editorial Apoyo.

———. 1999. *The Shining Path: A history of the millenarian war in Peru*. Chapel Hill: University of North Carolina Press.

Gose, P. 1994. *Deathly waters and hungry mountains: Agrarian ritual and class formation in an Andean town*. Toronto: University of Toronto Press.

Government of India. 1985. *A Decade of ICDS: Integrated Child Development Services*. New Delhi: Ministry of Human Resources Development, Department of Women's Welfare.

Gramsci, Antonio 1971. *Selections from the prison notebooks*. London: Lawrence and Wishart.

Greenhalgh, Susan. 1999. Planned births, unplanned persons: "Population." In *The making of Chinese modernity*. Unpublished manuscript.

Griffiths, Anne M. O. 1997. *In the shadow of marriage: Gender and justice in an African community*. Chicago: University of Chicago Press.

Griffiths, John. 1986. What is legal pluralism? *Journal of Legal Pluralism and Unofficial Law* 24: 1–55.

Grist, Nicola. 1985. Ladakh, a trading state. In *Ladakh, Himalaya occidental: Ecologie, ethnologie. Proceedings of the 2nd colloquium of the International Association for Ladakh Studies*, ed. C. Dendaletche and P. Kaplanian. Pau, France: Centre Pyrénéen de Biologie et Anthropologie des Montagnes.

———. 1994. The use of obligatory labour for porterage in pre-independence Ladakh. In *Tibetan studies: Proceedings of the 7th seminar of the International Association for Tibetan Studies, Fagernes 1992*, ed. P. Kvaerne. Oslo: Institute for Comparative Research in Human Culture.

Guha, Ranajit. 1999 (1983). *Elementary aspects of peasant insurgency in colonial India*. Foreword by James Scott. Durham, NC: Duke University Press.

Gupta, Akhil. 1995. Blurred boundaries: The discourse of corruption, the culture of politics, and the imagined state. *American Ethnologist* 22(2): 375–402.

———. 1998. *Postcolonial developments*. Durham, NC: Duke University Press.

Gupta, Akhil, and James Ferguson. 1992. Beyond culture: Space, identity and the politics of difference. *Cultural Anthropology* 7(1): 6–23.

Hacking, Ian. 1982. Biopower and the avalanche of printed numbers. *Humanities in Society* 5(3): 279–95.

———. 1990. The taming of chance. In *Ideas in context*, ed. Richard Rorty. Cambridge, England: Cambridge University Press.

Hadot, Pierre. 1995. *Philosophy as a way of life*. Oxford: Basil Blackwell.

Hale, Charles. 1996. Political ideas and ideologies in Latin America, 1870–1930. In *Ideas and ideologies in twentieth century Latin America*, ed. Leslie Bethell. Cambridge, England: Cambridge University Press.

———. 1997. Consciousness, violence, and the politics of memory in Guatemala. *Current Anthropology* 38(5): 817–38.

Hansen, Thomas Blom. 1996. Recuperating masculinity: Hindu nationalism, violence and the exorcism of the Muslim "other." *Critique of Anthropology* 16(2): 137–72.

———. 1997a. Inside the romanticist episteme. *Thesis Eleven* 48: 21–41.

———. 1997b. *Segmented worlds: Work, livelihood and identity in central Mumbai*. Paper delivered at the conference Workers in Mumbai, Mumbai, 20–23 November.

———. 1998. BJP and the politics of Hindutva in Maharashtra. In *The BJP and compulsions of politics in India*, ed. T. B. Hansen and C. Jaffrelot. Delhi: Oxford University Press.

———. 1999. *The saffron wave: Hindu nationalism and democracy in modern India*. Princeton, NJ: Princeton University Press.

———. 2000. Predicaments of secularism: Muslim identities and politics in Mumbai. *Journal of the Royal Anthropological Institute* 6(2): 255–72.

Harding, C. 1987. Antonio Diaz Martinez and the ideology of Sendero Luminoso. *Bulletin of Latin American Research* 7(1): 65–73.

Handy, Jim. 1994. *Revolution in the countryside: Rural conflict and agrarian reform in Guatemala, 1944–1954*. Chapel Hill: University of North Carolina Press.

Hayner, Priscilla. 1994. Fifteen truth commissions, 1974 to 1994: A comparative study. *Human Rights Quarterly* 16: 597–655.

———. 1996. Commissioning the truth: Further research questions. *Third World Quarterly* 17(1): 19–29.

———. 1997. *International guidelines for the creation and operation of the truth commissions: A preliminary proposal*. New York: World Policy Institute, New School for Social Research.

Heaver, Richard. 1989. *Improving family planning, health, and nutrition outreach in India*. World Bank Discussion Papers no. 59. Washington, DC: World Bank.

Henry, Gray, ed. 1997. *Islam in Tibet and the illustrated narrative Tibetan caravans*. Louisville, KY: Fons Vitae.

Hepple, Leslie. 1992. Metaphor, geopolitical discourse and the military in South America. In *Writing worlds*, ed. J. Duncan and T. Barnes. London: Routledge.

Herzfeld, Michael. 1992. *The social production of indifference: Exploring the symbolic roots of Western bureaucracy*. Chicago: University of Chicago Press.

———. 1998. Factual fissures: Claims and contexts. *Annals of the American Academy of Political and Social Sciences* 560: 69–82.

Hindess, Barry. 1996. *Discourses of power: From Hobbes to Foucault*. London: Blackwell.

———. 1997. Politics and governmentality. *Economy and Society* 26(2): 257–72.

———. 1998. Divide and govern. *European Journal of Social Theory* 1(1): 57–70.

Hinojosa, I. 1998. On poor relations and the nouveau riche: Shining Path and the radical Peruvian left. In *Shining Path and other paths: War and society in Peru, 1980–1995*, eds. Stern. Durham, NC: Duke University Press.

Hirsh, Susan F. 1998. *Pronouncing and persevering: Gender and the discourse of disputing in an African Islamic court*. Chicago: University of Chicago Press.

Hobbes, Thomas. 1968 (1651). *Leviathan*. London: Penguin.

Hobsbawm, Eric. 1965. *Primitive rebels: Studies in archaic forms of social movement in 19th and 20th centuries*. London: Norton.

———. 1990. *Nations and nationalism since 1780*. Cambridge, England: Cambridge University Press.

Holiday, David, and William Sanley (forthcoming). *From fragmentation to a national project? Peace implementation in Guatemala*. Stanford, CA: Stanford Center for International Studies, International Peace Academy.

Holomisa, Bantu. 1998. Richmond violence: The UDM position. *Sunday Independent*, 2 August 1998.

Hooker, M. B. 1975. *Legal pluralism: An introduction to colonial and neo-colonial laws*. Oxford: Clarendon Press.

Hooson, David, ed. 1994. *Geography and national identity*. Oxford: Blackwell.

Horkheimer, Max, and Theodor W. Adorno. 1969 (1944). *Dialektik der Aufklärung: Philosophische Fragmente*. Frankfurt am Main: S. Fischer Verlag.

Human Rights Committee and Network of Independent Monitors (HRC/NIM). 1998. *Richmond: Role of security forces*. Commissioned report. Johannesburg: HRC/NIM.

Huntington, Samuel. 1968. *Political order in changing societies.* New Haven: Yale University Press.

Ibarra, Alicia. 1992. *Los indígenas y el estado en el Ecuador.* Quito, Ecuador: Abya-Yala.

Institute of Democratic Alternative in South Africa (IDASA). 1998. *IDASA Opinion Poll 99.* Cape Town: IDASA.

Institute for Security Studies (ISS). 1998. *Crime in Cape Town: Results of a city victim survey.* Monograph series no. 23. Pretoria, South Africa: ISS.

Iyob, Ruth. 1995. *The Eritrean struggle for independence: Domination, resistance, nationalism 1941–1993.* Cambridge, England: Cambridge University Press.

Jaffrelot, Christophe. 1996. *The Hindu nationalist movement in Indian politics.* New York: Columbia University Press.

Jalal, Ayesha. 1995. *Democracy and authoritarianism in South Asia.* Cambridge, England: Cambridge University Press.

James, P. 1996. *Nation formation: Towards a theory of abstract community.* London: Sage.

Jammu and Kashmir Government 1932a. *Report of the commission appointed under the orders of H.H. the Maharaja Bahadur, November 12, 1931, to enquire into grievances and complaints.* Jammu, India: Ranbir Government Press.

———. 1932b. *Report of the Kashmir constitutional reforms conference.* Jammu, India: Ranbir Government Press.

———. 1934. *Report of the Franchise Committee.* Jammu, India: Ranbir Government Press.

Jensen, Steffen. 1999a. Discourses of violence: Coping with violence on the Cape flats. *Social Dynamics* 25(2): 74–97.

———. 1999b. *Privatizing space: On social control and the emergence of private security in South Africa.* Cape Town, South Africa: University of Cape Town, Institute of Criminology.

Jensen, Steffen, and Simon Turner. 1996. *A place called Heideveld: Strategies and identities among coloureds in Cape Town, South Africa.* Research report no. 112. Roskilde: Roskilde University, Institutes of Geography and International Development Studies.

Jessop, Bob. 1990. *State theory: Putting capitalist states in their place.* Cambridge, England: Polity Press.

Jones, K. W. 1981. Religious identity and the Indian census. In *The census in British India: New perspectives,* ed. N. G. Barrier. New Delhi: Manohar.

Jordan, Z. Pallo. 1998. *The national question in post-1994 South Africa.* A discussion paper in preparation for the ANC's 50th national conference. Available at www.anc.org.za/ancdocs/discussion/natquestion.html.

Joseph, Gilbert, and Daniel Nugent. 1994a. Popular culture and state formation in revolutionary Mexico. In *Everyday forms of state formation: Revolution and the negotiation of rule in modern Mexico,* ed. G. Joseph and D. Nugent. Durham, NC: Duke University Press.

———, eds. 1994b. *Everyday forms of state formation: Revolution and the negotiation of rule in modern Mexico.* Durham, NC: Duke University Press.

Kantorowicz, Ernst 1957. *The king's two bodies.* Princeton, NJ: Princeton University Press.

Kashmir Raj Bodhi Maha Sabha (KRBMS). 1935. *Triennial report of the Kashmir Raj Bodhi Maha Sabha.* Srinagar: KRBMS.

Kaul, Shridhar, and H. N. Kaul. 1992. *Ladakh through the ages: Towards a new identity.* New Delhi: Indus Publishing Company.

Kaviraj, Sudipta. 1992. The imaginary institution of India. In *Subaltern Studies 7*, ed. P. Chatterjee and G. Pandey. Delhi: Oxford University Press.

———. 1994. On the construction of colonial power: Structure, discourse, hegemony. In *Contesting colonial hegemony*, ed. Dagmar Engels and Shula Marks. London: British Academic Press.

———. 1997a. The modern state in India. In *Dynamics of state formation: India and Europe compared*, ed. M. Dornboos and S. Kaviraj. New Delhi: Sage Publications.

———. 1997b. Religion and identity in India. *Ethnic and Racial Studies* 20(2): 325–44.

———. 1998. Filth and the "public sphere": Concepts and practices about space in the city of Calcutta. *Public Culture* 10(1).

Kaye, M. 1997. The role of truth commissions in the search for justice, reconciliation and democratisation: The Salvadorean and Honduran cases. *Journal of Latin American Studies* 4.

Khilnani, Sunil. 1997. *The idea of India*. Harmondsworth, England: Penguin.

Klarén, P. 1986. The origins of modern Peru: 1880–1930. In *The Cambridge history of Latin America*. Vol. 5. Cambridge, England: Cambridge University Press.

———. 1973. *Modernization, dislocation and aprismo*. Latin American Monographs no. 32. Austin: University of Texas, Institute of Latin American Studies.

———. 2000. *Peru: Society and nationhood in the Andes*. New York: Oxford University Press.

Kobrak, P. H. R. 1997. *Village troubles: The civil patrols in Aguacatán, Guatemala*. Ph.D. diss. University of Michigan.

Krishnaswamy, J. 1966. *A riot in Bombay, Aug. 11, 1893: A study of Hindu-Muslim relations in Western India in the nineteenth century*. University of Chicago: Department of History (microfilm).

Krog, A. 1995. The South African road. In *The Healing of a Nation?*, ed. A. Boraine and J. Levy, Cape Town, South Africa: Justice in Transition.

Laclau, Ernesto. 1990. *New reflections on the revolution of our time*. London: Verso.

———. 1996. *Emancipation(s)*. Chicago: University of Chicago Press.

Laclau, Ernesto, and Chantal Mouffe. 1985. *Hegemony and socialist strategy: Towards a radical democratic politics*. London: Verso.

Lan, David. 1985. *Guns and rain: Guerrillas and spirit mediums in Zimbabwe*. London: James Currey.

Latour, Bruno. 1986. The powers of association. In *Power, action and belief: A new sociology of knowledge*, ed. John Law. London: Routledge.

———. 1993. *We have never been modern*. Cambridge, MA: Harvard University Press.

Lavie, S., and T. Swedenburg, eds. 1996. *Displacement, diaspora and the geographies of identity*. London: Duke University Press.

Lefebvre, H. 1991. [1974]. *The Production of space*. Oxford: Blackwell Publishers.

Lefort, Claude. 1988. *Democracy and political theory*. Cambridge, England: Polity Press.

Lele, Jayant. 1995. Saffronization of Shiv Sena: The political economy of city, state and nation. In *Bombay: Metaphor of modern India*, ed. Sujata Patel and Alice Thorner. Bombay: Oxford University Press.

Letter to Soweto: Close to fire. 1995. *Electronic Mail and Guardian*, 24 February. www.mg.co.za.

Linares, A. 1988. La maraña bureaucratico-legislativo y la situación de los llamados "Polos de Desarollo y Servicios." In *CIEDEG Guatemala: Polos de Desarollo*. Ciudad de Mexico, Mexico: Editorial Praxis.

Livingstone, David N. 1992. *The geographical tradition: Episodes in the history of a contested enterprise*. Oxford: Blackwell.

Lowenthal, Abraham. 1975. Peru's ambiguous revolution. In *The Peruvian experiment: Continuity and change under military rule*, ed. A. Lowenthal. Princeton, NJ: Princeton University Press.

Lui-Bright, Robyn. 1997. International/National: Sovereignty, governmentality and international relations. *Australian Political Studies* (conference proceedings) 2: 581–97.

Maiguashca, Juan. 1983. La cuestión regional en la historia ecuatoriana (1830–1972). In *Nueva Historia del Ecuador*, Vol. 12, *Ensayos generales*, ed. E. Ayala Mora. Quito, Ecuador: Corporación Editora Nacional.

Majumdar, D. N. 1961. *Races and cultures of India*. Bombay: Asia Publishing House.

Malan, Rian. 1990. *My traitor's heart*. London: Vintage.

Mallon, Florencia. 1983. *The defense of community in Peru's Central Highlands*. Princeton, NJ: Princeton University Press.

———. 1994. Reflections on the ruins: Everyday forms of state Formation in nineteenth-century Mexico. In G. M. Joseph and D. Nugent, eds. *Everyday forms of state Formation: Revolution and the negotiation of rule in modern Mexico*. Durham, NC: Duke University Press.

———. 1995. *Peasant and nation: The making of postcolonial Mexico and Peru*. Berkeley: University of California Press.

———. 1999. *Decoding the parchments of the Latin American nation-state: Peru, Mexico and Chile in comparative perspective*. Paper presented to the conference The Formation of the Nation-State in Latin America, Institute of Latin American Studies, University of London, May.

Mamdani, Mahmoud. 1996a. *Citizen and subject*. Princeton, NJ: Princeton University Press.

———. 1996b. Reconciliation without justice. *Southern Review of Books*, no. 46, November–December.

———. 1997. From justice to reconciliation: Making sense of the African experience. In *Crisis and reconstruction: African perspectives*, ed. Colin Leys and Mahmood Mamdani. Discussion paper 8. Uppsala: Nordiska Afrikainstitutet.

Mandela, Nelson. 1994. *One Nation, many cultures*. Pretoria: Government of South Africa.

Mann, M. 1988. *States, war and capitalism: Studies in political sociology*. Oxford: Basil Blackwell.

Mann, R. S. 1986. The Ladakhis: A cultural ecological perspective. In *Ecology, economy and religion of the Himalayas*, ed. by L. P. Vidyarthi and M. Jha. Delhi: Orient Publications.

Manrique, N. 1995a. La caída de la cuarta espada y los senderos que bifurcan. *Márgnes* 8(13–14): 11–42.

———. 1995b. Political violence, ethnicity and racism in Peru in time of war. *Journal of Latin American Cultural Studies* 4(1): 5–18.

Massey, Doreen, John Allen, and Phillip Sarre, eds. 1999. *Human geography today*. Cambridge, England: Polity Press.

Mbeki, Thabo. 1999. Statements to the Afrikanerbond. Pretoria. 27 July. Available at www.anc.org.za.

Mbembe, Achille. 1992. Provisional notes on the postcolony. *Africa* 62(1): 3–37.

McCreery, David. 1994. *Rural Guatemala 1760–1940*. Stanford, CA: Stanford University Press.

McMichael, Philip D. 1996. Development and social change: A global perspective. In *Sociology for a new century*, ed. W. G. Charles Ragi and Larry Griffin. Thousand Oaks, CA: Pine Forge Press.

Meiring G. L. N.d. *Address to the Truth and Reconciliation Commission by the chief of the South African National Defence Force, General G. L. Meiring*. See www.truth.org.za/submit/sandf.htm.

Merry, Sally Engle. 1988. Legal pluralism. *Law and Society Review* 22: 869–96.

———. 1992. Anthropology, law and processes. *Annual Review of Anthropology* 21: 357–79.
———. 1993. Legal pluralism and transnational culture. In *Human rights, culture and context*, ed. Richard Wilson. London: Pluto Press.
Merwe, H. van der, P. Dewhirst, and B. Hamber. 1999. Non-governmental organisations and the Truth and Reconciliation Commission: An impact assessment. *Politikon* 26(10).
Metcalf, Thomas R. 1994. Ideologies of the Raj. In *The new Cambridge history of India*, vol. 3, ed. G. Johnson. Cambridge, England: Cambridge University Press.
Midgley, James. 1975. *Crime and punishment in South Africa*. Johannesburg: McGraw-Hill.
Migdal, Joel. 1988. *Strong societies and weak states*. Princeton, NJ: Princeton University Press.
Miller, Peter, and Nikolas Rose. 1990. Governing economic life. *Economy and Society* 19(1): 1–31.
———. 1997. *National evaluation of integrated child development services*. New Delhi: NIPCCD.
Mische, Ann. 1995. Projecting democracy: The formation of citizenship across youth networks in Brazil. *Citizenship, Identity and Social History, International Review of Social History* 40(3): 131–58.
Mision de Las Naciones Unidas en Guatemala (MINUGUA), ed. 1995. *Acuerdo sobre identidad y derechos de los pueblos, 31 de marzo de 1995*. Guatemala: MINUGUA.
———. 1998. Unpublished data on lynchings in Guatemala.
Mitchell, Timothy. 1988. *Colonizing Egypt*. Cambridge, England: Cambridge University Press.
———. 1990. Everyday metaphors of power. *Theory and Society* 19: 545–77.
———. 1991. The limits of the state: Beyond statist approaches and their critics. *American Political Science Review* 85(1): 77–96.
———. 1999. Economy and the state effect. In *State/Culture: State formation after the cultural turn*, ed. George Steinmetz. Ithaca, NY: Cornell University Press.
Moore, Sally Falk. 1986. *Social facts and fabrications: Customary law on Kilimanjaro, 1880–1980*. New York: Cambridge University Press.
Montero, C. 1990. *La escuela rural: Variaciones sobre un tema*. Lima: FAO.
Nader, Laura. 1990. *Harmony ideology, justice and control in a Zapotec mountain village*. Stanford, CA: Stanford University Press.
Nasr, Seyyed Vali Reza. 1992. Democracy and the crisis of governability in Pakistan. *Asian Survey* 32(6): 521–37.
National Crime Prevention Strategy (NCPS; South Africa). 1996. *Government Printer*. Pretoria.
Nedcor Project. 1996. *The Nedcor Project on crime, violence and investment: Final report*. Johannesburg: Nedcor Project.
Nelson, Diane. 1999. *A finger in the wound: Body politics in quincentennial Guatemala*. Berkeley: University of California Press.
Nina, Daniel. 1995. *Re-thinking popular justice: Self regulation and civil society in South Africa*. Cape Town, South Africa: Community Peace Foundation.
Norval, Aletta J. 1990. Postscript: Post-apartheid? In *New reflections on the revolution of our time*, ed. Ernesto Laclau. London: Verso.
———. 1996. *Deconstructing apartheid discourse*. London: Verso.
———. 1998a. Memory, identity and the (im)possibility of reconciliation: The work of the Truth and Reconciliation Commission in South Africa. *Constellations* 5(2): 250–65.
———. 1998b. Reinventing the politics of cultural recognition: The freedom front and the de-

mand for a *Volkstaat*. In *South Africa in transition: New theoretical perspectives*, ed. D. Howarth and Aletta J. Norval. London: Macmillan.

———. 1999a. Rethinking ethnicity: Identification, hybridity and democracy. In *Ethnicity and nationalism in Africa: Constructivist reflections and contemporary politics*, ed. P. Yeros. London: Macmillan.

———. 1999b. Truth and reconciliation: The birth of the present and the reworking of history. *Journal of Southern African Studies* 25(3): 499–519.

Nugent, David. 1988. *The mercantile transformation of provincial urban life: Labor, value and time in the northern Peruvian sierra*. Ph.D. diss., Columbia University.

———. 1994. Building the state, making the nation: The bases and limits of state centralization in "modern Peru." *American Anthropologist* 96(2): 333–69.

———. 1995. Artisanal cooperation, forms of labor, and the global economy: Chachapoyas, 1930s to the 1990s. *Journal of Historical Sociology* 8(1): 36–58.

———. 1996. From devil pacts to drug deals: Commerce, unnatural accumulation and moral community in "modern" Peru. *American Ethnologist* 23(2): 258–90.

———. 1997. *Modernity at the edge of empire: State, individual, and nation in the northern Peruvian Andes, 1885–1935*. Stanford, CA: Stanford University Press.

———. 1999. State and shadow state in turn-of-the-century Peru: Illegal political networks and the problem of state boundaries. In *States and Illegal Practices*, ed. Josiah Heyman. London: Berg.

———. n.d. *Beyond modernity and the nation-state: Post and transnational processes in the Northern Peruvian Andes*. Unpublished manuscript.

Nuijten, Monique. 1998. *In the name of the land: Organization, transnationalism, and the culture of the state in a Mexican ejido*. Ph.D. diss., University of Wageningen, Holland.

Ochoa Garcia, C., ed. 1993. *Los contextos actuales del poder local: Governabilidad y municipalismo*. Guatemala City, Guatemala: IRIPAZ.

O'Donnell, Guillermo. 1996. The state, democratization and some conceptual problems. In *Latin American political economy in the age of neoliberal reform: Theoretical and comparative perspectives for the 1990s*. Miami: University of Miami, North-South Center.

O'Malley, Pat. 1998. Indigenous governance. In *Governing Australia: Studies in contemporary rationalities of government*, ed. Mitchell Dean and Barry Hindess. New York: Cambridge University Press.

O'Malley, Pat, Lorna Weir, and Clifford Shearing. 1997. Governmentality, criticism, politics. *Economy and Society* 26(4): 501–17.

Omar, Dullah. 1995. Building a new future. In *The healing of a nation?*, ed. A. Boraine and J. Levy. Cape Town, South Africa: Justice in Transition.

Ortner, Sherry. 1995. Resistance and the problem of ethnographic refusal. *Comparative Studies in Society and History* 37: 173–93.

Osiel, M. 1997. *Mass atrocities, collective memory and the law*. New Brunswick, NJ: Transaction Publishers.

Padgaonkar, Dilip, ed. 1993. *When Bombay burned*. Delhi: UPSD Press.

Painter, Jo, and Chris Philo. 1995. Spaces of citizenship. *Political Geography* 14(2): 107–70.

Palencia, Tania. 1997. Entre los hilos de la nueva cultura. In *Guatemala 1983–1997: Hacia dónde va la transición?*, ed. Jeremy Armon et al. Cuadernos de Debate no. 38. Guatemala City: FLACSO.

Palmer, David Scott. 1994. *Shining Path of Peru*. 2nd ed. New York: St. Martin's Press.

———. 1998. *Democracia incompleta y política informal en el Peru: El caso de Ayacucho*. Paper presented at the LASA congress, Chicago. 28–30 September.

Pandey, Gyanendra. 1990. *The colonial construction of communalism in colonial North India*. Delhi: Oxford University Press.

Payeras, Mario. 1991. *Los fusiles de octubre: Ensayos y articulos militares sobre la revolución guatemalteca 1985–88*. Mexico City: Juan Pablos Editor.

Pedersen, Poul. 1986. Khatri: Vaishya, or Kshatriya? An essay in colonial adminstration and cultural identity. *Folk* 28: 19–31.

Pels, Peter. 1997. The anthropology of colonialism: Culture, history, and the emergence of Western governmentality. *Annual Review of Anthropology* 26: 163–83.

Perelli, C. 1993. The power of memory and the memory of power. In *Repression, exile and democracy: Uruguayan culture*, ed. S. Sosnowski and L. Popkin. Durham, NC: Duke University Press.

Peters, Michael. 1995. "After Auschwitz": Ethics and educational policy. *Discourse* 16(2): 237–51.

Peukert, Detlev. 1989. *Inside Nazi Germany*. Harmondsworth, England: Penguin.

———. 1993. The genesis of the "Final Solution" from the spirit of science. In *Reevaluating the Third Reich*, ed. T. Childers and J. Caplan. New York: Holmes and Meier.

Philpott, Simon. 1997. *Knowing Indonesia: Orientalism and the discourse of Indonesian politics*. Ph.D. diss., Australian National University.

Pinault, David. 1999. Muslim-Buddhist relations in a ritual context: An analysis of the muharram procession in Leh Township, Ladakh. In *Ladakh: Culture, history, and development between Himalaya and Karakoram. Recent research on Ladakh 8*, ed. M. van Beek, K. Bertelsen, and P. Pedersen. Aarhus, Denmark: Aarhus University Press.

Pine, Lisa. 1997. *Nazi family policy 1933–45*. Oxford: Berg.

Pinnock, Don. 1984. *The brotherhoods: Street gangs and state control in Cape Town*. Cape Town, South Africa: David Philip.

Plant, Roger. 1998. Ethnicity and the Guatemalan peace process: Conceptual and practical challenges. In *Guatemala after the peace accords*, ed. Rachel Sieder. London: Institute of Latin American Studies.

Poley, J. A., ed. 1985. *Selected writings on the freedom charter 1955–1985*. London: African National Congress.

———, ed. 1988. *The freedom charter and the future*. Johannesburg: A. D. Donker.

Police "sat on" Nkabinde docket. 1999. *Mail and Guardian*, 20–26 August.

Poole, D., and G. Renique. 1991. The new chroniclers of Peru: U.S. scholars and their "Shining Path" of peasant rebellion. *Bulletin of Latin American Research* 10(1): 133–91.

———. 1992. *Peru, time of fear*. London: Latin American Bureau.

Portocarrero, G. 1998. *Razones de sangre: Aproximaciones a la violencia politica*. Lima: Fondo Editorial, Pontificia Universidad Católica del Peru.

Portocarrero G., and P. Oliarte. 1989. *El Perú desde la escuela*. Lima, Peru: Instituto de Apoyo Agrario.

Posel, D. 1991. *The making of apartheid 1948–1961*. Oxford: Clarendon Press.

Pratt, Gerr. 1992. Spatial metaphors and speaking positions. *Environment and Planning D: Society and Space* 10: 241–44.

Price, Pamela. 1996. *Kingship and political practice in colonial India*. Cambridge, England: Cambridge University Press.

Primov, G. 1980. The political role of mestizo schoolteachers in Indian communities. In *Land and power in Latin America: Agrarian economics and social processes in the Andes*, ed. Benjamin Orlove and Glynn Custred. New York: Holmes and Meier.

Pritchard, Diana. 1995. The legacy of conflict: Refugee repatriation and reintegration in Central America. In *Central America: Fragile transition*, ed. Rachel Sieder. Basingstoke, England: Macmillan.

Promotion of National Unity and Reconciliation Act (South Africa) 1997. Act no. 18. *Government Printer*. Pretoria.

Quintero, Luis, and Erika Silva. 1991. *Ecuador: Una nación en ciernes*. Quito: FLACSO.

Rabinow, P., ed. 1984. *The Foucault reader*. Harmondsworth, England: Penguin.

Radcliffe, Sarah A. 1996. Imaginative geographies, postcolonialism and national identities: Contemporary discourses of the nation in Ecuador. *Ecumene* 3(1): 23–42.

———. 1998. Frontiers and popular nationhood: Geographies of identities in the 1995 Ecuador-Peru border dispute. *Political Geography* 17(3): 273–93.

———. 1999. Popular and state discourses of power. In *Human geography today*, ed. D. Massey, J. Allen, and P. Sarre. Cambridge, England: Polity Press.

Radcliffe, Sarah A., and Sallie Westwood. 1996. *Re-making the nation: Place, politics and identity in Latin America*. London: Routledge.

Radhu, Abdul Wahid. 1981. *Caravane tibétaine: Adapté en français par Roger du Pasquier*. La Bibliothèque des Voyageurs. Paris: Fayard.

Ransom, John. 1997. *Foucault's discipline*. Durham, NC: Duke University Press.

Recinos, Adrian. 1913. *Monografía del Departamento de Huehuetenango, República de Guatemala*. Guatemala City: Tipografía Sanchez and de Guise.

Reno, William. 1998. *Warlord politics and African states*. Boulder, CO: Lynne Rienner.

Restrepo, M. 1993. El problema de la frontera en la construcción del espacio amazónico. In *Amazonía: Escenarios y conflictos*, ed. Lucy Ruiz. Quito, Ecuador: Cedime.

Richards, Paul. 1996. *Fighting for the rainforest: War, youth, and resources in Sierra Leone*. London: James Currey.

Risley, Herbert. 1969. (1915). *The people of India*. Delhi: Oriental Books Reprint Co.

Rizvi, Janet. 1994. The Trans-Karakoram trade in the nineteenth and twentieth centuries. *Indian Economic and Social History Review* 31(1).

———. 1997. Leh to Yarkand: Travelling the Trans-Karakoram trade route. In *Recent Research on Ladakh 7: Proceedings of the 7th Colloquium of the International Association for Ladakh Studies, Bonn/St. Augustin, 12–15 June 1995*, ed. T. Dodin and H. Räther. Ulm, Germany: Universität Ulm.

———. 1999. *Transhimalayan caravans: Merchant princes and peasant traders in Ladakh*. Delhi: Oxford University Press.

Robins, S. 1998. Silence in my father's house: Memory, nationalism, and narratives of the body. In *Negotiating the past: The making of memory in South Africa*, ed. S. Nuttall and C. Coetzee. Cape Town, South Africa: Oxford University Press.

Rønsbo, H. 1997. State formation and property: Reflections on the political technologies of space in Central America. *Journal of Historical Sociology* 10(1): 56–74.

Rose, Nikolas. 1985. *The psychological complex: Politics, psychology and society in England, 1869–1939.* London: Routledge and Keegan Paul.

———. 1996. The death of the social? Re-figuring the territory of government. *Economy and Society* 25(3): 327–56.

Roseberry, William. 1994. Hegemony and the language of contention. In *Everyday forms of state formation: Revolution and the negotiation of rule in modern Mexico*, ed. G. Joseph and D. Nugent. Durham, NC: Duke University Press.

———. 1996. Hegemony, power, and languages of contention. In *The politics of difference: Ethnic premises in a world of power*, ed. Edwin N. Wilmsen and Patrick McAllister. Chicago: University of Chicago Press.

Rowe, William, and Vivian Schelling. 1991. *Memory and modernity: Popular culture in Latin America.* London: Verso.

Saff, Grant. 1998. *Changing Cape Town: Urban dynamics, policy, and planning during the political transition in South Africa.* Boston: University Press of America.

Sahlins, Peter. 1989. *Boundaries: The making of France and Spain in the Pyrenees.* Berkeley: University of California Press.

Said, Edward. 1983. *Orientalism.* London: Verso.

Sanchez, R. 1981. *Toma de tierras y conciencia politica campesina.* Lima, Peru: Instituto de Estudios Campesinos.

Santana, Robert. 1995. *Ciudadanos en la etnicidad? Los indios en la política y la política de los indios.* Quito, Ecuador: Abya-Yala.

Santos, Boaventura de Sousa. 1987. Law: A map of misreading. Toward a post-modern conception of law. *Journal of Law and Society* 14(3): 279–302.

———. 1995. *Toward a new common sense: Law, science and politics in the paradigmatic transition.* New York: Routledge.

Sarakinsky, I. 1988. *A web on national manipulation.* Unpublished manuscript.

Schärf, Wilfried. 1997. *Specialist courts and community courts.* Position paper submitted to the Ministry of Justice, the Planning Unit, Institute of Criminology, Cape Town University.

Schirmer, Jennifer. 1998. *The Guatemalan military project: A violence called democracy.* Philadelphia: University of Pennsylvania Press.

Schmidt, Lars-Henrik. 1993. *Setting the values.* Working paper no. 1. Aarhus, Denmark: Center for Kulturforskning.

Scott, James C. 1985. *Weapons of the weak: Everyday forms of resistance.* New Haven: Yale University Press.

———. 1990. *Domination and the art of resistance.* New Haven: Yale University Press.

———. 1994. Foreword. In *Everyday forms of state formation: Revolution and the negotiation of rule in modern Mexico*, ed. G. Joseph and D. Nugent. Durham, NC: Duke University Press.

———. 1998. *Seeing like a state: How certain schemes to improve the human condition have failed.* New Haven: Yale University Press.

———. 1999. Foreword. In *Elementary aspects of peasant insurgency in colonial India*, ed. Ranajit Guha. Durham, NC: Duke University Press.

Selected writings on the freedom charter 1955–1985. 1985. London: African National Congress.

Sen, Amartya. 1986. Critical assessment of monitoring and evaluation in Integrated Child Development Services programme and profile of suggested indicators in the social components. *Indian Journal of Social Work* 47(3): 303–13.

———. 1990. More than 100 million women are missing. *New York Review of Books*, 20 December.

———. 1994. Population: Delusion and reality. *New York Review of Books*, 22 September.

Serrano, F. 1993. Las organizaciones indígenas de la Amazonía ecuatoriana. In *Amazonía: escenarios y conflictos*, ed. Lucy Ruiz. Quito, Ecuador: Cedime.

Sharma, Urmil. 1986. A critical assessment of monitoring and evaluation in Integrated Child Development Services Programme and profile of suggested indicators in the social components. In *The Indian journal of social work* 47(3): 303–13.

Shaw, Mark. 1997. South Africa: Crime in transition. In *Terrorism and political violence* 8(4): 156–75.

Shearing, Clifford, and Mike Brogden. 1993. *Policing for a new South Africa*. London: Routledge.

Sieder, Rachel. 1996. *Derecho consuetudinario y transición democrática en Guatemala*. Ciudad de Guatemala, Guatemala: Facultad Latinoamericana de Ciencias Sociales.

———. ed. 1998. *Guatemala after the peace accords*. London: Institute of Latin American Studies.

Sieder, Rachel, and Jessica Witchell. 2001. Advancing indigenous demands through the law: Reflections on the Guatemalan peace process. In *Culture and rights*, ed. Jane Cowan, Marie Dembour, and Richard Wilson. Cambridge, England: Cambridge University Press.

Sigley, Gary. 1996. Governing Chinese bodies: The significance of studies in the concept of governmentality for the analysis of government in China. *Economy and Society* 25(4): 457–82.

Simmel, Georg. 1950. The secret and the secret society. In *The sociology of Georg Simmel*, ed. K. H. Wolff. New York: Free Press.

Singh, Karan. 1982. *Heir apparent: An autobiography*. Delhi: Oxford University Press.

Skinner, Quentin. 1985. Introduction: The return of grand theory in the human sciences. In *The return of grand theory in the human sciences*, ed. Q. Skinner. Cambridge, England: Cambridge University Press.

Slater, David. 1997. Re-thinking the spatialities of social movements: Questions of (b)orders in global times. In *Cultures of politics: Politics of culture*, ed. S. Alvarez et al. Princeton, NJ: Princeton University Press.

Smith, Anthony. 1991. *National identity*. Harmondsworth, England: Penguin.

Smith, Carol A., ed. 1990. *Guatemalan Indians and the state 1540–1988*. Austin: University of Texas Press.

Smith, Gavin. 1989. *Livelihood and resistance: Peasants and the politics of land in Peru*. Berkeley: University of California Press.

Sonntag, Selma. 1999. Autonomous councils in India: Contesting the liberal nation-state. *Alternatives* 24(4): 415–34.

South African Police Service (SAPS). 1997a. *Police plan, 1996–97*. Pretoria: SAPS.

———. 1997b. *Status report: The transformation of the South African Police Service*. Pretoria: SAPS.

Sparks, Allister. 1990. *The mind of South Africa*. London: William Heineman.

Srikrishna, B. N. 1998. *Report of the Srikrishna Commission*. Vols. 1 and 2. Mumbai, India: Punwani and Vrijendra.

Starn, O. 1991. Missing the revolution: Anthropologists and the war in Peru. *Cultural Anthropology* 6(1): 466–504.

Starr, June, and Jane Collier. 1989. *History and power in the study of law: New directions in legal anthropology*. Ithaca, NY: Cornell University Press.

Stavenhagen, Rodolfo. 1996. Indigenous rights: Some conceptual problems. In *Constructing democracy: Human rights, citizenship, and society in Latin America*, ed. Elizabeth Jelin and Eric Hershberg. Boulder, CO: Westview Press.

Stein, Steve. 1980. *Populism in Peru: The emergence of the masses and the politics of social control*. Madison: University of Wisconsin Press.

Stepputat, Finn. 1992. *Beyond relief? Life in a Guatemalan refugee settlement in Mexico*. Ph.D. diss., University of Copenhagen.

———. 1999a. Politics of displacement in Guatemala. *Journal of Historical Sociology* 12(1): 54–80.

———. 1999b. Repatriation and everyday forms of state formation in Guatemala. In *The end of the refugee cycle? Refugee repatriation and reconstruction*, ed. Richard Black and Khalid Koser. New York: Berghahn Books.

———. 2000. At the frontiers of the modern state in post-war Guatemala. In *Anthropology, development and modernities: Exploring discourses, counter-tendencies and violence*, ed. Norman Long and Arturo Arce. London: Routledge.

Stern, S., ed. 1998. *Shining Path and other paths: War and society in Peru, 1980–1995*. Durham, NC: Duke University Press.

Stoler, Ann Laura. 1995. *Race and the education of desire*. Durham, NC: Duke University Press.

Stoll, David. 1993. *Between two fires in the Ixil towns of Guatemala*. New York: Columbia University Press.

Strudsholm, Jesper. 1997. Man lod en leder gå amok. *Politiken*, December (Copenhagen).

———. 1999. Attentat på en voldelig vendekåbe. *Politiken*, January (Copenhagen).

Submission to the TRC by Mr. F. W. de Klerk, leader of the National Party. http://www.truth.org.za/np-truth.html. Accessed February 15, 1997.

Sulmont, Denis. 1977. *Historia del movimiento obrero Peruano, 1890–1977*. Lima: Tarea.

Swilling, M., and M. Phillips. 1988. State power in the 1980s: From "total strategy" to "counterrevolutionary warfare." In *War and society: The militarisation of South Africa*, ed. J. Cock and L. Nathan. Cape Town, South Africa: David Phillip.

Tambiah, Stanley J. 1996. *Levelling crowds*. Berkeley: University of California Press.

Tandon, B. N., K. Ramachandran, and S. Bhatnagar. 1981. Integrated Child Development Services in India: Objectives, organization and baseline survey of the project population. *Indian Journal of Medical Research* 73: 374–84.

Tapia, C. 1997. *Las fuerzas armadas y Sendero Luminoso: Dos estrategias y un final*. Lima, Peru: Instituto de Estudios Peruanos.

Taracena, Arturo. 1995. Nación y republica en Centroamérica (1821–1865). In *Identidades nacionales y estado moderno en Centroamérica*, Arturo Taracena and Jean Piel, eds., San José: Costa Rica: Editorial de la Universidad de Costa Rica.

Taussig, Michael. 1993a. Maleficium: State fetishism. In *Fetishism as cultural discourse*, ed. E. Apter and W. Pietz. Ithaca, NY: Cornell University Press.

———. 1993b. *Mimesis and alterity: A particular history of the senses*. London: Routledge.

———. 1997. *The magic of the state*. New York: Routledge.

Taylor, Lewis. 1986. *Bandits and politics in Peru: Landlord and peasant violence in Hualgayoc 1900–1930*.

Cambridge, England: Cambridge University Press, Centre of Latin American Studies.

———. 1998. Counter-insurgency strategy, the PCP–Sendero Luminoso and the civil war in Peru, 1980–1996. *Bulletin of Latin American Research* 17(1): 35–59.

Terán, F. 1983. *Estudios de historia y geografía*. Quito, Ecuador: Biblioteca Ecuatoriana.

Theissen, Gunnar. 1999. *Common past, divided truth: The Truth and Reconciliation Commission in South Africa public opinion*. Paper presented at the international conference The TRC: Commissioning the Past, 11–14 June, University of the Witwatersrand, Johannesburg.

Third Force of the Cape flats. 1997. *Electronic Mail and Guardian*, 30 September. www.mg.co.za.

Torpey, John. 2000. *The invention of the passport: Surveillance, citizenship and the state*. Cambridge, England: Cambridge University Press.

Trinquier, Roger. 1964 (1961). *Modern warfare: A French view of counterinsurgency*. New York: Praeger.

Truth and Reconciliation Commission of South Africa (TRC). 1996. *Interim report*. Pretoria: Government Printer.

———. 1998a. *Final report*. Cape Town, South Africa: Juta and Co.

———. 1998b. *The South African Truth and Reconciliation Commission Proposal for Reparation and Rehabilitation*. Pretoria: Government Printer.

———. 2000. *TRC: Current status and statistics*. December 9, 1999. (TRC Mailing List: http://www.truth.org.za)

———. website. 1998. CD, November.

———. *Truth and Reconciliation Commission: Information pack*. Pretoria: Government Printer.

Tsing, Anna, L. 1993. *In the realm of the diamond queen: Marginality in an out-of-the-way place*. Princeton, NJ: Princeton University Press.

Tully, James. 1995. *Strange multiplicity: Constitutionalism in an age of diversity*. Cambridge, England: Cambridge University Press.

Tutu, D. 1996a. Healing a nation. *Index on Censorship*, 5.

———. 1996b. Letter to the *Sunday Times* of South Africa. 4 December.

United Nations Development Program (UNDP). 2000. *Human development report*. New York: United Nations.

Uquillas, Jorge. 1993. Estructuración del espacio y actividad productiva indígena en la Amazonía ecuatoriana. In *Amazonía: Escenarios y conflictos*, ed. Lucy Ruiz. Quito, Ecuador: Cedime.

Urban, Greg, and Joel Sherzer, eds. 1991. *Nation-states and Indians in Latin America*. Austin: University of Texas Press.

Valverde, Mariana. 1996. "Despotism" and ethical governance. *Economy and Society* 25(3): 357–72.

van Beek, Martijn. 1996. *Identity fetishism and the art of representation: The long struggle for regional autonomy in Ladakh*. Ph.D. diss., Cornell University, Ithaca, NY.

———. 1997a. *Beyond identity fetishism: "Communal" conflict in Ladakh and the limits of autonomy*. Paper presented at the SSRC MacArthur Foundation Program on Peace and International Security in a Changing World, Cornell University, Ithaca, NY.

———. 1997b. Contested classifications of people in Ladakh: An analysis of the census of Kashmir, 1873–1941. In *Tibetan studies: Proceedings of the seventh seminar of the International Association for Tibetan Studies, Graz 1995*, ed. H. Krasser, M. T. Much, E. Steinkellner, and H. Tauscher. Vienna: Verlag der Östereichen Akademie der Wissenschaften.

———. 1998. True patriots: Justifying autonomy for Ladakh. *Himalayan Research Bulletin* 18(1): 35–45.

———. 1999. Hill councils, development, and democracy: Assumptions and experiences from Ladakh. *Alternatives* 24(4): 435–59.

van der Veer, Peter. 1994. *Religious nationalism: Hindus and Muslims in India*. Berkeley: University of California Press.

van Krieken, Robert 1996. Proto-governmentalization and the historical formation of organizational subjectivity. *Economy and Society* 25(2): 195–221.

Van Neiuwkoop, Martien, and Jorge Uquillas. 2000. *Defining ethnodevelopment in operational terms: Lessons from the Ecuador Indigenous and Afro-Ecuadoran Peoples Development Project*. Washington, DC: World Bank.

Van Oss, Adrian C. 1986. *Catholic colonialism. A parish history of Guatemala 1524–1821*. Cambridge, England: Cambridge University Press.

Vanaik, Achin. 1997. *Communalism contested: Religion, modernity and secularization*. New Delhi: Vistaar.

Vazquez, M. 1965. *Educación rural en el valle del Callejón de Huaylas, Vicos*. Lima: Instituto de Estudios Peruanos.

Verdery, Katherine. 1996. *What was socialism, and what comes next?* Princeton, NJ: Princeton University Press.

Verkaaik, Oskar. 1999. *Inside the citadel: Fun, violence, and religious nationalism in Hyderabad, Pakistan*. Ph.D. diss., University of Amsterdam.

Vincent, Joan. 1990. *Anthropology and politics: Visions, traditions, and trends*. Tucson: University of Arizona Press.

Visvanathan, Shiv. 1988a. On the annals of the laboratory state. In *Science, hegemony and violence: A requiem for modernity*, ed. A. Nandy. Delhi: Oxford University Press.

———. 1988b. The early years. In *Foul play: Chronicles of corruption, 1974–1997*. New Delhi: Banyan Books.

Visvanathan, Shiv, and Harsh Sethi, eds. 1998. *Foul play: Chronicles of corruption 1947–97*. New Delhi: Banyan Books.

Wagner, P. 1994. *A sociology of modernity: Liberty and discipline*. London: Routledge.

Walt, B. J. van der, and T. van der Walt. 1996. *Die waarheids: En versoeningskommissie*. Potchefstroom, South Africa: Institute for Reformational Studies.

Warikoo, Kulbushan. 1985. Ladakh: An entrepôt of Indo-Central Asian trade during the Dogra rule. *South Asian Studies* 20(2).

———. 1990. Ladakh's trade relations with Tibet under the Dogras. *China Report* 26(2): 137–43.

———. 1995. Gateway to Central Asia: The transhimalayan trade of Ladakh, 1846–1947. In *Recent research on Ladakh 4 and 5: Proceedings of the Fourth and Fifth Colloquia on Ladakh*, ed. H. Osmaston and P. Denwood. Delhi: Motilal Banarsidass.

Warren, K. B. 1978. *The symbolism of subordination: Indian identity in a Guatemalan town*. Austin: University of Texas Press.

Warren, U. B. 1998. *Indigenous movements and their critics: Pan-Mayan activism in Guatemala*. Princeton, NJ: Princeton University Press.

Watanabe, J. M. 1992. *Maya saints and souls in a changing world*. Austin: University of Texas Press.

———. 1997. *Forging identities in an emerging nation-state: Bureaucratic procedures, policing, and punishment in Maya communities of late nineteenth-century western Guatemala*. Paper presented at the

20th international congress of the Latin American Studies Association, Guadelajara, Mexico, 19 April.

Wattal, C. L. 1948. Buddhists in Kashmir. *Maha-Bodhi*, May–June: 181–84.

Weber, Max. 1968a. Bureaucracy. In *From Max Weber: Essays in sociology*, ed. H. H. Gerth and C. Wright Mills. New York: Oxford University Press.

———. 1968b. *Economy and society: An outline of interpretive sociology*. Vol. 3, ed. G. Roth and C. Wittich. New York: Bedminister Press.

Werbner, Pnina, and Helene Basu. 1998. *Embodying charisma: Modernity, locality and the performance of emotion in Sufi cults*. London: Routledge.

Whitten, Norman, ed. 1981. *Cultural transformations and ethnicity in modern Ecuador*. Chicago: University of Illinois Press.

Willke, Helmut. 1992. *Ironie des Staates: Grundlinien einer Staatstheorie polyzentricher Gesellschaft*. Frankfurt am Main: Suhrkamp Verlag.

Wilson, Fiona. 1982. Property and ideology: A regional oligarchy in the Central Andes in the nineteenth century. In *Ecology and exchange in the Andes*, ed. David Lehmann. Cambridge, England: Cambridge University Press.

———. 2000. Representing the state? School and teacher in post-Sendero Peru. *Bulletin of Latin American Research* 19(3): 1–16.

Wilson, Richard. 1991. Machine guns and mountain spirits: The cultural effects of state repression among the Q'eqchi' of Guatemala. *Critique of Anthropology* 11(1): 33–61.

———. 1995a. Manufacturing legitimacy: The Truth and Reconciliation Commission and the rule of law. *Indicator SA* 13(1).

———. 1995b. *Mayan resurgence in Guatemala: Qeqchi experiences*. Norman: University of Oklahoma Press.

———. 1996. The Siswe will not go away: The Truth and Reconciliation Commission. Human rights and nation-building in South Africa. *African Studies* 55(2): 1–20.

Wolf, Eric R. 1966. *Peasants*. Englewood Cliffs, NJ: Prentice-Hall.

———. 1969. *Peasant wars in the twentieth century*. New York: Harper and Row.

Woods, D. 1997. Can the killers ever find peace? *The Guardian*, 1 February.

Woost, M. D. 1994. Developing a nation of villages: Rural community as state formation in Sri Lanka. *Critique of Anthropology* 14(1): 77–95.

A word, a nudge, a drink, a gun . . . then death. 1999. *Sunday Argus* (Cape Town), 24–25 April.

World Bank. 1997. *The state in a changing world*. New York: Oxford University Press.

Young, Crawford. 1994. *The African colonial state in comparative perspective*. New Haven: Yale University Press.

Young, J. E. 1992. The counter-monument: Memory against itself in Germany today. *Critical Inquiry* 18.

Zamosc, Leon. 1994. Agrarian protest and the Indian movement in the Ecuadorian highlands. *Latin American Research Review* 21(3): 37–69.

Zartman, W., ed. 1994. *Collapsed states: The disintegration and restoration of legitimate authority*. Boulder, CO: Lynne Rienner.

Žižek, Slavoj. 1989. *The sublime object of ideology*. London: Verso.

CONTRIBUTORS

THOMAS BLOM HANSEN is a reader in the Department of Social Anthropology at the University of Edinburgh.

LARS BUUR is a research fellow at the Centre for Development Research in Copenhagen.

MITCHELL DEAN is a professor of Sociology at Macquarie University in Australia.

AKHIL GUPTA is an associate professor in the Department of Cultural and Social Anthropology at Stanford University.

STEFFEN JENSEN is a research fellow at the Centre for Development Research in Copenhagen.

ALETTA J. NORVAL is a senior lecturer in the Department of Government at the University of Essex.

DAVID NUGENT is an associate professor in the Department of Anthropology at Colby College.

SARAH A. RADCLIFFE is a lecturer in the Department of Geography at the University of Cambridge.

RACHEL SIEDER is a senior lecturer at the Institute of Latin American Studies at the University of London.

FINN STEPPUTAT is a senior researcher at the Centre for Development Research in Copenhagen.

MARTIJN VAN BEEK is an associate professor in the Department of Ethnography and Social Anthropology at Aarhus University in Denmark.

OSKAR VERKAAIK is a lecturer on the Faculty of Social Studies at Vrije University in Amsterdam.

FIONA WILSON is a professor at the Centre for Development Research in Copenhagen.

INDEX

Library of Congress Cataloging-in-Publication Data
States of imagination : ethnographic explorations of the postcolonial state/
Thomas Blom Hansen and Finn Stepputat.
Includes bibliographical references and index.
ISBN 0-8223-2801-1 (cloth : alk. paper) — ISBN 0-8223-2798-8 (pbk. : alk. paper)
1. Political anthropology. 2. Anthropology—Field work. 3. Social sciences and state. 4. Postcolonialism. 5. Postcommunism. 6. Poststructuralism.
I. Hansen, Thomas Blom. II. Stepputat, Finn.
GN492.S75 2001 306.2—dc21 2001040348